Getting MEAN

Getting MEAN

with Mongo, Express, Angular, and Node

SIMON HOLMES

MANNING

SHELTER ISLAND

For online information and ordering of this and other Manning books, please visit
www.manning.com. The publisher offers discounts on this book when ordered in quantity.
For more information, please contact

> Special Sales Department
> Manning Publications Co.
> 20 Baldwin Road
> PO Box 761
> Shelter Island, NY 11964
> Email: orders@manning.com

Manning Publications Co.
20 Baldwin Road
PO Box 761
Shelter Island, NY 11964

Development editors:	Susie Pitzen, Susanna Kline, Karen Miller
Technical development editor:	Marius Butuc
Copyeditor:	Jodie Allen
Proofreader:	Alyson Brener
Technical proofreaders:	Steven Jenkins, Deepak Vohra
Typesetter:	Dennis Dalinnik
Cover designer:	Marija Tudor

ISBN: 9781617292033
Printed in the United States of America
1 2 3 4 5 6 7 8 9 10 – EBM – 20 19 18 17 16 15

brief contents

v

contents

preface

Back in 1995 I got my first taste of web development, putting together a few pages of simple HTML for a piece of university coursework. It was a small part of my course, which was a mixture of software engineering and communication studies. This was an unusual mixture. I learned the fundamentals of software development, database design, and programming. But I also learned about the importance of the audience and end-user and how to communicate with them, both verbally and non-verbally.

In 1998, on the communication studies side of the degree, I was required to write a publication for an organization of my choice. I decided to write a prospectus for the school where my mother was teaching at the time. But I decided to do it as a website. Again this was all front-end work. Fortunately I no longer have a copy of it, as I shudder at the thought of the code. We're talking HTML with frames, table layouts, inline styles, and a smattering of basic JavaScript. By today's standards it was shocking, but back then it was quite futuristic. I was the first person at the university to submit a website as a publication. I even had to tell my instructors how to open it in their browser from the floppy disk it was submitted on! After it was completed and marked, I sold the website to the school it was about. I figured there was probably a future in this web development thing.

During the following years I made use of both parts of my degree working as the "web guy" in a London design agency. Because it was a design agency, user-experience (before it was called UX) and the front end were crucial. But of course there has to be a back end to support the front end. As the only web guy I fulfilled both roles as the classic full-stack developer. There wasn't much separation of concerns in those days. The database was tightly coupled to the back end. Back-end logic, markup, and front-end logic all wove together tightly. This is largely because the project was thought of as a single thing: the website.

Many of the best practices from this book are borne of the pain of finding out the hard way over these years. Something that might seem harmless at the time, most definitely easier, or sometimes even sensible, can come back to bite you later on. Don't let this put you off from diving in and having a go. Mistakes are there to be made, and—in this arena at least—mistakes are a great way of learning. They say that intelligence is "learning from your mistakes." This is true, but you'll be a step ahead if you can also learn from others' mistakes.

The web development landscape changed over the years, but I was still heavily involved with creating—or managing the creation of—full websites and applications. I came to appreciate that there is a real art to gluing together applications made from different technologies. It is a skill in itself; just knowing the technologies and what they can do is only part of the challenge.

When Node.js came onto my radar I jumped right in and embraced the idea full on. I had done a lot of context switching between various languages, and the idea of having a single language to focus on and master was extremely compelling. I figured that if used in the right way it could streamline development by reducing the language context shifting. Playing with Node I started to create my own MVC framework, before discovering Express. Express solved a lot of the problems and challenges I faced when first trying to learn Node and use it to create a website or web application. In many ways adopting it was a no-brainer.

Naturally, behind pretty much any web application is a database. I didn't want to fall back on my previous go-to option of Microsoft SQL Server, as the cost made it quite prohibitive to launch small personal projects. Some research led me to the leading open source NoSQL database: MongoDB. It worked natively with JavaScript! I was more excited than I possibly should have been about a database. However MongoDB was different from all of the databases I had used before. My previous experience was all in relational databases; MongoDB is a document database, and that is something quite different, making the way you approach database design quite different as well. I had to retrain my brain to think in this new way, and eventually it all made sense.

There was just one piece missing. JavaScript in the browser was no longer just about enhancing functionality, it was about *creating* the functionality and managing the application logic. Out of the available options I was already leaning toward AngularJS. When I heard Valeri Karpov of MongoDB coin the term "MEAN stack" that was it. I knew that here was a next-generation stack.

I knew that the MEAN stack would be powerful. I knew that the MEAN stack would be flexible. I knew that the MEAN stack would capture the imagination of developers. Each of the individual technologies is great, but when you put them all together you have something exceptional on your hands. This is where *Getting MEAN* comes from. Getting the best out of the MEAN stack is more than just knowing the technologies, it's about knowing how to get those technologies working together.

acknowledgments

I must start with the people who mean the world to me, who inspire me to push myself, and who ultimately make everything worthwhile. I'm talking about my wife, Sally, and daughters, Eri and Bel. Everything I do starts and ends with these three ladies.

Thanks of course must go to the Manning team. I know it extends beyond the people I'm about to name, so if you were involved in any way then thank you! Here are the people I have personally dealt with.

Right from the beginning there was Robin de Jongh who was instrumental in getting the project started and also in shaping the book. And many thanks to Bert Bates for providing great insight and challenging me to justify my thinking and opinions from an early stage. Those were fun conversations.

Crucial to the momentum and feel of the book were my developmental editors, Susie Pitzen, Susanna Kline, and Karen Miller. And of course my technical developmental editor, Marius Butuc. Thanks all for sharp eyes, great ideas, and positive feedback.

The next two people really impressed me with their amount of effort and attention to detail. So thank you Kevin Sullivan and Jodie Allen for the copyediting and proofing, and for staying on top of everything under increasingly short timeframes.

Last but by no means least for the Manning team is Candace Gillhoolley, who has been keeping up the marketing pace on the book, giving me the sales numbers to maintain my motivation.

Manning must also be congratulated for having their Manning Early Access Program (MEAP) and associated online author forum. The comments, corrections, ideas, and feedback from early readers proved invaluable in improving the quality of this book. I don't have the names of everybody who contributed. You know who you are: thank you!

Special thanks for their insights and suggestions to the following peer reviewers who read the manuscript at various stages of its development: Andrea Tarocchi, Andy Knight, Blake Hall, Cynthia Pepper, Davide Molin, Denis Ndwiga, Devang Paliwal, Douglas Duncan, Filip Pravica, Filippo Veneri, Francesco Bianchi, Jesus Rodriguez Rodriguez, Matt Merkes, Rambabu Posa, and William E. Wheeler. Also to Steven Jenkins and Deepak Vohra for their final technical proofread of the chapters, shortly before they went into production.

A couple of extra shout-outs for putting up with me and my late-night technology discussions are to Tamas Piros and Marek Karwowski. Thanks guys!

about this book

JavaScript has come of age. Building an entire web application from front to back with just one language is now possible, using JavaScript. The MEAN stack is comprised of the best-of-breed technologies in this arena. You've got MongoDB for the database, Express for the server-side web-application framework, AngularJS for the client-side framework, and Node for the server-side platform.

This book introduces each of these technologies, as well as how to get them working well together as a stack. Throughout the book we build a working application, focusing on one technology at a time, seeing how they fit into the overall application architecture. So it's a very practical book designed to get you comfortable with all of the technologies and how to use them together.

A common theme running through the book is "best practice." This book is a springboard to building great things with the MEAN stack, so there is a focus on creating good habits, doing things the "right way," and planning ahead.

This book doesn't teach HTML, CSS, or basic JavaScript; previous knowledge of these are assumed. It does include a very brief primer on the Twitter Bootstrap CSS framework, and there's also a good, long appendix on JavaScript theory, best practice, tips, and gotchas. It's worth checking out early on. This appendix can be found online at www.manning.com/books/getting-mean-with-mongo-express-angular-and-node.

Roadmap

This book takes you on a journey through eleven chapters, as follows:

Chapter 1 takes a look at the benefits of learning full-stack development and explores the components of the MEAN stack.

Chapter 2 builds on this knowledge of the components and discusses options of how you can use them together to build different things.

Chapter 3 gets you going with creating and setting up a MEAN project, getting you acquainted with Express.

Chapter 4 provides a much deeper understanding of Express by building out a static version of the application.

Chapter 5 takes what we've learned about the application so far and works with MongoDB and Mongoose to design and build the data model we'll need.

Chapter 6 covers the benefits and processes of creating a data API, and we'll create a REST API using Express, MongoDB, and Mongoose.

Chapter 7 ties this REST API back into the application by consuming it from our static Express application.

Chapter 8 introduces Angular to the stack, and we'll see how to use it to build a component for an existing web page, including calling our REST API to get data.

Chapter 9 covers the fundamentals of creating a single-page application with Angular, showing how to build a modular, scalable, and maintainable application.

Chapter 10 builds on the foundations of chapter 9, developing the single-page application further by covering some critical concepts and increasing the complexity of the Angular application.

Chapter 11 touches every part of the MEAN stack as we add authentication to the application, enabling users to register and log in.

Code conventions

All source code in listings or in the text is in a `fixed-width font like this` to separate it from ordinary text. Method and function names, properties, JSON elements, and attributes in the text are also presented in this same font.

In some cases, the original source code has been reformatted to fit on the pages. In general, the original code was written with page-width limitations in mind, but sometimes you may find a slight formatting difference between the code in the book and that provided in the source download. In a few rare cases, where long lines could not be reformatted without changing their meaning, the book listings contain line continuation markers.

Code annotations accompany many of the listings, highlighting important concepts. In many cases, numbered bullets link to explanations that follow in the text.

Code downloads

The source code for the application built throughout the book is available to download via Manning's website, www.manning.com/books/getting-mean-with-mongo-express-angular-and-node. It is also available on GitHub, github.com/simonholmes/getting-MEAN.

There is a separate folder (branch on GitHub) for each of the stages of the application, typically at the end of a chapter. The folders (or branches) do not include the nodemodules folder—as is best practice. To run the application in any of the given folders you will need to install the dependencies using `npm install` in the command line. The book covers what this is and why it is necessary.

Author Online

The purchase of *Getting MEAN* includes free access to a private web forum run by Manning Publications, where you can make comments about the book, ask technical questions, and receive help from the author and from other users. To access the forum and subscribe to it, point your web browser to www.manning.com/books/getting-mean-with-mongo-express-angular-and-node. This page provides information on how to get on the forum once you are registered, what kind of help is available, and the rules of conduct on the forum.

Manning's commitment to our readers is to provide a venue where a meaningful dialogue between individual readers and between readers and the author can take place. It is not a commitment to any specific amount of participation on the part of the author, whose contribution to the forum remains voluntary (and unpaid). We suggest you try asking the author some challenging questions lest his interest stray!

The Author Online forum and the archives of previous discussions will be accessible from the publisher's website as long as the book is in print.

About the cover illustration

The figure on the cover of this book is captioned "Habit of a Lady of Constantinople ca. 1730." The illustration is taken from Thomas Jefferys's *A Collection of the Dresses of Different Nations, Ancient and Modern* (four volumes), London, published between 1757 and 1772. The title page states that these are hand-colored copperplate engravings, heightened with gum arabic. Thomas Jefferys (1719–1771) was called "Geographer to King George III." He was an English cartographer who was the leading map supplier of his day. He engraved and printed maps for government and other official bodies and produced a wide range of commercial maps and atlases, especially of North America. His work as a map maker sparked an interest in local dress customs of the lands he surveyed and mapped, and which are brilliantly displayed in this collection.

Fascination with faraway lands and travel for pleasure were relatively new phenomena in the late 18th century, and collections such as this one were popular, introducing both the tourist as well as the armchair traveler to the inhabitants of other countries. The diversity of the drawings in Jefferys's volumes speaks vividly of the uniqueness and individuality of the world's nations some 200 years ago. Dress codes have changed since then and the diversity by region and country, so rich at the time, has faded away. It is now often hard to tell the inhabitants of one continent from another. Perhaps, trying to view it optimistically, we have traded a cultural and visual diversity for a more varied personal life. Or a more varied and interesting intellectual and technical life.

At a time when it is hard to tell one computer book from another, Manning celebrates the inventiveness and initiative of the computer business with book covers based on the rich diversity of regional life of two centuries ago, brought back to life by Jefferys's pictures.

Part 1

Setting the baseline

Full-stack development is very rewarding when you get it right. There are many moving parts to an application and it's your job to get them working in harmony. The best first step you can take is to understand the building blocks you have to work with and look at the ways you can put them together to achieve different results.

This is what part 1 is all about. In chapter 1 we'll take a look at the benefits of learning full-stack development in a bit more detail and explore the components of the MEAN stack. Chapter 2 builds on this knowledge of the components and discusses how you can use them together to build different things.

By the end of part 1 you'll have a good understanding of possible software and hardware architectures for a MEAN-stack application, as well as the plan for the application we'll build throughout the book.

Introducing full-stack development

This chapter covers

- The benefits of full-stack development
- An overview of the MEAN stack components
- What makes the MEAN stack so compelling
- A preview of the application we'll build throughout this book

If you're like me then you're probably impatient to dive into some code and get on with building something. But let's take a moment first to clarify what is meant by *full-stack development,* and look at the component parts of the stack to make sure you understand each.

When I talk about full-stack development, I'm really talking about developing all parts of a website or application. The full stack starts with the database and web server in the back end, contains application logic and control in the middle, and goes all the way through to the user interface at the front end.

The MEAN stack is comprised of four main technologies, with a cast of supporting technologies:

- **M**ongoDB—the database
- **E**xpress—the web framework
- **A**ngularJS—the front-end framework
- **N**ode.js—the web server

MongoDB has been around since 2007, and is actively maintained by MongoDB Inc., previously known as 10gen.

Express was first released in 2009 by T. J. Holowaychuk and has since become the most popular framework for Node.js. It's open source with more than 100 contributors, and is actively developed and supported.

AngularJS is open source and backed by Google. It has been around since 2010 and is constantly being developed and extended.

Node.js was created in 2009, and its development and maintenance are sponsored by Joyent. Node.js uses Google's open source V8 JavaScript engine at its core.

1.1   Why learn the full stack?

So, indeed, why learn the full stack? It sounds like an awful lot of work! Well yes, it *is* quite a lot of work, but it's also very rewarding. And with the MEAN stack it isn't as hard as you might think.

1.1.1   A very brief history of web development

Back in the early days of the web, people didn't have high expectations of websites. Not much emphasis was given to presentation; it was much more about what was going on behind the scenes. Typically, if you knew something like Perl and could string together a bit of HTML then you were a web developer.

As use of the internet spread, businesses started to take more of an interest in how their online presence portrayed them. In combination with the increased browser support of Cascading Style Sheets (CSS) and JavaScript, this desire started to lead to more complicated front-end implementations. It was no longer a case of being able to string together HTML; you needed to spend time on CSS and JavaScript, making sure it looked right and worked as expected. And all of this needed to work in different browsers, which were much less compliant than they are today.

This is where the distinction between front-end developer and back-end developer came in. Figure 1.1 illustrates this separation over time.

While the back-end developers were focused on the mechanics behind the scenes, the front-end developers focused on building a good user experience. As time went on, higher expectations were made of both camps, encouraging this trend to continue. Developers often had to choose an expertise and focus on it.

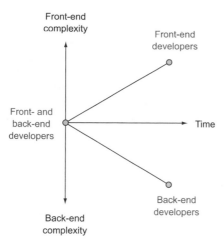

Figure 1.1 Divergence of front-end and back-end developers over time

HELPING DEVELOPERS WITH LIBRARIES AND FRAMEWORKS

During the 2000s libraries and frameworks started to become popular and prevalent for the most common languages, on both the front and back ends. Think Dojo and jQuery for front-end JavaScript, and CodeIgniter for PHP and Ruby on Rails. These frameworks were designed to make your life as a developer easier, lowering the barriers to entry. A good library or framework abstracts away some of the complexities of development, allowing you to code faster and requiring less in-depth expertise. This trend toward simplification has resulted in a resurgence of full-stack developers who build both the front end and the application logic behind it, as figure 1.2 shows.

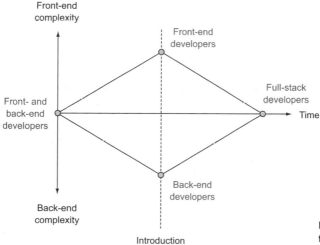

Figure 1.2 Impact of frameworks on the separated web development factions

Figure 1.2 illustrates a trend rather than proclaiming a definitive "all web developers should be full-stack developers" maxim. There have been, of course, full-stack developers throughout the entire history of the web, and moving forward it's most likely that some developers will choose to specialize on either front-end or back-end development. The intention is to show that through the use of frameworks and modern tools you no longer have to choose one side or the other to be a good web developer.

A huge advantage of embracing the framework approach is that you can be incredibly productive, as you'll have an all-encompassing vision of the application and how it ties together.

MOVING THE APPLICATION CODE FORWARD IN THE STACK

Continuing with the trend for frameworks, the last few years have seen an increasing tendency for moving the application logic away from the server and into the front end. Think of it as coding the back end in the front end. Some of the more popular JavaScript frameworks doing this are AngularJS, Backbone, and Ember.

Tightly coupling the application code to the front end like this really starts to blur the lines between traditional front-end and back-end developers. One of the reasons that people like to use this approach is that it reduces the load on the servers, thus reducing cost. What you're in effect doing is crowd-sourcing the computational power required for the application by pushing that load into the users' browsers.

I'll discuss the pros and cons of this approach later in the book, and cover when it may or may not be appropriate to use one of these technologies.

1.1.2 The trend toward full-stack developers

As discussed, the paths of front-end and back-end developers are merging, and it's entirely possible to be fully proficient in both disciplines. If you're a freelancer, consultant, or part of a small team, being multiskilled is extremely useful, increasing the value that you can provide for your clients. Being able to develop the full scope of a website or application gives you better overall control and can help the different parts work seamlessly together, as they haven't been built in isolation by separate teams.

If you work as part of a large team then chances are that you'll need to specialize in (or at least focus on) one area. But it's generally advisable to understand how your component fits with other components, giving you a greater appreciation of the requirements and goals of other teams and the overall project.

In the end, building on the full stack by yourself is very rewarding. Each part comes with its own challenges and problems to solve, keeping things interesting. The technology and tools available today enhance this experience, and empower you to build great web applications relatively quickly and easily.

1.1.3 Benefits of full-stack development

There are many benefits to learning full-stack development. For starters, there's the enjoyment of learning new things and playing with new technologies, of course. Then there's also the satisfaction of mastering something different and the thrill of being able to build and launch a full data-driven application all by yourself.

The benefits when working in a team include

- You're more likely to have a better view of the bigger picture by understanding the different areas and how they fit together.
- You'll form an appreciation of what other parts of the team are doing and what they need to be successful.
- Team members can move around more freely.

The additional benefits when working by yourself include

- You can build applications end-to-end by yourself with no dependencies on other people.
- You have more skills, services, and capabilities to offer customers.

All in all, there's a lot to be said for full-stack development. A majority of the most accomplished developers I've met have been full-stack developers. Their overall understanding and ability to see the bigger picture is a tremendous bonus.

1.1.4　Why the MEAN stack specifically?

The MEAN stack pulls together some of the "best-of-breed" modern web technologies into a very powerful and flexible stack. One of the great things about the MEAN stack is that it not only uses JavaScript in the browser, it uses JavaScript throughout. Using the MEAN stack, you can code both the front end and back end in the same language.

The principle technology allowing this to happen is Node.js, bringing JavaScript to the back end.

1.2　Introducing Node.js: The web server/platform

Node.js is the N in MEAN. Being last doesn't mean that it's the least important—it's actually the foundation of the stack!

In a nutshell, Node.js is a software platform that allows you to create your own web server and build web applications on top of it. Node.js isn't itself a web server, nor is it a language. It contains a built-in HTTP server library, meaning that you don't need to run a separate web server program such as Apache or Internet Information Services (IIS). This ultimately gives you greater control over how your web server works, but also increases the complexity of getting it up and running, particularly in a live environment.

With PHP, for example, you can easily find a shared-server web host running Apache, send some files over FTP, and—all being well—your site is running. This works because the web host has already configured Apache for you and others to use. With Node.js this isn't the case, as you configure the Node.js server when you create your application. Many of the traditional web hosts are behind the curve on Node.js support, but a number of new platform as a service (PaaS) hosts are springing up to address this need, including Heroku, Nodejitsu, and OpenShift. The approach to deploying live sites on these PaaS hosts is different from the old FTP model, but is quite easy when you get the hang of it. We'll be deploying a site live to Heroku as we go through the book.

An alternative approach to hosting a Node.js application is to do it all yourself on a dedicated server onto which you can install anything you need. But production server administration is a whole other book! And while you could independently swap out any of the other components with an alternative technology, if you take Node.js out then everything that sits on top of it would change.

1.2.1   JavaScript: The single language through the stack

One of the main reasons that Node.js is gaining broad popularity is that you code it in a language that most web developers are already familiar with: JavaScript. Until now, if you wanted to be a full-stack developer you had to be proficient in at least two languages: JavaScript on the front end and something else like PHP or Ruby on the back end.

Microsoft's foray into server-side JavaScript

In the late 1990s Microsoft released Active Server Pages (now known as Classic ASP). ASP could be written in either VBScript or JavaScript, but the JavaScript version didn't really take off. This is largely because, at the time, a lot of people were familiar with Visual Basic, which VBScript looks like. The majority of books and online resources were for VBScript, so it snowballed into becoming the "standard" language for Classic ASP.

With the release of Node.js you can leverage what you already know and put it to use on the server. One of the hardest parts of learning a new technology like this is learning the language, but if you already know some JavaScript then you're one step ahead!

There is, of course, a learning curve when taking on Node.js, even if you're an experienced front-end JavaScript developer. The challenges and obstacles in server-side programming are different from those in the front end, but you'll face those no matter what technology you use. In the front end you might be concerned about making sure everything works in a variety of different browsers on different devices. On the server you're more likely to be aware of the flow of the code, to ensure that nothing gets held up and that you don't waste system resources.

1.2.2   Fast, efficient, and scalable

Another reason for the popularity of Node.js is, when coded correctly, it's extremely fast and makes very efficient use of system resources. This enables a Node.js application to serve more users on fewer server resources than most of the other mainstream server technologies. So business owners also like the idea of Node.js because it can reduce their running costs, even at a large scale.

How does it do this? Node.js is light on system resources because it's single-threaded, whereas traditional web servers are multithreaded. Let's take a look at what that means, starting with the traditional multithreaded approach.

TRADITIONAL MULTITHREADED WEB SERVER

Most of the current mainstream web servers are multithreaded, including Apache and IIS. What this means is that every new visitor (or session) is given a separate "thread" and associated amount of RAM, often around 8 MB.

Thinking of a real-world analogy, imagine two people going into a bank wanting to do separate things. In a multithreaded model they'd each go to a separate bank teller who would deal with their requests, as shown in figure 1.3.

You can see in figure 1.3 that Simon goes to bank teller 1 and Sally goes to bank teller 2. Neither side is aware of or impacted by the other. Bank teller 1 deals with Simon throughout the entirety of the transaction and nobody else; the same goes for bank teller 2 and Sally.

This approach works perfectly well as long as you have enough tellers to service the customers. When the bank gets busy and the customers outnumber the tellers, that's when the service starts to slow down and the customers have to wait to be seen. While banks don't always worry about this too much, and seem happy to make you queue,

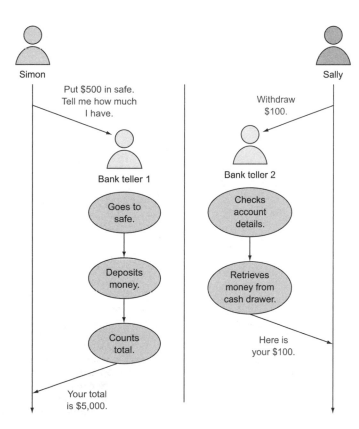

Figure 1.3　Example of a multithreaded approach: visitors use separate resources. Visitors and their dedicated resources have no awareness of or contact with other visitors and their resources.

the same isn't true of websites. If a website is slow to respond you're likely to leave and never come back.

This is one of the reasons why web servers are often overpowered and have so much RAM, even though they don't need it 90% of the time. The hardware is sct up in such a way as to be prepared for a huge spike in traffic. It's like the bank hiring an additional 50 full-time tellers and moving to a bigger building because they get busy at lunchtime.

Surely there's a better way, a way that's a bit more scalable? Here's where a single-threaded approach comes in.

A SINGLE-THREADED WEB SERVER

A Node.js server is single-threaded and works differently than the multithreaded way. Rather than giving each visitor a unique thread and a separate silo of resources, every visitor joins the same thread. A visitor and thread only interact when needed, when the visitor is requesting something or the thread is responding to a request.

Returning to the bank teller analogy, there would be only one teller who deals with all of the customers. But rather than going off and managing all requests end-to-end, the teller delegates any time-consuming tasks to "back office" staff and deals with the next request. Figure 1.4 illustrates how this might work, using the same two requests from the multithreaded example.

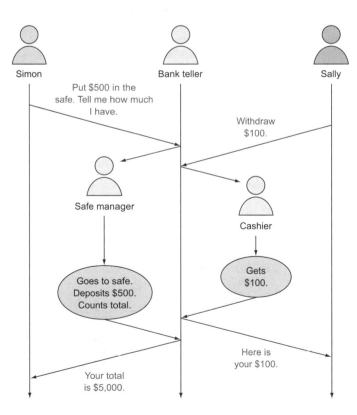

Figure 1.4   Example of a single-threaded approach: visitors use the same central resource. The central resource must be well disciplined to prevent one visitor from affecting others.

In the single-threaded approach shown in figure 1.4, Sally and Simon both give their requests to the same bank teller. But instead of dealing with one of them entirely before the next, the teller takes the first request and passes it to the best person to deal with it, before taking the next request and doing the same thing. When the teller is told that the requested task is completed, the teller then passes this straight back to the visitor who requested it.

Blocking versus nonblocking code

With the single-threaded model it's important to remember that all of your users use the same central process. To keep the flow smooth you need to make sure that nothing in your code causes a delay, blocking another operation. An example would be if the bank teller has to go to the safe to deposit the money for Simon, Sally would have to wait to make her request.

Similarly, if your central process is responsible for reading each static file (such as CSS, JavaScript, or images) it won't be able to process any other request, thus blocking the flow. Another common task that's potentially blocking is interacting with a database. If your process is going to the database each time it's asked, be it searching for data or saving data, it won't be able to do anything else.

So for the single-threaded approach to work you must make sure your code is non-blocking. The way to achieve this is to make any blocking operations run asynchronously, preventing them from blocking the flow of your main process.

Despite there being just a single teller, neither of the visitors is aware of the other, and neither of them is impacted by the requests of the other. This approach means that the bank doesn't need a large number of tellers constantly on hand. This model isn't infinitely scalable, of course, but it's more efficient. You can do more with fewer resources. This doesn't mean that you'll never need to add more resources.

This particular approach is possible in Node.js due to the asynchronous capabilities of JavaScript. You'll see this in action throughout the book, but if you're not sure on the theory, check out appendix D, particularly the section on callbacks.

1.2.3　*Using prebuilt packages via npm*

npm is a package manager that gets installed when you install Node.js. npm gives you the ability to download Node.js modules or "packages" to extend the functionality of your application. At the time of writing there are more than 46,000 packages available through npm, giving you an indication of just how much depth of knowledge and experience you can bring into the application.

Packages in npm vary widely in what they give you. We'll use some throughout this book to bring in an application framework and database driver with schema support. Other examples include helper libraries like *Underscore*, testing frameworks like *Mocha*, and other utilities like *Colors*, which adds color support to Node.js console logs.

We'll look more closely at npm and how it works when we get started building an application in chapter 3.

As you've seen, Node.js is extremely powerful and flexible, but it doesn't give you much help when trying to create a website or application. Express has been created to give you a hand here. Express is installed using npm.

1.3 Introducing Express: The framework

Express is the E in MEAN. As Node.js is a platform, it doesn't prescribe how it should be set up or used. This is one of its great strengths. But when creating websites and web applications there are quite a few common tasks that need doing every time. Express is a web application framework for Node.js that has been designed to do this in a well-tested and repeatable way.

1.3.1 Easing your server setup

As already noted, Node.js is a platform not a server. This allows you to get creative with your server setup and do things that other web servers can't do. It also makes it harder to get a basic website up and running.

Express abstracts away this difficulty by setting up a web server to listen to incoming requests and return relevant responses. In addition, it also defines a directory structure. One of these folders is set up to serve static files in a nonblocking way—the last thing you want is for your application to have to wait when somebody else requests a CSS file! You could configure this yourself directly in Node.js, but Express does it for you.

1.3.2 Routing URLs to responses

One of the great features of Express is that it provides a really simple interface for directing an incoming URL to a certain piece of code. Whether this is going to serve a static HTML page, read from a database, or write to a database doesn't really matter. The interface is simple and consistent.

What Express has done here is abstract away some of the complexity of doing this in native Node.js, to make code quicker to write and easier to maintain.

1.3.3 Views: HTML responses

It's likely that you'll want to respond to many of the requests to your application by sending some HTML to the browser. By now it will come as no surprise to you that Express makes this easier than it is in native Node.js.

Express provides support for a number of different templating engines that make it easier to build HTML pages in an intelligent way, using reusable components as well as data from your application. Express compiles these together and serves them to the browser as HTML.

1.3.4   *Remembering visitors with session support*

Being single-threaded, Node.js doesn't remember a visitor from one request to the next. It doesn't have a silo of RAM set aside just for you; it just sees a series of HTTP requests. HTTP is a stateless protocol, so there's no concept of storing a session state there. As it stands, this makes it difficult to create a personalized experience in Node.js or have a secure area where a user has to log in—it's not much use if the site forgets who you are on every page. You can do it, of course, but you have to code it yourself.

Or, you'll never guess what: Express has an answer to this too! Express comes with the ability to use *sessions* so that you can identify individual visitors through multiple requests and pages. Thank you Express!

Sitting on top of Node.js, Express gives you a great helping hand and a sound starting point for building web applications. It abstracts away a number of complexities and repeatable tasks that most of us don't need—or want—to worry about. We just want to build web applications.

1.4   *Introducing MongoDB: The database*

The ability to store and use data is vital for most applications. In the MEAN stack the database of choice is MongoDB, the M in MEAN. MongoDB fits into the stack incredibly well. Like Node.js, it's renowned for being fast and scalable.

1.4.1   *Relational versus document databases*

If you've used a relational database before, or even a spreadsheet, you'll be used to the concept of columns and rows. Typically, a column defines the name and data type and each row would be a different entry. See table 1.1 for an example of this.

Table 1.1   How rows and columns can look in a relational database table

firstName	middleName	lastName	maidenName	nickname
Simon	David	Holmes		Si
Sally	June	Panayiotou		
Rebecca		Norman	Holmes	Bec

MongoDB is *not* like that! MongoDB is a document database. The concept of rows still exists but columns are removed from the picture. Rather than a column defining what should be in the row, each row is a document, and this document both defines and holds the data itself. See table 1.2 for how a collection of documents might be listed (the indented layout is for readability, not a visualization of columns).

Table 1.2   Each document in a document database defines and holds the data, in no particular order.

firstName: "Simon"	middleName: "David"	lastName: "Holmes"	nickname: "Si"
lastName: "Panayiotou"	middleName: "June"	firstName: "Sally"	
maidenName: "Holmes"	firstName: "Rebecca"	lastName: "Norman"	nickname: "Bec"

This less-structured approach means that a collection of documents could have a wide variety of data inside. Let's take a look at a sample document so that you've got a better idea of what I'm talking about.

1.4.2   *MongoDB documents: JavaScript data store*

MongoDB stores documents as BSON, which is binary JSON (JavaScript Serialized Object Notation). Don't worry for now if you're not fully familiar with JSON—check out the relevant section in appendix D, which can be found online at https://www .manning.com/books/getting-mean-with-mongo-express-angular-and-node. In short, JSON is a JavaScript way of holding data, hence why MongoDB fits so well into the JavaScript-centric MEAN stack!

The following code snippet shows a very simple sample MongoDB document:

```
{
  "firstName" : "Simon",
  "lastName" : "Holmes",
  _id : ObjectId("52279effc62ca8b0c1000007")
}
```

Even if you don't know JSON that well, you can probably see that this document stores the first and last names of me, Simon Holmes! So rather than a document holding a data set that corresponds to a set of columns, a document holds name and value pairs. This makes a document useful in its own right, as it both describes and defines the data.

A quick word about _id. You most likely noticed the _id entry alongside the names in the preceding example MongoDB document. The _id entity is a unique identifier that MongoDB will assign to any new document when it's created.

We'll look at MongoDB documents in more detail in chapter 5 when we start to add the data into our application.

1.4.3   *More than just a document database*

MongoDB sets itself apart from many other document databases with its support for secondary indexing and rich queries. This means that you can create indexes on more than just the unique identifier field, and querying indexed fields is much faster. You can also create some fairly complex queries against a MongoDB database—not to the level of huge SQL commands with joins all over the place, but powerful enough for most use cases.

As we build an application through the course of this book, we'll get to have some fun with this, and you'll start to appreciate exactly what MongoDB can do.

1.4.4 *What is MongoDB not good for?*

MongoDB isn't a transactional database, and shouldn't be used as such. A transactional database can take a number of separate operations as one transaction. If any one of the operations in a transaction should fail the entire transaction fails, and none of the operations complete. MongoDB does *not* work like this. MongoDB will take each of the operations independently; if one fails then it alone fails and the rest of the operations will continue.

This is important if you need to update multiple collections or documents at once. If you're building a shopping cart, for example, you need to make sure that the payment is made and recorded, and also that the order is marked as confirmed to be processed. You certainly don't want to entertain the possibility that a customer might have paid for an order that your system thinks is still in the checkout. So these two operations need to be tied together in one *transaction*. Your database structure might allow you to do this in one collection, or you might code fallbacks and safety nets into your application logic in case one fails, or you might choose to use a transactional database.

1.4.5 *Mongoose for data modeling and more*

MongoDB's flexibility about what it stores in documents is a great thing for the database. But most applications need some structure to their data. Note that it's the application that needs the structure, not the database. So where does it make most sense to define the structure of your application data? In the application itself!

To this end, the company behind MongoDB created Mongoose. In their own words, Mongoose provides "elegant MongoDB object modeling for Node.js" (http://mongoosejs.com/).

WHAT IS DATA MODELING?

Data modeling, in the context of Mongoose and MongoDB, is defining what data *can* be in a document, and what data *must* be in a document. When storing user information you might want to be able to save the first name, last name, email address, and phone number. But you only *need* the first name and email address, and the email address must be unique. This information is defined in a schema, which is used as the basis for the data model.

WHAT ELSE DOES MONGOOSE OFFER?

As well as modeling data, Mongoose adds an entire layer of features on top of MongoDB that are useful when building web applications. Mongoose makes it easier to manage the connections to your MongoDB database, as well as to save data and read data. We'll use all of this later. We'll also discuss how Mongoose enables you to add data validation at the schema level, making sure that you only allow valid data to be saved in the database.

MongoDB is a great choice of database for most web applications because it provides a balance between the speed of pure document databases and the power of relational databases. That the data is effectively stored in JSON makes it the perfect data store for the MEAN stack.

1.5   Introducing AngularJS: The front-end framework

AngularJS is the A in MEAN. In simple terms, AngularJS is a JavaScript framework for working with data directly in the front end.

You could use Node.js, Express, and MongoDB to build a fully functioning data-driven web application. And we'll do just this throughout the book. But you can put some icing on the cake by adding AngularJS to the stack.

The traditional way of doing things is to have all of the data processing and application logic on the server, which then passes HTML out to the browser. AngularJS enables you to move some or all of this processing and logic out to the browser, sometimes leaving the server just passing data from the database. We'll take a look at this in a moment when we discuss two-way data binding, but first we need to address the question of whether AngularJS is like jQuery, the leading front-end JavaScript library.

1.5.1   jQuery versus AngularJS

If you're familiar with jQuery, you might be wondering if AngularJS works the same way. The short answer is no, not really. jQuery is generally added to a page to provide interactivity, after the HTML has been sent to the browser and the Document Object Model (DOM) has completely loaded. AngularJS comes in a step earlier and helps put together the HTML based on the data provided.

Also, jQuery is a library, and as such has a collection of features that you can use as you wish. AngularJS is what is known as an *opinionated framework*. This means that it forces its opinion on you as to how it needs to be used.

As mentioned, AngularJS helps put the HTML together based on the data provided, but it does more than this. It also immediately updates the HTML if the data changes, and can also update the data if the HTML changes. This is known as two-way data binding, which we'll now take a quick look at.

1.5.2   Two-way data binding: Working with data in a page

To understand two-way data binding let's start with a look at the traditional approach of one-way data binding. One-way data binding is what you're aiming for when looking at using Node.js, Express, and MongoDB. Node.js gets the data from MongoDB, and Express then uses a template to compile this data into HTML that's then delivered to the server. This process is illustrated in figure 1.5.

This one-way model is the basis for most database-driven websites. In this model most of the hard work is done on the server, leaving the browser to just render HTML and run any JavaScript interactivity.

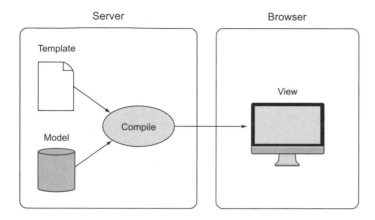

Figure 1.5 One-way data binding—the template and model are compiled on the server before being sent to the browser.

Two-way data binding is different. First, the template and data are sent independently to the browser. The browser itself compiles the template into the view and the data into a model. The real difference is that the view is "live." The view is bound to the model, so if the model changes the view changes instantly. On top of this, if the view changes then the model also changes. Two-way binding is illustrated in figure 1.6.

As your data store is likely to be exposed via an API and not tightly coupled to the application, there's typically some processing involved before adding it to the model. You want to make sure that you're binding the correct, relevant data to the view.

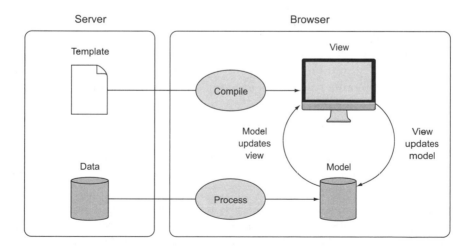

Figure 1.6 Two-way data binding—the model and the view are processed in the browser and bound together, each instantly updating the other.

As we go through part 3 of the book you'll really get to see—and use—this in action. Seeing is believing with this, and you won't be disappointed.

1.5.3   *Using AngularJS to load new pages*

Something that AngularJS has been specifically designed for is *single-page application* (SPA) functionality. In real terms, an SPA runs everything inside the browser and never does a full page reload. What this means is that all application logic, data processing, user flow, and template delivery can be managed in the browser.

Think Gmail. That's an SPA. Different views get shown in the page, along with a whole variety of data sets, but the page itself never fully reloads.

This approach can really reduce the amount of resources you need on your server, as you're essentially crowd-sourcing the computational power. Each person's browser is doing the hard work, and your server is basically just serving up static files and data on request.

The user experience can also be better when using this approach. Once the application is loaded there are fewer calls to be made to the server, reducing the potential of latency.

All this sounds great, but surely there's a price to pay? Why isn't everything built in AngularJS?

1.5.4   *Are there any downsides?*

Despite its many benefits, AngularJS isn't appropriate for every website. Front-end libraries like jQuery are best used for progressive enhancement. The idea is that your site will function perfectly well without JavaScript, and the JavaScript you do use makes the experience better. That isn't the case with AngularJS, or indeed any other SPA framework. AngularJS uses JavaScript to build the rendered HTML from templates and data, so if your browser doesn't support JavaScript, or if there's a bug in the code, then the site won't run.

This reliance on JavaScript to build the page also causes problems with search engines. When a search engine crawls your site it will not run any JavaScript, and with AngularJS the only thing you get before JavaScript takes over is the template from the server. If you want your content and data indexed by search engines rather than just your templates, you'll need to think whether AngularJS is right for that project.

There are ways to combat this issue—in short, you need your server to output compiled content as well as AngularJS—but if you don't *need* to fight this battle, I'd recommend against doing so.

One thing you can do is use AngularJS for some things and not others. There's nothing wrong with using AngularJS selectively in your project. For example, you might have a data-rich interactive application or section of your site that's ideal for building in AngularJS. You might also have a blog or some marketing pages around your application. These don't need to be built in AngularJS, and arguably would be better served from the server in the traditional way. So part of your site is served by Node.js, Express, and MongoDB, and another part also has AngularJS doing its thing.

This flexible approach is one of the most powerful aspects of the MEAN stack. With one stack you can achieve a great many different things.

1.6   Supporting cast

The MEAN stack gives you everything you need for creating data-rich interactive web applications, but you may want to use a few extra technologies to help you on the way. You can use Twitter Bootstrap to help create a good user interface, Git to help manage your code, and Heroku to help by hosting the application on a live URL. In later chapters we'll look at incorporating these into the MEAN stack. Here, we'll just cover briefly what each can do for you.

1.6.1   Twitter Bootstrap for user interface

In this book we're going to use Twitter Bootstrap to create a responsive design with minimal effort. It's not essential for the stack, and if you're building an application from existing HTML or a specific design then you probably won't want to add it in. But we're going to be building an application in a "rapid prototype" style, going from idea to application with no external influences.

Bootstrap is a front-end framework that provides a wealth of help for creating a great user interface. Among its features, Bootstrap provides a responsive grid system, default styles for many interface components, and the ability to change the visual appearance with themes.

RESPONSIVE GRID LAYOUT

In a responsive layout, you serve up a single HTML page that arranges itself differently on different devices. This is done through detecting the screen resolution rather than trying to sniff out the actual device. Bootstrap targets four different pixel-width breakpoints for their layouts, loosely aimed at phones, tablets, laptops, and external monitors. So if you give a bit of thought to how you set up your HTML and CSS classes, you can use one HTML file to give the same content in different layouts suited to the screen size.

CSS CLASSES AND HTML COMPONENTS

Bootstrap comes with a set of predefined CSS classes that can create useful visual components. These include things like page headers, flash-message containers, labels and badges, stylized lists … the list goes on! They've thought of a lot, and it really helps you quickly build an application without having to spend too much time on the HTML layout and CSS styling.

Teaching Bootstrap isn't an aim of this book, but I'll point out various features as we're using them.

ADDING THEMES FOR A DIFFERENT FEEL

Bootstrap has a default look and feel that provides a really neat baseline. This is so commonly used that your site could end up looking like anybody else's. Fortunately, it's possible to download themes for Bootstrap to give your application a different twist. Downloading a theme is often as simple as replacing the Bootstrap CSS file with a new one. We'll use a free theme in this book to build our application, but it's also possible to buy premium themes from a number of sites online to give an application a unique feel.

1.6.2 Git for source control

Saving code on your computer or a network drive is all very well and good, but that only ever holds the current version. It also only lets you, or others on your network, access it.

Git is a distributed revision control and source code management system. This means that several people can work on the same codebase at the same time on different computers and networks. These can be pushed together with all changes stored and recorded. It also makes it possible to roll back to a previous state if necessary.

HOW TO USE GIT

Git is typically used from the command line, although there are GUIs available for Windows and Mac. Throughout this book we'll use command-line statements to issue the commands that we need. Git is very powerful and we're barely going to scratch the surface of it in this book, but everything we do will be noted.

In a typical Git setup you'll have a local repository on your machine and a remote centralized master repository hosted somewhere like GitHub or BitBucket. You can pull from the remote repository into your local one, or push from local to remote. All of this is really easy in the command line, and both GitHub and BitBucket have web interfaces so that you can keep a visual track on everything committed.

WHAT ARE WE USING GIT FOR HERE?

In this book we're going to be using Git for two reasons.

First, the source code of the sample application in this book will be stored on GitHub, with different branches for various milestones. We'll be able to clone the master or the separate branches to use the code.

Second, we'll use Git as the method for deploying our application to a live web server for the world to see. For hosting we'll be using Heroku.

1.6.3 Hosting with Heroku

Hosting Node.js applications can be complicated, but it doesn't have to be. Many traditional shared hosting providers haven't kept up with the interest in Node.js. Some will install it for you so that you can run applications, but the servers are generally not set up to meet the unique needs of Node.js. To run a Node.js application successfully you either need a server that has been configured with that in mind, or you can use a PaaS provider that's aimed specifically at hosting Node.js.

In this book we're going to go for the latter. We're going to use Heroku (www.heroku.com) as our hosting provider. Heroku is one of the leading hosts for Node.js applications, and it has an excellent free tier that we'll be making use of.

Applications on Heroku are essentially Git repositories, making the publishing process incredibly simple. Once everything is set up you can publish your application to a live environment using a single command:

```
$ git push heroku master
```

I told you it didn't have to be complicated.

1.7 *Putting it together with a practical example*

As already mentioned a few times, throughout the course of this book we'll build a working application on the MEAN stack. This will give you a good grounding in each of the technologies, as well as showing how they all fit together.

1.7.1 *Introducing the example application*

So what are we actually going to be building as we go through the book? We'll be building an application called Loc8r. Loc8r will list nearby places with WiFi where people can go and get some work done. It will also display facilities, opening times, a rating, and a location map for each place. Users will be able to log in and submit ratings and reviews.

This application has some grounding in the real world. Location-based applications themselves are nothing particularly new and come in a few different guises. Foursquare and Facebook Check In list everything nearby that they can, and crowd-source data for new places and information updates. UrbanSpoon helps people find nearby places to eat, allowing a user to search on price bracket and type of cuisine. Even companies like Starbucks and McDonald's have sections of their applications to help users find the nearest one.

REAL OR FAKE DATA?

Okay, so we're going to fake the data for Loc8r in this book, but you could collate the data, crowd-source it, or use an external source if you wanted. For a rapid prototype approach you'll often find that faking data for the first private version of your application speeds up the process.

END PRODUCT

We'll use all layers of the MEAN stack to create Loc8r, including Twitter Bootstrap to help us create a responsive layout. Figure 1.7 shows some screenshots of what we're going to be building throughout the book.

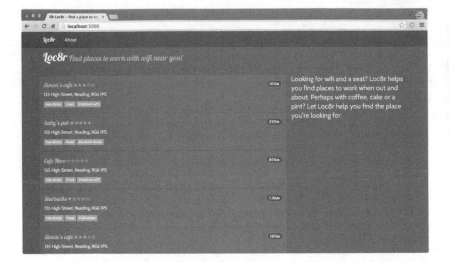

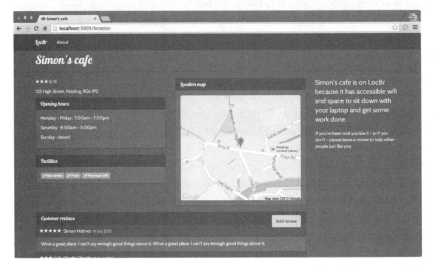

Figure 1.7 Loc8r is the application we're going to build throughout this book. It will display differently on different devices, showing a list of places and details about each place, and will allow visitors to log in and leave reviews.

1.7.2 How the MEAN stack components work together

By the time you've been through this book you'll have an application running on the MEAN stack, using JavaScript all of the way through. MongoDB stores data in binary JSON, which through Mongoose is exposed as JSON. The Express framework sits on top of Node.js, where the code is all written in JavaScript. In the front end is AngularJS, which again is JavaScript. Figure 1.8 illustrates this flow and connection.

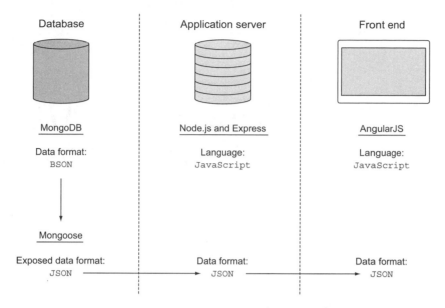

Figure 1.8 JavaScript is the common language throughout the MEAN stack, and JSON is the common data format.

We're going to explore various ways you can architect the MEAN stack and how we're going to build Loc8r in chapter 2.

1.8   Summary

In this chapter we've covered

- The different technologies making up the MEAN stack
- MongoDB as the database layer
- Node.js and Express working together to provide an application server layer
- AngularJS providing an amazing front-end, data-binding layer
- How the MEAN components work together
- A few ways to extend the MEAN stack with additional technologies

As JavaScript plays such a pivotal role in the stack, please take a look at appendix D (available online), which has a refresher on JavaScript pitfalls and best practices.

Coming up next in chapter 2 we're going to discuss how flexible the MEAN stack is, and how you can architect it differently for different scenarios.

Designing a MEAN
stack architecture

2

This chapter covers

- Introducing a common MEAN stack architecture
- Considerations for single-page applications
- Discovering alternative MEAN stack architectures
- Designing an architecture for a real application
- Planning a build based on the architecture design

In chapter 1 we took a look at the component parts of the MEAN stack and how they fit together. In this chapter we're going to look at how they fit together in more detail.

We'll start off by looking at what some people think of as *the* MEAN stack architecture, especially when they first encounter the stack. Using some examples we'll explore why you might use a different architecture, and switch things up a bit and move things around. MEAN is a very powerful stack and can be used to solve a diverse range of problems ... if you get creative with how you design your solutions.

2.1 A common MEAN stack architecture

A common way to architect a MEAN stack application is to have a representational state transfer (REST) API feeding a single-page application. The API is typically built with MongoDB, Express, and Node.js, with the SPA being built in AngularJS. This approach is particularly popular with those who come to the MEAN stack from an AngularJS background and are looking for a stack that gives a fast, responsive API. Figure 2.1 illustrates the basic setup and data flow.

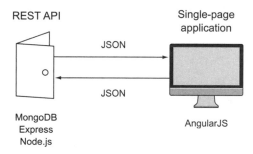

Figure 2.1 A common approach to MEAN stack architecture, using MongoDB, Express, and Node.js to build a REST API that feeds JSON data to an AngularJS SPA run in the browser

> ### What is a REST API?
>
> REST stands for REpresentational State Transfer, which is an architectural style rather than a strict protocol. REST is stateless—it has no idea of any current user state or history.
>
> API is an abbreviation for application program interface, which enables applications to talk to each other.
>
> So a REST API is a stateless interface to your application. In the case of the MEAN stack the REST API is used to create a stateless interface to your database, enabling a way for other applications to work with the data.

Figure 2.1 is a great setup, ideal if you have, or intend to build, an SPA as your user-facing side. AngularJS is designed with a focus on building SPAs, pulling in data from a REST API, as well as pushing it back. MongoDB, Express, and Node.js are also extremely capable when it comes to building an API, using JSON all the way through the stack including the database itself.

This is where many people start with the MEAN stack, looking for an answer to the question, "I've built an application in AngularJS; now where do I get the data?"

Having an architecture like this is great if you have an SPA, but what if you don't have or want to use an SPA? If this is the only way you think of the MEAN stack, you're going to get a bit stuck and start looking elsewhere. But the MEAN stack is very flexible. All four components are very powerful and have a lot to offer.

2.2 Looking beyond SPAs

Coding an SPA in AngularJS is like driving a Porsche along a coastal road with the roof down. Both are amazing. They're fun, fast, sexy, agile, and very, very capable. And it's most likely that both are a vast improvement on what you've been doing before.

But sometimes they're not appropriate. If you want to pack up the surfboards and take your family away for the week you're going to struggle with the sports car. As amazing as your car may be, in this case you're going to want to use something different. It's the same story with SPAs. Yes, building them in AngularJS is amazing, but sometimes it's not the best solution to your problem.

Let's take a brief look at some things to bear in mind about SPAs when designing a solution and deciding whether a full SPA is right for your project or not. This section isn't intended to be in any way "anti-SPA." SPAs generally offer a fantastic user experience while reducing the load on your servers, and therefore also your hosting costs. In sections 2.3.1 and 2.3.2 we'll look at a good use case for an SPA and a bad one, and we'll actually build one by the end of this book!

2.2.1 Hard to crawl

JavaScript applications are very hard for search engines to crawl and index. Most search engines look at the HTML content on a page but don't download or execute much JavaScript. For those that do, the actual crawling of JavaScript-created content is nowhere near as good as content delivered by the server. If all of your content is served via a JavaScript application then you cannot be sure how much of it will be indexed.

A related downside is that automatic previews from social-sharing sites like Facebook, LinkedIn, and Pinterest don't work very well. This is also because they look at the HTML of the page you're linking to and try to extract some relevant text and images. Like search engines they don't run JavaScript on the page, so content served by JavaScript won't be seen.

MAKING AN SPA CRAWLABLE

There are a couple of workarounds to make it look as though your site is crawlable. Both involve creating separate HTML pages that mirror the content of your SPA. You can have your server create an HTML-based version of your site and deliver that to crawlers, or you can use a headless browser such as PhantomJS to run your JavaScript application and output the resulting HTML.

Both of these require quite a bit of effort, and can end up being a maintenance headache if you have a large, complex site. There are also potential search engine optimization (SEO) pitfalls. If your server-generated HTML is deemed to be too different from the SPA content then your site will be penalized. Running PhantomJS to output the HTML can slow down the response speed of your pages, which is something for which search engines—Google in particular—downgrade you.

DOES IT MATTER?

Whether this matters or not depends on what you want to build. If the main growth plan for whatever you're building is through search engine traffic or social sharing then this is something you want to give a great deal of thought to. If you're creating something small that will stay small then managing the workarounds is achievable, whereas at a larger scale you'll struggle.

On the other hand, if you're building an application that doesn't need much SEO—or indeed if you *want* your site to be harder to scrape—then this isn't an issue you need to be concerned about. It could even be an advantage.

2.2.2 Analytics and browser history

Analytics tools like Google Analytics rely heavily on entire new pages loading in the browser, initiated by a URL change. SPAs don't work this way. There's a reason they're called *single-page* applications!

After the first page load, all subsequent page and content changes are handled internally by the application. So the browser never triggers a new page load, nothing gets added to the browser history, and your analytics package has no idea who's doing what on your site.

ADDING PAGE LOADS TO AN SPA

You can add page load events to an SPA using the HTML5 history API; this will help you integrate analytics. The difficulty comes in managing this and ensuring that everything is being tracked accurately, which involves checking for missing reports and double entries.

The good news is that you don't have to build everything from the ground up. There are several open source analytics integrations for AngularJS available online, addressing most of the major analytics providers. You still have to integrate them into your application and make sure that everything is working correctly, but you don't have to do everything from scratch.

IS IT A MAJOR PROBLEM?

The extent to which this is a problem depends on your need for undeniably accurate analytics. If you want to monitor trends in visitor flows and actions then you're probably going to find it easy to integrate. The more detail and definite accuracy you need, the more work it is to develop and test. While it's arguably much easier to just include your analytics code on every page of a server-generated site, analytics integration isn't likely to be the sole reason that you choose a non-SPA route.

2.2.3 Speed of initial load

SPAs have a slower first page load than server-based applications. This is because the first load has to bring down the framework and the application code before rendering the required view as HTML in the browser. A server-based application just has to push out the required HTML to the browser, reducing the latency and download time.

SPEEDING UP THE PAGE LOAD

There are some ways of speeding up the initial load of an SPA, such as a heavy approach to caching and lazy-loading modules when you need them. But you'll never get away from the fact that it needs to download the framework, at least some of the application code, and will most likely hit an API for data before displaying something in the browser.

SHOULD YOU CARE ABOUT SPEED?

The answer to whether you should care about the speed of the initial page load is, once again, "it depends." It depends on what you're building and how people are going to interact with it.

Think about Gmail. Gmail is an SPA and takes quite a while to load. Granted this is only normally a couple of seconds, but everyone online is impatient these days and expects immediacy. But people don't mind waiting for Gmail to load, as it's snappy and responsive once you're in. And once you're in, you often stay in for a while.

But if you have a blog pulling in traffic from search engines and other external links, you don't want the first page load to take a few seconds. People will assume your site is down or running slowly and click the back button before you've had the chance to show them content. I'm willing to bet that you know this happens because you've done it yourself!

2.2.4 To SPA or not to SPA?

Just a reminder that this wasn't an exercise in SPA-bashing; we're just taking a moment to think about some things that often get pushed to the side until it's too late. The three points about crawlability, analytics integration, and page load speed aren't designed to give clear-cut definitions about when to create an SPA and when to do something else. They're there to give a framework for consideration.

It might be the case that none of those things is an issue for your project, and that an SPA is definitely the right way to go. If you find that each point makes you pause and think, and it looks like you need to add in workarounds for all three, then an SPA probably isn't the way to go.

If you're somewhere in between then it's a judgment call about what is most important, and, crucially, what is the best solution for the project. As a rule of thumb, if your solution includes a load of workarounds at the outset then you probably need to rethink it.

Even if you decide that an SPA isn't right for you, that doesn't mean that you can't use the MEAN stack. Let's move on and take a look at how you can design a different architecture.

2.3 Designing a flexible MEAN architecture

If AngularJS is like having a Porsche then the rest of the stack is like also having an Audi RS6 in the garage. A lot of people may be focusing on your sports car out front and not give a second glance to the estate car in your garage. But if you do go into the garage and have a poke around, you'll find that there's a Lamborghini V10 engine under the hood. There's a lot more to that estate car than you might first think!

Only ever using MongoDB, Express, and Node.js together to build a REST API is like only ever using the Audi RS6 to do the school drop-off runs. They're all extremely capable and will do the job very well, but they have a lot more to offer.

We talked a little about what the technologies can do in chapter 1, but here are a few starting points:

- MongoDB can store and stream binary information.
- Node.js is particularly good for real-time connections using web sockets.
- Express is a web application framework with templating, routing, and session management built in.

There's also a lot more, and I'm certainly not going to be able to address the full capabilities of all of the technologies in this book. I'd need several books to do that! What I can do here is give you a simple example and show you how you can fit together the pieces of the MEAN stack to design the best solution.

2.3.1 Requirements for a blog engine

Let's take a look at the familiar idea of a blog engine, and see how you could best architect the MEAN stack to build one.

A blog engine typically has two sides to it. There's a public-facing side serving up articles to readers, and hopefully being syndicated and shared across the internet. A blog engine will also have an administrator interface where blog owners log in to write new articles and manage their blogs. Figure 2.2 shows some of the key characteristics for these two sides.

Looking at the lists in figure 2.2, it's quite easy to see a high level of conflict between the characteristics of the two sides. You've got content-rich, low interaction for the blog articles, but a feature-rich, highly interactive environment for the admin

Blog entries

Admin interface

Characteristics:
- Content-rich
- Low interaction
- Fast first load
- Short user duration
- Public and shareable

Characteristics:
- Feature-rich
- High interaction
- Fast response to actions
- Long user duration
- Private

Figure 2.2 Conflicting characteristics of the two sides of a blog engine, the public-facing blog entries and the private admin interface

interface. The blog articles should be quick to load to reduce bounce rates, whereas the admin area should be quick to respond to user input and actions. Finally, users typically stay on a blog entry for a short time, but may share it with others, whereas the admin interface is very private and an individual user could be logged in for a long time.

Taking what we've discussed about potential issues with SPAs, and looking at the characteristics of blog entries, you'll see quite a lot of overlap. It's quite likely that bearing this in mind you'd choose not to use an SPA to deliver your blog articles to readers. On the other hand, the admin interface is a perfect fit for an SPA.

So what do you do? Arguably the most important thing is to keep the blog readers coming—if they get a bad experience they won't come back and they won't share. If a blog doesn't get readers then the writer will stop writing or move to another platform. Then again, a slow and unresponsive admin interface will also see your blog owners jumping ship. So what do you do? How do you keep everybody happy and keep the blog engine in business?

2.3.2   A blog engine architecture

The answer lies in not looking for a one-size-fits-all solution. You effectively have two applications. You have public-facing content that should be delivered direct from the server and an interactive private admin interface that you want to build as an SPA. Let's start by looking at each of the two applications separately, starting with the admin interface.

ADMIN INTERFACE: AN ANGULARJS SPA

We've already discussed that this would be an ideal fit for an SPA built in AngularJS. So the architecture for this part of the engine will look very familiar: a REST API built with MongoDB, Express, and Node.js with an AngularJS SPA upfront. Figure 2.3 shows how this looks.

There's nothing particularly new shown in figure 2.3. The entire application is built in AngularJS and runs in the browser, with JSON data being passed back and forth between the AngularJS application and the REST API.

REST API   Admin interface

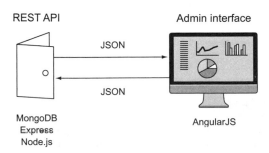

MongoDB   AngularJS
Express
Node.js

Figure 2.3   A familiar sight: the admin interface would be an AngularJS SPA making use of a REST API built with MongoDB, Express, and Node.js

BLOG ENTRIES: WHAT TO DO?

Looking at the blog entries, things get a little more difficult.

If you only think of the MEAN stack as an AngularJS SPA calling a REST API then you're going to get a bit stuck. You could build the public-facing site as an SPA anyway, because you want to use JavaScript and the MEAN stack. But it's not the best solution. You could decide that the MEAN stack isn't appropriate in this case and choose a different technology stack. But you don't want to do that! You want end-to-end JavaScript.

So let's take another look at the MEAN stack, and think about all of the components. You know that Express is a web application framework. You know that Express can use template engines to build HTML on the server. You know that Express can use URL routing and MVC patterns. You should start to think that perhaps Express has the answer!

BLOG ENTRIES: MAKING GOOD USE OF EXPRESS

In this blog scenario, delivering the HTML and content directly from the server is exactly what you want to do. Express does this particularly well, even offering a choice of template engines right from the get-go. The HTML content will require data from the database, so you'll use a REST API again for that (more on why it's best to take this approach in section 2.3.3). Figure 2.4 lays out the basis for this architecture.

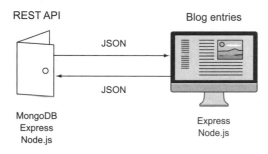

Figure 2.4 An architecture for delivering HTML directly from the server: an Express and Node.js application at the front, interacting with a REST API built in MongoDB, Express, and Node.js

This gives you an approach where you can use the MEAN stack, or part of it at least, to deliver database-driven content directly from the server to the browser. But it doesn't have to stop there. The MEAN stack is yet again more flexible.

BLOG ENTRIES: USING MORE OF THE STACK

You're looking at an Express application delivering the blog content to the visitors. If you want visitors to be able to log in, perhaps to add comments to articles, you need to track user sessions. You could use MongoDB with your Express application to do just this.

You might also have some dynamic data in the sidebar of your posts, such as related posts or a search box with type-ahead auto-completion. You could implement these in AngularJS. Remember, AngularJS isn't only for SPAs; it can also be used to add some rich data interactivity to an otherwise static page.

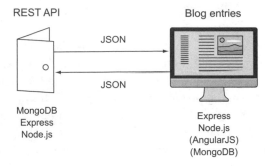

Figure 2.5 Adding the options of using AngularJS and MongoDB as part of the public-facing aspect of the blog engine, serving the blog entries to visitors

Figure 2.5 shows these optional parts of MEAN added to the blog entry architecture.

Now you have the possibility of a full MEAN application delivering content to visitors interacting with your REST API.

BLOG ENGINE: A HYBRID ARCHITECTURE

At this point there are two separate applications, each using a REST API. With a little bit of planning this can be a common REST API, used by both sides of the application.

Figure 2.6 shows what this looks like as a single architecture, with the one REST API interacting with the two front-end applications.

This is just a simple example to show how you can piece together the various parts of the MEAN stack into different architectures to answer the questions that your projects ask of you. Your options are only limited by your understanding of the components

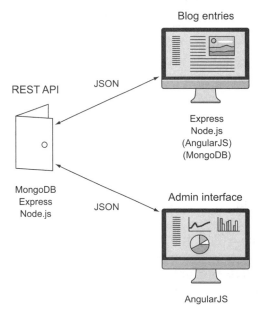

Figure 2.6 A hybrid MEAN stack architecture: a single REST API feeding two separate user-facing applications, built using different parts of the MEAN stack to give the most appropriate solution

and your creativity in putting them together. There's no one correct architecture for the MEAN stack.

2.3.3 Best practice: Build an internal API for a data layer

You've probably noticed that every version of the architecture includes an API to surface the data, and allows interaction between the main application and the database. There's a good reason for this.

If you were to start off by building your application in Node.js and Express, serving HTML directly from the server, it would be really easy to talk to the database directly from the Node.js application code. With a short-term view this is the easy way. But with a long-term view this becomes the difficult way, as it will tightly couple your data to your application code in a way that nothing else could use it.

The other option is to build your own API that can talk to the database directly and output the data you need. Your Node.js application can then talk with this API instead of directly with the database. Figure 2.7 shows a comparison of the two setups.

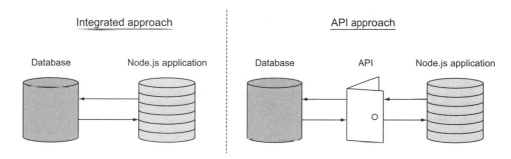

Figure 2.7   The short-term view of data integration into your Node.js application. You can set up your Node.js application to talk directly to your database, or you can create an API that interacts with the database and have your Node.js application talk only with the API.

Looking at figure 2.7 you could well be wondering why you'd want to go to the effort of creating an API just to sit in between your application and your database. Isn't it creating more work? At this stage, yes, it's creating more work—but you want to look further down the road here. What if you want to use your data in a native mobile application a little later? Or, for example, in an AngularJS front end?

You certainly don't want to find yourself in the position where you have to write separate but similar interfaces for each. If you've built your own API upfront that outputs the data you need, you can avoid all of this. If you have an API in place, when you want to integrate the data layer into your application you can simply make it reference your API. It doesn't matter if your application is Node.js, AngularJS, or iOS. It doesn't have to be a public API that anyone can use, so long as you can access it. Figure 2.8

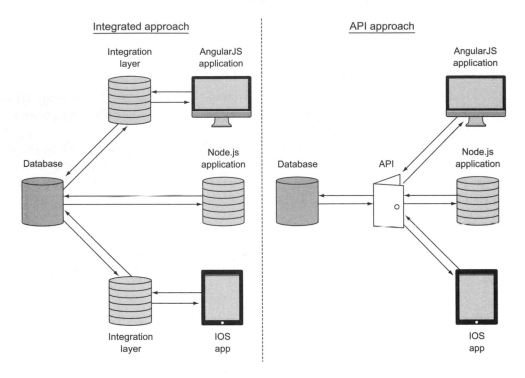

Figure 2.8   The long-term view of data integration into your Node.js application, and additional AngularJS and iOS applications. The integrated approach has now become fragmented, whereas the API approach is simple and maintainable.

shows a comparison of the two approaches when you have Node.js, AngularJS, and iOS applications all using the same data source.

As figure 2.8 shows, the previously simple integrated approach is now becoming fragmented and complex. You'll have three data integrations to manage and maintain, so any changes will have to be made in multiple places to retain consistency. If you have a single API you don't have any of these worries. So with a little bit of extra work at the beginning, you can make life much easier for yourself further down the road. We'll look at creating internal APIs in chapter 6.

2.4   *Planning a real application*

As we talked about in chapter 1, throughout the course of this book we'll build a working application on the MEAN stack called Loc8r. Loc8r will list nearby places with WiFi where people can go and get some work done. It will also display facilities, opening times, a rating, and a location map for each place. Visitors will be able to submit ratings and reviews.

For the sake of the demo application, we'll be creating fake data so that we can test it quickly and easily. So let's get planning.

2.4.1 *Planning the application at a high level*

The first step is to think about what screens we'll need in our application. We'll focus on the separate page views and the user journeys. We can do this at a very high level, not really concerning ourselves with the details of what is on each page. It is a good idea to sketch out this stage on a piece of paper or a whiteboard, as it helps to visualize the application as a whole. It also helps with organizing the screens into collections and flows, while serving as a good reference point for when we come to build it. As there's no data attached to the pages or application logic behind them, it's really easy to add and remove parts, change what is displayed where, and even change how many pages we want. The chances are that we won't get it right the first time; the key is to start and iterate and improve until we're happy with the separate pages and overall user flow.

PLANNING THE SCREENS

Let's think about Loc8r. As stated our aim is as follows:

> Loc8r will list nearby places with WiFi where people can go and get some work done. It will also display facilities, opening times, a rating, and a location map for each place. Visitors will be able to submit ratings and reviews.

From this we can get an idea about some of the screens we're going to need:

1. A screen that lists nearby places
2. A screen that shows details about an individual place
3. A screen for adding a review about a place

We'll probably also want to tell visitors what Loc8r is for and why it exists, so we should add another screen to the list:

4. A screen for "about us" information

DIVIDING THE SCREENS INTO COLLECTIONS

Next we want to take the list of screens and collate them where they logically belong together. For example, the first three in the list are all dealing with locations. The About page doesn't really belong anywhere so it can go in a miscellaneous Others collection. Sketching this out brings us something like figure 2.9.

Having a quick sketch like this is the first stage in planning, and we really need to go through this stage before we can start thinking about architecture. This stage gives us a chance to look at the basic pages, and to also think about the flow. Figure 2.9, for example, also shows a basic user journey in the Locations collection, going from the List page, to a Details page, and then onto the form to add a review.

Locations

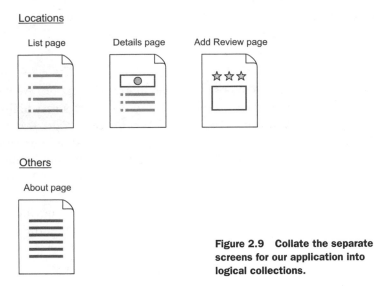

Others

Figure 2.9 **Collate the separate screens for our application into logical collections.**

2.4.2 *Architecting the application*

On the face of it Loc8r is a fairly simple application, with just a few screens. But we still need to think about how to architect it, as we're going to be transferring data from a database to a browser, letting users interact with the data, and allowing data to be sent back to the database.

STARTING WITH THE API

Because the application is going to be using a database and passing data around, we'll start building up the architecture with the piece we're definitely going to need. Figure 2.10 shows the starting point, a REST API built with Express and Node.js to enable interactions with the MongoDB database.

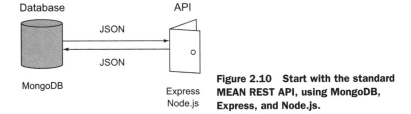

Figure 2.10 **Start with the standard MEAN REST API, using MongoDB, Express, and Node.js.**

As already discussed in this chapter, building an API to interface with our data is a bit of a given, and is the base point of the architecture. So the more interesting and difficult question is: How do we architect the application itself?

APPLICATION ARCHITECTURE OPTIONS

At this point we need to take a look at the specific requirements of our application, and how we can put together the pieces of the MEAN stack to build the best solution. Do we need something special from MongoDB, Express, AngularJS, or Node.js that will swing the decision a certain way? Do we want HTML served directly from the server, or is an SPA the better option?

For Loc8r there are no unusual or specific requirements, and whether or not it should be easily crawlable by search engines depends on the business growth plan. If the aim is to bring in organic traffic from search engines, then yes it needs to be crawlable. If the aim is to promote the application as an application and drive use that way, then search engine visibility is a lesser concern.

Thinking back to the blog example, we can immediately envisage three possible application architectures as shown in figure 2.11:

1. A Node.js and Express application
2. A Node.js and Express application with AngularJS additions for interactivity
3. An AngularJS SPA

With these three options in mind, which is the best for Loc8r?

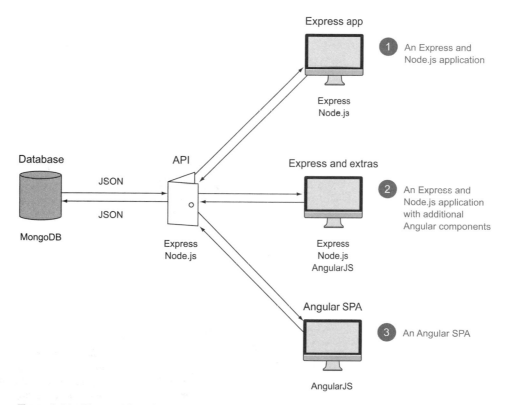

Figure 2.11 Three options for building the Loc8r application, ranging from a server-side Express and Node.js application to a full client-side AngularJS SPA

CHOOSING AN APPLICATION ARCHITECTURE

There are no specific business requirements pushing us to favor one particular architecture over another. It doesn't matter because we're going to do all three in this book. Building all three of the architectures will allow us to explore how each approach works, and will enable us to take a look at each of the technologies in turn, building up the application layer by layer.

We'll be building the architectures in the order they're shown in figure 2.11, starting with a Node.js and Express application, then moving on to add some AngularJS, before refactoring to an AngularJS SPA. While this isn't necessarily how you might build a site normally, it gives you a great opportunity for learning all aspects of the MEAN stack. We'll talk shortly in section 2.5 about the approach, and walk through the plan in a bit more detail.

2.4.3 *Wrapping everything in an Express project*

The architecture diagrams we've been looking at so far imply that we'll have separate Express applications for the API and the application logic. This is perfectly possible, and is a good way to go for a large project. If we're expecting large amounts of traffic we might even want our main application and our API on different servers. An additional benefit of this is that we can have more specific settings for each of the servers and applications that are best suited to the individual needs.

Another way is to keep things simple and contained and have everything inside a single Express project. With this approach we only have one application to worry about hosting and deploying, and one set of source code to manage. This is what we'll be doing with Loc8r, giving us one Express project containing a few subapplications. Figure 2.12 illustrates this particular approach.

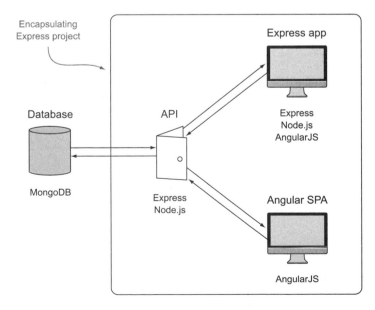

Figure 2.12 The architecture of the application with the API and application logic wrapped inside the same Express project

When putting together an application in this way it's important to organize our code well so that the distinct parts of the application are kept separate. As well as making our code easier to maintain, it also makes it easier to split it out into separate projects further down the line if we decide that's the right route. This is a key theme that we'll keep coming back to throughout the book.

2.4.4 The end product

As you can see, we'll use all layers of the MEAN stack to create Loc8r. We'll also include Twitter Bootstrap to help us create a responsive layout. Figure 2.13 shows some screenshots of what we're going to be building throughout the book.

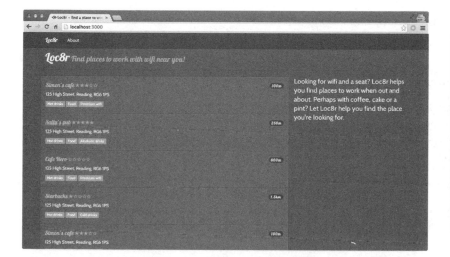

Figure 2.13   Loc8r is the application we're going to build throughout this book. It will display differently on different devices, showing a list of places and details about each place, and will enable visitors to log in and leave reviews.

2.5 *Breaking the development into stages*

In this book we have two aims:

1 Build an application on the MEAN stack
2 Learn about the different layers of the stack as we go

We'll approach the project in the way I'd personally go about building a rapid proto-type, but with a few tweaks to give you the best coverage of the whole stack. We'll start by looking at the five stages of rapid prototype development, and then see how we can use this approach to build up Loc8r layer by layer, focusing on the different technolo-gies as we go.

2.5.1 *Rapid prototype development stages*

Let's break down the process into a number of stages, which lets us concentrate on one thing at a time, increasing our chances of success. I find this approach works well for making an idea a reality.

STAGE 1: BUILD A STATIC SITE

The first stage is to build a static version of the application, which is essentially a num-ber of HTML screens. The aims of this stage are

- To quickly figure out the layout
- To ensure that the user flow makes sense

At this point we're not concerned with a database or flashy effects on the user inter-face; all we want to do is create a working mockup of the main screens and journeys that a user will take through the application.

STAGE 2: DESIGN THE DATA MODEL AND CREATE THE DATABASE

Once we have a working static prototype that we're happy with, the next thing to do is look at any hard-coded data in the static application and put it into a database. The aims of this stage are

- To define a data model that reflects the requirements of the application
- To create a database to work with the model

The first part of this is to define the data model. Stepping back to a bird's-eye view, what are the objects we need data about, how are the objects connected, and what data is held in them?

If we try to do this stage before building the static prototype then we're dealing with abstract concepts and ideas. Once we have a prototype, we can see what is hap-pening on different pages and what data is needed where. Suddenly this stage becomes much easier. Almost unknown to us, we've done the hard thinking while building the static prototype.

STAGE 3: BUILD OUR DATA API

After stages 1 and 2 we have a static site on one hand and a database on the other. This stage and the next take the natural steps of linking them together. The aim of stage 3 is

- To create a REST API that will allow our application to interact with the database

STAGE 4: HOOK THE DATABASE INTO THE APPLICATION

When we get to this stage we have a static application and an API exposing an interface to our database. The aim of this stage is

- To get our application to talk to our API

When this stage is complete the application will look pretty much the same as it did before, but the data will be coming from the database. When it's done, we'll have a data-driven application!

STAGE 5: AUGMENT THE APPLICATION

This stage is all about embellishing the application with additional functionality. We might add authentication systems, data validation, or methods for displaying error messages to users. It could include adding more interactivity to the front end or tightening up the business logic in the application itself.

So, really, the aims of this stage are

- To add finishing touches to our application
- To get the application ready for people to use

These five stages of development provide a great methodology for approaching a new build project. Let's take a look at how we'll follow these steps to build Loc8r.

2.5.2 The steps to build Loc8r

In building Loc8r throughout this book we have two aims. First, of course, we want to build a working application on the MEAN stack. Second, we want to learn about the different technologies, how to use them, and how to put them together in different ways.

So throughout the book we'll be following the five stages of development, but with a couple of twists so that we get to see the whole stack in action. Before we look at the steps in detail, let's quickly remind ourselves of the proposed architecture as shown in figure 2.14.

STEP 1: BUILD A STATIC SITE

We'll start off by following stage 1 and building a static site. I recommend doing this for any application or site, as you can learn a lot with relatively little effort. When building the static site, it's good to keep one eye on the future, keeping in mind what the final architecture will be. We've already defined the architecture for Loc8r as shown in figure 2.14.

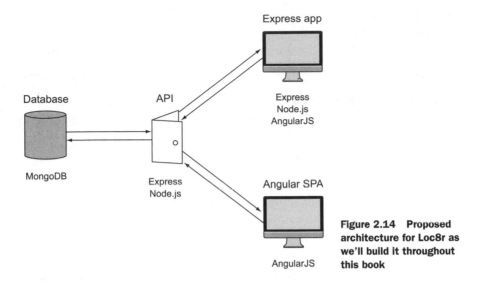

Figure 2.14   Proposed architecture for Loc8r as we'll build it throughout this book

Based on this architecture we'll build the static application in Node and Express, using that as our starting point into the MEAN stack. Figure 2.15 highlights this step in the process as the first part of developing the proposed architecture.

This step is covered in chapters 3 and 4.

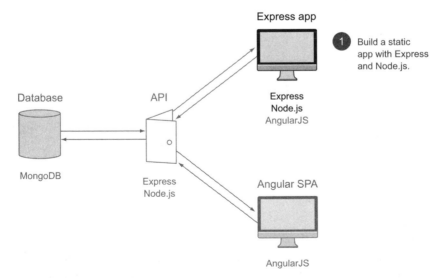

Figure 2.15   The starting point for our application is building the user interface in Express and Node.js.

STEP 2: DESIGN THE DATA MODEL AND CREATE THE DATABASE

Still following the stages of development we'll continue to stage 2 by creating the database and designing the data model. Again, any application is likely to need this step, and you'll get much more out of it if you've been through step 1 first.

Figure 2.16 illustrates how this step adds to the overall picture of building up the application architecture.

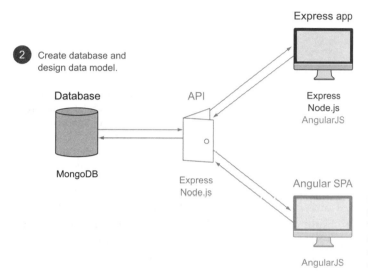

Figure 2.16   After the static site is built we'll use the information gleaned to design the data model and create the MongoDB database.

In the MEAN stack we'll use MongoDB for this step, relying heavily on Mongoose for the data modeling. The data models themselves will actually be defined inside the Express application. This step will be covered in chapter 5.

STEP 3: BUILD OUR REST API

When we've built the database and defined the data models we'll want to create a REST API so that we can interact with the data through making web calls. Pretty much any data-driven application will benefit from having an API interface, so this is another step you'll want to have in most build projects.

You can see where this step fits into building the overall project in figure 2.17.

In the MEAN stack this step is mainly done in Node.js and Express, with quite a bit of help from Mongoose. We'll use Mongoose to interface with MongoDB rather than dealing with MongoDB directly. This step will be covered in chapter 6.

STEP 4: USE THE API FROM OUR APPLICATION

This step matches stage 4 of the development process and is where Loc8r will start to come to life. The static application from step 1 will be updated to use the REST API from step 3 to interact with the database created in step 2.

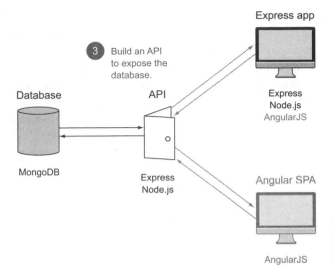

Figure 2.17 **Use Express and Node.js to build an API, exposing methods of interacting with the database.**

To learn about all parts of the stack, and the different ways in which we can use them, we'll be using Express and Node.js to make calls to the API. If, in a real-world scenario, you were planning to build the bulk of an application in AngularJS then you'd hook your database into AngularJS instead. We'll cover that in chapters 8, 9, and 10.

At the end of this step we'll have an application running on the first of the three architectures: an Express and Node.js application. Figure 2.18 shows how this step fits together the two sides of the architecture.

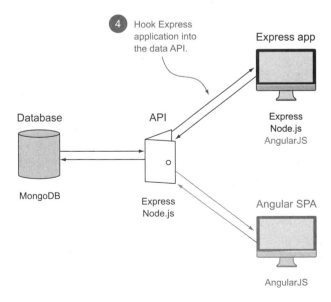

Figure 2.18 **Update the static Express application by hooking it into the data API, allowing the application to be database-driven.**

In this build we'll be doing the majority of this step in Node.js and Express, and it will be covered in chapter 7.

STEP 5: EMBELLISH THE APPLICATION

Step 5 relates to stage 5 in the development process where we get to add extra touches to the application. We're going to use this step to take a look at AngularJS, and we'll see how we can integrate AngularJS components into an Express application.

You can see this addition to the project architecture highlighted in figure 2.19.

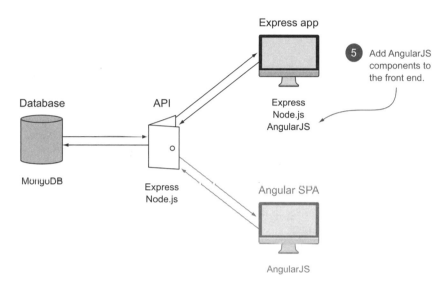

Figure 2.19   One way to use AngularJS in a MEAN application is to add components to the front end in an Express application.

This step is all about introducing and using AngularJS. To support this we'll most likely also change some of our Node.js and Express setup. This step will be covered in chapter 8.

STEP 6: REFACTOR THE CODE INTO AN ANGULARJS SPA

In step 6 we'll radically change the architecture by replacing the Express application and moving all of the logic into an SPA using AngularJS. Unlike all of the previous steps, this replaces some of what has come before it, rather than building upon it.

This would be an unusual step in a normal build process, to develop an application in Express and then redo it in AngularJS, but it suits the learning approach in this book particularly well. We'll be able to focus on AngularJS as we already know what the application should do, and there's a data API ready for us.

Figure 2.20 shows how this change affects the overall architecture.

This step is once again focused on AngularJS, and will be covered in chapters 9 and 10.

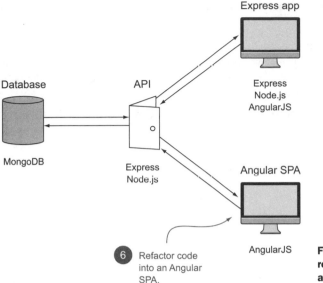

Figure 2.20   Effectively rewriting the application as an AngularJS SPA

STEP 7: ADD AUTHENTICATION

In step 7 we'll add functionality to the application and enable users to register and log in, and also see how to make use of the user's data whilst they are using the application. We'll build on everything we've done so far and add authentication to the Angular SPA. As a part of this we'll save user information in the database and secure certain API end points so that they can only be used by authenticated users.

Figure 2.21 shows what we'll be working with in the architecture.

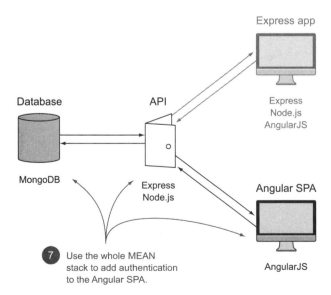

Figure 2.21   Using all of the MEAN stack to add authentication to the AngularJS SPA

In this step we'll work with all of the MEAN technologies; this is covered in chapter 11.

2.6　*Hardware architecture*

No discussion about architecture would be complete without a section on hardware. You've seen how all of the software and code components can be put together, but what type of hardware do you need to run it all?

2.6.1　*Development hardware*

The good news is that you don't need anything particularly special to run a development stack. Just a single laptop, or even a virtual machine (VM), is enough to develop a MEAN application. All components of the stack can be installed on Windows, Mac OS X, and most Linux distributions.

I've successfully developed applications on Windows and Mac OS X laptops, and also on Ubuntu VMs. My personal preference is native development in OS X, but I know of others who swear by using Linux VMs.

If you have a local network and a number of different servers you can run different parts of your application across them. For example, it's possible to have one machine as a database server, another for the REST API, and a third for the main application code itself. So long as the servers can talk to each other this isn't a problem.

2.6.2　*Production hardware*

The approach to production hardware architecture isn't all that different from development hardware. The main difference is that production hardware is normally higher spec, and is open to the internet to receive public requests.

STARTER SIZE
It's quite possible to have all parts of your application hosted and running on the same server. You can see a basic diagram of this in figure 2.22.

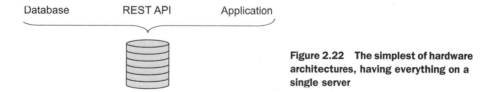

Figure 2.22　The simplest of hardware architectures, having everything on a single server

This architecture is okay for applications with low amounts of traffic, but isn't generally advised as your application grows, because you don't want your application and database fighting over the same resources.

GROWING UP: A SEPARATE DATABASE SERVER
One of the first things to be moved onto a separate server is often the database. So now you have two servers: one for the application code and one for the database. Figure 2.23 illustrates this approach.

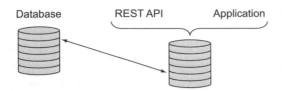

Figure 2.23   A common hardware architecture approach: one server to run the application code and API, and a second, separate database server

This is quite a common model, particularly if you choose to use a platform as a service (PaaS) provider for your hosting. We'll be using this approach in this book.

GOING FOR SCALE

Much like we talked about in the development hardware, you can have a different server for the different parts of your application—a database server, an API server, and an application server. This will allow you to deal with more traffic as the load is spread across three servers, as illustrated in figure 2.24.

Figure 2.24   A decoupled architecture using three servers: one for the database, one for the API, and one for the application code

But it doesn't stop there. If your traffic starts to overload your three servers, you can have multiple instances—or clusters—of these servers, as shown in figure 2.25.

Setting up this approach is a little more involved than the previous methods because you need to ensure that your database remains accurate, and that the load is balanced across the servers. Once again, PaaS providers offer a convenient route into this type of architecture.

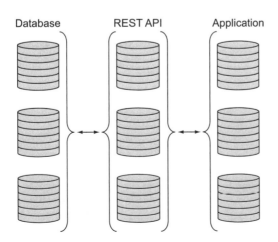

Figure 2.25   You can scale MEAN applications by having clusters of servers for each part of your entire application.

2.7 *Summary*

In this chapter we've covered

- A common MEAN stack architecture with an AngularJS SPA using a REST API built in Node.js, Express, and Mongo
- Points to consider when deciding whether to build an SPA or not
- How to design a flexible architecture in the MEAN stack
- The best practice of building an API to expose a data layer
- The steps we're going to take to build the sample application Loc8r
- Development and production hardware architectures

We'll get started on the journey in chapter 3 by creating the Express project that will hold everything together.

Part 2

Building a Node web application

Node.js underpins any MEAN application, so that's where we'll start. Throughout part 2 we'll build a data-driven web application using Node.js, Express, and MongoDB. We'll learn the individual technologies as we go, steadily building up the application to a point where we have a fully functioning Node web application.

In chapter 3 we'll get going by creating and setting up a MEAN project, getting acquainted with Express, before getting a much deeper understanding of Express by building out a static version of the application in chapter 4. Taking what we've learned about the application so far, in chapter 5 we'll work with MongoDB and Mongoose to design and build the data model we'll need.

Good application architecture should include a data API rather than tightly coupling the database interactions with the application logic. In chapter 6 we'll create a REST API using Express, MongoDB, and Mongoose, before tying this back into the application by consuming the REST API from our static application. As we get to the end of part 2 we'll have a data-driven website using Node.js, MongoDB, and Express, and also a fully functioning REST API.

Creating and setting up a MEAN project

3

This chapter covers

- Managing dependencies by using a package.json file
- Creating and configuring Express projects
- Setting up an MVC environment
- Adding Twitter Bootstrap for layout
- Publishing to a live URL and using Git and Heroku

Now we're really ready to get underway, and in this chapter we'll get going on building our application. Remember from chapters 1 and 2 that throughout this book we're going to build an application called Loc8r. This is going to be a location-aware web application that will display listings near users and invite people to login and leave reviews.

In the MEAN stack Express is the Node web application framework. Together Node and Express underpin the entire stack, so let's start here. In terms of building

Getting the source code

The source code for this application is on GitHub at github.com/simonholmes/getting-MEAN. Each chapter with a significant update will have its own branch. I encourage you to build it up from scratch, through the course of the book, but if you wish you can get the code we'll be building throughout this chapter from GitHub on the chapter-03 branch. In a fresh folder in terminal the following two commands will clone it, if you already have Git installed:

```
$ git clone -b chapter-03 https://github.com/simonholmes/getting-MEAN.git
```

This will give you a copy of the code that's stored on GitHub. To run the application you'll need to install some dependencies with the following commands:

```
$ cd getting-MEAN
$ npm install
```

Don't worry if some of this doesn't make sense just yet, or if some of the commands aren't working. During this chapter we'll install these technologies as we go.

up the application architecture, figure 3.1 shows where we'll be focusing in this chapter. We'll be doing two things:

1. Creating the project and encapsulating the Express application that will house everything else except the database
2. Setting up the main Express application

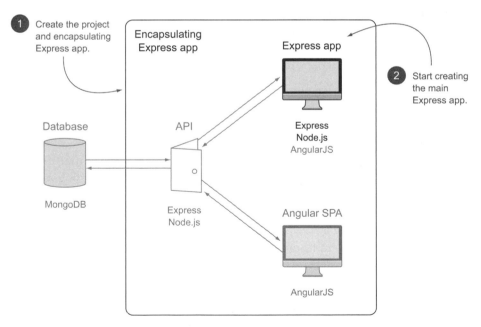

Figure 3.1   Creating the encapsulating Express application, and starting to set up the main Express application

We'll start with a bit of groundwork by looking at Express and seeing how we can manage dependencies and modules using npm and a package.json file. We'll need this background knowledge to get going and set up an Express project.

Before we can really do anything we'll make sure that you have everything you need installed on your machine. When that's all done we'll look at creating new Express projects from the command line, and the various options we can specify at this point.

Express is great, but you can make it better—and get to know it better—by tinkering a little and changing some things around. This ties into a quick look at model-view-controller (MVC) architecture. Here's where we'll get under the hood of Express a little, and see what it's doing by modifying it to have a very clear MVC setup.

When the framework of Express is set up as we want it, we'll next include Twitter's Bootstrap framework, and make the site responsive by updating the Jade templates. In the final step of this chapter we'll push the modified, responsive MVC Express application to a live URL using Heroku and Git.

3.1 A brief look at Express, Node, and npm

As mentioned before, Express is a web application framework for Node. In basic terms, an Express application is simply a Node application that happens to use Express as the framework. Remember from chapter 1 that npm is a package manager that gets installed when you install Node, which gives you the ability to download Node modules or packages to extend the functionality of your application.

But how do these things work together, and how do you use them? A key piece to understanding this puzzle is the package.json file.

3.1.1 Defining packages with package.json

In every Node application there should be a file in the root folder of the application called *package.json*. This file can contain various metadata about a project, including the packages that it depends on to run. The following listing shows an example package.json file that you might find in the root of a new Express project.

> **Listing 3.1 Example package.json file in a new Express project**

```
{
  "name": "application-name",
  "version": "0.0.0",
  "private": true,
  "scripts": {                          Various metadata
    "start": "node ./bin/www"           defining application
  },
  "dependencies": {
    "express": "~4.9.0",                Package dependencies
    "body-parser": "~1.8.1",            needed for application
    "cookie-parser": "~1.3.3",          to run
    "morgan": "~1.3.0",
```

```
    "serve-favicon": "~2.1.3",
    "debug": "~2.0.0",
    "jade": "~1.6.0"
  }
}
```

△ **Package dependencies needed for application to run**

This is the file in its entirety, so it's not particularly complex. There's various metadata at the top of the file followed by the dependencies section. In this default installation of an Express project there are quite a few dependencies. Express itself is modular so that you can add in components or upgrade them individually.

WORKING WITH DEPENDENCY VERSIONS IN PACKAGE.JSON
Alongside the name of each dependency is the version number that the application is going to use. Notice that they're all prefixed with a ~.

Let's take a look at the dependency definition for Express 4.9.0. It specifies a particular version at three levels:

- Major version (4)
- Minor version (9)
- Patch version (0)

Prefixing the whole version number with a ~ is like replacing the patch version with a wildcard, which means that the application will use the latest patch version available. This is considered best practice, as patches should only contain fixes that won't have any impact on the application. But different major and minor versions could well include changes that cause problems with the application, so you want to avoid automatically using later versions of these.

3.1.2 *Installing Node dependencies with npm*

Any Node application or module can have dependencies defined in a package.json file. Installing them is really easy, and is done in the same way regardless of the application or module.

Using a terminal prompt in the same folder as the package.json file you simply need to run the following command:

```
$ npm install
```

This tells npm to install all of the dependencies listed in the package.json file. When you run it, npm will download all of the packages listed as dependencies and install them into a specific folder in the application called *node_modules*. Figure 3.2 illustrates the three key parts.

npm will install each package into its own subfolder because each one is effectively a Node package in its own right. As such, each package also has its own package.json file defining the metadata including the specific dependencies. It's quite common for a package to have its own node_modules folder. You don't need to worry about manually installing all of the nested dependencies though, because this is all handled by the original npm install command.

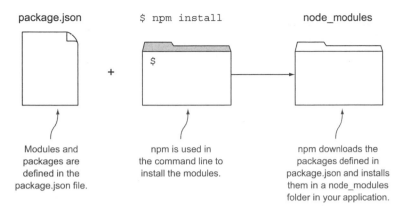

Figure 3.2 The npm modules defined in a package.json file are downloaded and installed into the application's node_modules folder when you run the npm install terminal command.

ADDING MORE PACKAGES TO AN EXISTING PROJECT

You're unlikely to have the full list of dependencies for a project right from the outset. It's far more likely that you'll start off with a few key ones that you know you'll need, and perhaps some that you always use in your workflow.

Using npm, it's really easy to add more packages to the application whenever you want. You simply find the name of the package you want to install and open a command prompt in the same folder as the package.json file. You then run a simple command like this:

```
$ npm install --save package-name
```

With this command npm will download and install the new package into the node_ modules folder. The --save flag tells npm to add this package to the list of dependencies in the package.json file.

UPDATING PACKAGES TO LATER VERSIONS

The only time npm downloads and reinstalls existing packages is when you're upgrading to a new version. When you run npm install, npm will go through all of the dependencies and check the following:

- The version defined in the package.json file
- The latest patch version on npm (assuming you used the ~)
- The version installed in the node_modules folder (if at all)

If your installed version is different from the definition in the package.json file, npm will download and install the version defined in package.json. Similarly, if you're using a patch wildcard and there's a later patch version available, npm will download and install it in place of the previous version.

With that knowledge under your belt, we can start creating our first Express project.

3.2   Creating an Express project

All journeys must have a starting point, which for building a MEAN application is to create a new Express project. To create an Express project you'll need to have five key things installed on your development machine:

- Node and npm
- The Express generator installed globally
- Git
- Heroku
- New command-line interface (CLI) or terminal

3.2.1   Installing the pieces

If you don't have Node, npm, or the Express generator installed yet, see appendix A for instructions and pointers to online resources. They can all be installed on Windows, Mac OS X, and most mainstream Linux distributions.

By the end of this chapter we'll also have used Git to manage the source control of our Loc8r application, and pushed it to a live URL using Heroku. Please take a look through appendix B, which guides you through setting up Git and Heroku.

Depending on your operating system you may need to install a new CLI or terminal. See appendix B to find out if this applies to you or not.

> **NOTE**   Throughout this book I'll often refer to the CLI as *terminal*. So when I say "run this command in terminal," simply run it in whichever CLI you're using. When terminal commands are included as code snippets throughout this book, they'll start with a $. You shouldn't type this into terminal; it's simply there to denote that this is a command-line statement. For example, using the echo command $ echo 'Welcome to Getting MEAN', you'd just type in echo 'Welcome to Getting MEAN'.

VERIFYING THE INSTALLATIONS

To create a new Express project you must have Node and npm installed, and also have the Express generator installed globally. You can verify this by checking for the version numbers in the terminal using the following commands:

```
$ node --version
$ npm --version
$ express --version
```

Each of these commands should output a version number to terminal. If one of them fails, head back to appendix A on how to install it again.

3.2.2   Creating a project folder

Assuming all is good, let's start by creating a new folder on your machine called *loc8r*. This can be on your desktop, in your documents, in a Dropbox folder—it doesn't really matter, as long as you have full read and write access rights to the folder.

I personally do a lot of my MEAN development in Dropbox folders so that it's immediately backed up and accessible on any of my machines. If you're in a corporate environment this may not be suitable for you, so create the folder wherever you think best.

3.2.3 Configuring an Express installation

An Express project is installed from the command line, and the configuration is passed in using parameters on the command that you use. If you're not familiar with using the command line, don't worry, none of what we'll go through in the book is particularly complex, and it's all pretty easy to remember. Once you've started using it you'll probably start to love how it makes some operations so fast!

For example—don't do this just yet—you can install Express into a folder with a simple command:

```
$ express
```

This would install the framework with default settings into your current folder. This is probably a good start, but let's take a look at some configuration options first.

CONFIGURATION OPTIONS WHEN CREATING AN EXPRESS PROJECT

What can you configure when creating an Express project? When creating an Express project in this way, you can specify the following:

- Which HTML template engine to use
- Which CSS preprocessor to use
- Whether to add support for sessions

A default installation will use the Jade template engine, but it will have no CSS preprocessing or session support. You can specify a few different options as laid out in table 3.1.

Table 3.1 Command-line configuration options when creating a new Express project

Configuration command	Effect
`--css less|stylus`	Adds a CSS preprocessor to your project, either Less or Stylus, depending on which you type in the command.
`--ejs`	Changes the HTML template engine from Jade to EJS.
`--jshtml`	Changes the HTML template engine from Jade to JsHtml.
`--hogan`	Changes the HTML template engine from Jade to Hogan.

For example—and this isn't what we're going to do here—if you want to create a project that uses the Less CSS preprocessor and the Hogan template engine you'd run the following command in terminal:

```
$ express --css less --hogan
```

To keep things simple in our project we won't use CSS preprocessing, so we can stick with the default of plain CSS. But we do need to use a template engine, so let's take a quick look at the options.

DIFFERENT TEMPLATE ENGINES

When using Express in this way there are four template options available: Jade, EJS, JsHtml, and Hogan. The basic workflow of a template engine is that you create the HTML template, including placeholders for data, and then pass it some data. The engine will then compile the two together to create the final HTML markup that the browser will receive.

All of the engines have their own merits and quirks, and if you already have a preferred one then that's fine. In this book we're going to be using Jade. Jade is very powerful and provides all of the functionality we're going to need. As it's the default template engine in Express you'll also find that most examples and projects online use it, so it's very helpful to be familiar with it. Finally, Jade's minimal style makes it ideal for code samples in a book!

A QUICK LOOK AT JADE

Jade is unusual when compared to the other template engines in that it doesn't actually contain HTML tags in the templates. Instead, Jade takes a rather minimalist approach, using tag names, indentation, and a CSS-inspired reference method to define the structure of the HTML. The exception to this is the `<div>` tag. Because it's so common, if the tag name is omitted from the template, Jade will assume that you want a `<div>`.

> **TIP**   Jade templates must be indented using spaces, not tabs.

The following code snippet shows a simple example of a Jade template and the compiled output:

```
#banner.page-header
  h1 My page
  p.lead Welcome to my page
```
Jade template contains
no HTML tags

```
<div id="banner" class="page-header">
  <h1>My page</h1>
  <p class="lead">Welcome to my page</p>
</div>
```
Compiled output is
recognizable HTML

From the first lines of the input and output you should be able to see that

- With no tag name specified, a `<div>` is created.
- `#banner` in Jade becomes `id="banner"` in HTML.
- `.page-header` in Jade becomes `class="page-header"` in HTML.

So with that starting knowledge behind us, it's time for us to create a project.

3.2.4 *Creating an Express project and trying it out*

So we know the basic command for creating an Express project, and have decided to use the default configuration options, so let's go ahead and create a new project. In section 3.2.2 you should have created a new folder called loc8r. Navigate to this folder in your terminal, and run the following command:

```
$ express
```

This will create a bunch of folders and files inside the loc8r folder that will form the basis of our Loc8r application. But we're not quite ready yet. Next you'll need to install the dependencies. As you may remember, this is simply done by running the following command from a terminal prompt in the same folder as the package.json file:

```
$ npm install
```

As soon as you run it you'll see your terminal window light up with all of the things it's downloading. Once it has finished, the application is ready for a test drive.

TRYING IT OUT

Running the application is a piece of cake. We'll take a look at a better way of doing this in just a moment, but if you're impatient like me, you'll want to see that what you've done so far works.

In terminal, in the loc8r folder, run the following command:

```
$ npm start
```

You should see a confirmation similar to this:

```
loc8r@0.0.0 start /path/to/your/application/folder
```

This means that the Express application is running! You can see it in action by opening a browser and heading over to localhost:3000. Hopefully you'll see something like the screenshot in figure 3.3.

Figure 3.3 Landing page for a barebones Express project

Admittedly, this is not exactly ground-breaking stuff right now, but getting the Express application up and running to the point of working in a browser was pretty easy, right?

If you head back to terminal now you should see a couple of log statements confirming that the page has been requested, and that a stylesheet has been requested. To get to know Express a little better, let's take a look at what's going on here.

HOW EXPRESS HANDLES THE REQUESTS

The default Express landing page is pretty simple. There's a small amount of HTML, of which some of the text content is pushed as data by the Express route. There's also a CSS file. The logs in terminal should confirm that this is what Express has had requested and has returned to the browser. But how does it do it?

About Express middleware

In the middle of the app.js file there are a bunch of lines that start with `app.use`. These are known as *middleware*. When a request comes in to the application it passes through each piece of middleware in turn. Each piece of middleware may or may not do something with the request, but it's always passed on to the next one until it reaches the application logic itself, which returns a response.

Take `app.use(express.cookieParser());` for example. This will take an incoming request, parse out any of the cookie information, and then attach the data to the request in a way that makes it easy to reference it in the controller code.

You don't really need to know what each piece does right now, but you may well find yourself adding to this list as you build out applications.

All requests to the Express server run through the middleware defined in the app.js file (see the sidebar "About Express middleware"). As well as doing other things, there's a default piece of middleware that looks for paths to static files. When the middleware matches the path against a file, Express will return this asynchronously, ensuring that the Node.js process isn't tied up with this operation and therefore blocking other operations. When a request runs through all of the middleware, Express will then attempt to match the path of the request against a defined route. We'll get into this in a bit more detail later in this chapter.

Figure 3.4 illustrates this flow, using the example of the default Express homepage from figure 3.3.

The flow in figure 3.4 shows the separate requests made and how Express handles them differently. Both requests run through the middleware as a first action, but the outcomes are very different.

3.2.5   *Restarting the application*

A Node application compiles before running, so if you make changes to the application code while it's running, they won't be picked up until the Node process is stopped

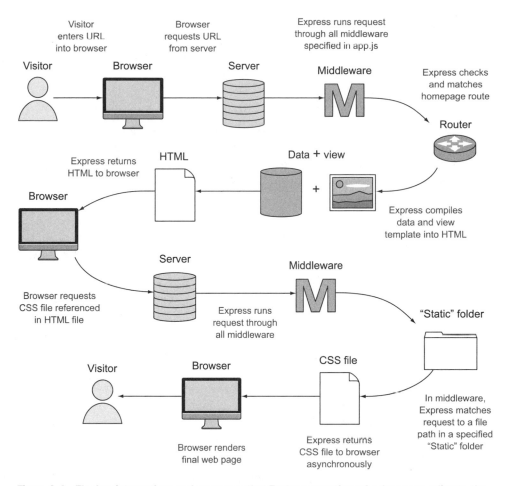

Figure 3.4 The key interactions and processes that Express goes through when responding to the request for the default landing page. The HTML page is processed by Node to compile data and a view template, and the CSS file is served asynchronously from a static folder.

and restarted. Note that this is only true for application code; Jade templates, CSS files, and client-side JavaScript can all be updated on-the-fly.

Restarting the Node process is a two-step procedure. First you have to stop the running process. You do this in terminal by pressing Ctrl-C. Then you have to start the process again in terminal using the same command as before: npm start.

This doesn't sound problematic, but when you're actively developing and testing an application, having to do these two steps every time you want to check an update actually becomes quite frustrating. Fortunately there's a better way.

AUTOMATICALLY RESTARTING THE APPLICATION WITH NODEMON

There are some services out there that have been developed to monitor application code that will restart the process when it detects that changes have been made. One such service, and the one we'll be using in this book, is *nodemon*. nodemon simply wraps the Node application, and other than monitoring for changes causes no interference.

To use nodemon you start off by installing it globally, much like you did with Express. This is done using npm in terminal:

```
$ npm install -g nodemon
```

When the installation has finished, you'll be able to use nodemon wherever you wish. Using it's really simple. Instead of typing node to start the application, you type nodemon. So, making sure you're in the loc8r folder in terminal—and that you've stopped the Node process if it's still running—enter the following command:

```
$ nodemon
```

You should see that a few extra lines are output to terminal confirming that nodemon is running, and that it has started node ./bin/www. If you head back over to your browser and refresh, you should see that the application is still there.

> **NOTE**   nodemon is only intended for easing the development process in your development environment, and shouldn't really be used in a live production environment.

3.3 *Modifying Express for MVC*

First off, what is MVC architecture? MVC stands for model-view-controller, and it's an architecture that aims to separate out the data (model), the display (view), and the application logic (controller). This separation aims to remove any tight coupling between the components, theoretically making code more maintainable and reusable. A bonus is that these components fit very nicely into our rapid prototype development approach and allow us to concentrate on one aspect at a time as we discuss each part of the MEAN stack.

There are whole books dedicated to the nuances of MVC, but we're not going to go into that depth here. We'll keep the discussion of MVC at a high level, and see how we can use it with Express to build our Loc8r application.

3.3.1 *A bird's eye view of MVC*

Most applications or sites that you build will be designed to take an incoming request, do something with it, and return a response. At a simple level, this loop in an MVC architecture works like this:

1 A request comes into the application.
2 The request gets routed to a controller.
3 The controller, if necessary, makes a request to the model.
4 The model responds to the controller.
5 The controller sends a response to a view.
6 The view sends a response to the original requester.

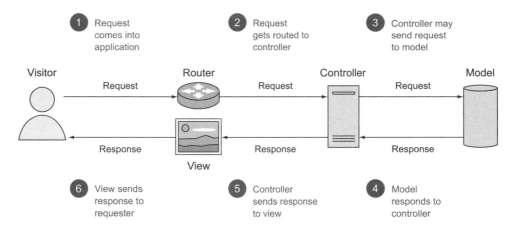

Figure 3.5   Request–response flow of a basic MVC architecture

In reality, depending on your setup, the controller may actually compile the view before sending the response back to the visitor. The effect is the same though, so keep this simple flow in mind as a visual for what will happen in our Loc8r application. See figure 3.5 for an illustration of this loop.

Figure 3.5 highlights the individual parts of the MVC architecture and how they link together. It also illustrates the need for a routing mechanism along with the model, view, and controller components. So now that you've seen how we want the basic flow of our Loc8r application to work, it's time to modify the Express setup to make this happen.

3.3.2   *Changing the folder structure*

If you look inside the newly created Express project in the loc8r folder, you should see a file structure including a views folder, and even a routes folder, but no mention of models or controllers. Rather than going ahead and cluttering up the root level of the application with some new folders, let's keep things tidy with one new folder for all of our MVC architecture. Follow three quick steps here:

1 Create a new folder called app_server.
2 In app_server create two new folders called models and controllers.
3 Move the views and routes folders from the root of the application into the app_server folder.

Figure 3.6 illustrates these changes and shows the folder structures before and after the modifications.

Now we have a really obvious MVC setup in the application, which makes it easier to separate our concerns. But if you try to run the application now it won't work, as

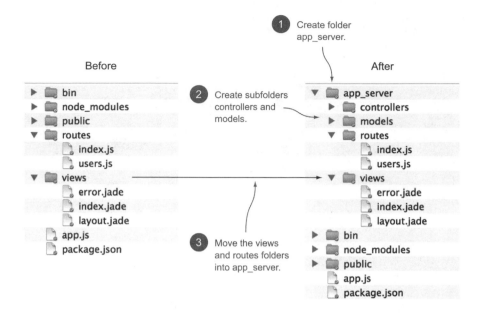

Figure 3.6   Changing the folder structure of an Express project into an MVC architecture

we've just broken it. So let's fix it. Express doesn't know that we've added in some new folders, or have any idea what we want to use them for. So we need to tell it.

3.3.3   *Using the new views and routes folders*

The first thing we need to do is tell Express that we've moved the views and routes folders, because Express will be looking for folders and files that no longer exist.

USING THE NEW VIEWS FOLDER LOCATION

Express will be looking in /views but we've just moved it to /app_server/views. Changing it's really simple. In app.js find the following line:

```
app.set('views', path.join(__dirname, 'views'));
```

and change it to the following (modifications in bold):

```
app.set('views', path.join(__dirname, 'app_server', 'views'));
```

Our application still won't work just yet because we've moved the routes, so let's tell Express about them too.

USING THE NEW ROUTES FOLDER LOCATION

Express will be looking in /routes but we've just moved it to /app_server/routes. Changing this is also really simple. In app.js find the following lines:

```
var routes = require('./routes/index');
var users = require('./routes/users');
```

and change them to the following (modifications in bold):

```
var routes = require('./app_server/routes/index');
var users = require('./app_server/routes/users');
```

If you save this and run the application again, you'll find that we've fixed it and the application works once more!

3.3.4 *Splitting controllers from routes*

In a default Express setup, controllers are very much part of the routes, but we want to separate them out. Controllers should manage the application logic, and routing should map URL requests to controllers.

UNDERSTANDING ROUTE DEFINITION

To understand how routes work let's take a look at the route already set up for delivering the default Express homepage. Inside index.js in app_server/routes you should see the following code snippet:

```
/* GET home page. */
router.get('/', function(req, res) {
  res.render('index', { title: 'Express' });
});
```

1 Where router looks for URL

2 Controller content, albeit very basic right now

In the code at **1** you can see `router.get('/',` which is where the router looks for a get request on the homepage URL path, which is just `'/'`. The anonymous function that runs the code **2** is really the controller. This is a very basic example with no application code to speak of. So **1** and **2** are the pieces we want to separate here.

Rather than diving straight in and putting the controller code into the controllers folder, we'll test out the approach in the same file first. To do this, we can take the anonymous function from the route definition and define it as a named function. We'll then pass the name of this function through as the callback in the route definition. Both of these steps are in the following listing, which you can put into place inside app_server/routes/index.js.

Listing 3.2 Taking the controller code out of the route: step 1

```
var homepageController = function (req, res) {
  res.render('index', { title: 'Express' });
};
```

Take anonymous function and define it as a named function

```
/* GET home page. */
router.get('/', homepageController);
```

Pass name of function through as a callback in route definition

---

If you refresh your homepage now it should still work just as before. We haven't changed anything in how the site works, just moved a step toward separating concerns.

Understanding `res.render`

We'll look at this more in chapter 4, but `render` is the Express function for compiling a view template to send as the HTML response that the browser will receive. The `render` method takes the name of the view template and a JavaScript data object in the following construct:

JavaScript object containing
data for template to use

```
res.render('index', {title:'express'});
```

Name of template file to use—in
this case referencing index.jade

Note that the template file doesn't need to have the file extension suffix, so `index` `.jade` can just be referenced as `index`. You also don't need to specify the path to the view folder because you've already done this in the main Express setup.

Now that we're clear about how the route definition works, it's time to put the controller code into its proper place.

MOVING THE CONTROLLER OUT OF THE ROUTES FILE

In Node, to reference code in an external file you create a module in your new file and then `require` it in the original file. See the following sidebar for some overarching principles behind this process.

Creating and using Node modules

Taking some code out of a Node file to create an external module is fortunately pretty simple. In essence, you create a new file for your code, choose which bits of it you want to expose to the original file, and then `require` your new file in your original file.

In your new module file you expose the parts of the code that you wish to by using the `module.exports` method, like so:

```
module.exports = function () {
  console.log("This is exposed to the requester");
};
```

You'd then `require` this in your main file like so:

```
require('./yourModule');
```

If you want your module to have separate named methods exposed, then you can do so by defining them in your new file in the following way:

```
module.exports.logThis = function(message){
  console.log(message);
};
```

> To reference this in your original file you need to assign your module to a variable name, and then invoke the method. For example, in your main file
>
> ```
> var yourModule = require('./yourModule');
> yourModule.logThis("Hooray, it works!");
> ```
>
> This assigns your new module to the variable `yourModule`. The exported function `logThis` is now available as a method of `yourModule`.
>
> When using the `require` function, note that you don't need to specify a file extension. The `require` function will look for a couple of things: a JavaScript file of the same name or an index.js file inside a folder of the given name.

So the first thing we need to do is create a file to hold the controller code. Create a new file called main.js in app_server/controllers. In this file we'll create an export method called `index` and use it to house the `res.render` code as shown in the following listing.

Listing 3.3 Setting up the homepage controller in app_server/controllers/main.js

```
/* GET home page */
module.exports.index = function(req, res){          ◁── Create an index
  res.render('index', { title: 'Express' });                export method
};                                                  ◁── Include controller
                                                        code for homepage
```

That's all there is to creating the controller export. The next step is to `require` this controller module in the routes file so that we can use the exposed method in the route definition. The following listing shows how the main routes file index.js should now look.

Listing 3.4 Updating the routes file to use external controllers

```
var express = require('express');
var router = express.Router();
var ctrlMain = require('../controllers/main');    ◁──❶ Require main
                                                         controllers file
/* GET home page. */
router.get('/', ctrlMain.index);        ◁──┐ Reference index
                                            │ method of controllers
module.exports = router;                  ❷   in route definition
```

This links the route to the new controller by "requiring" the controller file ❶ and referencing the controller function in the second parameter of the `router.get` function ❷.

We now have the routing and controller architecture, as illustrated in figure 3.7, where app.js `requires` routes/index.js, which in turn `requires` controllers/main.js.

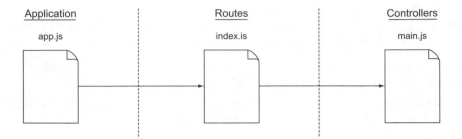

Figure 3.7   Separating the controller logic from the route definitions

If you test this out now in your browser, you should see that the default Express home-page displays correctly once again.

That's everything set up with Express for now, so it's almost time to start the building process. But before that there are a couple more things that we need to do, first of which is adding Twitter Bootstrap to the application.

3.4   Import Bootstrap for quick, responsive layouts

As discussed in chapter 1, our Loc8r application will make use of Twitter's Bootstrap framework to speed up the development of a responsive design. We'll also make the application stand out by using a theme. The aim here is to help us keep moving forward quickly with building the application, and not get side-tracked with the semantics of developing a responsive interface.

3.4.1   Download Bootstrap and add it to the application

Instructions for downloading Bootstrap, getting a custom theme, and adding the files into the project folder are all found in appendix B. A key point here's that the Bootstrap files are all static files to be sent directly to the browser; they don't need any processing by the Node engine. Your Express application will already have a folder for this purpose: the *public* folder. When you have it ready, the public folder should look something like figure 3.8.

Bootstrap also requires jQuery for some of the interactive components to load. You can reference it directly from a CDN, but we'll download it at http://jquery.com/download/ so that we've got it in our application. We're going to use the latest 1.x version, which at the time of writing is 1.11.1. So go ahead and download jQuery, saving it in the public/javascripts folder of the application.

3.4.2   Using Bootstrap in the application

Now that all of the Bootstrap pieces are sitting in the application, it's time to hook it up to the front end. This means taking a look at the Jade templates.

Figure 3.8 Structure of the public folder in the Express application after adding Bootstrap

WORKING WITH JADE TEMPLATES

Jade templates are often set up to work by having a main layout file that has defined areas for other Jade files to extend. This makes a great deal of sense when building a web application, because there are often many screens or pages that have the same underlying structure with different content in the middle.

This is how Jade appears in a default Express installation. If you look in the views folder in the application you'll see two files, layout.jade and index.jade. The index.jade file is controlling the content for the index page of the application. Open it up, and there's not much in there; the entire contents are shown in the following listing.

Listing 3.5 The complete index.jade file

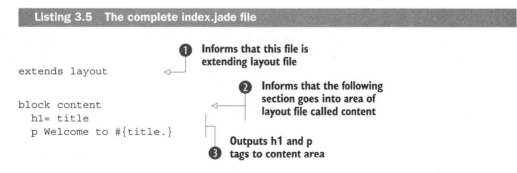

There's more going on here than meets the eye. Right at the top of the file is a statement declaring that this file is an extension of another file ❶, in this case the layout file. Following this is a statement defining a block of code ❷ that belongs to a specific area of the layout file, an area called `content` in this instance. Finally, there's the minimal content that's displayed on the Express index page, a single `<h1>` tag and a single `<p>` tag ❸.

There are no references to <head> or <body> tags here, nor any stylesheet references. These are all handled in the layout file, so that's more likely where you want to go to add in global scripts and stylesheets to the application. Open up layout.jade and you should see something similar to the following listing.

Listing 3.6   Default layout.jade file

```
doctype html
html
  head
    title= title
    link(rel='stylesheet', href='/stylesheets/style.css')
  body
    block content
```

> **Empty named block can be used by other templates**

Listing 3.6 shows the layout file being used for the basic index page in the default Express installation. You'll see that there's a head section and a body section, and within the body section there's a block content line with nothing inside it. This named block can be referenced by other Jade templates, such as the index.jade file in listing 3.5. The block content from the index file gets pushed into the block content area of the layout file when the views are compiled.

ADDING BOOTSTRAP TO THE ENTIRE APPLICATION

If you want to add some external reference files to the entire application, then using the layout file makes sense in the current setup. So in layout.jade you need to accomplish four things:

- Reference the Bootstrap CSS file.
- Reference the Bootstrap JavaScript file.
- Reference jQuery, which Bootstrap requires.
- Add viewport metadata so that the page scales nicely on mobile devices.

The CSS file and the viewport metadata should both be in the head of the document, and the two script files should be at the end of the body section. The following listing shows all of this in place in layout.jade, with the new lines in bold.

Listing 3.7   Updated layout.jade including Bootstrap references

```
doctype html
html
  head
    meta(name='viewport', content='width=device-width, initial-scale=1.0')
    title= title
    link(rel='stylesheet', href='/bootstrap/css/amelia.bootstrap.css')
    link(rel='stylesheet', href='/stylesheets/style.css')
  body
    block content
```

> **Set viewport metadata for better display on mobile devices**

> **Include themed Bootstrap CSS**

```
script(src='/javascripts/jquery-1.11.1.min.js')          Bring in jQuery
script(src='/bootstrap/js/bootstrap.min.js')             as it's needed by
                                                         Bootstrap
                                Bring in Bootstrap
                                JavaScript file
```

With that done, any new template that you create will automatically have Bootstrap included and will scale on mobile devices—as long as your new templates extend the layout template, of course.

Finally, before testing it all out, delete the contents of the style.css file in /public/ stylesheets/. This will prevent the default Express styles from overriding the Bootstrap files. We'll want to add our own styles in to the Loc8r application somewhere a little later down the line, so there's no need to delete the file.

VERIFY THAT IT WORKS

If the application isn't already running with nodemon, start it up and view it in your browser. The content hasn't changed, but the appearance should have. You should now have something looking like figure 3.9.

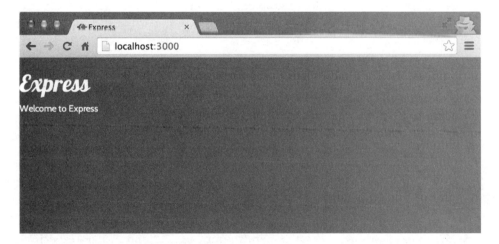

Figure 3.9 Bootstrap theme having an effect on the default Express index page

Remember you can get the source code of the application so far from GitHub on the chapter-03 branch. In a fresh folder in terminal the following command will clone it:

```
$ git clone -b chapter-03 https://github.com/simonholmes/getting-MEAN.git
```

Now we've got something working locally; let's see how we can get it running on a live production server.

3.5   *Make it live on Heroku*

A common perceived headache with Node applications is deploying them to a live production server. We're going to get rid of that headache early on and push our Loc8r application onto a live URL already. As we iterate and build it up we can keep pushing out the updates. For prototyping this is great because it makes it really easy to show our progress to others.

As mentioned in chapter 1 there are a few platform as a service providers such as Google Cloud Platform, Nodejitsu, OpenShift, and Heroku. We're going to use Heroku here, but there's nothing stopping you from trying out other options.

3.5.1   *Getting Heroku set up*

Before you can use Heroku, you'll need to sign up for a free account and install the Heroku Toolbelt on your development machine. Appendix B has more detailed information on how to do this. You'll also need a bash-compatible terminal; the default terminal for Mac users is fine, but the default CLI for Windows users won't do. If you're on Windows you'll need to download something like the GitHub terminal, which comes as part of the GitHub desktop application.

Once you have everything set up, we can continue and get the application ready to push live.

UPDATING PACKAGE.JSON

Heroku can run applications on all different types of codebases, so we need to tell it what our application is running. As well as telling it that we're running a Node application using npm as the package manager, we need to tell it which version we're running to ensure that the production setup is the same as the development setup.

If you're not sure which versions of Node and npm you're running you can find out with a couple of terminal commands:

```
$ node --version
$ npm --version
```

At the time of writing, these commands return v4.2.1 and 2.2.0, respectively. Using the ~ syntax to add a wildcard for a patch version as you've seen previously, you need to add these to a new engines section in the package.json file. The complete updated package.json file is shown in the following listing, with the added section in bold.

Listing 3.8   Adding an engines section to package.json

```
{
  "name": "Loc8r",
  "version": "0.0.1",
  "private": true,
  "scripts": {
    "start": "node ./bin/www"
  },
```

```
"engines": {
  "node": "~4.2.1",
  "npm": "~2.2.0"
},
"dependencies": {
  "express": "~4.9.0",
  "body-parser": "~1.8.1",
  "cookie-parser": "~1.3.3",
  "morgan": "~1.3.0",
  "serve-favicon": "~2.1.3",
  "debug": "~2.0.0",
  "jade": "~1.6.0"
  }
}
```

> **Add an engines section to package.json to tell Heroku which platform your application is on, and which version to use**

When pushed up to Heroku, this will tell Heroku that our application uses the latest patch version of Node, 4.2, and the latest patch version of npm, 2.2.

CREATING A PROCFILE

The package.json file will tell Heroku that the application is a Node application, but it doesn't tell it how to start it. For this we need to use a Procfile. A Procfile is used to declare the process types used by our application, and the commands used to start them.

For Loc8r we want a web process, and we want it to run the Node application. So in the root folder of the application create a file called Procfile—this is case-sensitive and has no file extension. Enter the following line into the Procfile file:

```
web: npm start
```

When pushed up to Heroku, this file will simply tell Heroku that the application needs a web process and that it should run npm start.

TESTING IT LOCALLY WITH FOREMAN

The Heroku Toolbelt comes with a utility called Foreman. We can use Foreman to verify our setup and run our application locally before pushing the application up to Heroku. If the application is currently running, stop it by pressing Ctrl-C in the terminal window running the process. Then in the terminal window enter the following command:

```
$ foreman start
```

All being well with the setup, this will start the application running on localhost again, but this time on a different port: 5000. The confirmation you get in terminal should be along these lines:

```
16:09:01 web.1  | started with pid 91976
16:09:02 web.1  | > loc8r@0.0.1 start /path/to/your/application/folder
16:09:02 web.1  | > node ./bin/www
```

If you fire up a browser and head over to localhost:5000—note that the port is 5000 instead of 3000—you should be able to see the application up and running once again.

Now that we know the setup is working it's time to push our application up to Heroku.

3.5.2 *Pushing the site live using Git*

Heroku uses Git as the deployment method. If you already use Git you'll love this approach; if you haven't you may feel a bit apprehensive about it, as the world of Git can be quite complex. But it doesn't need to be, and once you get going you'll love this approach too!

STORING THE APPLICATION IN GIT

The first action is to store the application in Git, on your local machine. This is a three-step process, as you need to

1 Initialize the application folder as a Git repository.
2 Tell Git which files you want to add to the repository.
3 Commit these changes to the repository.

This might sound complex, but it really isn't. You just need a single short terminal command for each step. If the application is running locally, stop it in terminal (Ctrl-C). Then, ensuring you're still in the root folder of the application, stay in terminal and run the following commands:

These three things together will create a local Git repository containing the entire codebase for the application. When we go to update the application later on, and we want to push some changes live, we'll use the second two commands, with a different message, to update the repository.

Your local repository is now ready. It's time to create the Heroku application.

CREATING THE HEROKU APPLICATION

This next step will create an application on Heroku, as a remote Git repository of your local repository. All this is done with a single terminal command:

```
$ heroku create
```

When this is done, you'll see a confirmation in terminal of the URL that the application will be on, the Git repository address, and the name of the remote repository. For example

```
http://shrouded-tor-1673.herokuapp.com/ | git@heroku.com:shrouded-tor-
    1673.git
Git remote heroku added
```

If you log in to your Heroku account in a browser you'll also see that the application exists there. So you now have a container on Heroku for the application, and the next step is to push the application code up.

DEPLOYING THE APPLICATION TO HEROKU

By now you have the application stored in a local Git repository, and you've created a new remote repository on Heroku. The remote repository is currently empty, so you need to push the contents of your local repository into the heroku remote repository.

If you don't know Git, there's a single command to do this, which has the following construct:

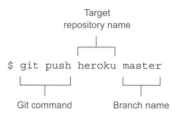

This command will push the contents of your local Git repository to the heroku remote repository. Currently, you only have a single branch in your repository, which is the master branch, so that's what you'll push to Heroku. See the following sidebar for more information on Git branches.

When you run this, terminal will display a load of log messages as it goes through the process, eventually ending up with a confirmation that the application has been deployed to Heroku. This will be something like the following, except you'll have a different URL of course:

```
http://shrouded-tor-1673.herokuapp.com deployed to Heroku
```

What are Git branches?

If you just work on the same version of the code and push it up to a remote repository like Heroku or GitHub periodically, you're working on the *master* branch. This is absolutely fine for linear development with just one developer. If you have multiple developers or your application is already published, then you don't really want to be doing your development on the master branch. Instead, you start a new branch from the master code in which you can continue development, add fixes, or build a new feature.

When work on a branch is complete it can be merged back into the master branch.

STARTING A WEB DYNO ON HEROKU

Heroku uses the concept of dynos for running and scaling an application. The more dynos you have, the more system resources and processes you have available to your application. Adding more dynos when your application gets bigger and more popular is really easy.

Heroku also has a great free tier, which is perfect for application prototyping and building a proof-of-concept. You get one web dyno for free, which is more than adequate for our purposes here. Before you can view the application online you need to add a single web dyno. This is easily done with a simple terminal command:

```
$ heroku ps:scale web=1
```

When you've run this, terminal will display a confirmation:

```
Scaling web dynos... done, now running 1
```

Now let's check out the live URL.

VIEWING THE APPLICATION ON A LIVE URL

Everything is now in place, and the application is live on the internet! You can see it by typing in the URL given to you in the confirmation, via your account on the Heroku website, or by using the following terminal command:

```
$ heroku open
```

This will launch the application in your default browser, and you should see something like figure 3.10.

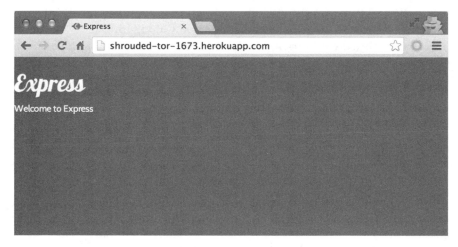

Figure 3.10   MVC Express application running on a live URL

Your URL will be different, of course, and within Heroku you can change it to use your domain name instead of the address it has given you. In the application settings on the Heroku website you can also change it to use a more meaningful subdomain of herokuapp.com.

Having your prototype on an accessible URL is very handy for cross-browser and cross-device testing, as well as sending it out to colleagues and partners.

A SIMPLE UPDATE PROCESS

Now that the Heroku application is set up, updating it will be really easy. Every time you want to push some new changes through, you just need three terminal commands:

```
$ git add .
$ git commit -m "Commit message here"
$ git push heroku master
```

That's all there's to it, for now at least. Things might get a bit more complex if you have multiple developers and branches to deal with, but the actual process of pushing the code to Heroku using Git remains the same.

3.6 *Summary*

In this chapter we've covered

- Creating a new Express application
- Managing application dependencies with npm and the package.json file
- Modifying Express to meet an MVC approach to architecture
- Routes and controllers
- Creating new Node modules
- Publishing an Express application live onto Heroku using Git

In the next chapter you'll get to know Express even more when we build out a prototype of the Loc8r application.

Building a static site
with Node and Express

4

This chapter covers

- Prototyping an application through building
  a static version
- Defining routes for application URLs
- Creating views in Express using Jade and
  Bootstrap
- Using controllers in Express to tie routes
  to views
- Passing data from controllers to views

In chapter 3 you should have had an Express application running, set up in an MVC way, with Bootstrap included to help with building page layouts. Our next step is to build on this base, creating a static site that you can click through. This is a critical step in putting together any site or application. Even if you've been given a design or some wireframes to work from, there's no substitute for rapidly creating a realistic prototype that you can use in the browser. Something always comes to light in terms of layout or usability that hadn't been noticed before. From this static prototype, we'll take the data out from the views and put it into the controllers. By the end of this chapter we'll have intelligent views that can display data passed to them, and controllers passing hard-coded data to the views.

> **Getting the source code**
>
> If you haven't yet built the application from chapter 3, you can get the code from GitHub on the chapter-03 branch at github.com/simonholmes/getting-MEAN. In a fresh folder in terminal the following commands will clone it and install the npm module dependencies:
>
> ```
> $ git clone -b chapter-03 https://github.com/simonholmes/getting-MEAN.git
> $ cd getting-MEAN
> $ npm install
> ```

In terms of building up the application architecture, this chapter will be focusing on the Express application as shown in figure 4.1.

As there are two main steps being taken in this chapter, there are two versions of the source code available. The first version contains all of the data in the views and represents the application as it stands at the end of section 4.4. This is available from GitHub on the chapter-04 views branch.

The second version has the data in the controllers, in the state the application will be at the end of this chapter. This is available from GitHub on the chapter-04 branch.

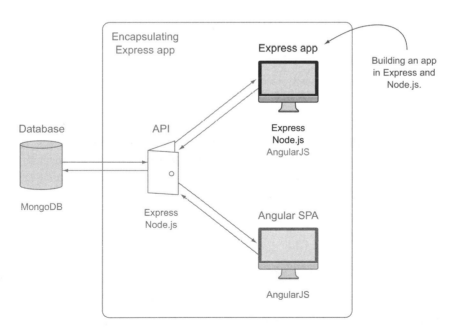

Figure 4.1 Using Express and Node to build a static site for testing views

To get one of these use the following commands in a fresh folder in terminal, remembering to specify the branch that you want:

```
$ git clone -b chapter-04 https://github.com/simonholmes/getting-MEAN.git
$ cd getting-MEAN
$ npm install
```

Okay, let's get back into Express.

4.1   *Defining the routes in Express*

In chapter 2 we planned out the application and decided on the four pages we are going to build. There's a collection of Locations pages and a page in the Others collection as shown in figure 4.2.

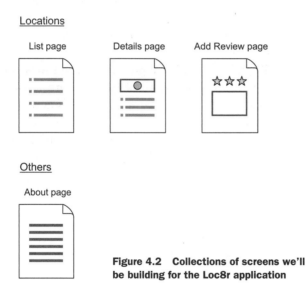

Figure 4.2   **Collections of screens we'll be building for the Loc8r application**

Having a set of screens is great, but these need to relate to incoming URLs. Before we do any coding it's a good idea to map this out and to get a good standard in place. Take a look at table 4.1. It shows a simple mapping of the screens against URLs. These will form the basis of the routing for our application.

Table 4.1   **Defining a URL path, or route, for each of the screens in the prototype**

Collection	Screen	URL path
Locations	List of locations (this will be the homepage)	`/`
Locations	Location detail	`/location`
Locations	Location review form	`/location/review/new`
Others	About Loc8r	`/about`

For example, when somebody visits the homepage we want to show them a list of places, but when somebody visits the /about URL path we want to show them the information about Loc8r.

4.1.1 Different controller files for different collections

In chapter 3 you'll recall we moved any sense of controller logic out of the route definitions and into an external file. Looking to the future we know that our application will grow, and we don't want to have all the controllers in one file. A logical starting point for splitting them up is to divide them by collections.

So looking at the collections we've decided upon, we'll split the controllers up into Locations and Others. To see how this might work from a file architecture point of view, we can sketch out something like figure 4.3. Here the application includes the routes file, which in turn includes multiple controller files, each named according to the relevant collection.

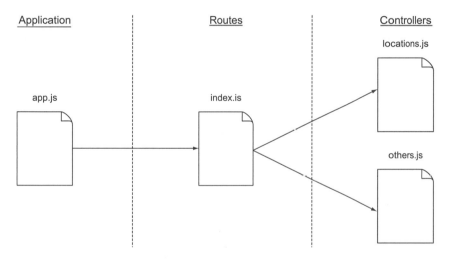

Figure 4.3 Proposed file architecture for routes and controllers in our application

Here we have a single route file and one controller file for each logical collection of screens. This setup is designed to help us organize our code in line with how our application is organized. We'll look at the controllers shortly, but first we'll deal with the routes.

The time for planning is over; now it's time for action! So head back over to your development environment and open the application. We'll start off working in the routes file index.js.

REQUIRING THE CONTROLLER FILES

As shown in figure 4.3 we want to reference two controller files in this routes file. We haven't created these controller files yet; we'll do that shortly.

These files will be called locations.js and others.js and will be saved in app_server/controllers. In index.js we'll `require` both of these files and assign each to a relevant variable name, as shown in the following listing.

Listing 4.1   Requiring the controller files in routes/index.js

```
var express = require('express');
var router = express.Router();
var ctrlLocations = require('../controllers/locations');
var ctrlOthers = require('../controllers/others');
```

> **Replace existing ctrlMain reference with two new requires**

Now we have two variables we can reference in the route definitions, which will contain different collections of routes.

SETTING UP THE ROUTES

In index.js you'll need to have the routes for the three screens in the Locations collection, and also the About page in the Others collection. Each of these routes will also need a reference to the controllers. Remember that routes simply serve as a mapping service, taking the URL of an incoming request and mapping it to a specific piece of application functionality.

From table 4.1 we already know which paths we want to map, so it's a case of putting it all together into the routes/index.js file. What you need to have in the file is shown in entirety in the following listing.

Listing 4.2   Defining the routes and mapping them to controllers

```
var express = require('express');
var router = express.Router();
var ctrlLocations = require('../controllers/locations');
var ctrlOthers = require('../controllers/others');

/* Locations pages */
router.get('/', ctrlLocations.homelist);
router.get('/location', ctrlLocations.locationInfo);
router.get('/location/review/new', ctrlLocations.addReview);

/* Other pages */
router.get('/about', ctrlOthers.about);

module.exports = router;
```

> **Require controller files**

> **Define location routes and map them to controller functions**

> **Define other routes**

This routing file maps the defined URLs to some specific controllers, although we haven't created those yet. So let's take care of that now and create the controllers.

4.2   *Building basic controllers*

At this point we're going to make the controllers really basic so that our application will run and we can test the different URLs and routing.

4.2.1 Setting up controllers

We currently have one file, the main.js file in the controllers folder (in the app_server folder) that has a single function that's controlling the homepage. This is shown in the following code snippet:

```
/* GET 'home' page */
module.exports.index = function(req, res){
  res.render('index', { title: 'Express' });
};
```

We don't actually want a "main" controller file anymore, but we can use this as a template. Start by renaming this as *others.js*.

ADDING THE OTHERS CONTROLLERS

Recall from listing 4.2 that we want one controller in others.js called about. So rename the existing index controller to about, keep the same view template for now, and update the title property to be something relevant. This will help you easily test that the route is working as expected. The following listing shows the full contents of the others.js controller file following these couple of little changes.

Listing 4.3 Others controller file

```
/* GET 'about' page */
module.exports.about = function(req, res){          Define route using same view
  res.render('index', { title: 'About' });          template but changing title to About
};
```

That's the first one done, but the application still won't work, as there aren't any controllers for the Locations routes yet.

ADDING THE LOCATIONS CONTROLLERS

Adding the controllers for the Locations routes is going to be pretty much the same process. In the routes file we specified the name of the controller file to look for, and the name of the three controller functions.

In the controllers folder create a file called locations.js, and create three basic controller functions: homelist, locationInfo, and addReview. The following listing shows how this should look.

Listing 4.4 Locations controller file

```
/* GET 'home' page */
module.exports.homelist = function(req, res){
  res.render('index', { title: 'Home' });
};

/* GET 'Location info' page */
module.exports.locationInfo = function(req, res){
  res.render('index', { title: 'Location info' });
};
```

```
/* GET 'Add review' page */
module.exports.addReview = function(req, res){
  res.render('index', { title: 'Add review' });
};
```

That looks like everything is in place, so let's test it.

4.2.2   Testing the controllers and routes

Now that the routes and basic controllers are in place you should be able to start and run the application. If you don't already have it running with nodemon, head to the root folder of the application in the terminal and start it up:

```
$ nodemon
```

> ### Troubleshooting
>
> If you're having problems restarting the application at this point, the main thing to check is that all of the files, functions, and references are named correctly. Look at the error messages you're getting in the terminal window and see if they give you any clues. Sometimes they're more helpful than others! Take a look at the following possible error, and we'll pick out the parts that are interesting to us:
>
> ```
> module.js:340
>     throw err;
>     ^
> Error: Cannot find module '../controllers/other'          ① Clue one: a
>     at Function.Module._resolveFilename (module.js:338:15)    module can't
>     at Function.Module._load (module.js:280:25)               be found
>     at Module.require (module.js:364:17)
>     at require (module.js:380:17)
>     at module.exports (/Users/sholmes/Dropbox/Manning/Getting-MEAN/Code/
>            Loc8r/BookCode/routes/index.js:2:3)           ◄─┐
>     at Object.<anonymous> (/Users/sholmes/Dropbox/Manning/Getting-MEAN/
>            Code/Loc8r/BookCode/app.js:26:20)
>     at Module._compile (module.js:456:26)              Clue two: file
>     at Object.Module._extensions..js (module.js:474:10)  throwing
>     at Module.load (module.js:356:32)                      error  ②
>     at Function.Module._load (module.js:312:12)
> ```
>
> First, you can see that a module called other can't be found ①. Further down the stack trace you can see the file where the error originated ②. So you'd then open the routes/index.js file and discover that you'd written require('../controllers/other') when the file you want to require is others.js. So to fix the problem you'd simply need to correct the reference by changing it to require('../controllers/others').

All being well, this should give you no errors, meaning that all of the routes are pointing to controllers. So you can head over to your browser and check each of the four routes we've created, such as localhost:3000 for the homepage and localhost:3000/location for the location information page. Because we changed the data being

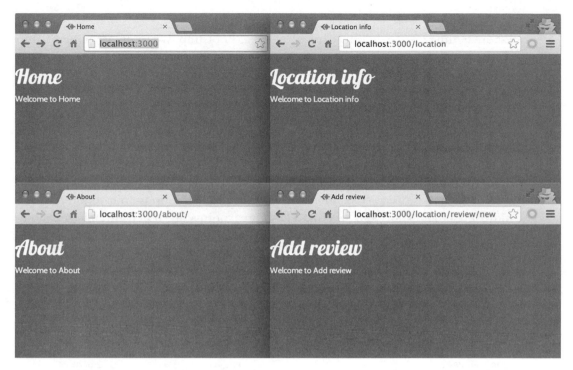

Figure 4.4   Screenshots of the four routes created so far, with different heading text coming through from the specific controllers associated with each route

sent to the view template by each of the controllers, we'll easily be able to see that each one is running correctly because the title and heading should be different on each page. Figure 4.4 shows a collection of screenshots of the newly created routes and controllers.

From this we can see that each route is getting unique content, so we know that the routing and controller setup has worked.

The next stage in this prototyping process is to put some HTML, layout, and content onto each screen. We'll do this using views.

4.3   Creating some views

When you have your empty pages, paths, and routes sorted out, it's time to get some content and layout into our application. This is where we really bring it to life and can start to see our idea become reality. For this step, the technologies that we're going to use are Jade and Bootstrap. Jade is the default template engine in Express (although you can use others if you prefer) and Bootstrap is a front-end layout framework that makes it really easy to build a responsive website that looks different on desktop and mobile devices.

4.3.1   A look at Bootstrap

Before getting started, let's take a quick look at Bootstrap. We're not going to go into all the details about Bootstrap and everything it can do, but it's useful to see some of the key concepts before we try to throw it into a template file.

BOOTSTRAP RESPONSIVE GRID SYSTEM

Bootstrap uses a 12-column grid. No matter the size of the display you're using, there will always be these 12 columns. On a phone each column will be narrow, and on a large external monitor each column will be wide. The fundamental concept of Bootstrap is that you can define how many columns an element will use, and this can be a different number for different screen sizes.

Bootstrap has various CSS references that let you target up to four different pixel-width breakpoints for your layouts. These breakpoints are noted in table 4.2 along with the example device that you'd be targeting at each size.

Table 4.2   Breakpoints that Bootstrap targets for different types of devices

Breakpoint name	CSS reference	Example device	Width in pixels
Extra-small devices	xs	Phones	Less than 768
Small devices	sm	Tablets	768 or more
Medium devices	md	Laptops	992 or more
Large devices	lg	External monitors	1,200 or more

To define the width of an element you combine a CSS reference from table 4.2 with the number of columns you wish it to span. A class denoting a column is constructed like this:

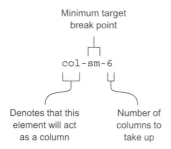

This class of col-sm-6 will make the element it's applied to take up 6 columns on screens of size sm and larger. So on tablets, laptops, and monitors this column will take up half of the available width.

To get the responsive side of things to work, you can apply multiple classes to a single element. So if you wanted a div to span the entire width of the screen on the phone, but only half of the width on tablets and larger, you could use the following code snippet:

```
<div class="col-xs-12 col-sm-6"></div>
```

The `col-xs-12` class tells the layout to use 12 columns on extra-small devices, and the `col-sm-6` class tells the layout to use 6 columns for small devices and above. Figure 4.5 illustrates the effect this has on different devices if you have two of these, one after another on the page, like this:

```
<div class="col-xs-12 col-sm-6">DIV ONE</div>
<div class="col-xs-12 col-sm-6">DIV TWO</div>
```

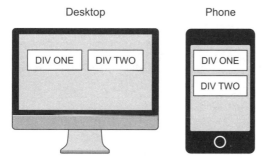

Figure 4.5 Bootstrap's responsive column system on a desktop and mobile device. CSS classes are used to determine the number of columns out of 12 that each element should take up at different screen resolutions.

This approach allows for a very semantic way of putting together responsive templates, and we'll rely heavily on this for the Loc8r pages. Speaking of which, let's make a start.

4.3.2 Setting up the HTML framework with Jade templates and Bootstrap

There are some common requirements across all of the pages we'll have in the application. At the top of the page we'll want a navigation bar and logo, at the bottom of the page we'll have a copyright notice in the footer, and we'll have a content area in the middle. What we're aiming for here is something like figure 4.6.

Figure 4.6 Basic structure of the reusable layout, comprising a standard navigation bar and footer with an extendable and changeable content area in between

This framework for a layout is pretty simple, but it suits our needs. It will give a consistent look and feel, while allowing for all types of content layouts to go in the middle.

As you saw in chapter 3, Jade templates use the concept of extendable layouts, enabling you to define this type of repeatable structure just once in a layout file. In the layout file you can specify which parts can be extended; once you have this layout file set up you can extend it as many times as you want. Creating the framework in a layout file means that you only have to do it once, and only have to maintain it in one place.

LOOKING AT THE LAYOUT

To build the common framework then, we're mainly going to be working with the layout.jade file in the app_server/views folder. This is currently pretty minimal and looks like this code snippet:

```
doctype html
html
  head
    meta(name='viewport', content='width=device-width, initial-scale=1.0')
    title= title
    link(rel='stylesheet', href='/bootstrap/css/amelia.bootstrap.css')
    link(rel='stylesheet', href='/stylesheets/style.css')
  body
    block content

    script(src='/javascripts/jquery-1.11.1.min.js')
    script(src='/bootstrap/js/bootstrap.min.js')
```

There isn't any HTML content in the body area at all yet, just a single extendable block called content and a couple of script references. We want to keep all of this, but need to add a navigation section above the content block, and a footer below it.

BUILDING THE NAVIGATION

Bootstrap offers a collection of elements and classes that can be used to create a sticky navigation bar that's fixed to the top, and collapses the options into a dropdown menu on mobile devices. We're not going to explore the details of Bootstrap's CSS classes here, as we really just need to grab the example code from the Bootstrap website, tweak it a little, and update it with the correct links.

In the navigation we want to have

1 The Loc8r logo linking to the homepage
2 An About link on the left, pointing to the /about URL page

The code to do all of this is in the following snippet, and can be placed in the layout.jade file above the block content line:

```
.navbar.navbar-default.navbar-fixed-top      ◁──  Set up a Bootstrap navigation
  .container                                        bar fixed to top of window
    .navbar-header
      a.navbar-brand(href='/') Loc8r          ◁──  Add a brand-styled
                                                    link to homepage
```

```
        button.navbar-toggle(type='button', data-toggle='collapse', data-
    target='#navbar-main')
        span.icon-bar
        span.icon-bar
        span.icon-bar
    #navbar-main.navbar-collapse.collapse
      ul.nav.navbar-nav
        li
          a(href='/about/') About
```

Set up collapsing navigation for smaller screen resolutions

Add About link to left side of bar

If you pop that in and run it you'll notice that the navigation now overlays the page heading. This will be fixed when we build the layouts for the content area in sections 4.3.3 and 4.4, so it's nothing to worry about.

> **TIP** Remember that Jade doesn't include any HTML tags, and that correct indentation is critical to provide the expected outcome.

And that's it for the navigation bar; it's all we'll need for a while. If Jade and Bootstrap are new to you it might take a little while to get used to the approach and the syntax, but as you can see, you can achieve a lot with little code.

WRAPPING THE CONTENT
Working down the page from top to bottom the next area is the content block. There isn't much to do with this, as other Jade files will decide the contents. As it stands though, the content block is anchored to the left margin and is unconstrained, meaning that it will stretch the full width of any device.

Addressing this is easy with Bootstrap. You simply need to wrap the content block in a container div like so:

```
.container
  block content
```

The div with a class of container will be centered in the window, and constrained to sensible maximum widths on large displays. The contents of a container div will remain aligned to the left as normal though.

ADDING THE FOOTER
At the bottom of the page we want to add a standard footer. We could add a bunch of links in here, terms and conditions, or a privacy policy. For now we'll just add a copyright notice and keep things simple. As it's going in the layout file it will be really easy to update this across all of the pages should we need to at a later date.

The following code snippet shows all the code needed for our simple footer:

```
footer
  .row
    .col-xs-12
      small &copy; Simon Holmes 2014
```

This will be best placed inside the container div that holds the content block, so when you add it in make sure that the footer line is at the same level of indentation as the block content line.

ALL TOGETHER NOW

Now that the navigation bar, content area, and footer are all dealt with, that's the complete layout file. The full code for layout.jade is shown in the following listing (modifications in bold).

> **Listing 4.5   Final code for the layout framework in app_server/views/layout.jade**

```jade
doctype 5
html
  head
    meta(name='viewport', content='width=device-width, initial-scale=1.0')
    title= title
    link(rel='stylesheet', href='/bootstrap/css/amelia.bootstrap.css')
    link(rel='stylesheet', href='/stylesheets/style.css')
  body
    .navbar.navbar-default.navbar-fixed-top              ◁─┐ Starting layout with
      .container                                             fixed navigation bar
        .navbar-header
          a.navbar-brand(href='/') Loc8r
          button.navbar-toggle(type='button', data-toggle='collapse',
        data-target='#navbar-main')
            span.icon-bar
            span.icon-bar
            span.icon-bar
        #navbar-main.navbar-collapse.collapse
          ul.nav.navbar-nav
            li
              a(href='/about/') About          ◁─┐ Extendable content
    .container                                     block now wrapped
      block content                          ◁─┘ in a container div

      footer                        ◁─┐ Simple copyright footer in same
        .row                             container as content block
          .col-xs-12
            small &copy; Simon Holmes 2014
    script(src='/javascripts/jquery-1.11.1.min.js')
    script(src='/bootstrap/js/bootstrap.min.js')
```

That's all it takes to create a responsive layout framework using Bootstrap, Jade, and Express. If you've got that all in place and run the application you should see something like the screenshots in figure 4.7, depending on your device.

You'll see that the navigation still overlays the content, but we'll address that very soon when we start looking at the content layouts. It's a good indication that the navigation is working as we want it to though—we want the navigation to be ever-present, fixed to the top of the window. Also notice how Bootstrap has collapsed the navigation into a dropdown menu on the smaller screen of the phone. Pretty nice isn't it, for very little effort on our part?

> **TIP**   If you can't access your development site on a phone you can always try resizing your browser window, or Google Chrome allows you to emulate various different mobile devices through the JavaScript console.

Figure 4.7 **The homepage after the layout template has been set up. Bootstrap has automatically collapsed the navigation on the small screen size of the phone. The navigation bar overlaps the content, but that will be fixed when the content layouts are created.**

Now that the generic layout template is complete, it's time to start building out the actual pages of our application.

4.3.3 Building a template

When building templates, start with whichever one makes the most sense to you. This might be the most complicated or the most simple, or just the first in the main user journey. For Loc8r a good place to start is the homepage; this is the example we'll go through in most detail.

DEFINING A LAYOUT

The primary aim for the homepage is to display a list of locations. Each location will need to have a name, an address, the distance away, users' ratings, and a facilities list. We'll also want to add a header to the page, and some text to put the list in context, so that users know what they're looking at when they first visit.

You may find it useful, as I do, to sketch out a layout or two on a piece of paper or a whiteboard. I find this really helpful for creating a starting point for the layout, making sure you've got all of the pieces you need on a page without getting bogged down in the technicalities of any code. Figure 4.8 shows what I've sketched for the homepage of Loc8r.

You'll see that there are two layouts, a desktop and a phone. It's worth making the responsive distinction at this point, with your understanding of what Bootstrap can do and how it works in the back of your mind.

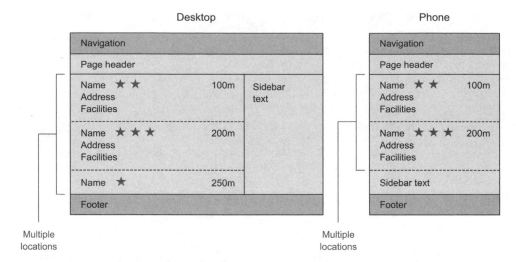

Figure 4.8 Desktop and mobile layout sketches for the homepage. Sketching out the layouts for a page can give you a quick idea of what you're going to build, without getting distracted by the intricacies of Photoshop or technicalities of code.

At this stage, the layouts are by no means final and we may well find that we'll tweak them and change them as we build the code. But any journey is easier if there's a destination and a map; this is what the sketches give us. We can start off our coding in the right direction. The few minutes it takes to do this upfront can save us hours later on—moving parts around, or even throwing them out and starting again, is much easier with a sketch than with a load of code.

Now that we've got an idea of the layout and the pieces of content required, it's time to put it together in a new template.

SETTING UP THE VIEW AND THE CONTROLLER

The first step is to create a new view file and link it to the controller. So in the app_server/views folder make a copy of the index.jade view and save it in the same folder as locations-list.jade. It's best not calling it "homepage" or something similar, as at some point we may change our mind about what should be displayed on the homepage. This way, the name of the view is clear, and it can be used anywhere without confusion.

The second step is to tell the controller for the homepage that we want to use this new view. The controller for the homepage is in the locations.js file in app_server/ controllers. Update this to change the view called by the homelist controller. This should look like the following code snippet (modifications in bold):

```
module.exports.homelist = function(req, res){
  res.render('locations-list', { title: 'Home' });
};
```

Now let's build the view template.

CODING THE TEMPLATE: PAGE LAYOUT

When actually writing the code for the layouts, I prefer to start with the big pieces, and then move toward the detail. As we're extending the layout file, the navigation bar and footer are already done, but there's still the page header, the main area for the list, and the sidebar to consider.

At this point we need to take a first stab at how many of the 12 Bootstrap columns we want each element to take up on which devices. The following code snippet shows the layout of the three distinct areas of the Loc8r List page:

```
#banner.page-header
  .row
    .col-lg-6
      h1 Loc8r
        small  Find places to work with wifi near you!
.row
  .col-xs-12.col-sm-8
    p List area.
  .col-xs-12.col-sm-4
    p.lead Loc8r helps you find places to work when out and about.
```

Page header that fills entire width, containing a column that limits text width to 6 columns on large screens for readability

Container for list of locations, spanning all 12 columns on extra-small devices and 8 columns on small devices and larger

Container for secondary or sidebar information, spanning all 12 columns on extra-small devices and 4 columns on small devices and larger

I did go back and forth a bit, testing the columns at various resolutions until I was happy with them. Having device simulators can make this process easier, but a really simple method is to just change the width of your browser window to force the different Bootstrap breakpoints. When you've got something you think is probably okay, you can push it up to Heroku and test it out for real on your phone or tablet.

CODING THE TEMPLATE: LOCATIONS LIST

Now that the containers for the homepage are defined, it's time for the main area. We have an idea of what we want in here from the sketches drawn for the page layout. Each place should show the name, address, its rating, how far away it is, and the key facilities.

Because we're creating a clickable prototype all of the data will be hard-coded into the template for now. It's the quickest way of putting a template together and ensuring that we have the information we want displayed the way we want. We'll worry about the data side of it later. If you're working from an existing data source, or have constraints around what data you can use, then naturally you'll have to bear that in mind when creating the layouts.

Again, getting a layout you're happy with will take a bit of testing, but Jade and Bootstrap working together make this process considerably easier than it might be. The following code snippet shows what I've come up with for a single location:

```
.row.list-group
  .col-xs-12.list-group-item
    h4
      a(href="/location") Starcups
      small  
        span.glyphicon.glyphicon-star
        span.glyphicon.glyphicon-star
        span.glyphicon.glyphicon-star
        span.glyphicon.glyphicon-star-empty
        span.glyphicon.glyphicon-star-empty
      span.badge.pull-right.badge-default 100m
    p.address 125 High Street, Reading, RG6 1PS
    p
      span.label.label warning Hot drinks
       
      span.label.label-warning Food
       
      span.label.label-warning Premium wifi
       
```

Set up a Bootstrap list group and create a single item spanning full 12 columns

Name of listing and a link to location

Use Bootstrap's badge helper class to hold distance away

Use Bootstrap's glyphicons to output a star rating

Address of location

Facilities of location, output using Bootstrap's label classes

Once again you can see how much you can achieve with relatively little effort and code, all thanks to the combination of Jade and Bootstrap. To give you an idea of what the preceding code snippet does, it will render like figure 4.9.

Figure 4.9   Onscreen rendering of a single location on the List page

This section is set to go across the full width of the available area, so 12 columns on all devices. Remember, though, that this section is nested inside a responsive column, so that full width is the full width of the containing column, not necessarily the browser viewport.

This will probably make more sense when we put it all together and see it in action.

CODING THE TEMPLATE: PUTTING IT TOGETHER

So we've got the layout of page elements, the structure of the list area, and some hard-coded data. Let's see what it looks like all together. To get a better feel of the layout in the browser it will be a good idea to duplicate and modify the List page so that we have a number of locations showing up. The code, including just a single location for brevity, is shown in the following listing.

Listing 4.6   Complete template for app_server/views/locations-list.jade

```
extends layout

block content                          ← Start header
  #banner.page-header                     area
    .row
      .col-lg-6
        h1 Loc8r
          small  Find places to work with wifi near you!  ← Start responsive
    .row                                    main listing
      .col-xs-12.col-sm-8                   column section
        .row.list-group
          .col-xs-12.list-group-item
            h4
              a(href="/location") Starcups
              small  
                span.glyphicon.glyphicon-star
                span.glyphicon.glyphicon-star
                span.glyphicon.glyphicon-star
                span.glyphicon.glyphicon-star-empty    ← An individual
                span.glyphicon.glyphicon-star-empty       listing; duplicate
              span.badge.pull-right.badge-default 100m    this section to
            p.address 125 High Street, Reading, RG6 1PS   create list of
            p                                             multiple items
              span.label.label-warning Hot drinks
              |  
              span.label.label-warning Food
              |  
              span.label.label-warning Premium wifi
              |  
      .col-xs-12.col-sm-4    ← Set up sidebar area and populate with some content
        p.lead Looking for wifi and a seat? Loc8r helps you find places to work
          when out and about. Perhaps with coffee, cake or a pint? Let Loc8r help
          you find the place you're looking for.
```

When you've got this all in place, you've got the homepage listing template all done. If you run the application and head to localhost:3000 you should see something like figure 4.10.

See how the layout changes between a desktop view and a mobile view? That's all thanks to Bootstrap's responsive framework and our choice of CSS classes. Scrolling down in the mobile view you'll see the sidebar text content between the main list and the footer. On the smaller screen it's more important to display the list in the available space than the text.

So that's great; we've got a responsive layout for the homepage using Jade and Bootstrap in Express and Node. Let's quickly add the other views.

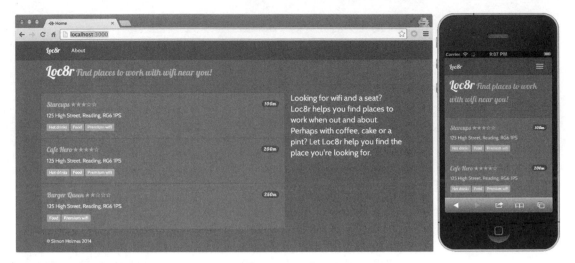

Figure 4.10   Responsive template for the homepage in action on different devices

4.4   Adding the rest of the views

The Locations collection's List page is done, so we now need to look at creating the other pages to give users a site they can click through. In this section we'll cover adding these pages:

1 Details
2 Add Review
3 About

We won't go through the process in so much detail for all of them though, just a bit of explanation, the code, and the output. You can always download the source code from GitHub if you prefer.

4.4.1   Details page

The logical step, and arguably the next most important page to look at, is the Details page for an individual location.

This page needs to display all of the information about a location, including

- Name
- Address
- Rating
- Opening hours
- Facilities
- Location map

Anythink Wright Farms

5877 E 120th Ave
Thornton, CO 80602
303-405-3200
Mon-Thu 9:30 am-8:30 pm
Fri-Sat 9:30 am-5:30 pm
Sun 1:00 pm-5:00 pm

---

te: 10/30/2019 Time: 12:29:13 PM

---

ems checked out this session: 2

---

le: React quickly : painless web apps wi
rcode: 33021032004662
ie Date: 11/20/19

le: Getting MEAN With Mongo, Express, An
rcode: 33021029042402
ie Date: 11/20/19

Page 1 of 1

... where anything is possible.

- Reviews, each with
  - Rating
  - Reviewer name
  - Review date
  - Review text
- Button to add a new review
- Text to set the context of the page

That's quite a lot of information! This is the most complicated single template that we'll have in our application.

PREPARATION

The first step is to update the controller for this page to use a different view. Look for the `locationInfo` controller in the locations.js file in app_server/controllers. Change the name of the view to be `location-info`, as per the following code snippet:

```
module.exports.locationInfo = function(req, res){
  res.render('location-info', { title: 'Location info' });
};
```

Remember, if you run the application at this point it won't work because Express can't find the view template. Not surprising really, as we haven't created it yet. That's the next part.

THE VIEW

Create a new file in app_server/views and save it as location-info.jade. The content for this is shown in listing 4.7. This is the largest listing in this book. Remember that for the purposes of this stage in the prototype development, we're generating clickable pages with the data hard-coded directly into them.

Listing 4.7 View for the Details page, app_server/views/location-info.js

```
extends layout

block content
  .row.page-header                          Start with
    .col-lg-12                              page header
      h1 Starcups
  .row
    .col-xs-12.col-md-9          ⟵┐  Set up nested
      .row                        │  responsive columns
        .col-xs-12.col-sm-6      ⟵┘  needed for template
          p.rating
            span.glyphicon.glyphicon-star
            span.glyphicon.glyphicon-star
            span.glyphicon.glyphicon-star
            span.glyphicon.glyphicon-star-empty
            span.glyphicon.glyphicon-star-empty
```

```
          p 125 High Street, Reading, RG6 1PS
          .panel.panel-primary
            .panel-heading
              h2.panel-title Opening hours
            .panel-body
              p Monday - Friday : 7:00am - 7:00pm
              p Saturday : 8:00am - 5:00pm
              p Sunday : closed
          .panel.panel-primary
            .panel-heading
              h2.panel-title Facilities
            .panel-body
              span.label.label-warning
                span.glyphicon.glyphicon-ok
                |   Hot drinks
              |   
              span.label.label-warning
                span.glyphicon.glyphicon-ok
                |   Food
              |   
              span.label.label-warning
                span.glyphicon.glyphicon-ok
                |   Premium wifi
              |   
      .col-xs-12.col-sm-6.location-map
        .panel.panel-primary
          .panel-heading
            h2.panel-title Location map
          .panel-body
            img.img-responsive.img-rounded(src='http://maps.googleapis.com/
maps/api/staticmap?center=51.455041,-
0.9690884&zoom=17&size=400x350&sensor=false&markers=51.455041,-
0.9690884&scale=2')
    .row
      .col-xs-12
        .panel.panel-primary.review-panel
          .panel-heading
            a.btn.btn-default.pull-right(href='/location/review/new') Add
review
            h2.panel-title Customer reviews
          .panel-body.review-container
            .row
              .review
                .well.well-sm.review-header
                  span.rating
                    span.glyphicon.glyphicon-star
                    span.glyphicon.glyphicon-star
                    span.glyphicon.glyphicon-star
                    span.glyphicon.glyphicon-star
                    span.glyphicon.glyphicon-star
                  span.reviewAuthor Simon Holmes
                  small.reviewTimestamp 16 July 2013
                .col-xs-12
```

One of several Bootstrap panel components used to define information areas, in this case opening hours

Use static Google Maps image, including coordinates in the query string 51.455041,-0.9690884

Create link to Add Review page using Bootstrap's button helper class

```
                p What a great place. I can't say enough good things about
  it.
            .row
              .review
                .well.well-sm.review-header
                  span.rating
                    span.glyphicon.glyphicon-star
                    span.glyphicon.glyphicon-star
                    span.glyphicon.glyphicon-star
                    span.glyphicon.glyphicon-star-empty
                    span.glyphicon.glyphicon-star-empty
                  span.reviewAuthor Charlie Chaplin
                  small.reviewTimestamp 16 June 2013
                .col-xs-12
                  p It was okay. Coffee wasn't great, but the wifi was fast.
 .col-xs-12.col-md-3
  p.lead Simon's cafe is on Loc8r because it has accessible wifi and space
  to sit down with your laptop and get some work done.
  p If you've been and you like it - or if you don't - please leave a
  review to help other people just like you.
```

Final responsive column for sidebar contextual information

So that's a pretty long template, and we'll look at how we can shorten that soon. But the page itself is pretty complex and contains a lot of information, and a few nested responsive columns. Imagine how much longer it would be if it was written in full HTML, though!

ADDING A BIT OF STYLE

This template will look okay as it is, but there are some little stylistic issues that can easily be addressed with a few lines of CSS. When we set up the project we left the default Express stylesheet where it was for just this reason, even though we took all of the content out of it. The file is called style.css and is in the folder public/stylesheets. Enter the following code snippet into the file and save it:

```
.review {padding-bottom: 5px;}
.panel-body.review-container {padding-top: 0;}
.review-header {margin-bottom: 10px;}
.reviewAuthor {margin: 0 5px;}
.reviewTimestamp {color: #ccc;}
```

With this saved, the Details page layout is complete, and you can head over to localhost:3000/location to check it out. Figure 4.11 shows how this layout looks in a browser and on a mobile device.

The next step in this user journey is the Add Review page, which has much simpler requirements.

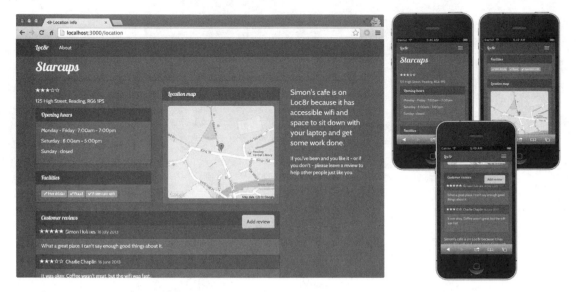

Figure 4.11   Details page layout on desktop and mobile devices

4.4.2   Adding Review page

This will be a pretty straightforward page. It only really needs to hold a form containing the user's name and a couple of input fields for the rating and review.

The first step is to update the controller to reference a new view. In app_server/controllers/locations.js change the `addReview` controller to use a new view `location-review-form`, like in the following code snippet:

```
module.exports.addReview = function(req, res){
  res.render('location-review-form', { title: 'Add review' });
};
```

The second step is to create the view itself. In the views folder app_server/views create a new file called location-review-form.jade. Because this is designed to be a clickable prototype we're not going to be posting the form data anywhere, so the aim is just to get the action to redirect to the Details page that displays the review data. In the form then, we'll set the action to be `/location` and the method to `get`. This will give us the functionality we need for now. The entire code for the review form page is shown in the following listing.

Listing 4.8   View for the Add Review page, app_server/views/location-review.form.js

```
extends layout

block content
  .row.page-header
    .col-lg-12
      h1 Review Starcups
```

```
.row
  .col-xs-12.col-md-6
    form.form-horizontal(action="/location", method="get", role="form")
      .form-group
        label.col-xs-10.col-sm-2.control-label(for="name") Name
        .col-xs-12.col-sm-10
          input#name.form-control(name="name")
      .form-group
        label.col-xs-10.col-sm-2.control-label(for="rating") Rating
        .col-xs-12.col-sm-2
          select#rating.form-control.input-sm(name="rating")
            option 5
            option 4
            option 3
            option 2
            option 1
      .form-group
        label.col-sm-2.control-label(for="review") Review
        .col-sm-10
          textarea#review.form-control(name="review", rows="5")
      button.btn.btn-default.pull-right Add my review
  .col-xs-12.col-md-4
```

Set form action to /location and method to get →

Input field for reviewer to leave name ←

Dropdown select box for rating 1 to 5

Submit button for form →

Text area for text content of review ←

Bootstrap has a lot of helper classes for dealing with forms, which are evident in listing 4.8. But it's a pretty simple page, and when you run it, it should look like figure 4.12.

The Add Review page marks the end of the user journey through the Locations collection of screens. There is just the About page left to do.

Figure 4.12 Complete Add Review page in a desktop and mobile view

4.4.3   *The About page*

The final page of the static prototype is the About page. This is just going to be a page with a header and some content, so nothing complicated. The layout might be useful for other pages further down the line, such as a privacy policy or terms and conditions, so we're best off creating a generic, reusable view.

The controller for the About page is in the others.js file in app_server/controllers. You're looking for the controller called about, and you want to change the name of the view to generic-text, like in the following code snippet:

```
module.exports.about = function(req, res){
  res.render('generic-text', { title: 'About' });
};
```

Next, create the view generic-text.jade in app_server/views. It's a pretty small template, and should look like the following listing.

> **Listing 4.9   View for text only pages, app_server/views/generic-text.jade**

```
extends layout

block content
  #banner.page-header
    .row
      .col-md-6.col-sm-12
        h1= title
    .row
      .col-md-6.col-sm-12
        p
          | Loc8r was created to help people find places to sit down and get a
        bit of work done.
          | <br /><br />
          | Lorem ipsum dolor sit amet, consectetur adipiscing elit. Nunc sed
        lorem ac nisi dignissim accumsan.
```

Use | to create lines of plain text within a \<p> tag

Listing 4.9 is a very simple layout. Don't worry about including page-specific content into a generic view at this point; we'll take that on soon and make the page reusable. For now, for the purposes of finishing the clickable static prototype, it's okay.

You'll probably want to add some additional lines in there, so that the page looks like it has real content. Notice that the lines starting with the pipe character (|) can contain HTML tags if you want them to. Figure 4.13 shows how this might look in the browser with a bit more content in it.

And that's the last one of the four pages we need for the static site. You can now push this up to Heroku and have people visit the URL and click around. If you've forgotten how to do this, the following code snippet shows the terminal commands you need, assuming you've already set up Heroku. In terminal, you need to be in the root folder of the application.

```
$ git add .
$ git commit -m "Adding the view templates"
$ git push heroku master
```

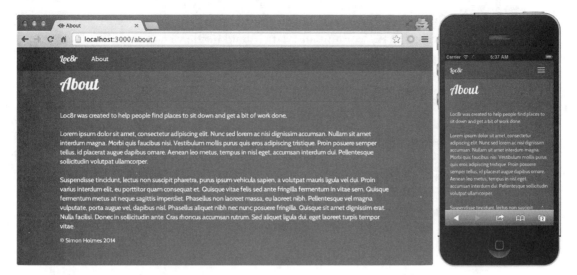

Figure 4.13 Generic text template rendering the About page

Get the source code

The source code for the application as it stands at this point is available on GitHub in the chapter-04-views branch. In a fresh folder in terminal the following commands will clone it and install the npm module dependencies:

```
$ git clone  b chapter 04 views https://github.com/simonholmes/getting-
    MEAN.git
$ cd getting-MEAN
$ npm install
```

So what's next? The routes, views, and controllers are set up for a static site that you can click through. And you've just pushed it up to Heroku so that others can also try it out. In some ways this is the end goal for this stage, and you can stop here while you play with the journeys and get feedback. This is definitely the easiest point in the process to make large sweeping changes.

If you were definitely going to be building an Angular SPA, and assuming you're happy with what you've done to this point, then you probably wouldn't go any further with creating a static prototype. Instead, you'd start to create an application in Angular.

But the next step we're going to take now will continue down the road of creating the Express application. So while keeping with the static site, we'll be removing the data from the views and putting them into the controllers.

4.5   *Take the data out of the views and make them smarter*

At the moment, all of the content and data is held in the views. This is perfect for testing stuff out and moving things around, but we need to move forward. An end goal of the MVC architecture is to have views without content or data. The views should simply be fed data that they present to the end users, while being agnostic of the data they're fed. The views will need a data structure, but what is inside the data doesn't matter to the view itself.

If you think about the MVC architecture, the model holds the data, the controller then processes the data, and finally the view renders the processed data. We're not dealing with the model yet—that will come soon, starting in chapter 5. For now we're working with the views and controllers. To make the views smarter, and do what they're intended to do, we need to take the data and content out of the views and into the controllers. Figure 4.14 illustrates the data flow in an MVC architecture, and the changes we want to make to get us a step closer.

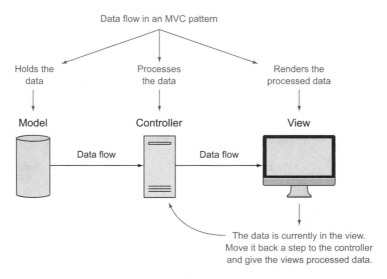

Figure 4.14   How the data should flow in an MVC pattern, from the model through the controller to the view. At this point in the prototype our data is in the view, but we want to move it a step back into the controller.

Making these changes now will allow us to finalize the views and be ready for the next step. As a bonus, we'll start thinking about how the processed data should look in the controllers. So rather than starting with a data structure, we'll start off with the ideal front end and slowly reverse-engineer the data back through the MVC steps as our understanding of the requirements solidifies.

So how are we going to do this? Starting with the homepage we'll take every piece of content out of the Jade view. We'll update the Jade file to contain variables in place

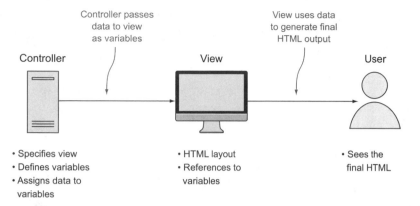

Figure 4.15   When the controller specifies the data, it passes the data to the view as variables; the view then uses that data to generate the final HTML that's delivered to the user.

of the content, and put the content as variables into the controller. The controller can then pass these values into the view. The result should end up looking the same in the browser, and end users shouldn't be able to spot a difference. The roles of the various parts and the movement and use of data are shown in figure 4.15.

At the end of this stage, the data will still be hard-coded, but in the controllers instead of the views. The views will now be smarter and able to accept and display whatever data is sent to them, providing it's in the correct format, of course.

4.5.1   How to move data from the view to the controller

We're going to start with the homepage, and take the data out of the `locations-list.jade` view into the `homelist` function in the locations.js controllers file. Let's start at the top with something pretty simple, the page header. The following code snippet shows the page header section of the `list.jade` view, which has two pieces of content:

```
#banner.page-header
  .row
    .col-lg-6
      h1 Loc8r
        small  Find places to work with wifi near you!
```

Large font page title

Smaller font strapline for page

These two pieces of content are the first that we'll move into the controller. The homepage controller currently looks like the following:

```
module.exports.homelist = function(req, res){
  res.render('locations-list', { title: 'Home' });
};
```

This is already sending one piece of data to the view. Remember that the second parameter in the `render` function is a JavaScript object containing the data to send to the view. Here the homelist controller is sending the data object { title: 'Home' } to the view. This is being used by the layout file to put the string Home into the HTML <title>, which isn't necessarily the best choice of text.

UPDATE THE CONTROLLER

So let's change the title to something more appropriate for the page, and also add in the two data items for the page header. Make these changes to the controller first, as follows (modifications in bold):

```
module.exports.homelist = function(req, res){
  res.render('locations-list', {
    title: 'Loc8r - find a place to work with wifi',
    pageHeader: {                                          New nested pageHeader
      title: 'Loc8r',                                      object containing
      strapline: 'Find places to work with wifi near you!' properties for title and
    }                                                      strapline of page
  });
};
```

For neatness and future manageability the title and the strapline are grouped together within a pageHeader object. This is a good habit to get into, and will make the controllers easier to update and maintain further down the line.

UPDATE THE VIEW

Now that the controller is passing these pieces of data to the view, we can update the view to reference them in place of the hard-coded content. Nested data items like this are referenced using the dot syntax. So to reference the page header strapline in the list.jade view we'll use pageHeader.strapline. The following code snippet shows the page header section of the view (modifications in bold):

```
#banner.page-header                = signifies that following    #{} delimiters are
  .row                             content is buffered code, in  used to insert data into
    .col-lg-6                      this case a JavaScript object a specific place, like
      h1= pageHeader.title    ◁┘                                part of a piece of text
        small  #{pageHeader.strapline}              ◁┘
```

The code is outputting pageHeader.title and pageHeader.strapline in the relevant places in the view. See the following sidebar for details about the different methods of referencing data in Jade templates.

Referencing data in Jade templates

There are two key syntaxes for referencing data in Jade templates. The first is called *interpolation*, and it's typically used to insert data into the middle of some other content. Interpolated data is defined by the opening delimiter #{ and the end delimiter }. You'd normally use it like this:

```
h1 Welcome to #{pageHeader.title}
```

If your data contains HTML, this will be escaped for security reasons. This means that the end users will see any HTML tags displayed as text, and the browser will not interpret them as HTML. If you want the browser to render any HTML contained in the data you can use the following syntax:

```
h1 Welcome to !{pageHeader.title}
```

This poses potential security risks and should only be done from data sources that you trust. You shouldn't allow user inputs to display like this, for example, with some additional security checks.

The second method of outputting the data is with *buffered code*. Instead of inserting the data into a string, you build the string using JavaScript. This is done by using the = sign directly after the tag declaration, like this:

```
h1= "Welcome to " + pageHeader.title
```

Again, this will escape any HTML for security reasons. If you want to have unescaped HTML in your output you can use slightly different syntax like this:

```
h1!= "Welcome to " + pageHeader.title
```

Once again, be careful using this. Whenever possible you should try to use one of the escaped methods just to be on the safe side.

If you run the application now and head back to the homepage, the only change you should notice is that the `<title>` has been updated. Everything else still looks the same; it's just that some of the data is now coming from the controller.

This section served as a simple example of what we're doing at this point, and how we're doing it. The complicated part of the homepage is the listing section, so let's look at how we can approach that.

4.5.2 *Dealing with complex, repeating data*

This first thing to bear in mind with the listing section is that there are multiple entries, all following the same data pattern and layout pattern. Like we've just done with the page header, we'll start with the data, taking it from the view to the controller.

In terms of JavaScript data, a repeatable pattern lends itself nicely to the idea of an array of objects. We'll look to have one array holding multiple objects, with each single object containing all of the relevant information for an individual listing.

ANALYZING THE DATA IN THE VIEW

Let's take a look at a listing and see what information we need the controller to send. Figure 4.16 reminds us how a listing looks in the homepage view.

**Figure 4.16
An individual listing,
showing the data
that we need**

From this screenshot we can see that an individual listing on the homepage has the following data requirements:

- Name
- Rating
- Distance away
- Address
- List of facilities

Taking the data from the screenshot in figure 4.16 and creating a JavaScript object from it, we could come up with something simple like the following code snippet:

```
{
  name: 'Starcups',
  address: '125 High Street, Reading, RG6 1PS',
  rating: 3,
  facilities: ['Hot drinks', 'Food', 'Premium wifi'],
  distance: '100m'
}
```

List of facilities is sent as an array of string values

That's all the data needed for a single location. For multiple locations we'll need an array of these.

ADDING THE REPEATING DATA ARRAY TO THE CONTROLLER

So we just need to create an array of the single location objects—taking the data you currently have in the view if you want—and add it to the data object passed to the render function in the controller. The following code snippet shows the updated homelist controller including the array of locations:

```
module.exports.homelist = function(req, res){
  res.render('locations-list', {
    title: 'Loc8r - find a place to work with wifi',
    pageHeader: {
      title: 'Loc8r',
      strapline: 'Find places to work with wifi near you!'
    },
    locations: [{
      name: 'Starcups',
      address: '125 High Street, Reading, RG6 1PS',
      rating: 3,
      facilities: ['Hot drinks', 'Food', 'Premium wifi'],
      distance: '100m'
    },{
      name: 'Cafe Hero',
      address: '125 High Street, Reading, RG6 1PS',
      rating: 4,
      facilities: ['Hot drinks', 'Food', 'Premium wifi'],
      distance: '200m'
    },{
      name: 'Burger Queen',
      address: '125 High Street, Reading, RG6 1PS',
      rating: 2,
```

Array of locations is being passed as locations to view for rendering

```
      facilities: ['Food', 'Premium wifi'],
      distance: '250m'
   }]
 });
};
```

Here we've got the details for three locations being sent in the array. You can add many more, of course, but this is as good a start as any. Now we need to get the view to render this information, instead of the data currently hard-coded inside it.

LOOPING THROUGH ARRAYS IN A JADE VIEW

The controller is sending an array to Jade as the variable `locations`. Jade offers a very simple syntax for looping through an array. In one line we specify which array to use and what variable name we want to use as the key. The key is simply a named reference to the current item in the array, so the contents of it change as the loop progresses through the array. The construct of a Jade loop is like so:

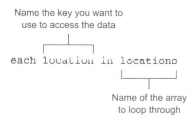

Anything nested inside this line in Jade will be iterated through for each item in the array. Let's take a look at an example of using this, using the locations data and part of the view we want. In the view file, each location starts off with the code in the following snippet, just with a different name each time:

```
.col-xs-12.list-group-item
   h4
      a(href="/location") Starcups
```

We can use Jade's each/in syntax to loop through all of the locations in the `locations` array, and output the name of each. How this works is shown in the next code snippet:

```
                                           Set up loop, defining
                                           variable location as key
each location in locations      ←
   .col-xs-12.list-group-item              Nested items are all
      h4                                   looped through
         a(href="/location")= location.name      ←
                                                       Output name of each
                                                       location, accessing the name
                                                       property of each location
```

Given the controller data we've got, with three locations in it, using that with the preceding code would result in the following HTML:

```html
<div class="col-xs-12 list-group-item">
  <h4>
    <a href="/location">Starcups</a>
  </h4>
</div>
<div class="col-xs-12 list-group-item">
  <h4>
    <a href="/location">Cafe Hero</a>
  </h4>
</div>
<div class="col-xs-12 list-group-item">
  <h4>
    <a href="/location">Burger Queen</a>
  </h4>
</div>
```

As you can see, the HTML construct—the div, h4, and a tags—are repeated three times. But the name of the location is different in each one, corresponding to the data in the controller.

So looping through arrays is pretty easy, and with that little test we've already got the first few lines of the updated view text we need. Now we just need to follow this through with the rest of the data used in the listings. We can't deal with the ratings stars like this, so we'll ignore those for now and deal with them shortly.

Dealing with the rest of the data we can produce the following code snippet, which will output all of the data for each listing. As the facilities are being passed as an array, we'll need to loop through that array for each listing:

```
each location in locations
  .col-xs-12.list-group-item
    h4
      a(href="/location")= location.name
      small  
        span.glyphicon.glyphicon-star
        span.glyphicon.glyphicon-star
        span.glyphicon.glyphicon-star
        span.glyphicon.glyphicon-star-empty
        span.glyphicon.glyphicon-star-empty
      span.badge.pull-right.badge-default= location.distance
    p.address= location.address
    p
      each facility in location.facilities
        span.label.label-warning= facility
         
```

Looping through a nested array to output facilities for each location

Looping through the facilities array is no problem, and Jade handles this with ease. Pulling out the rest of the data like the distance and the address is pretty straightforward, using the techniques we've already looked at.

The only part left to deal with is the ratings stars. For that, we're going to need a bit of inline JavaScript code.

4.5.3   *Manipulating the data and view with code*

For the star ratings the view is outputting spans with different classes using Bootstrap's Glyphicon system. There are a total of five stars, which are either solid or empty, depending on the rating. For example, a rating of five will show five solid stars, a rating of three will show three solid stars and two empty stars, as shown in figure 4.17, and a rating of zero will show five empty stars.

Figure 4.17   The Glyphicon star rating system in action, showing a rating of three out of five stars

To generate this type of output, we're going to use some code inside the Jade template. The code is essentially JavaScript, with some Jade-specific conventions thrown in. To add a line of inline code to a Jade template we prefix the line with a dash or hyphen. This tells Jade to run the JavaScript code rather than passing it through to the browser.

To generate the output for the stars we're going to use a couple of for loops. The first loop will output the correct number of solid stars and the second loop will output the remaining empty stars. The following code snippet shows how this looks and works in Jade:

```
- for (var i = 1; i <= location.rating; i++)
  span.glyphicon.glyphicon-star
- for (i = location.rating; i < 5; i++)
  span.glyphicon.glyphicon-star-empty
```

Notice that the syntax is very familiar JavaScript, but there are no curly brackets defining the block of code to run. Instead, the block of code is defined by indentation, like the rest of Jade. Also notice the mixture of code and Jade. The lines of code are saying "for every time I evaluate as true, render the indented Jade content." This is a really nice approach, as you don't have to try to construct your HTML using JavaScript.

That's all of the content and layout for the homepage sorted, so we can move on. Except, there's one more thing we can do to improve what we've got and make some of the code reusable.

4.5.4   *Using includes and mixins to create reusable layout components*

The star rating code that we've just written is going to be quite useful on other layouts. We're going to want it on the Details page, for example, and maybe in more places in the future. We don't want to have to manually add it to every page. What if we decide that we don't like the Glyphicons anymore and want to change the markup? We certainly don't want to have to change it separately on every single page that shows a rating, not if we can help it.

Fortunately, Jade enables you to create reusable components using *mixins* and *includes.*

DEFINING JADE MIXINS

A *mixin* in Jade is essentially a function. You can define a mixin at the top of your file and use it in multiple places. A mixin definition is really straightforward: you simply define the name of the mixin, and then nest the content of it with indentation. The following code snippet shows a basic mixin definition:

```
mixin welcome
  p Welcome
```

This will output the "Welcome" text inside a <p> tag wherever it's invoked.

Mixins are also able to accept parameters, just like a JavaScript function. This is going to be very useful for creating the mixin we need to display the rating, as the HTML output will be different depending on the actual rating. The following code snippet shows how this can work, defining the mixin we want to use on the homepage to output the ratings stars:

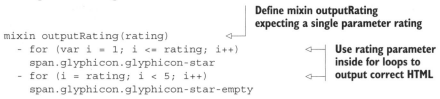

```
mixin outputRating(rating)      ◁——  Define mixin outputRating
  - for (var i = 1; i <= rating; i++)      expecting a single parameter rating
    span.glyphicon.glyphicon-star                    ◁——  Use rating parameter
  - for (i = rating; i < 5; i++)                           inside for loops to
    span.glyphicon.glyphicon-star-empty      ◁——  output correct HTML
```

In a sense, this works just like a JavaScript function. When you define the mixin you can specify the parameters that it expects. Within the mixin you can then use this parameter. You can take the preceding code snippet and pop it into the top of the locations-list.jade file, between the extends layout and block content lines.

CALLING JADE MIXINS

After defining the mixin, you're going to want to use it, of course. The syntax for calling a mixin is to simply place a + before its name. If you have no parameters, such as the welcome mixin we've just looked at, this looks like the following:

```
+welcome
```

This will call the welcome mixin and output the text "Welcome" inside a <p> tag.

Calling a mixin with parameters is just as easy. You simply send the values of the parameters through inside brackets, just like you'd do when calling a JavaScript function. In the location-listings.jade file, at the point where we're outputting the ratings, the value of the rating is held in the variable location.rating, as shown in the following code snippet:

```
small  
  - for (var i - 1; i <= location.rating; i++)
    span.glyphicon.glyphicon-star
  - for (i = location.rating; i < 5; i++)
    span.glyphicon.glyphicon-star-empty
```

We can replace this code with a call to our new mixin `outputRating`, sending the `location.rating` variable as the parameter. This looks like the following code snippet:

```
small  
  +outputRating(location.rating)
```

This will now output the exact same HTML as before, but we've taken a part of the code outside of the contents of the layout. Right now, this is only reusable within the same file, but next we're going to use includes to make it accessible to other files.

USING INCLUDES IN JADE

To allow our new mixin to be called from other Jade templates, we need to make it an include file. This is super easy.

Within the app_server/views folder, create a subfolder called _includes. Within this folder create a new file called sharedHTMLfunctions.jade, and paste into it the `outputRating` mixin definition, as follows:

```
mixin outputRating(rating)
  - for (var i = 1; i <= rating; i++)
    span.glyphicon.glyphicon-star
  - for (i = rating; i < 5; i++)
    span.glyphicon.glyphicon-star-empty
```

Save the file, and that's your include created. To use an include file in a Jade layout there is a very simple syntax. Simply use the keyword `include`, followed by the relative path to the include file. The following code snippet shows the line of code that we can use to replace the mixin code at the top of location-listings.jade:

```
include _includes/sharedHTMLfunctions
```

Now, rather than having the mixin code inline in the template, we're calling it in from an include file. Notice that you can omit the .jade file extension when calling the include. So now, when we create a new template that needs to have ratings stars on it, we can easily reference this include file and call the `outputRatings` mixin.

And now, we're really done with the homepage!

4.5.5 The finished homepage

We've made quite a lot of changes to the homepage template throughout this section. So let's see what we've ended up with. First let's take a look at the updated controller. The following listing shows the final `homelist` controller, incorporating the hard-coded data.

Listing 4.10 The `homelist` controller, passing hard-coded data to the view

```
module.exports.homelist = function(req, res){
  res.render('locations-list', {
    title: 'Loc8r - find a place to work with wifi',          ◁──  Update text for
    pageHeader: {                                                   HTML <title>
      title: 'Loc8r',
      strapline: 'Find places to work with wifi near you!'     Add text for page
    },                                                         header as two items
                                                               inside an object
```

```
    sidebar: "Looking for wifi and a seat? Loc8r helps you find places
    to work when out and about. Perhaps with coffee, cake or a pint?
    Let Loc8r help you find the place you're looking for.",
    locations: [{                                        ◁
      name: 'Starcups',                                              Add text
      address: '125 High Street, Reading, RG6 1PS',                 for sidebar
      rating: 3,
      facilities: ['Hot drinks', 'Food', 'Premium wifi'],
      distance: '100m'                                       Create an array of
    },{                                                      one object for each
      name: 'Cafe Hero',                                     location in list
      address: '125 High Street, Reading, RG6 1PS',
      rating: 4,
      facilities: ['Hot drinks', 'Food', 'Premium wifi'],
      distance: '200m'
    },{
      name: 'Burger Queen',
      address: '125 High Street, Reading, RG6 1PS',
      rating: 2,
      facilities: ['Food', 'Premium wifi'],
      distance: '250m'
    }]
  });
};
```

Seeing this all together you can start to appreciate where we're going with this approach. We've got a clear picture of all of the data required for the homepage of Loc8r. This is going to come in handy in the next chapter. This controller contains the text for the sidebar. We didn't talk about this step, but taking it from the view to the controller is as simple as creating a new variable for it in the controller and referencing it in the view.

Something important that we've achieved through this process is the removal of data from the view. Building the view with data in was great as a first step, as it allowed us to focus on the end-user experience without getting distracted by the technicalities. Now that we've moved the data from the view into the controller we have a much smarter, dynamic view. The view knows what pieces of data it needs, but it doesn't care what is in those pieces of data. The following listing shows the final view for the homepage.

Listing 4.11   Final view for the homepage, app_server/views/locations-list.jade

```
extends layout
                                          Bring in external
include _includes/sharedHTMLfunctions   ◁  include file containing
                                           outputRating mixin
block content
  #banner.page-header
    .row
      .col-lg-6
        h1= pageHeader.title                Output page header text
          small  #{pageHeader.strapline}   using different methods
```

```
.row
  .col-xs-12.col-sm-8
    .row.list-group
      each location in locations          ◁─┐  Loop through
        .col-xs-12.list-group-item              array of locations
          h4
            a(href="/location")= location.name    Call outputRating mixin for
            small                             each location, passing value
              +outputRating(location.rating)  ◁─┘  of current location's rating
            span.badge.pull-right.badge-default= location.distance
          p.address= location.address
          p
            each facility in location.facilities
              span.label.label-warning= facility
              |  
  .col-xs-12.col-sm-4                    Reference sidebar
    p.lead= sidebar               ◁─┐    content from controller
```

That's a pretty small template, right? Especially considering everything it's doing. This is a testament to the power of Jade and Bootstrap working together. Not to mention a side effect of removing all of the content (notice that the sidebar content is being pulled from the controller too).

We're one step closer to the MVC—and general development—goal of separation of concerns. With the homepage at least.

4.5.6 Updating the rest of the views and controllers

We've stepped through the process for the homepage in quite some detail here, but we're not going to spend so much time on each of the other pages. Before we can move to the next stage of development—building the data model—we need to go through the process on all of the pages, though. The end goal is to have no data in any of the views; instead the views will be smarter and the data will be hard-coded into the relevant controllers.

The process for each page will be

1 Look at the data in the view.
2 Create a structure for that data in the controller.
3 Replace the data in the view with references to the controller data.
4 Look for opportunities to reuse code.

Appendix C goes through the process for each of the three remaining pages, showing what the controller and view code should look like for each one. When you've finished, none of your views should contain any hard-coded data; the controller for each page should be passing the required data. Figure 4.18 shows a collection of screenshots of the final pages you should have at the end of this stage.

This puts us at the end of the first phase of our rapid prototype development, and primed to start the next phase.

Figure 4.18   Screenshots of all four pages in the static prototype, using smart views and data hard-coded into the controllers

> **Get the source code**
>
> The source code of the application so far is available from GitHub on the chapter-04 branch of the getting-MEAN repository. In a fresh folder in terminal the following commands will clone it and install the dependencies:
>
> ```
> $ git clone -b chapter-04 https://github.com/simonholmes/getting-MEAN.git
> $ cd getting-MEAN
> $ npm install
> ```

4.6   *Summary*

In this chapter we've covered

- Defining and organizing routes in Express
- Creating Node modules to hold the controllers
- Using multiple sets of controllers with the routes
- Creating views using Jade and Bootstrap
- Making reusable Jade components, mixins
- Displaying dynamic data in Jade templates
- Passing data from controllers to views

Coming up in chapter 5 we're going to continue the journey of moving the data back up through the MVC architecture by using MongoDB and Mongoose to create a data model. That's right, it's database time!

Building a data model with
MongoDB and Mongoose

This chapter covers

- How Mongoose helps bridge an Express/Node application to a MongoDB database
- Defining schemas for a data model using Mongoose
- Connecting an application to a database
- Managing databases using the MongoDB shell
- Pushing a database into a live environment
- Using the correct database depending on the environment, distinguishing between local and live versions of an application

In chapter 4 we ended up by moving our data out of the views and backward down the MVC path into the controllers. Ultimately, the controllers will pass data to the views, but they shouldn't store it. Figure 5.1 recaps the data flow in an MVC pattern.

For storing the data we'll need a database, specifically MongoDB. So this is our next step in the process: creating a database and data model.

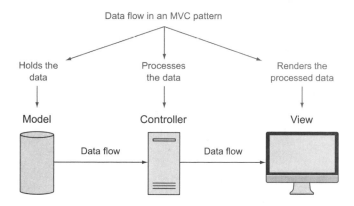

Figure 5.1 In an MVC pattern, data is held in the model, processed by a controller, and then rendered by a view.

NOTE If you haven't yet built the application from chapter 4, you can get the code from GitHub on the chapter-04 branch at github.com/simonholmes/getting-MEAN. In a fresh folder in terminal the following command will clone it:

```
$ git clone -b chapter-04 https://github.com/simonholmes/getting-MEAN.git
```

We'll start by connecting our application to a database before using Mongoose to define schemas and models. When we're happy with the structure we can add some test data directly to the MongoDB database. The final step will be making sure that this also works when pushed up to Heroku. Figure 5.2 shows the flow of these four steps.

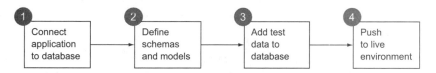

Figure 5.2 Four main steps in this chapter, from connecting our application to a database to pushing the whole thing into a live environment

For those of you who are worried that you've missed a section or two, don't worry—we haven't created a database yet. And we don't need to. In various other technology stacks this can present an issue and throw errors. But with MongoDB we don't need to create a database before connecting to it. MongoDB will create a database when we first try to use it.

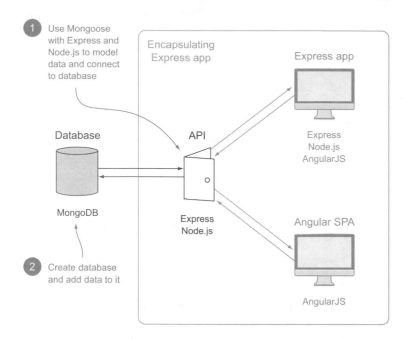

Figure 5.3 The MongoDB database and using Mongoose inside Express to model the data and manage the connection to the database

Figure 5.3 shows where this chapter will focus in terms of the overall architecture.

We'll, of course, be working with a MongoDB database, but most of the work will be in Express and Node. In chapter 2 we discussed the benefits of decoupling the data integration by creating an API rather than tightly integrating it into the main Express app. So although we'll be working in Express and Node, and still within the same encapsulating application, we'll actually be starting the foundations of our API layer.

NOTE   To follow through this chapter you'll need to have MongoDB installed. If you haven't done so already, you can find the instructions for this in appendix A.

The source code of the application as it will be at the end of this chapter is available from GitHub on the chapter-05 branch. In a fresh folder in terminal the following commands will clone it and install the npm module dependencies:

```
$ git clone -b chapter-05 https://github.com/simonholmes/getting-MEAN.git
$ cd getting-MEAN
$ npm install
```

5.1   Connecting the Express application to MongoDB using Mongoose

We could connect our application directly to MongoDB and have the two interact with each other using the native driver. While the native MongoDB driver is very powerful it isn't particularly easy to work with. It also doesn't offer a built-in way of defining and maintaining data structures. Mongoose exposes most of the functionality of the native driver, but in a more convenient way, designed to fit into the flows of application development.

Where Mongoose really excels is in the way it enables us to define data structures and models, maintain them, and use them to interact with our database. All from the comfort of our application code. As part of this approach Mongoose includes the ability to add validation to our data definitions, meaning that we don't have to write validation code into every place in our application where we send data back to the database.

So Mongoose fits into the stack inside the Express application by being the liaison between the application and the database, as shown in figure 5.4.

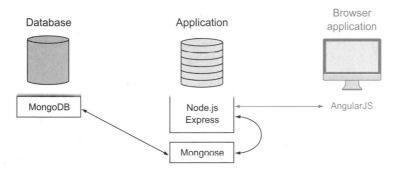

Figure 5.4   The data interactions in the MEAN stack and where Mongoose fits in. The Node/Express application interacts with MongoDB through Mongoose, and Node and Express can then also talk to Angular.

MongoDB only talks to Mongoose, and Mongoose in turn talks to Node and Express. Angular will not talk directly to MongoDB or Mongoose, but only to the Express application.

You should already have MongoDB installed on your system (covered in appendix A), but not Mongoose. Mongoose isn't installed globally, but is instead added directly to our application. We'll do that now.

5.1.1   Adding Mongoose to our application

Mongoose is available as an npm module. As you saw in chapter 3, the quickest and easiest way to install an npm module is through the command line. We can install Mongoose and add it to our list of dependencies in package.json with one command.

So head over to terminal and make sure the prompt is at the root folder of the application, where the package.json file is, and run the following command:

```
$ npm install --save mongoose
```

The --save flag is what tells npm to add Mongoose to the dependency list in package.json. When that command has finished running you'll be able to see a new *mongoose* folder inside the *node_modules* folder of the application, and the dependencies section of the package.json file should look like the following code snippet:

```
"dependencies": {
  "express": "~4.9.0",
  "body-parser": "~1.8.1",
  "cookie-parser": "~1.3.3",
  "morgan": "~1.3.0",
  "serve-favicon": "~2.1.3",
  "debug": "~2.0.0",
  "jade": "~1.6.0",
  "mongoose": "~3.8.20"
}
```

You may have slightly different version numbers, of course, but at the time of writing the latest stable version of Mongoose is 3.8.20. Now that Mongoose is installed, let's get it connected.

5.1.2   *Adding a Mongoose connection to our application*

At this stage we're going to connect our application to a database. We haven't created a database yet, but that doesn't matter because MongoDB will create a database when we first try to use it. This can seem a little odd, but for putting an application together it's a great advantage: we don't need to leave our application code to mess around in a different environment.

MONGODB AND MONGOOSE CONNECTION

Mongoose opens a pool of five reusable connections when it connects to a MongoDB database. This pool of connections is shared between all requests. Five is just the default number and can be increased or decreased in the connection options if you need to.

> **BEST-PRACTICE TIP**   Opening and closing connections to databases can take a little bit of time, especially if your database is on a separate server or service. So it's best to only run these operations when you need to. The best practice is to open the connection when your application starts up, and to leave it open until your application restarts or shuts down. This is the approach we're going to take.

SETTING UP THE CONNECTION FILE

When we first sorted out the file structure for the application we created three folders inside the app_server folder: *models, views,* and *controllers.* For working with data and models, we'll be predominantly based in the app_server/models folder.

Setting up the connection file is a two-part process: creating the file and requiring it into the application so that it can be used.

Step one: create a file called db.js in app_server/models and save it. For now we'll just `require` Mongoose in this file, with the following single command line:

```
var mongoose = require( 'mongoose' );
```

Step two: bring this file into the application by requiring it in app.js. As the actual process of creating a connection between the application and the database can take a little while, we want to do this early on in the setup. So amend the top part of app.js to look like the following code snippet (modifications in bold):

```
var express = require('express');
var path = require('path');
var favicon = require('serve-favicon');
var logger = require('morgan');
var cookieParser = require('cookie-parser');
var bodyParser = require('body-parser');
require('./app_server/models/db');
```

We're not going to export any functions from db.js, so we don't need to assign it to a variable when we `require` it. We need it to be there in the application, but we're not going to need to hook into any methods of it from within app.js.

If you restart the application it should run just as before, but now you have Mongoose in the application. If you get an error, check that the path in the `require` statement matches the path to the new file, that your package.json includes the Mongoose dependency, and that you've run `npm install` from terminal in the root folder of the application.

CREATING THE MONGOOSE CONNECTION

Creating a Mongoose connection can be as simple as declaring the URI for your database and passing it to Mongoose's `connect` method. A database URI is a string following this construct:

```
mongodb://username:password@localhost:27027/database
```

| MongoDB protocol | Login credentials for database | Server address | Port | Database name |

The username, password, and port are all optional. So on your local machine your database URI is going to be quite simple. For now, assuming that you have MongoDB installed on your local machine, adding the following code snippet to db.js will be all you need to create a connection:

```
var dbURI = 'mongodb://localhost/Loc8r';
mongoose.connect(dbURI);
```

If you run the application with this addition to db.js it should still start and function just as before. So how do you know your connection is working correctly? The answer lies in connection events.

MONITORING THE CONNECTION WITH MONGOOSE CONNECTION EVENTS

Mongoose will publish events based on the status of the connection, and these are really easy to hook into so that you can see what's going on. We're going to use events to see when the connection is made, when there's an error, and when the connection is disconnected. When any one of these events occurs we'll log a message to the console. The following code snippet shows the code required to do this:

```
mongoose.connection.on('connected', function () {
  console.log('Mongoose connected to ' + dbURI);
});
mongoose.connection.on('error',function (err) {
  console.log('Mongoose connection error: ' + err);
});
mongoose.connection.on('disconnected', function () {
  console.log('Mongoose disconnected');
});
```

Monitoring for successful connection through Mongoose

Checking for connection error

Checking for disconnection event

With this added to db.js, when you restart the application you should see the following confirmations logged to the terminal window:

```
Express server listening on port 3000
Mongoose connected to mongodb://localhost/Loc8r
```

If you restart the application again, however, you'll notice that you don't get any disconnection messages. This is because the Mongoose connection doesn't automatically close when the application stops or restarts. We need to listen for changes in the Node process to deal with this.

CLOSING A MONGOOSE CONNECTION

Closing the Mongoose connection when the application stops is as much a part of the best practice as opening the connection when it starts. The connection has two ends: one in your application and one in MongoDB. MongoDB needs to know when you want to close the connection so that it doesn't keep redundant connections open.

To monitor when the application stops we need to listen to the Node.js process, listening for an event called SIGINT.

Listening for SIGINT on Windows

SIGINT is an operating system–level signal that fires on Unix-based systems like Linux and Mac OS X. It also fires on some later versions of Windows. If you're running on Windows and the disconnection events don't fire, you can emulate them. If you need to emulate this behavior on Windows you first add a new npm package to your application, readline. So in your package.json file update the dependencies section like this:

```
"dependencies": {
  "express": "3.4.x",
```

```
    "jade": "*",
    "mongoose": "3.8.x",
    "readline": "0.0.x"
}
```

When that's done, install it into the application by running `npm install` from the command line, based in the same folder as your package.json file.

In the db.js file, above the event listener code, add the following:

```
var readLine = require ("readline");
if (process.platform === "win32"){
    var rl = readLine.createInterface ({
        input: process.stdin,
        output: process.stdout
    });
    rl.on ("SIGINT", function (){
        process.emit ("SIGINT");
    });
}
```

This will emit the SIGINT signal on Windows machines, allowing you to capture it and gracefully close down anything else you need to before the process ends.

If you're using nodemon to automatically restart the application then you'll also have to listen to a second event on the Node process called SIGUSR2. Heroku uses another different event, SIGTERM, so we'll need to listen for that as well.

CAPTURING THE PROCESS TERMINATION EVENTS

With all of these events, once we've captured them we prevent the default behavior from happening, so we need to make sure that we manually restart the behavior required. After closing the Mongoose connection, of course.

To do this, we need three event listeners and one function to close the database connection. Closing the database is an asynchronous activity, so we're going to need to pass through whatever function is required to restart or end the Node process as a callback. While we're at it, we can output a message to the console confirming that the connection is closed, and the reason why. We can wrap this all in a function called gracefulShutdown in db.js, as in the following code snippet:

Close Mongoose connection, passing through an anonymous function to run when closed

Define function to accept message and callback function

```
var gracefulShutdown = function (msg, callback) {
  mongoose.connection.close(function () {
    console.log('Mongoose disconnected through ' + msg);
    callback();
  });
};
```

Output message and call callback when Mongoose connection is closed

Now we need to call this function when the application terminates, or when nodemon restarts it. The following code snippet shows the two event listeners we need to add to db.js for this to happen:

Listen for SIGINT emitted on application termination

Listen for SIGTERM emitted when Heroku shuts down process

Listen for SIGUSR2, which is what nodemon uses

Send message to graceful-Shutdown and callback to kill process, emitting SIGUSR2 again

Send message to gracefulShutdown and callback to exit Node process

```
process.once('SIGUSR2', function () {
  gracefulShutdown('nodemon restart', function () {
    process.kill(process.pid, 'SIGUSR2');
  });
});

process.on('SIGINT', function () {
  gracefulShutdown('app termination', function () {
    process.exit(0);
  });
});

process.on('SIGTERM', function() {
  gracefulShutdown('Heroku app shutdown', function () {
    process.exit(0);
  });
});
```

Now when the application terminates, it gracefully closes the Mongoose connection before it actually ends. Similarly, when nodemon restarts the application due to changes in the source files, the application closes the current Mongoose connection first. The nodemon listener is using process.once as opposed to process.on, as we only want to listen for the SIGUSR2 event once. nodemon also listens for the same event and we don't want to capture it each time, preventing nodemon from working.

> **TIP** It's important to manage opening and closing your database connections properly in every application you create. If you use an environment with different process termination signals you should ensure that you listen to them all.

COMPLETE CONNECTION FILE

That's quite a lot of stuff we've added to the db.js file, so let's take a moment to recap. So far we have

- Defined a database connection string
- Opened a Mongoose connection at application startup
- Monitored the Mongoose connection events
- Monitored some Node process events so that we can close the Mongoose connection when the application ends

All together the db.js file should look like the following listing. Note that this doesn't include the extra code required by Windows to emit the SIGINT event.

Listing 5.1 Complete database connection file db.js in app_server/models

```
var mongoose = require( 'mongoose' );                    Define database connection
var gracefulShutdown;                                    string and use it to open
var dbURI = 'mongodb://localhost/Loc8r';                 Mongoose connection
mongoose.connect(dbURI);

mongoose.connection.on('connected', function () {
  console.log('Mongoose connected to ' + dbURI);
});                                                      Listen for Mongoose
mongoose.connection.on('error',function (err) {          connection events
  console.log('Mongoose connection error: ' + err);      and output statuses
});                                                      to console
mongoose.connection.on('disconnected', function () {
  console.log('Mongoose disconnected');
});

gracefulShutdown = function (msg, callback) {
  mongoose.connection.close(function () {                Reusable function
    console.log('Mongoose disconnected through ' + msg); to close Mongoose
    callback();                                          connection
  });
},

// For nodemon restarts
process.once('SIGUSR2', function () {
  gracefulShutdown('nodemon restart', function () {
    process.kill(process.pid, 'SIGUSR2');
  });
});                                                      Listen to Node
// For app termination                                   processes for
process.on('SIGINT', function() {                        termination or
  gracefulShutdown('app termination', function () {      restart signals,
    process.exit(0);                                     and call
  });                                                    gracefulShutdown
});                                                      function when
// For Heroku app termination                            appropriate,
process.on('SIGTERM', function() {                       passing a
  gracefulShutdown('Heroku app shutdown', function () {  continuation
    process.exit(0);                                     callback
  });
});
```

Once you have a file like this you can easily copy it from application to application, because the events you're listening for are always the same. All you'll have to do each time is change the database connection string. Remember that we also *required* this file into app.js, right near the top, so that the connection opens up early on in the application's life.

Using multiple databases

What you've seen so far is known as the default connection, and is well suited to keeping a single connection open throughout the uptime of an application. But if you want to connect to a second database, say for logging or managing user sessions, then you can use a named connection. In place of the `mongoose.connect` method you'd use a different method called `mongoose.createConnection`, and assign this to a variable. You can see this in the following code snippet:

```
var dbURIlog = 'mongodb://localhost/Loc8rLog';
var logDB = mongoose.createConnection(dbURIlog);
```

This creates a new Mongoose connection object called `logDB`. You can interact with this in the same ways as you would with `mongoose.connection` for the default connection. Here are a couple of examples:

```
logDB.on('connected', function () {                    Monitoring connection
  console.log('Mongoose connected to ' + dbURIlog);    event for named
});                                                    connection
logDB.close(function () {                               Closing named
  console.log('Mongoose log disconnected');            connection
});
```

5.2 *Why model the data?*

In chapter 1 we talked about how MongoDB is a document store, rather than a traditional table-based database using rows and columns. This allows MongoDB great freedom and flexibility, but sometimes we want—that is, we *need*—structure to our data.

Take the Loc8r homepage, for example. The listing section shown in figure 5.5 contains a specific data set that's common to all locations.

Figure 5.5   Listing section of the homepage has very defined data requirements and structure

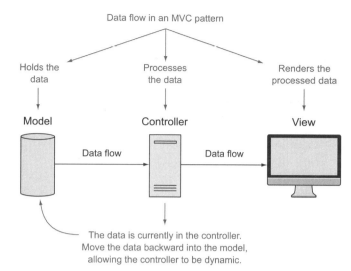

Figure 5.6 How data should flow in an MVC pattern, from the model, through the controller, into the view. At this point in our prototype our data is in the controller, so we want to move it a step back into the model.

The page needs these data items for all locations, and the data record for each location must have a consistent naming structure. Without this, the application wouldn't be able to find the data and use it. At this point in the development the data is held in the controller and being passed into the view. In terms of MVC architecture, we started off with the data in the *view* and then moved it back a step to the *controller*. Now what we need to do is move it back one final step to where it should belong, in the *model*. Figure 5.6 illustrates our current position, highlighting the end goal.

One of the outcomes of moving the data back through the MVC flow step-by-step as we've done so far is that it helps solidify the requirements of the data structure. This ensures the data structure accurately reflects the needs of our application. If you try to define your model first you end up second-guessing what the application will look like and how it will work.

So when we talk about modeling data, what we're really doing is describing how we want the data to be structured. In our application we could create and manage the definitions manually and do the heavy lifting ourselves, or we could use Mongoose and let it do the hard work for us.

5.2.1 What is Mongoose and how does it work?

Mongoose was built specifically as a MongoDB Object-Document Modeler (ODM) for Node applications. One of the key principles is that you can manage your data model from within your application. You don't have to mess around directly with databases or external frameworks or relational mappers; you can just define your data model in the comfort of your application.

First off, let's get some naming conventions out of the way:

- In MongoDB each entry in a database is called a *document*.
- In MongoDB a collection of documents is called a *collection* (think "table" if you're used to relational databases).
- In Mongoose the definition of a document is called a *schema*.
- Each individual data entity defined in a schema is called a *path*.

Using the example of a stack of business cards, figure 5.7 illustrates these naming conventions, and how each is related to the other.

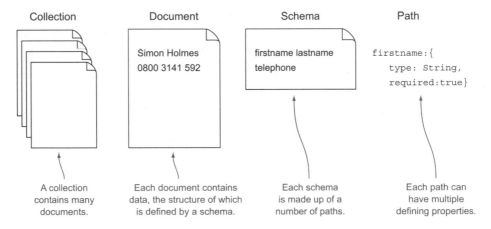

Figure 5.7   Relationships among collections, documents, schemas, and paths in MongoDB and Mongoose, using a business card metaphor

One final definition is for models. A *model* is the compiled version of a schema. All data interactions using Mongoose go through the model. We'll work with models more in chapter 6, but for now we're focusing on building them.

HOW DOES MONGOOSE MODEL DATA?

If we're defining our data in the application, how are we going to do it? In JavaScript, of course! JavaScript objects to be precise. We've already had a sneak peak in figure 5.7, but let's take a look at a simple MongoDB document and see what the Mongoose schema for it might look like. The following code snippet shows a MongoDB document, followed by the Mongoose schema:

```
{
  "firstname" : "Simon",
  "surname" : "Holmes",
  _id : ObjectId("52279effc62ca8b0c1000007")
}
```

Example MongoDB document

```
{
  firstname : String,
  surname : String
}
```

**Corresponding
Mongoose schema**

As you can see, the schema bears a very strong resemblance to the data itself. The schema defines the name for each data path, and the data type it will contain. In this example we've simply declared the paths firstname and surname as strings.

About the _id path

You may have noticed that we haven't declared the id path in the schema. id is the unique identifier—the primary key if you like—for each document. MongoDB automatically creates this path when each document is created and assigns it a unique ObjectId value. The value is designed to always be unique by combining the time since the Unix epoch with machine and process identifiers and a counter.

It's possible to use your own unique key system if you prefer, if you have a preexisting database, for example. In this book and the Loc8r application we're going to stick with the default ObjectId.

BREAKING DOWN A SCHEMA PATH

The basic construct for an individual path definition is the path name followed by a properties object. What we've just looked at is actually shorthand for when you just want to define the data type for that particular path. So a schema path is constructed of two parts, the path name and the properties object, like this:

```
firstname: {type:String}
```

Path name   Properties object

Allowed schema types

The schema type is the property that defines the data type for a given path. It's required for all paths. If the only property of a path is the type, then the shorthand definition can be used. There are eight schema types that you can use:

- String—Any string, UTF-8 encoded
- Number—Mongoose doesn't support long or double numbers, but it can be extended to do so using Mongoose plugins; the default support is enough for most cases
- Date—Typically returned from MongoDB as an ISODate object
- Boolean—True or false
- Buffer—For binary information such as images

> **(continued)**
>
> - `Mixed`—Any data type
> - `Array`—Can either be an array of the same data type, or an array of nested sub-documents
> - `ObjectId`—For a unique ID in a path other than `_id`; typically used to reference `_id` paths in other documents
>
> If you do need to use a different schema type it's possible to write your own custom schema types or to use an existing Mongoose plugin from http://plugins.mongoosejs.com.

The path name follows JavaScript object definition conventions and requirements. So there are no spaces or special characters and you should try to avoid reserved words. My convention is to use camelCase for path names. If you're using an existing database use the names of the paths already in the documents. If you're creating a new database, the path names in the schema will be used in the documents, so think carefully.

The properties object is essentially another JavaScript object. This one defines the characteristics of the data held in the path. At a minimum this contains the data type, but it can include validation characteristics, boundaries, default values, and more. We'll explore and use some of these options over the next few chapters as we turn Loc8r into a data-driven application.

But let's get moving and start defining the schemas we want in the application.

5.3   *Defining simple Mongoose schemas*

We've just discussed that a Mongoose schema is essentially a JavaScript object, which we define from within the application. Let's start by setting up and including the file so that it's done and out of the way, leaving us to concentrate on the schema.

As you'd expect we're going to define the schema in the model folder alongside db.js. In fact, we're going to `require` it into db.js to expose it to the application. So inside the models folder in app_server create a new empty file called locations.js. You need Mongoose to define a Mongoose schema, naturally, so enter the following line into locations.js:

```
var mongoose = require( 'mongoose' );
```

We're going to bring this file into the application by requiring it in db.js, so at the very end of db.js add the following line:

```
require('./locations');
```

And with that, we're set up and ready to go.

5.3.1 The basics of setting up a schema

Mongoose gives you a constructor function for defining new schemas, which you typically assign to a variable so that you can access it later. It looks like the following line:

```
var locationSchema = new mongoose.Schema({ });
```

In fact, that's exactly the construct we're going to use, so go ahead and add that to the locations.js model, below the line requiring Mongoose, of course. The empty object inside the mongooseSchema({ }) brackets is where we'll define the schema.

DEFINING A SCHEMA FROM CONTROLLER DATA

One of the outcomes in moving the data back from the view to the controller is that the controller ends up giving us a good idea of the data structure we need. Let's start simple and take a look at the homelist controller in app_server/controllers/locations.js. The homelist controller passes the data to be shown on the homepage into the view. Figure 5.8 shows how one of the locations looks on the homepage.

Figure 5.8   A single location as displayed on the homepage list

The following code snippet shows the data for this location, as found in the controller:

```
locations: [{                         name is a string              address is
  name: 'Starcups',                                                 another string
  address: '125 High Street, Reading, RG6 1PS',
  rating: 3,                                                        rating is a number
  facilities: ['Hot drinks', 'Food', 'Premium wifi'],
  distance: '100m'                                                  facilities is an
}]                                                                  array of strings
```

We'll come back to the distance a bit later, as that will need to be calculated. The other four data items are fairly straightforward: two strings, one number, and one array of strings. Taking what you know so far you can use this information to define a basic schema, like in the following:

```
var locationSchema = new mongoose.Schema({
  name: String,
  address: String,                       ❶ Declare an array of same
  rating: Number,                          schema type by declaring that
  facilities: [String]                     type inside square brackets
});
```

Note the simple approach to declaring facilities as an array ❶. If your array will only contain one schema type, such as `String`, then you can simply define it by wrapping the schema type in square brackets.

ASSIGNING DEFAULT VALUES

In some cases it's useful to set a default value when a new MongoDB document is created based on your schema. In the `locationSchema` the `rating` path is a good candidate for this. When a new location is added to the database, it won't have had any reviews, so it won't have a rating. But our view expects a rating between zero and five stars, which is what the controller will need to pass through.

So what we'd like to do is set a default value of `0` for the rating on each new document. Mongoose lets you do this from within the schema. Remember how `rating: Number` is shorthand for `rating: {type: Number}`? Well you can add other options to the definition object, including a default value. This means that you can update the rating path in the schema as follows:

```
rating: {type: Number, "default": 0}
```

The word `default` doesn't *have* to be in quotes, but it's a reserved word in JavaScript so it's a good idea to do so.

ADDING SOME BASIC VALIDATION: REQUIRED FIELDS

Through Mongoose you can quickly add some basic validation at the schema level. This helps toward maintaining data integrity and can protect your database from problems of missing or malformed data. Mongoose's helpers make it really easy to add some of the most common validation tasks, meaning that you don't have to write or import the code each time.

The first example of this type of validation ensures that required fields aren't empty before saving the document to the database. Rather than writing the checks for each required field in code, you can simply add a `required: true` flag to the definition objects of each path that you decide should be mandatory. In the `locationSchema`, we certainly want to ensure that each location has a name, so we can update the name path like this:

```
name: {type: String, required: true}
```

If you try to save a location without a name, Mongoose will return a validation error that you can capture immediately in your code, without needing a roundtrip to the database.

ADDING SOME BASIC VALIDATION: NUMBER BOUNDARIES

You can also use a similar technique to define the maximum and minimum values you want for a number path. These validators are called `max` and `min`. Each location we have has a rating assigned to it, which we have just given a default value of `0`. The value should never be less than `0` or greater than `5`, so you can update the `rating` path as follows:

```
rating: {type: Number, "default": 0, min: 0, max: 5}
```

With this update Mongoose will not let you save a rating value of less than 0 or greater than 5. It will return a validation error that you can handle in your code. One great thing about this approach is that the application doesn't have to make a roundtrip to the database to check the boundaries. Another bonus is that you don't have to write validation code into every place in the application where you might add, update, or calculate a rating value.

5.3.2   Using geographic data in MongoDB and Mongoose

When we first started to map our application's data from the controller into a Mongoose schema we left the question of distance until later. Now it's time to discuss how we're going to handle geographic information.

MongoDB can store geographic data as longitude and latitude coordinates, and can even create and manage an *index* based on this. This ability, in turn, enables users to do fast searches of places that are near to each other, or near a specific longitude and latitude. This is very helpful indeed for building a location-based application!

> ### About MongoDB indexes
> Indexes in any database system enable faster and more efficient queries, and MongoDB is no different. When a path is indexed, MongoDB can use this index to quickly grab subsets of data without having to scan through all documents in a collection.
>
> Think of a filing system you might have at home, and imagine you need to find a particular credit card statement. You might keep all of your paperwork in one drawer or cabinet. If it's all just thrown in there randomly you'll have to sort through all types of irrelevant documents until you find what you're looking for. If you've "indexed" your paperwork into folders, you can quickly find your "credit card" folder. Once you've picked this out you just look through this one set of documents, making your search much more efficient.
>
> This is akin to how indexing works in a database. In a database, though, you can have more than one index for each document, enabling you to search efficiently on different queries.
>
> Indexes do take maintenance and database resources, though, just as it takes time to correctly file your paperwork. So for best overall performance, try to limit your database indexes to the paths that really need indexing and are used for most queries.

The data for a single geographical location is stored according to the GeoJSON format specification, which we'll see in action shortly. Mongoose supports this data type allowing you to define a geospatial path inside a schema. As Mongoose is an abstraction layer on top of MongoDB it strives to make things easier for you. All you have to do to add a GeoJSON path in your schema is

1 Define the path as an array of the Number type.
2 Define the path as having a 2dsphere index.

To put this into action you can add a `coords` path to your location schema. If you follow the two preceding steps, your schema should be looking like the following code snippet:

```
var locationSchema = new mongoose.Schema({
  name: {type: String, required: true},
  address: String,
  rating: {type: Number, "default": 0, min: 0, max: 5},
  facilities: [String],
  coords: {type: [Number], index: '2dsphere'}
});
```

The `2dsphere` here is the critical part, as that's what enables MongoDB to do the correct calculations when running queries and returning results. It allows MongoDB to calculate geometries based on a spherical object. We'll work more with this in chapter 6 when we build our API and start to interact with the data.

> **TIP**   To meet the GeoJSON specification, a coordinate pair must be entered into the array in the correct order: longitude then latitude.

We've now got the basics covered and our schema for Loc8r currently holds everything needed to satisfy the homepage requirements. Next it's time to take a look at the Details page. This page has more complex data requirements, and we'll see how to handle them with Mongoose schemas.

5.3.3   *Creating more complex schemas with subdocuments*

The data we've used so far has been pretty simple, and can be held in a fairly flat schema. We've used a couple of arrays for the facilities and location coordinates, but again those arrays are simple, containing just a single data type each. Now we're going to look at what happens when we have a slightly more complicated data set to work with.

Let's start by reacquainting ourselves with the Details page, and the data that it shows. Figure 5.9 shows a screenshot of the page and shows all the different areas of information.

The name, rating, and address are right at the top, and a little further down are the facilities. On the right side there's a map, based on the geographic coordinates. All of this we've covered already with the basic schema. The two areas that we don't have anything for are *opening hours* and *customer reviews.*

The data powering this view is currently held in the `locationInfo` controller in app_server/controllers/locations.js. The following listing shows the relevant portion of the data in this controller.

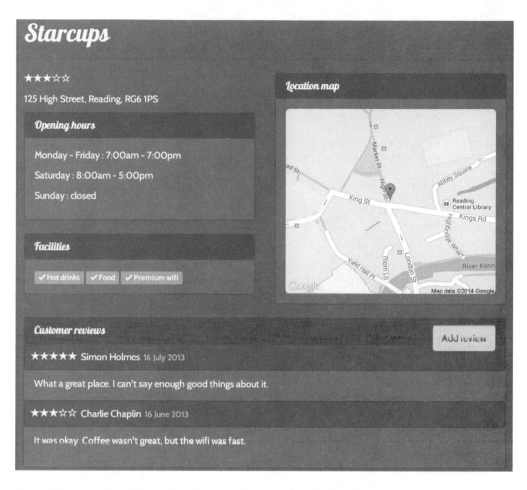

Figure 5.9   The information displayed for a single location on the Details page

Listing 5.2   Data in the controller powering the Details page

```
location: {
  name: 'Starcups',
  address: '125 High Street, Reading, RG6 1PS',
  rating: 3,
  facilities: ['Hot drinks', 'Food', 'Premium wifi'],
  coords: {lat: 51.455041, lng: -0.9690884},
  openingTimes: [{
    days: 'Monday - Friday',
    opening: '7:00am',
    closing: '7:00pm',
    closed: false
  },{
    days: 'Saturday',
    opening: '8:00am',
```

Already covered with existing schema

Data for opening hours is held as an array of objects

```
          closing: '5:00pm',
          closed: false
        },{
          days: 'Sunday',
          closed: true
        }],
        reviews: [{
          author: 'Simon Holmes',
          rating: 5,
          timestamp: '16 July 2013',
          reviewText: 'What a great place. I can\'t say enough good things about it.'
        },{
          author: 'Charlie Chaplin',
          rating: 3,
          timestamp: '16 June 2013',
          reviewText: 'It was okay. Coffee wasn\'t great, but the wifi was fast.'
        }]
      }
```

Data for opening hours is held as an array of objects

Reviews are also passed to the view as array of objects

So here we have arrays of objects for the opening hours and for the reviews. In a relational database you'd create these as separate tables, and `join` them together in a query when you need the information. But that's not how document databases work, including MongoDB. In a document database anything that belongs specifically to a parent document should be contained *within* that document. Figure 5.10 illustrates the conceptual difference between the two approaches.

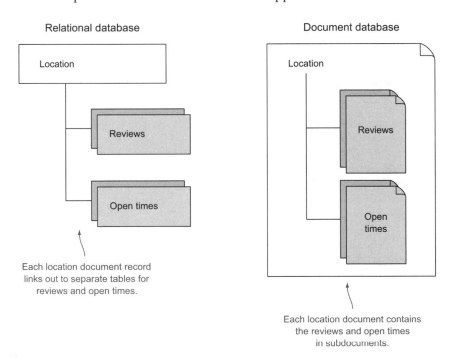

Figure 5.10 Differences between how a relational database and document database store repeating information relating to a parent element

MongoDB offers the concept of *subdocuments* to store this repeating, nested data. Subdocuments are very much like documents in that they have their own schema and each is given a unique _id by MongoDB when created. But subdocuments are nested inside a document and they can only be accessed as a path of that parent document.

USING NESTED SCHEMAS IN MONGOOSE TO DEFINE SUBDOCUMENTS

Subdocuments are defined in Mongoose by using nested schemas. So that's one schema nested inside another. Let's create one to see how that works in code. The first step is to define a new schema for a subdocument. We'll start with the opening times and create the following schema. Note that this needs to be in the same file as the locationSchema definition, and, importantly, must be *before* the locationSchema definition.

```
var openingTimeSchema = new mongoose.Schema({
  days: {type: String, required: true},
  opening: String,
  closing: String,
  closed: {type: Boolean, required: true}
});
```

Options for storing time information

In the opening time schema we have an interesting situation where we want to save time information, such as 7:30 a.m., but without a date associated with it.

Here we're using a String method, as it doesn't require any processing before being put into the database or after being retrieved. It also makes each record easy to understand. The downside is that it would make it harder to do any computational processing with it.

One option is to create a date object with an arbitrary data value assigned to it, and manually set the hours and minutes, such as

```
var d = new Date();
d.setHours(15);
d.setMinutes(30);
```
⟵ **d is now Wed Apr 09 2014 15:30:40 GMT+0100 (BST)**

Using this method we could easily extract the time from the data. The downside is storing unnecessary data, and it's technically incorrect.

A second option is to store the number of minutes since midnight. So 7:30 a.m. is $(7 \times 60) + 30 = 450$. This is a fairly simple computation to make when putting data into the database and pulling it back out again. But the data at a glance is meaningless.

But this second option would be my preference for making the dates smarter and could be a good extension if you want to try out something new. For the sake of readability and avoiding distractions we'll keep using the String method through the book.

This schema definition is again pretty simple, and maps over from the data in the controller. We have two required fields, the `closed` Boolean flag and the `days` each subdocument is referring to.

Nesting this schema inside the location schema is another straightforward task. We need to add a new path to the parent schema, and define it as an array of our subdocument schema. The following code snippet shows how to nest the `openingTimeSchema` inside the `locationSchema`:

```
var locationSchema = new mongoose.Schema({
  name: {type: String, required: true},
  address: String,
  rating: {type: Number, "default": 0, min: 0, max: 5},
  facilities: [String],
  coords: {type: [Number], index: '2dsphere'},
  openingTimes: [openingTimeSchema]          ◁──  Add nested schema
});                                                by referencing
                                                   another schema
                                                   object as an array
```

With this in place we could now add multiple opening time subdocuments to a given location, and they would be stored within that location document. An example document from MongoDB based on this schema is shown in the following code snippet, with the subdocuments for the opening times in bold:

```
{
  "_id": ObjectId("52ef3a9f79c44a86710fe7f5"),
  "name": "Starcups",
  "address": "125 High Street, Reading, RG6 1PS",
  "rating": 3,
  "facilities": ["Hot drinks", "Food", "Premium wifi"],
  "coords": [-0.9690884, 51.455041],
  "openingTimes": [{
    "_id": ObjectId("52ef3a9f79c44a86710fe7f6"),
    "days": "Monday - Friday",
    "opening": "7:00am",
    "closing": "7:00pm",
    "closed": false
  }, {                                        In a MongoDB
    "_id": ObjectId("52ef3a9f79c44a86710fe7f7"),    document nested
    "days": "Saturday",                       opening times
    "opening": "8:00am",                      subdocuments live
    "closing": "5:00pm",                      inside location
    "closed": false                           document
  }, {
    "_id": ObjectId("52ef3a9f79c44a86710fe7f8"),
    "days": "Sunday",
    "closed": true
  }]
}
```

With the schema for the opening times taken care of, we'll move on and look at adding a schema for the review subdocuments.

ADDING A SECOND SET OF SUBDOCUMENTS

Neither MongoDB nor Mongoose limit the number of subdocument paths in a document. This means we're free to take what we've done for the opening times and replicate the process for the reviews.

Step one: take a look at the data used in a review, shown in the following code snippet:

```
{
  author: 'Simon Holmes',
  rating: 5,
  timestamp: '16 July 2013',
  reviewText: 'What a great place. I can\'t say enough good things about it.'
}
```

Step two: map this into a new reviewSchema in app_server/models/location.js:

```
var reviewSchema = new mongoose.Schema({
  author: String,
  rating: {type: Number, required: true, min: 0, max: 5},
  reviewText: String,
  createdOn: {type: Date, "default": Date.now}
});
```

Step three: add this reviewSchema as a new path to locationSchema:

```
var locationSchema = new mongoose.Schema({
  name: {type: String, required: true},
  address: String,
  rating: {type: Number, "default": 0, min: 0, max: 5},
  facilities: [String],
  coords: {type: [Number], index: '2dsphere'},
  openingTimes: [openingTimeSchema],
  reviews: [reviewSchema]
});
```

Once we've defined the schema for reviews and added it to our main location schema we have everything we need to hold the data for all locations in a structured way.

5.3.4 *Final schema*

Throughout this section we've done quite a bit in the file, so let's take a look at it all together and see what's what. The following listing shows the contents of the locations.js file in app_server/models, defining the schema for the location data.

> **Listing 5.3 Final location schema definition, including nested schemas**

Require Mongoose so that we can use its methods

```
var mongoose = require( 'mongoose' );

var reviewSchema = new mongoose.Schema({
  author: String
  rating: {type: Number, required: true, min: 0, max: 5},
  reviewText: String,
  createdOn: {type: Date, default: Date.now}
});
```

Define a schema for reviews

```
var openingTimeSchema = new mongoose.Schema({
  days: {type: String, required: true},
  opening: String,
  closing: String,
  closed: {type: Boolean, required: true}
});
```
Define a schema for opening times

```
var locationSchema = new mongoose.Schema({
  name: {type: String, required: true},
  address: String,
  rating: {type: Number, "default": 0, min: 0, max: 5},
  facilities: [String],
  coords: {type: [Number], index: '2dsphere'},
  openingTimes: [openingTimeSchema],
  reviews: [reviewSchema]
});
```
Start main location schema definition

Use 2dsphere to add support for GeoJSON longitude and latitude coordinate pairs

Reference opening times and reviews schemas to add nested subdocuments

Documents and subdocuments all have a schema defining their structure, and we've also added in some default values and basic validation. To make this a bit more real, the following listing shows an example MongoDB document based on this schema.

Listing 5.4   Example MongoDB document based on the location schema

```
{
  "_id": ObjectId("52ef3a9f79c44a86710fe7f5"),
  "name": "Starcups",
  "address": "125 High Street, Reading, RG6 1PS",
  "rating": 3,
  "facilities": ["Hot drinks", "Food", "Premium wifi"],
  "coords": [-0.9690884, 51.455041],
  "openingTimes": [{
    "_id": ObjectId("52ef3a9f79c44a86710fe7f6"),
    "days": "Monday - Friday",
    "opening": "7:00am",
    "closing": "7:00pm",
    "closed": false
  }, {
    "_id": ObjectId("52ef3a9f79c44a86710fe7f7"),
    "days": "Saturday",
    "opening": "8:00am",
    "closing": "5:00pm",
    "closed": false
  }, {
    "_id": ObjectId("52ef3a9f79c44a86710fe7f8"),
    "days": "Sunday",
    "closed": true
  }],
```
Coordinates are stored as a GeoJSON pair [longitude, latitude]

Opening times are stored as nested array of objects— these are subdocuments

```
  "reviews": [{
    "_id": ObjectId("52ef3a9f79c44a86710fe7f9"),
    "author": "Simon Holmes",
    "rating": 5,
    "createdOn": ISODate("2013-07-15T23:00:00Z"),
    "reviewText": "What a great place. I can't say enough good
     things about it."
  }, {
    "_id": ObjectId("52ef3a9f79c44a86710fe7fa"),
    "author": "Charlie Chaplin",
    "rating": 3,
    "createdOn": ISODate("2013-06-15T23:00:00Z"),
    "reviewText": "It was okay. Coffee wasn't great, but the wifi was fast."
  }]
}
```

Reviews are also array of subdocuments

That should give you an idea of what a MongoDB document looks like, including subdocuments, when based on a known schema. In a readable form like this it's a JSON object, although technically MongoDB stores it as BSON, which is Binary JSON.

5.3.5 *Compiling Mongoose schemas into models*

An application doesn't interact with the schema directly when working with data, data interaction is done through models.

In Mongoose, a model is a compiled version of the schema. Once compiled, a single instance of the model maps directly to a single document in your database. It's through this direct one-to-one relationship that the model can create, read, save, and delete data. Figure 5.11 illustrates this arrangement.

This approach makes Mongoose a breeze to work with and we'll really get our teeth into it in chapter 6 when we build the internal API for the application.

COMPILING A MODEL FROM A SCHEMA

Anything with the word "compiling" in it tends to sound a bit complicated. In reality, compiling a Mongoose model from a schema is a really simple one-line task. You just need to ensure that the schema is complete before you invoke the model command. The model command follows this construct:

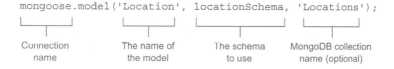

```
mongoose.model('Location', locationSchema, 'Locations');
```

| Connection name | The name of the model | The schema to use | MongoDB collection name (optional) |

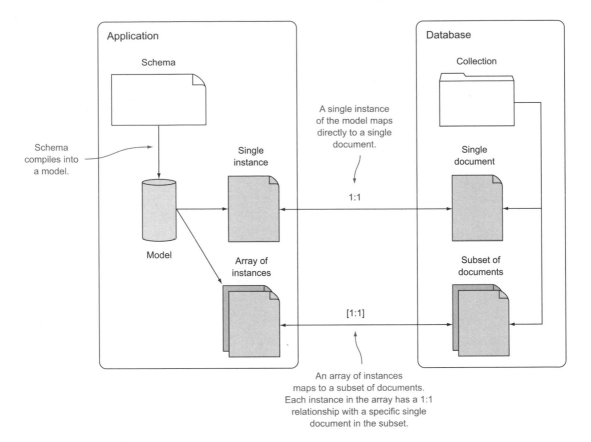

Figure 5.11   The application and database talk to each other through models. A single instance of a model has a one-to-one relationship with a single document in the database. It's through this relationship that the creating, reading, updating, and deleting of data is managed.

TIP   The MongoDB collection name is optional. If you exclude it Mongoose will use a lowercase pluralized version of the model name. For example, a model name of `Location` would look for a collection name of `locations` unless you specify something different.

As we're creating a database and not hooking into an existing data source we can use a default collection name, so we don't need to include that parameter into the `model` command. So to build a model of our location schema we can add the following line to the code, just below the `locationSchema` definition:

```
mongoose.model('Location', locationSchema);
```

That's all there is to it. We've defined a data schema for the locations, and complied the schema into a model that we can use in the application. What we need now is some data.

5.4   Using the MongoDB shell to create a MongoDB database and add data

For building the Loc8r app we're going to create a new database and manually add some test data. This means that you get to create your own personal version of Loc8r for testing, and at the same time get to play directly with MongoDB.

5.4.1   MongoDB shell basics

The MongoDB shell is a command-line utility that gets installed with MongoDB, and allows you to interact with any MongoDB databases on your system. It's quite powerful and can do a lot—we're just going to dip our toes in with the basics to get up and running.

STARTING THE MONGODB SHELL
Drop into the shell by running the following line in terminal:

```
$ mongo
```

This should respond in terminal with a couple of lines like these next two, confirming the shell version and that it's connecting to a test database:

```
MongoDB shell version: 2.4.6
connecting to: test
```

> **TIP**   When you're in the shell new lines start with a > to differentiate from the standard command-line entry point. The shell commands printed in this section will start with > instead of $ to make it clear that we're using the shell, but like the $ you don't need to type it in.

LISTING ALL LOCAL DATABASES
Next is a simple command that will show you a list of all of the local MongoDB databases. Enter the following line into the shell:

```
> show dbs
```

This will return a list of the local MongoDB database names and their sizes. If you haven't created any databases at this point you'll still see the two default ones, something like this:

```
local    0.078125GB
test     (empty)
```

USING A SPECIFIC DATABASE
When starting the MongoDB shell it automatically connects to the empty test database. If you want to switch to a different database, such as the default one called local, you can use the use command, like this:

```
> use local
```

The shell will respond with a message, along these lines:

```
switched to db local
```

This message confirms the name of the database the shell has connected to.

LISTING THE COLLECTIONS IN A DATABASE

Once you're using a particular database, it's really easy to output a list of the collections using the following command:

```
> show collections
```

If you're using the local database you'll probably see a single collection name output to terminal: `startup_log`.

SEEING THE CONTENTS OF A COLLECTION

The MongoDB shell also lets you query the collections in a database. The construct for a query or find operation is as follows:

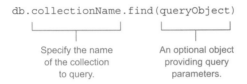

```
db.collectionName.find(queryObject)
```

Specify the name of the collection to query.

An optional object providing query parameters.

The `query` object is used to specify what you're trying to find in the collection, and we'll look at examples of this `query` object later in chapter 6 (Mongoose also uses the `query` object). The simplest query is an empty query, which will return all of the documents in a collection. Don't worry if your collection is large, as MongoDB will return a subset of documents that you can page through. Using the `startup_log` collection as an example, you can run the following command:

```
> db.startup_log.find()
```

This will return a number of documents from the MongoDB startup log, the content of which isn't interesting enough to show here. This command is useful for when you're getting your database up and running, and making sure that things are being saved as you expect.

5.4.2 *Creating a MongoDB database*

You don't actually have to *create* a MongoDB database; you just start to use it. For the Loc8r application it makes sense to have a database called Loc8r. So in the shell, you use it with the following command:

```
> use Loc8r
```

If you run the show collections command it won't return anything yet, but if you run show dbs you should see that it has been added to the list of databases, and is currently empty:

```
Loc8r    (empty)
local    0.078125GB
test     (empty)
```

This message shows it has been added to the list of databases.

CREATING A COLLECTION AND DOCUMENTS

Similarly, you don't have to explicitly create a collection as MongoDB will create it for you when you first save data into it.

> **Location data more personal to you**
>
> Loc8r is all about location-based data, and the examples are all fictitious places, geographically close to where I live in the United Kingdom. You can make your version more personal to you by changing the names, addresses, and coordinates.
>
> To get your current coordinates you can visit http://whatsmylatlng.com. There's a button on the page to find your location using JavaScript, which will give you a much more accurate location than the first attempt. Note that the coordinates are shown to you in latitude–longitude order, and you need to flip them round for the database, so that longitude is first.
>
> To get the coordinates of any address you can use http://mygeoposition.com. This will let you enter an address or drag and drop a pointer to give you the geographic coordinates. Again, remember that the pairs in MongoDB must be longitude then latitude.

To match the Location model you'll want a locations collection, remember that the default collection name is a lowercase pluralized version of the model name. You can create and save a new document by passing a data object into the save command of a collection, like in the following code snippet:

```
> db.locations.save({                          ◁── Note collection name
    name: 'Starcups',                              specified as part of
    address: '125 High Street, Reading, RG6 1PS',  save command
    rating: 3,
    facilities: ['Hot drinks', 'Food', 'Premium wifi'],
    coords: [-0.9690884, 51.455041],
    openingTimes: [{
      days: 'Monday - Friday',
      opening: '7:00am',
      closing: '7:00pm',
      closed: false
    }, {
      days: 'Saturday',
      opening: '8:00am',
```

```
    closing: '5:00pm',
    closed: false
  }, {
    days: 'Sunday',
    closed: true
  }]
})
```

In one step this will have created a new `locations` collection, and also the first document within the collection. If you run `show collections` in the MongoDB shell now you should see the new `locations` collection being returned, alongside an automatically generated `system.indexes` collection. For example

```
> show collections
locations
system.indexes
```

You can now query the collection to find all of the documents—there's only one in there right now, so the returned information will be quite small. You can use the `find` command on the collection as well:

```
> db.locations.find()
{
  "_id": ObjectId("530efe98d382e7fa4345f173"),
  "address": "125 High Street, Reading, RG6 1PS",
  "coords": [-0.9690884, 51.455041],
  "facilities": ["Hot drinks", "Food", "Premium wifi"],
  "name": "Starcups",
  "openingTimes": [{
    "days": "Monday - Friday",
    "opening": "7:00am",
    "closing": "7:00pm",
    "closed": false
  }, {
    "days": "Saturday",
    "opening": "8:00am",
    "closing": "5:00pm",
    "closed": false
  }, {
    "days": "Sunday",
    "closed": true
  }],
  "rating": 3,
}
```

Remember to run the find operation on collection itself

MongoDB has automatically added a unique identifier for this document

This code snippet has been formatted for readability; the document that MongoDB returns to the shell won't have the line breaks and indentation. But the MongoDB shell can prettify it for you if you add `.pretty()` to the end of the command like this:

```
> db.locations.find().pretty()
```

Notice that the order of the data in the returned document doesn't match the order of the data in the object you supplied. As the data structure isn't column-based it doesn't matter how MongoDB stores the individual paths within a document. The data is always still there in the correct paths, and data held inside arrays always maintains the same order.

ADDING SUBDOCUMENTS

You've probably noticed that our first document doesn't have the full data set—there are no review subdocuments. You can actually add these to the initial `save` command like we've done with the opening times, or you can update an existing document and push them in.

MongoDB has an `update` command that accepts two arguments, the first being a query so that it knows which document to update, and the second contains the instructions on what to do when it has found the document. At this point we can do a really simple query and look for the location by name (Starcups), as we know that there aren't any duplicates. For the instruction object we can use a `$push` command to add a new object to the reviews path; it doesn't matter if the reviews path doesn't exist yet, MongoDB will add it as part of the push operation.

Putting it all together shows something like the following code snippet:

```
> db.locations.update({          Start with query object to
    name: 'Starcups'             find correct document
}, {
    $push: {                     When document is found, push a
      reviews: {                 subdocument into the reviews path
        author: 'Simon Holmes',
        id: ObjectId(),
        rating: 5,                                    Subdocument
        timestamp: new Date("Jul 16, 2013"),         contains this
        reviewText: "What a great place. I can't say enough good    data
        things about it."
      }
    }
})
```

If you run that command in the MongoDB shell while using the `Loc8r` database, it will add a review to the document. You can repeat it as often as you like, changing the data to add multiple reviews.

Note the `new Date` command for setting the timestamp of the review. Using this ensures that MongoDB stores the date as an ISO date object, not a string—this is what our schema expects and allows greater manipulation of dates data.

REPEAT THE PROCESS

These few commands have given us one location to test the application with, but ideally we need a couple more. So go ahead and add some more locations to your database.

When you're done with that and your data is set, you're just about at the point where you can start using it from the application—in this case we'll be building an API. But before we jump into that in chapter 6, there's just one more piece of house-keeping. We want to keep pushing regular updates into Heroku, and now that we've added a database connection and data models to our application we need to make sure that these are supported in Heroku.

5.5   *Getting our database live*

If you've got your application out in the wild it's no good having your database on your local host. Your database also needs to be externally accessible. In this section we're going to push our database into a live environment, and update our Loc8r application so that it uses the published database from the published site, and the local host database from the development site. We'll start by using the free tier of a service called MongoLab, which can be used as an add-on to Heroku. If you have a different preferred provider or your own database server, that's no problem. The first part of this section runs through setting up on MongoLab, but the following parts—migrating the data and setting the connection strings in the Node application—aren't platform-specific.

5.5.1   *Setting up MongoLab and getting the database URI*

The first goal is to get an externally accessible database URI so that we can push data to it and add it to the application. We're going to use MongoLab here as it has a good free tier, excellent online documentation, and a very responsive support team.

There are a couple of ways to set up a database on MongoLab. The quickest and easiest way is to use an add-on via Heroku. This is what we'll run through here, but this does require you to register a valid credit card with Heroku. Heroku makes you do this when using add-ons through their ecosystem to protect themselves from abusive behavior. Using the free sandbox tier of MongoLab will not incur any charges. If you're not comfortable doing this, check out the following sidebar for setting up MongoLab manually.

Setting up MongoLab manually

You don't have to use the Heroku add-on system if you don't want to. What you really want to do is to set up a MongoDB database in the cloud and get a connection string for it.

You can follow through the MongoLab documentation to guide you through this: http://docs.mongolab.com/.

In short, the steps are

1 Sign up for a free account.
2 Create a new database (select Single Node, Sandbox for the free tier).
3 Add a user.
4 Get the database URI (connection string).

The connection string will look something like this:

```
mongodb://dbuser:dbpassword@ds059957.mongolab.com:59957/loc8r-dev
```

All of the parts will be different for you, of course, and you'll have to swap out the username and password with what you specified in step 3.

> Once you have your full connection string you should save it as part of your Heroku configuration. With a terminal prompt in the root folder of your application you can do this with the following command:
>
> ```
> $ heroku config:set MONGOLAB_URI=your_db_uri
> ```
>
> Replace `your_db_uri` with your full connection string, including the `mongodb://` protocol. The quick and easy way automatically creates the `MONGOLAB_URI` setting in your Heroku configuration. These manual steps bring you to the same point as the quick way, and you can now jump back to the main text.

ADDING MONGOLAB TO THE HEROKU APPLICATION

The quickest way to add MongoLab as a Heroku add-on is through terminal. Make sure you're in the root folder of your application and run the following command:

```
$ heroku addons:add mongolab
```

Unbelievably, that's it! You now have a MongoDB database ready and waiting for you out in the cloud. You can prove this to yourself and open up a web interface to this new database using the following command:

```
$ heroku addons:open mongolab
```

To use the database, you'll need to know its URI.

GETTING THE DATABASE URI

You can get the full database URI also using the command line. This will give you the full connection string that you can use in the application, and also show you the various components that you'll need to push data up to the database.

The command to get the database URI is

```
$ heroku config:get MONGOLAB_URI
```

This will output the full connection string, which looks something like this:

```
mongodb://heroku_app20110907:4rqhlidfdqq6vgdi06c15jrlpf@ds033669
.mongolab.com:33669/heroku_app20110907
```

Keep your version handy, as you'll use it in the application soon. First we need to break it down into the components.

BREAKING DOWN THE URI INTO ITS COMPONENTS

This looks like quite a random mess of characters, but we can break it down to make sense of it. From section 5.2.2 we know that this is how a database URI is constructed:

So taking the URI that MongoLab has given you, you can break it down into something like the following:

- Username: `heroku_app20110907`
- Password: `4rqhlidfdqq6vgdi06c15jrlpf`
- Server address: `ds033669.mongolab.com`
- Port: `33669`
- Database name: `heroku_app20110907`

These are from the example URI, so yours will be different, of course, but make a note of them and they'll be useful.

5.5.2   Pushing up the data

Now that you have an externally accessible database set up, and know all of the details for connecting to it, you can push up data to it. The steps to do this are as follows:

1   Create a temporary directory to hold the data dump.
2   Dump the data from your development Loc8r database.
3   Restore the data to your live database.
4   Test the live database.

All of these steps can be achieved quickly through terminal, so that's what we'll do. It saves jumping around between environments.

CREATING A TEMPORARY FOLDER

A really simple first step, which you can do in your operating system interface if you prefer, is to create a temporary folder into which you can dump your data. The following command does it on Mac or Linux:

```
$ mkdir -p ~/tmp/mongodump
```

Now you have a place for the data dump.

DUMPING THE DATA FROM THE DEVELOPMENT DATABASE

Dumping the data sounds like you're deleting everything from your local development version, but this isn't the case. The process is more of an export than a trashing.

The command used is `mongodump`, which accepts the following three parameters:

- `-h`—The host server (and port)
- `-d`—The database name
- `-o`—The output destination folder

Putting it all together, and using the default MongoDB port of `27017`, you should end up with a command like the following:

```
$ mongodump -h localhost:27017 -d Loc8r -o ~/tmp/mongodump
```

Run that and you have a temporary dump of the data.

RESTORING THE DATA TO YOUR LIVE DATABASE

The process of pushing up the data to your live database is similar, this time using the mongorestore command. This command expects the following parameters:

- -h—Live host and port
- -d—Live database name
- -u—Username for the live database
- -p—Password for the live database
- Path to the dump directory and database name (this comes at the end of the command and doesn't have a corresponding flag like the other parameters)

Putting all of this together, using the information you have about the database URI, you should have a command like the following:

```
$ mongorestore -h ds033669.mongolab.com:33669 -d heroku_app20110907 -u
heroku_app20110907 -p 4rqhlidfdqq6vgdi06c15jrlpf ~/tmp/mongodump/Loc8r
```

Yours will look a bit different, of course, because you'll have a different host, live database name, username, and password. When you run your mongorestore command it will push up the data from the data dump into your live database.

TESTING THE LIVE DATABASE

The MongoDB shell isn't restricted to only accessing databases on your local machine. You can also use the shell to connect to external databases, if you have the right credentials, of course.

To connect the MongoDB shell to an external database you use the same mongo command, but add information about the database you want to connect to. You need to include the hostname, port, and database names, and you can supply a username and password if required. This is put together in the following construct:

```
$ mongo hostname:port/database_name -u username -p password
```

For example, using the setup we've been looking at in this section would give you this command:

```
$ mongo ds033669.mongolab.com:33669/heroku_app20110907 -u heroku_app20110907
-p 4rqhlidfdqq6vgdi06c15jrlpf
```

This will connect you to the database through the MongoDB shell. When the connection is established you can use the commands you've already been using to interrogate it, such as

```
> show collections
> db.locations.find()
```

Now you've got two databases and two connection strings; it's important to use the right one at the right time.

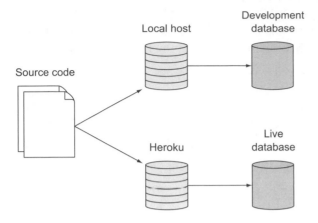

Figure 5.12 The source code runs in two locations, each of which needs to connect to a different database.

5.5.3 *Making the application use the right database*

So you have your original development database on your local machine plus your new live database up on MongoLab (or elsewhere). We want to keep using the development database while we're developing our application, and we want the live version of our application to use the live database. Yet they both use the same source code. Figure 5.12 shows the issue.

So we have one set of source code running in two environments, each of which should use a different database. The way to handle this is through using a Node environment variable, NODE_ENV.

THE NODE_ENV ENVIRONMENT VARIABLE

Environment variables affect the way the core process runs, and the one we're going to look at and use here is NODE_ENV. The application already uses NODE_ENV; you just don't see it exposed anywhere. By default, Heroku should set NODE_ENV to production so that the application will run in production mode on their server.

> **Ensuring Heroku is using production mode**
>
> In certain instances, depending on how the application was set up, the Heroku application might not be running in production mode. You can ensure that the Heroku environment variable is set correctly with the following terminal command:
>
> ```
> $ heroku config:set NODE_ENV=production
> ```

You can read NODE_ENV from anywhere in the application by using the following statement:

```
process.env.NODE_ENV
```

Unless specified in your environment this will come back as `undefined`. You can specify different environment variables when starting the Node application by prepending the assignment to the launch command. For example

```
$ NODE_ENV=production nodemon
```

This command will start up the application in production mode, and the value of `process.env.NODE_ENV` will be set to `production`.

TIP Don't set `NODE_ENV` from inside the application, only read it.

SETTING THE DATABASE URI BASED ON THE ENVIRONMENT

The database connection for our application is held in the db.js file in app_server/models. The connection portion of this file currently looks like the following code snippet:

```
var dbURI = 'mongodb://localhost/Loc8r';
mongoose.connect(dbURI);
```

Changing the value of `dbURI` based on the current environment is as simple as using an `if` statement to check `NODE_ENV`. The next code snippet shows how you can do this to pass in your live MongoDB connection. Remember to use your own MongoDB connection string rather than the one in this example.

```
var dbURI = 'mongodb://localhost/Loc8r';
if (process.env.NODE_ENV === 'production') {
  dbURI = 'mongodb://
    heroku_app20110907:4rqhlidfdqq6vgdi06c15jrlpf@ds033669.mongolab.com:3366
    9/heroku_app20110907';
}
mongoose.connect(dbURI);
```

If the source code is going to be in a public repository then you probably don't want to be giving everybody the login credentials to your database. A way around this is to use an environment variable. With MongoLab on Heroku you automatically have one set up—it's how we originally got access to the connection string (if you set your MongoLab account up manually, this is the Heroku configuration variable that you set). If you're using a different provider that hasn't added anything to the Heroku configuration, you can add in your URI with the `heroku config:set` command that we used to ensure Heroku is running in production mode.

The following code snippet shows how you can use the connection string set in the environment variables:

```
var dbURI = 'mongodb://localhost/Loc8r';
if (process.env.NODE_ENV === 'production') {
  dbURI = process.env.MONGOLAB_URI;
}
mongoose.connect(dbURI);
```

This now means that you can share your code, but only you retain access to your database credentials.

TESTING BEFORE LAUNCHING

You can test this update to the code locally before pushing the code to Heroku by setting the environment variable as you start up the application from terminal. The Mongoose connection events we set up earlier output a log to the console when the database connection is made, verifying the URI used.

Starting the application normally from terminal looks like this:

```
$ nodemon
Express server listening on port 3000
Mongoose connected to mongodb://localhost/Loc8r
```

In comparison, starting the application in production mode looks like this:

```
$ NODE_ENV=production nodemon
Express server listening on port 3000
Mongoose connected to mongodb://
heroku_app20110907:4rqhlidfdqq6vgdi06c15jrlpf@ds033669.mongolab.com:33669/
heroku_app20110907
```

When running these commands you'll probably notice that the Mongoose connection confirmation takes longer to appear in the production environment. This is due to the latency of using a separate database server and is why it's a good idea to open the database connection at application startup and leave it open.

Note that the preceding production test may fail on some versions of Windows and the occasional flavor of Linux. This happens when your system is unable to pull down the Heroku configuration variables. You can still test against the production database by prepending the MONGOLAB_URI to the application start command, which looks like the following code snippet (note that this should all be entered as one line):

```
$ NODE_ENV=production MONGOLAB_URI=mongodb://
<username>:<password>@<hostname>:<port>/<database> nodemon start
```

Whatever OS you're running you should now be able to run the application locally and connect to the production database.

TESTING ON HEROKU

If your local tests are successful, and you can connect to your remote database by temporarily starting the application in production mode, then you're ready to push it up to Heroku. Use the same commands as normal to push the latest version of the code up:

```
$ git add .
$ git commit -m "Commit message here"
$ git push heroku master
```

Heroku lets you easily look at the latest 100 lines of logs by running a terminal command. You can check in those logs to see the output of your console log messages, one of which will be your "Mongoose connected to ..." logs. To view the logs run the following command in terminal:

```
$ heroku logs
```

This will output the latest 100 rows to the terminal window, with the very latest messages at the bottom. Scroll up until you find the "Mongoose connected to ..." message that looks something like this:

```
2014-03-08T08:19:42.269603+00:00 app[web.1]: Mongoose connected to mongodb://
heroku_app20110907:4rqhlidfdqq6vgdi06c15jrlpf@ds033669.mongolab.com:33669/
heroku_app20110907
```

When you see this, you know that the live application on Heroku is connecting to your live database.

So that's the data defined and modeled, and our Loc8r application is now connected to the database. But we're not interacting with the database at all yet—that comes next!

> **Get the source code**
>
> The source code of the application so far is available from GitHub on the chapter-05 branch of the getting-MEAN repository. In a fresh folder in terminal the following commands will clone it and install the npm module dependencies:
>
> ```
> $ git clone -b chapter-05 https://github.com/simonholmes/getting-MEAN.git
> $ cd getting-MEAN
> $ npm install
> ```

5.6   *Summary*

In this chapter we've covered

- Using Mongoose to connect an Express application to MongoDB
- Best practices for managing Mongoose connections
- How to model data using Mongoose schemas
- Compiling schemas into models
- Using the MongoDB shell to work directly with the database
- Pushing your database to a live URI
- Connecting to different databases from different environments

Coming up next in chapter 6 we're going to use Express to create a REST API, so that we can then access the database through web services.

Writing a REST API: Exposing the MongoDB database to the application

6

This chapter covers

- Rules of REST APIs
- API patterns
- Typical CRUD functions (create, read, update, delete)
- Using Express and Mongoose to interact with MongoDB
- Testing API endpoints

As we come in to this chapter we have a MongoDB database set up, but we can only interact with it through the MongoDB shell. During this chapter we'll build a REST API so that we can interact with our database through HTTP calls and perform the common CRUD functions: create, read, update, and delete.

We'll mainly be working with Node and Express, using Mongoose to help with the interactions. Figure 6.1 shows where this chapter fits into the overall architecture.

We'll start off by looking at the rules of a REST API. We'll discuss the importance of defining the URL structure properly, the different request methods (GET, POST, PUT, and DELETE) that should be used for different actions, and how an API should respond with data and an appropriate HTTP status code. Once we have

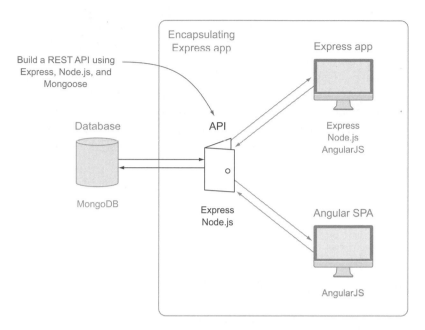

Figure 6.1 This chapter will focus on building the API that will interact with the database, exposing an interface for the applications to talk to.

that knowledge under our belts we'll move on to building our API for Loc8r, covering all of the typical CRUD operations. As we go, we'll discuss a lot about Mongoose, and get into some Node programming and more Express routing.

> **NOTE** If you haven't yet built the application from chapter 5, you can get the code from GitHub on the chapter-05 branch at github.com/simonholmes/ getting-MEAN. In a fresh folder in terminal the following commands will clone it and install the npm module dependencies:

```
$ git clone -b chapter-05 https://github.com/simonholmes/getting-MEAN.git
$ cd getting-MEAN
$ npm install
```

6.1 The rules of a REST API

Let's start with a recap of what a REST API is. From chapter 2 you may remember:

- REST stands for REpresentational State Transfer, which is an architectural style rather than a strict protocol. REST is stateless—it has no idea of any current user state or history.
- API is an abbreviation for application program interface, which enables applications to talk to each other.

So a REST API is a stateless interface to your application. In the case of the MEAN stack the REST API is used to create a stateless interface to your database, enabling a way for other applications to work with the data.

REST APIs have an associated set of standards. While you don't have to stick to these for your own API it's generally best to, as it means that any API you create will follow the same approach. It also means you're used to doing things in the "right" way if you decide you're going to make your API public.

In basic terms a REST API takes an incoming HTTP request, does some processing, and always sends back an HTTP response, as shown in figure 6.2.

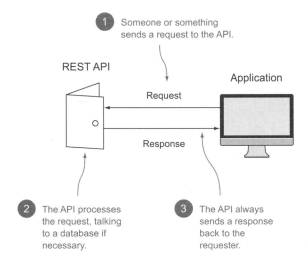

Figure 6.2   **A REST API takes incoming HTTP requests, does some processing, and returns HTTP responses.**

The standards that we're going to follow for Loc8r revolve around the requests and the responses.

6.1.1   *Request URLs*

Request URLs for a REST API have a simple standard. Following this standard will make your API easy to pick up, use, and maintain.

The way to approach this is to start thinking about the collections in your database, as you'll typically have a set of API URLs for each collection. You may also have a set of URLs for each set of subdocuments. Each URL in a set will have the same basic path, and some may have additional parameters.

Within a set of URLs you need to cover a number of actions, generally based around the standard CRUD operations. The common actions you'll likely want are

- Create a new item
- Read a list of several items
- Read a specific item

- Update a specific item
- Delete a specific item

Using Loc8r as an example, the database has a Locations collection that we want to interact with. Table 6.1 shows how the URLs and parameters might look for this collection.

Table 6.1 URL paths and parameters for an API to the Locations collection; all have the same base path, and several have the same location ID parameter

Action	URL path	Parameters	Example
Create new location	`/locations`		http://loc8r.com/api/locations
Read list of locations	`/locations`		http://loc8r.com/api/locations
Read a specific location	`/locations`	`locationid`	http://loc8r.com/api/locations/123
Update a specific location	`/locations`	`locationid`	http://loc8r.com/api/locations/123
Delete a specific location	`/locations`	`locationid`	http://loc8r.com/api/locations/123

As you can see from table 6.1, each action has the same URL path, and three of them expect the same parameter to specify a location. This poses a very obvious question: How do you use the same URL to initiate different actions? The answer lies in request methods.

6.1.2 Request methods

HTTP requests can have different methods that essentially tell the server what type of action to take. The most common type of request is a GET request—this is the method used when you enter a URL into the address bar of your browser. Another common method is POST, often used when submitting form data.

Table 6.2 shows the methods we'll be using in our API, their typical use cases, and what you'd expect returned.

Table 6.2 Four request methods used in a REST API

Request method	Use	Response
POST	Create new data in the database	New data object as seen in the database
GET	Read data from the database	Data object answering the request
PUT	Update a document in the database	Updated data object as seen in the database
DELETE	Delete an object from the database	Null

The four HTTP methods that we'll be using are POST, GET, PUT, and DELETE. If you look at the first word in the "Use" column you'll notice that there's a different method for each of the four CRUD operations.

TIP   Each of the four CRUD operations uses a different request method.

The method is important, because a well-designed REST API will often have the same URL for different actions. In these cases it's the method that tells the server which type of operation to perform. We'll discuss how to build and organize the routes for this in Express later in this chapter.

So if we take the paths and parameters and map across the appropriate request method we can put together a plan for our API, as shown in table 6.3.

Table 6.3   Request method is used to link the URL to the desired action, enabling the API to use the same URL for different actions

Action	Method	URL path	Parameters	Example
Create new location	POST	`/locations`		http://loc8r.com/api/locations
Read list of locations	GET	`/locations`		http://loc8r.com/api/locations
Read a specific location	GET	`/locations`	`locationid`	http://loc8r.com/api/locations/123
Update a specific location	PUT	`/locations`	`locationid`	http://loc8r.com/api/locations/123
Delete a specific location	DELETE	`/locations`	`locationid`	http://loc8r.com/api/locations/123

Table 6.3 shows the paths and methods we'll use for the requests to interact with the location data. As there are five actions but only two different URL patterns, we can use the request methods to get the desired results.

Loc8r only has one collection right now, so this is our starting point. But the documents in the Locations collection do have reviews as subdocuments, so let's quickly map those out too.

API URLs FOR SUBDOCUMENTS
Subdocuments are treated in a similar way, but require an additional parameter. Each request will need to specify the ID of the location, and some will also need to specify the ID of a review. Table 6.4 shows the list of actions and their associated methods, URL paths, and parameters.

Table 6.4   API URL specifications for interacting with subdocuments; each base URL path must contain the ID of the parent document

Action	Method	URL path	Parameters	Example

Create new review	POST	`/locations/`
		`locationid/`
		`reviews`
			`locationid`	http://loc8r.com/api/locations/
				123/reviews

Table 6.4 API URL specifications for interacting with subdocuments; each base URL path must contain the ID of the parent document

Action	Method	URL path	Parameters	Example

Read a specific review	GET	`/locations/`
		`locationid/`
		`reviews`
			`locationid`
			`reviewid`
				http://loc8r.com/api/locations/
				123/reviews/abc

Update a specific review	PUT	`/locations/`
		`locationid/`
		`reviews`
			`locationid`
			`reviewid`
				http://loc8r.com/api/locations/
				123/reviews/abc

Delete a specific review	DELETE	`/locations/`
		`locationid/`
		`reviews`
			`locationid`
			`reviewid`
				http://loc8r.com/api/locations/
				123/reviews/abc

You may have noticed that for the subdocuments we don't have a "read a list of reviews" action. This is because we'll be retrieving the list of reviews as part of the main document. The preceding tables should give you an idea of how to create basic API request specifications. The URLs, parameters, and actions will be different from one application to the next, but the approach should remain consistent.

That's requests covered. The other half of the flow, before we get stuck in some code, is responses.

6.1.3 *Responses and status codes*

A good API is like a good friend. If you go for a high-five a good friend will not leave you hanging. The same goes for a good API. If you make a request, a good API will always respond and not leave you hanging. Every single API request should return a response. This contrast is shown in figure 6.3.

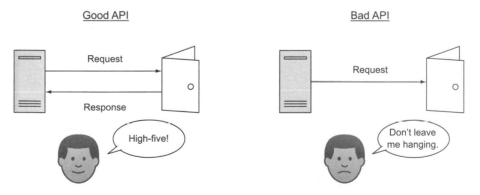

Figure 6.3 A good API always returns a response and shouldn't leave you hanging.

For a successful REST API, standardizing the responses is just as important as standardizing the request format. There are two key components to a response:

- The returned data
- The HTTP status code

Combining the returned data with the appropriate status code correctly should give the requester all of the information required to continue.

RETURNING DATA FROM AN API

Your API should return a consistent data format. Typical formats for a REST API are XML and JSON. We'll be using JSON for our API because it's the natural fit for the MEAN stack, and it's more compact than XML, so it can help speed up the response times of an API.

Our API will return one of three things for each request:

- A JSON object containing data answering the request query
- A JSON object containing error data
- A null response

During this chapter we'll discuss how to do all of these things as we build the Loc8r API. As well as responding with data, any REST API should return the correct HTTP status code.

USING HTTP STATUS CODES

A good REST API should return the correct HTTP status code. The status code most people are familiar with is 404, which is what is returned by a web server when a user requests a page that can't be found. This is probably the most prevalent error code on the internet, but there are dozens of other codes relating to client errors, server errors, redirections, and successful requests. Table 6.5 shows the 10 most popular HTTP status codes and where they might be useful when building an API.

Table 6.5   Most popular HTTP status codes and how they might be used when sending responses to an API request

Status code	Name	Use case
200	OK	A successful GET or PUT request
201	Created	A successful POST request
204	No content	A successful DELETE request
400	Bad request	An unsuccessful GET, POST, or PUT request, due to invalid content
401	Unauthorized	Requesting a restricted URL with incorrect credentials
403	Forbidden	Making a request that isn't allowed
404	Not found	Unsuccessful request due to an incorrect parameter in the URL
405	Method not allowed	Request method not allowed for the given URL

Table 6.5   Most popular HTTP status codes and how they might be used when sending responses to an API request

Status code	Name	Use case
409	Conflict	Unsuccessful POST request when another object already exists with the same data
500	Internal server error	Problem with your server or the database server

As we go through this chapter and build the Loc8r API we'll make use of several of these status codes, while also returning the appropriate data.

6.2   Setting up the API in Express

We've already got a good idea about the actions we want our API to perform, and the URL paths needed to do so. As we know from chapter 4, to get Express to do something based on an incoming URL request we need to set up controllers and routes. The controllers will do the action, and the routes will map the incoming requests to the appropriate controllers.

We have files for routes and controllers already set up in the application, so we could use those. A better option, though, is to keep the API code separate so that we don't run the risk of confusion and complication in our application. In fact, this is one of the reasons for creating an API in the first place. Also, by keeping the API code separate it makes it easier to strip it out and put it into a separate application at a future point, should you choose to do so. We really do want easy decoupling here.

So the first thing we want to do here is create a separate area inside the application for the files that will create the API. At the top level of the application *create a new folder called app_api*. If you've been following along and building up the application as you go, this will sit alongside the app_server folder.

This folder will hold everything specific to the API: routes, controllers, and models. When you've got this all set up we'll have a look at some ways to test these API placeholders.

6.2.1   Creating the routes

Like we did with the routes for the main Express application, we'll have an index.js file in the app_api/routes folder that will hold all of the routes we'll use in the API. Let's start by referencing this file in the main application file app.js.

INCLUDING THE ROUTES IN THE APPLICATION

The first step is to tell our application that we're adding more routes to look out for, and when it should use them. We already have a line in app.js to require the server application routes, which we can simply duplicate and set the path to the API routes as follows:

```
var routes = require('./app_server/routes/index');
var routesApi = require('./app_api/routes/index');
```

Next we need to tell the application when to use the routes. We currently have the following line in app.js telling the application to check the server application routes for all incoming requests:

```
app.use('/', routes);
```

Notice the `'/'` as the first parameter. This enables us to specify a subset of URLs for which the routes will apply. For example, we'll define all of our API routes starting with /api/. By adding the line shown in the following code snippet we can tell the application to use the API routes only when the route starts with /api:

```
app.use('/', routes);
app.use('/api', routesApi);
```

Okay, let's set up these URLs.

SPECIFYING THE REQUEST METHODS IN THE ROUTES

Up to now we've only used the GET method in the routes, like in the following code snippet from our main application routes:

```
router.get('/location', ctrlLocations.locationInfo);
```

Using the other methods of POST, PUT, and DELETE is as simple as switching out the `get` with the respective keywords of `post`, `put`, and `delete`. The following code snippet shows an example using the POST method for creating a new location:

```
router.post('/locations', ctrlLocations.locationsCreate);
```

Note that we don't specify /api at the front of the path. We specify in app.js that these routes should only be used if the path starts with /api, so it's assumed that all routes specified in this file will be prefixed with /api.

SPECIFYING REQUIRED URL PARAMETERS

It's quite common for API URLs to contain parameters for identifying specific documents or subdocuments—locations and reviews in the case of Loc8r. Specifying these parameters in routes is really simple; you just prefix the name of the parameter with a colon when defining each route.

Say you're trying to access a review with the ID abc that belongs to a location with the ID 123; you'd have a URL path like this:

```
/api/locations/123/reviews/abc
```

Swapping out the IDs for the parameter names (with a colon prefix) gives you a path like this:

```
/api/locations/:locationid/reviews/:reviewid
```

With a path like this Express will only match URLs that match that pattern. So a location ID must be specified and must be in the URL between locations/ and /reviews, and a review ID must also be specified at the end of the URL. When a path like this is assigned to a controller the parameters will be available to use in the code, with the names specified in the path, `locationid` and `reviewid` in this case.

We'll review exactly how you get to them in just a moment, but first we need to set up the routes for our Loc8r API.

DEFINING THE LOC8R API ROUTES

Now we know how to set up routes to accept parameters, and we also know what actions, methods, and paths we want to have in our API. So we can combine all of this to create the route definitions for the Loc8r API.

If you haven't done so yet, you should create an index.js file in the app_api/routes folder. To keep the size of individual files under control we'll separate the locations and reviews controllers into different files. The following listing shows how the defined routes should look.

Listing 6.1   Routes defined in app_api/routes/locations.js

```
var express = require('express');
var router = express.Router();
var ctrlLocations = require('../controllers/locations');    │ Include controller file
var ctrlReviews = require('../controllers/reviews');        │ (we'll create this next)

// locations
router.get('/locations', ctrlLocations.locationsListByDistance);
router.post('/locations', ctrlLocations.locationsCreate);                   │ Define
router.get('/locations/:locationid', ctrlLocations.locationsReadOne);       │ routes for
router.put('/locations/:locationid', ctrlLocations.locationsUpdateOne);     │ locations
router.delete('/locations/:locationid', ctrlLocations.locationsDeleteOne);

// reviews
router.post('/locations/:locationid/reviews', ctrlReviews.reviewsCreate);
router.get('/locations/:locationid/reviews/:reviewid',
    ctrlReviews.reviewsReadOne);                                            │ Define
router.put('/locations/:locationid/reviews/:reviewid',                      │ routes for
    ctrlReviews.reviewsUpdateOne);                                          │ reviews
router.delete('/locations/:locationid/reviews/:reviewid',
    ctrlReviews.reviewsDeleteOne);

module.exports = router;          ◁─│ Export
                                     routes
```

In this router file we need to `require` the related controller files. We haven't created these controller files yet, and will do so in just a moment. This is a good way to approach it, because by defining all of the routes and declaring the associated controller functions here we develop a high-level view of what controllers are needed.

The application now has two sets of routes: the main Express application routes and the new API routes. The application won't start at the moment though, because none of the controllers referenced by the API routes exist.

6.2.2 *Creating the controller placeholders*

To enable the application to start we can create placeholder functions for the controllers. These functions won't really do anything, but they will stop the application from falling over while we're building the API functionality.

The first step, of course, is to create the controller files. We know where these should be and what they should be called because we've already declared them in the app_api/routes folder. We need two new files called locations.js and reviews.js in the app_api/controllers folder.

You can create a placeholder for each of the controller functions as a blank export function, like in the following code snippet. Remember to put each controller into the correct file, depending on whether it's for a location or a review.

```
module.exports.locationsCreate = function (req, res) { };
```

To test the routing and the functions, though, we'll need to return a response.

RETURNING JSON FROM AN EXPRESS REQUEST

When building the Express application we rendered a view template to send HTML to the browser, but with an API we instead want to send a status code and some JSON data. Express makes this task really easy with the following commands:

```
res.status(status);
res.json(content);
```

> Send response status code, such as 200

> Send response data, such as {"status" : "success"}

You can use these two commands in the placeholder functions to test the success, as shown in the following code snippet:

```
module.exports.locationsCreate = function (req, res) {
  res.status(200);
  res.json({"status" : "success"});
};
```

Returning JSON and a response status is a very common task for an API, so it's a good idea to move these two statements into their own function. It also makes the code easier to test. So create a sendJsonResponse function in both controller files and call this from each of the controller placeholders as follows:

```
var sendJsonResponse = function(res, status, content) {
  res.status(status);
  res.json(content);
};
```

> New utility function that accepts response object, a status code, and a data object

```
module.exports.locationsCreate = function (req, res) {
  sendJsonResponse(res, 200, {"status" : "success"});
};
```

> Calling new function from each controller function

Now we can send a JSON response and associated status code with a single line. We'll use this a lot in our API!

6.2.3 *Including the model*

It's vitally important that the API can talk to the database; without it the API isn't going to be much use! To do this with Mongoose, we first need to `require` Mongoose into the controller files, and then bring in the Location model. Right at the top of the controller files, above all of the placeholder functions, add the following two lines:

```
var mongoose = require('mongoose');
var Loc = mongoose.model('Location');
```

The first line gives the controllers access to the database connection, and the second brings in the Location model so that we can interact with the Locations collection.

If we take a look at the file structure of our application, we see the app_api/models folder containing the database connection and the Mongoose setup is inside the app_server folder. But it's the API that's dealing with the database, not the main Express application. If the two applications were separate the model would be kept part of the API, so that's where it should live.

Just move the app_api/models folder from the app_server folder into the app_api folder, giving the folder structure like that shown in figure 6.4.

We need to tell the application that we've moved the app_api/models folder, of course, so we need to update the line in app.js that requires the model to point to the correct place:

```
require('./app_api/models/db');
```

Figure 6.4 Folder structure of the application at this point: app_api has models, controllers, and routes, and app_server has views, controllers, and routes

With that done, the application should start again and still connect to your database. The next question is, how can we test the API?

6.2.4   *Testing the API*

You can quickly test the GET routes in your browser by heading to the appropriate URL, such as http://localhost:3000/api/locations/1234. You should see the success response being delivered to the browser as shown in figure 6.5.

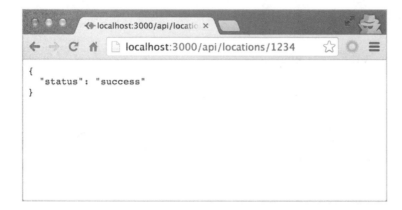

Figure 6.5   Testing a GET request of the API in the browser

This is okay for testing GET requests, but it doesn't get you very far with POST, PUT, and DELETE methods. There are a few tools to help you test API calls like this, but my current favorite is an extension for Chrome called Postman REST Client.

Postman enables you to test API URLs with a number of different request methods, allowing you to specify additional query string parameters or form data. After you click the Send button it will make a request to the URL you've specified and display the response data and status code.

Figure 6.6 shows a screenshot of Postman making a PUT request to the same URL as before.

It's a good idea to get Postman or another REST client up and running now. You'll need to use one a lot during this chapter as we build up a REST API. Let's get started by using the GET requests to read data from MongoDB.

6.3   *GET methods: Reading data from MongoDB*

GET methods are all about querying the database and returning some data. In our routes for Loc8r we have three GET requests doing different things, as listed in table 6.6.

We'll look at how to find a single location first, because it provides a good introduction to the way Mongoose works. Next we'll locate a single document using an ID, and then we'll expand into searching for multiple documents.

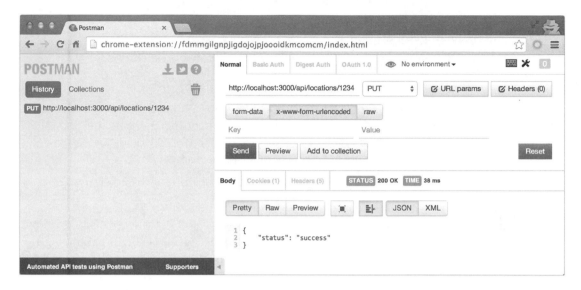

Figure 6.6   Using the Postman REST Client in Chrome to test a PUT request to the API

Table 6.6   Three GET requests of the Loc8r API

Action	Method	URL path	Parameters	Example
Read list of locations	GET	`/locations`		http://loc8r.com/api/ locations
Read a specific location	GET	`/locations`	`locationid`	http://loc8r.com/api/ locations/123
Read a specific review	GET	`/locations/ locationid/ reviews`	`locationid reviewid`	http://loc8r.com/api/ locations/123/reviews/abc

6.3.1   Finding a single document in MongoDB using Mongoose

Mongoose interacts with the database through its models, which is why we imported the Locations model as `Loc` at the top of the controller files. A Mongoose model has several associated methods to help manage the interactions as noted in the following sidebar.

For finding a single database document with a known ID in MongoDB, Mongoose has the `findById` method.

Mongoose query methods

Mongoose models have several methods available to them to help with querying the database. Here are some of the key ones:

- `find`—General search based on a supplied query object
- `findById`—Look for a specific ID
- `findOne`—Get the first document to match the supplied query
- `geoNear`—Find places geographically close to the provided latitude and longitude
- `geoSearch`—Add query functionality to a `geoNear` operation

We'll use some of these but not all of them in this book.

APPLYING THE FINDBYID METHOD TO THE MODEL

The `findById` method is relatively straightforward, accepting a single parameter, the ID to look for. As it's a model method, it's applied to the model like this:

```
Loc.findById(locationid)
```

This will not start the database query operation; it just tells the model what the query will be. To start the database query Mongoose models have an `exec` method.

RUNNING THE QUERY WITH THE EXEC METHOD

The `exec` method executes the query and passes a callback function that will run when the operation is complete. The callback function should accept two parameters, an error object and the instance of the found document. As it's a callback function the names of these parameters can be whatever you like.

The methods can be chained as follows:

```
Loc
  .findById(locationid)            ◁──  Apply findById method to
  .exec(function(err, location) {       Location model using Loc
    console.log("findById complete");   ◁──  Execute query
  });
                                    Log message
                                    when complete
```

This approach ensures that the database interaction is asynchronous, and therefore doesn't block the main Node process.

> **TIP** If you're not 100% comfortable with callbacks, scopes, and where the variables come from, take a look online at appendix D, section D.4, "Understanding JavaScript Callbacks."

Using the findById method in a controller

The controller we're working with to find a single location by ID is `locationsReadOne`, in the locations.js file in app_api/controllers.

We know the basic construct of the operation: apply the `findById` and `exec` methods to the Location model. To get this working in the context of the controller we need to do two things:

- Get the `locationid` parameter from the URL and pass it to the `findById` method.
- Provide an output function to the `exec` method.

Express makes it really easy to get the URL parameters we defined in the routes. The parameters are held inside a `params` object attached to the request object. With our route being defined like so

```
app.get('/api/locations/:locationid', ctrlLocations.locationsReadOne);
```

we can access the `locationid` parameter from inside the controller like this:

```
req.params.locationid
```

For the output function we can use the `sendJsonResponse` function that we created earlier. Putting this all together gives us the following:

```
module.exports.locationsReadOne = function(req, res) {
  Loc
    .findById(req.params.locationid)
    .exec(function(err, location) {
      sendJsonResponse(res, 200, location);
    });
};
```

Get locationid from URL parameters and give it to findById method

Define callback to accept possible parameters

Send document found as a JSON response

And now we have a very basic API controller. You can try it out by getting the ID of one of the locations in MongoDB and going to the URL in your browser, or by calling it in Postman. To get one of the ID values you can run the command `db.locations.find()` in the Mongo shell and it will list all of the locations you have, which will each include the `_id` value. When you've put the URL together the output should be a full location object as stored in MongoDB; you should see something like figure 6.7.

Did you try out the basic controller? Did you put an invalid location ID into the URL? If you did you'll have seen that you got nothing back. No warning, no message, just a `200` status telling you that everything is okay, but no data returned.

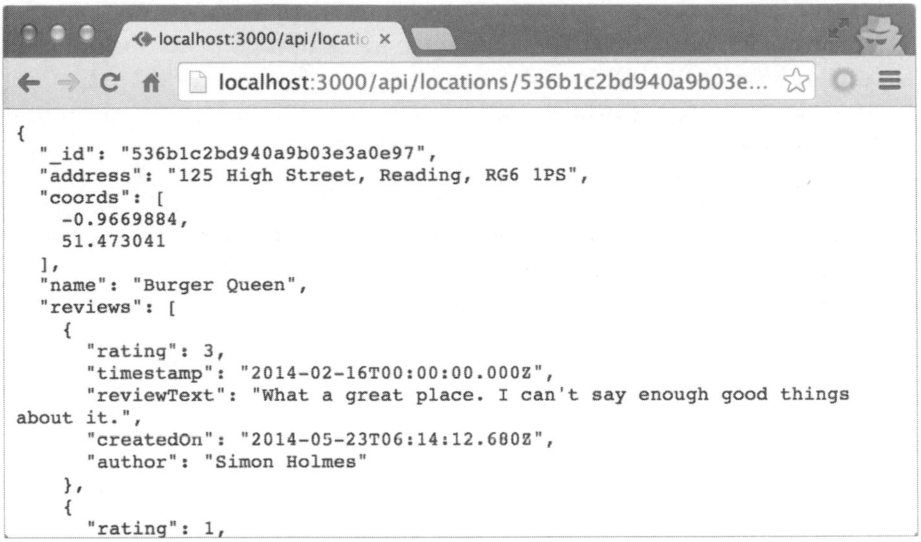

```
{
  "_id": "536b1c2bd940a9b03e3a0e97",
  "address": "125 High Street, Reading, RG6 1PS",
  "coords": [
    -0.9669884,
    51.473041
  ],
  "name": "Burger Queen",
  "reviews": [
    {
      "rating": 3,
      "timestamp": "2014-02-16T00:00:00.000Z",
      "reviewText": "What a great place. I can't say enough good things
about it.",
      "createdOn": "2014-05-23T06:14:12.680Z",
      "author": "Simon Holmes"
    },
    {
      "rating": 1,
```

Figure 6.7   Basic controller for finding a single location by ID returns a JSON object to the browser if the ID is found

CATCHING ERRORS

The problem with that basic controller is that it only outputs a success response, regardless of whether it was successful or not. This isn't good behavior for an API. A good API should respond with an error code when something goes wrong.

To respond with error messages the controller needs to be set up to trap potential errors and send an appropriate response. Error trapping in this fashion typically involves if statements. Every if statement must either have a corresponding else statement, or it must include a return statement.

> **TIP**   Your API code must never leave a request unanswered.

With our basic controller there are three errors we need to trap:

- The request parameters don't include locationid.
- The findById method doesn't return a location.
- The findById method returns an error.

The status code for an unsuccessful GET request is 404. Bearing this in mind the final code for the controller to find and return a single location looks like the following listing.

Listing 6.2   locationsReadOne controller

```
module.exports.locationsReadOne = function(req, res) {
  if (req.params && req.params.locationid) {
    Loc
      .findById(req.params.locationid)
      .exec(function(err, location) {
        if (!location) {
          sendJsonResponse(res, 404, {
            "message": "locationid not found"
          });
          return;
        } else if (err) {
          sendJsonResponse(res, 404, err);
          return;
        }
        sendJsonResponse(res, 200, location);
      });
  } else {
    sendJsonResponse(res, 404, {
      "message": "No locationid in request"
    });
  }
},
```

① Error trap 1: check that locationid exists in request parameters

② Error trap 2: if Mongoose doesn't return a location, send 404 message and exit function scope using return statement

③ Error trap 3: if Mongoose returned an error, send it as 404 response and exit controller using return statement

④ If Mongoose didn't error, continue as before and send location object in a 200 response

⑤ If request parameters didn't include locationid, send appropriate 404 response

Listing 6.2 uses both of the two methods of trapping with `if` statements. Error trap 1 **①** uses an `if` to check that the `params` object exists in the request object, and that the `params` object contains a `locationid` value. This loop is closed off with an `else` **⑤** for when either the `params` object or the `locationid` value isn't found. Error trap 2 **②** and error trap 3 **③** both use an `if` to check for an error returned by Mongoose. Each `if` includes a `return` statement, which will prevent any following code in the callback scope from running. If no error was found the `return` statement is ignored and the code moves on to send the successful response **④**.

Each of these traps provides a response for success and failure, leaving no room for the API to leave a requester hanging. If you wish you can also throw in a few `console.log` statements so that it's easier to track what's going on in terminal; the source code in GitHub will have some.

Figure 6.8 shows the difference between a successful request and a failed request, using the Postman extension in Chrome.

That's one complete API route dealt with. Now it's time to look at the second GET request to return a single review.

6.3.2 *Finding a single subdocument based on IDs*

To find a subdocument you first have to find the parent document like we've just done to find a single location by its ID. Once you've found the document you can look for a specific subdocument.

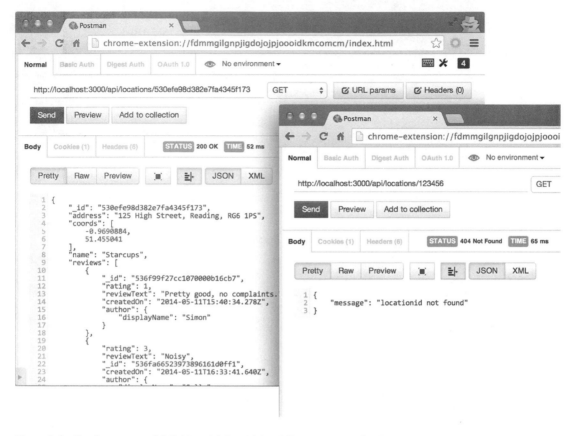

Figure 6.8   Testing successful (left) and failed (right) API responses using Postman

This means that we can take the `locationsReadOne` controller as the starting point and add a few modifications to create the `reviewsReadOne` controller. These modifications are

- Accept and use an additional `reviewid` URL parameter.
- Select only the name and reviews from the document, rather than having MongoDB return the entire document.
- Look for a review with a matching ID.
- Return the appropriate JSON response.

To do these things we can use a couple of new Mongoose methods.

LIMITING THE PATHS RETURNED FROM MONGODB

When you retrieve a document from MongoDB you don't always need the full document; sometimes you just want some specific data. Limiting the data being passed around is also better for bandwidth consumption and speed.

Mongoose does this through a `select` method chained to the model query. For example, the following code snippet will tell MongoDB that we only want to get the name and the reviews of a location:

```
Loc
  .findById(req.params.locationid)
  .select('name reviews')
  .exec();
```

The `select` method accepts a space-separated string of the paths we want to retrieve.

USING MONGOOSE TO FIND A SPECIFIC SUBDOCUMENT

Mongoose also offers a helper method for finding a subdocument by ID. Given an array of subdocuments Mongoose has an id method that accepts the ID you want to find. The `id` method will return the single matching subdocument, and it can be used as follows:

```
Loc
  .findById(req.params.locationid)
  .select('name reviews')
  .exec(
    function(err, location) {
      var review;
      review = location.reviews.id(req.params.reviewid);    ◁── Pass reviewid
    }                                                             from parameters
);                                                                into id method
```

In this code snippet a single review would be returned to the review variable in the callback.

ADDING SOME ERROR TRAPPING AND PUTTING IT ALL TOGETHER

Now we've got the ingredients needed to make the `reviewsReadOne` controller. Starting with a copy of the `locationsReadOne` controller we can make the modifications required to return just a single review.

The following listing shows the `reviewsReadOne` controller in review.js (modifications in bold).

Listing 6.3   Controller for finding a single review

```
module.exports.reviewsReadOne = function(req, res) {
  if (req.params && req.params.locationid && req.params.reviewid) {    ◁── Verify that
    Loc                                                                    reviewid
      .findById(req.params.locationid)                                     exists as a
      .select('name reviews')    ◁── Add Mongoose                          parameter
      .exec(                         select method
        function(err, location) {   to model query,
          var response, review;     stating that we
          if (!location) {          want to get name
            sendJsonResponse(res, 404, {  of location and
              "message": "locationid not found"  its reviews
            });
            return;
```

```
      } else if (err) {
        sendJsonResponse(res, 400, err);
        return;
      }
      if (location.reviews && location.reviews.length > 0) {
        review = location.reviews.id(req.params.reviewid);
        if (!review) {
          sendJsonResponse(res, 404, {
            "message": "reviewid not found"
          });
        } else {
          response = {
            location : {
              name : location.name,
              id : req.params.locationid
            },
            review : review
          };
          sendJsonResponse(res, 200, response);
        }
      } else {
        sendJsonResponse(res, 404, {
          "message": "No reviews found"
        });
      }
    }
  );
} else {
  sendJsonResponse(res, 404, {
    "message": "Not found, locationid and reviewid are both required"
  });
}
}
};
```

Check that returned location has reviews

Use Mongoose subdocument .id method as a helper for searching for matching ID

If review isn't found return an appropriate response

If review is found build response object returning review and location name and ID

If no reviews are found return an appropriate error message

When this is saved and ready you can test it using Postman again. You need to have correct ID values, which you can get directly from MongoDB via the Mongo shell. The command db.locations.find() will return all of the locations and their reviews. You can test what happens if you put in a false ID for a location or a review, or try a review ID from a different location.

6.3.3 *Finding multiple documents with geospatial queries*

The homepage of Loc8r should display a list of locations based on the user's current geographical location. MongoDB and Mongoose have some special geospatial query methods to help find nearby places.

Here we'll use the Mongoose method geoNear to find a list of locations close to a specified point, up to a specified maximum distance. geoNear is a model method that accepts three parameters:

- A geoJSON geographical point
- An options object
- A callback function

The following code snippet shows the basic construct:

```
Loc.geoNear(point, options, callback);
```

Unlike the `findById` method, `geoNear` doesn't have an `exec` method. Instead, `geoNear` is executed immediately and the code to run on completion is sent through in the callback.

CONSTRUCTING A GEOJSON POINT

The first parameter of the `geoNear` method is a `geoJSON` point. A `geoJSON` point is a simple JSON object containing a latitude and a longitude in an array. The construct for a `geoJSON` point is shown in the following code snippet:

```
var point = {
  type: "Point",
  coordinates: [lng, lat]
};
```

Declare object ← Declare object

Define it as type "Point"

Set longitude and latitude coordinates in an array, longitude first

The route set up here to get a list of locations doesn't have the coordinates in the URL parameters, meaning that they'll have to be specified in a different way. A query string is ideal for this data type, meaning that the request URL will look more like this:

```
api/locations?lng=-0.7992599&lat=51.378091
```

Express, of course, gives you access to the values in a query string, putting them into a query object attached to the `request` object—for example, `req.query.lng`. The longitude and latitude values will be strings when retrieved, but they need to be added to the `point` object as numbers. JavaScript's `parseFloat` function can see to this. Putting it all together, the following code snippet shows how to get the coordinates from the query string and create the `geoJSON` point required by the `geoNear` function:

```
module.exports.locationsListByDistance = function(req, res) {
  var lng = parseFloat(req.query.lng);
  var lat = parseFloat(req.query.lat);
  var point = {
    type: "Point",
    coordinates: [lng, lat]
  };
  Loc.geoNear(point, options, callback);
};
```

Get coordinates from query string and convert from strings to numbers

Create geoJSON point

Send point as first parameter in geoNear method

Naturally, this controller will not work yet as `options` and `callback` are both currently undefined. We'll work on these now, starting with the options.

ADDING REQUIRED QUERY OPTIONS TO GEONEAR

The `geoNear` method only has one required option: `spherical`. This determines whether the search will be done based on a spherical object or a flat plane. It's generally accepted these days that Earth is round, so we'll set the `spherical` option to be `true`.

In creating an object to hold the options we have the following code snippet:

```
var geoOptions = {
  spherical: true
};
```

Now the search will be based on coordinates on a sphere.

LIMITING GEONEAR RESULTS BY NUMBER

You'll often want to look after the API server—and the responsiveness seen by end users—by limiting the number of results when returning a list. In the `geoNear` method adding an option called `num` does this. You simply specify the maximum number of results you want to have returned.

The following code snippet shows this added to the previous `geoOptions` object, limiting the size of the returned data set to 10 objects:

```
var geoOptions = {
  spherical: true,
  num: 10
};
```

Now the search will bring back no more than the 10 closest results.

LIMITING GEONEAR RESULTS BY DISTANCE

When returning location-based data, another way to keep the processing of the API under control is to limit the list of results by distance from the central point. In theory, this is just a case of adding another option called `maxDistance`. The challenge is that MongoDB does the calculations in radians rather than meters or miles, and expects the `maxDistance` to be supplied as radians. This allows MongoDB to easily do these calculations on any size sphere, not just Earth, but that doesn't help us here.

The calculations to convert between physical distances and radians are quite straight-forward, as shown in figure 6.9.

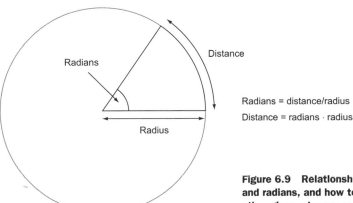

Radians = distance/radius

Distance = radians · radius

Figure 6.9   Relationship between distance and radians, and how to convert one to the other given a known radius

The radius of Earth is 6,371 kilometers, or 3,959 miles, but we'll be using kilometers in this book because, frankly, they're easier to work with! Given this information we can create a function called theEarth, exposing two methods to make the calculations for us. The following code snippet should go near the top of the API controller locations.js file, just after the Mongoose is required and the model set up:

```
var theEarth = (function(){                          Define fixed value
  var earthRadius = 6371; // km, miles is 3959        for radius of Earth

  var getDistanceFromRads = function(rads) {          Create function to convert
    return parseFloat(rads * earthRadius);            radians to distance
  };

  var getRadsFromDistance = function(distance) {      Create function to convert
    return parseFloat(distance / earthRadius);        distance to radians
  };

  return {
    getDistanceFromRads : getDistanceFromRads,        Expose these
    getRadsFromDistance : getRadsFromDistance          two functions
  };
})();
```

Now we have some reusable functions for making the distance calculations.

> **TIP** If this pattern of coding isn't familiar to you take a look at appendix D, section D.5, "Writing Modular JavaScript."

We can now add the maxDistance value to the options, and add these options to the controller as follows:

```
module.exports.locationsListByDistance = function(req, res) {
  var lng = parseFloat(req.query.lng);
  var lat = parseFloat(req.query.lat);
  var point = {
    type: "Point",
    coordinates: [lng, lat]
  };
  var geoOptions = {                                  Create options
    spherical: true,                                  object, including
    maxDistance: theEarth.getRadsFromDistance(20),    setting maximum
    num: 10                                           distance to 20 km
  };
  Loc.geoNear(point, geoOptions, callback);           Update geoNear function
};                                                    to use geoOptions object
```

> **Extra credit**
>
> Try taking the maximum distance from a query string value instead of hard-coding it into the function. The code on GitHub for this chapter has the answer to this.

That's the last of the options we need for our geoNear database search, so now it's time to start working with the output.

LOOKING AT THE GEONEAR OUTPUT

The completion callback for the geoNear method has three parameters, in this order:

1 An error object
2 A results object
3 A stats object

With a successful query the error object will be undefined, the results object will contain an array of results, and the stats object will contain information about the query, like time taken, number of documents scanned, the average distance, and the maximum distance of the documents returned. We'll start by working with a successful query before adding in the error trapping.

Following a successful geoNear query MongoDB returns an array of objects. Each object contains a distance value and a returned document from the database. In other words, MongoDB doesn't add the distance to the data. The following code snippet shows an example of the returned data, truncated for brevity:

```
[{
  dis: 0.002532674663406363,
  obj: {
    name: 'Starcups',
    address: '125 High Street, Reading, RG6 1PS'
  }
}]
```

This array only has one object, but a successful query is likely to have several objects returned at once. The geoNear method actually returns the entire document in the obj object. There are two problems here:

- The API shouldn't return more data than necessary.
- We want to return the distance in a meaningful way (not radians) as an integral part of the returned data set.

So rather than simply sending the returned data back as the response there's some processing to do first.

PROCESSING THE GEONEAR OUTPUT

Before the API can send a response we need to make sure it's sending the right thing, and only what's needed. We know what data is needed by the homepage listing as we've already built the homepage controller in app_server/controllers/location.js. The homelist function sends a number of location objects like the following example:

```
{
  name: 'Starcups',
  address: '125 High Street, Reading, RG6 1PS',
  rating: 3,
```

```
  facilities: ['Hot drinks', 'Food', 'Premium wifi'],
  distance: '100m'
}
```

To create an object along these lines from the results, we simply need to loop through the results and push the relevant data into a new array. This processed data can then be returned with a status 200 response. The following code snippet shows how this might look:

```
Loc.geoNear(point, options, function (err, results, stats) {
  var locations = [];
  results.forEach(function(doc) {
    locations.push({
      distance: theEarth.getDistanceFromRads(doc.dis),
      name: doc.obj.name,
      address: doc.obj.address,
      rating: doc.obj.rating,
      facilities: doc.obj.facilities,
      _id: doc.obj._id
    });
  });
  sendJsonResponse(res, 200, locations);
});
```

Create new array to hold processed results data

Loop through geoNear query results

Get distance and convert from radians to kilometers, using helper function previously created

Push rest of required data into return object

Send processed data back as a JSON response

If you test this API route with Postman—remembering to add longitude and latitude coordinates to the query string—you'll see something like figure 6.10.

> ### Extra credit
> Try passing the results to an external named function to build the list of locations. This function should return the processed list, which can then be passed into the JSON response.

If you test this by sending coordinates too far away from the test data you should still get a 200 status, but the returned array will be empty.

ADDING THE ERROR TRAPPING
Once again we've started by building the success functionality, and now we need to add in some error traps to make sure that the API always sends the appropriate response.

The traps we need to set should check that

- The parameters have all been sent correctly.
- The geoNear function hasn't returned an error.

The listing on the next page shows the final controller all put together, including these error traps.

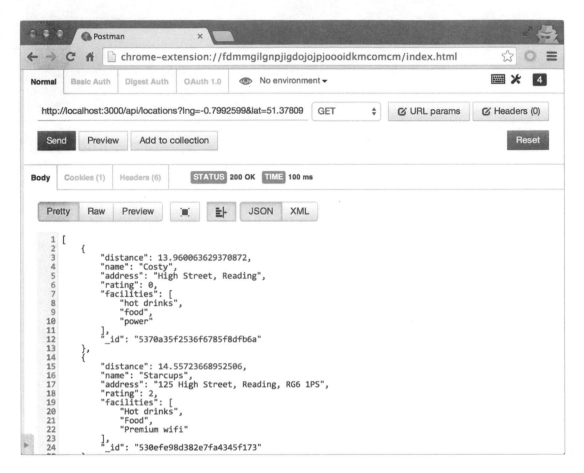

Figure 6.10   Testing the location list route in Postman should give a `200` status and a list of results, depending on the geographical coordinates sent in the query string.

Listing 6.4   Locations list controller `locationsListByDistance`

```
module.exports.locationsListByDistance = function(req, res) {
  var lng = parseFloat(req.query.lng);
  var lat = parseFloat(req.query.lat);
  var point = {
    type: "Point",
    coordinates: [lng, lat]
  };
  var geoOptions = {
    spherical: true,
    maxDistance: theEarth.getRadsFromDistance(20),
    num: 10
  };
```

```
if (!lng || !lat) {
    sendJsonResponse(res, 404, {
        "message": "lng and lat query parameters are required"
    });
    return;
}
Loc.geoNear(point, geoOptions, function(err, results, stats) {
    var locations = [];
    if (err) {
        sendJsonResponse(res, 404, err);
    } else {
        results.forEach(function(doc) {
            locations.push({
                distance: theEarth.getDistanceFromRads(doc.dis),
                name: doc.obj.name,
                address: doc.obj.address,
                rating: doc.obj.rating,
                facilities: doc.obj.facilities,
                _id: doc.obj._id
            });
        });
        sendJsonResponse(res, 200, locations);
    }
});
};
```

> **Check lng and lat query parameters exist in right format; return a 404 error and message if not**

> **If geoNear query returns error, send this as response with 404 status**

This completes the GET requests that our API needs to service, so moving forward it's time to tackle the POST requests.

6.4   *POST methods: Adding data to MongoDB*

POST methods are all about creating documents or subdocuments in the database, and then returning the saved data as confirmation. In the routes for Loc8r we have two POST requests doing different things, listed in Table 6.7.

Table 6.7   Two POST requests of the Loc8r API

Action	Method	URL path	Parameters	Example
Create new location	POST	`/locations`		http://api.loc8r.com/locations
Create new review	POST	`/locations/ locationid/ reviews`	`locationid`	http://api.loc8r.com/locations/ 123/reviews

POST methods work by taking form data posted to them and adding it to the database. In the same way that URL parameters are accessed using `req.params` and query strings are accessed via `req.query`, Express controllers access posted form data via `req.body`.

Let's make a start by looking at how to create documents.

6.4.1   *Creating new documents in MongoDB*

In the database for Loc8r each location is a document, so this is what we'll be creating in this section. Mongoose really couldn't make the process of creating MongoDB documents much easier for you. You take your model, apply the `create` method, and send it some data and a callback function. This is the minimal construct, as it would be attached to our `Loc` model:

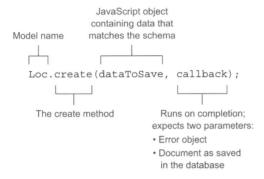

So that's pretty simple. There are two main steps to the creation process:

1   Take the posted form data and use it to create a JavaScript object that matches the schema.
2   Send an appropriate response in the callback depending on the success or failure of the `create` operation.

Looking at step 1 we already know that we can get data sent to us in a form by using `req.body`, and step 2 should be pretty familiar by now. So let's jump straight into the code. The following listing shows the full `locationsCreate` controller for creating a new document.

Listing 6.5   **Complete controller for creating a new location**

```
module.exports.locationsCreate = function(req, res) {
  Loc.create({                                               ◁─┐  Apply create
    name: req.body.name,                                          method to model
    address: req.body.address,
    facilities: req.body.facilities.split(","),          ▷
    coords: [parseFloat(req.body.lng), parseFloat(req.body.lat)],    ◁─┐
    openingTimes: [{
      days: req.body.days1,                                   Parse coordinates from
      opening: req.body.opening1,                                 strings to numbers
      closing: req.body.closing1,
      closed: req.body.closed1,
    }, {
      days: req.body.days2,
      opening: req.body.opening2,
```

Create array of facilities by splitting a comma-separated list

```
        closing: req.body.closing2,
        closed: req.body.closed2,
    }]
}, function(err, location) {
    if (err) {
        sendJsonResponse(res, 400, err);
    } else {
        sendJsonResponse(res, 201, location);
    }
});
};
```

Supply callback function, containing appropriate responses for success and failure

This shows how easy it can be to create a new document in MongoDB and save some data. For the sake of brevity we've limited the `openingTimes` array to two entries, but this could easily be extended, or better yet put into a loop checking for the existence of the values.

You might also notice that there's no `rating` being set. Remember in the schema that we set a default of 0, as in the following snippet:

```
rating: {type: Number, "default": 0, min: 0, max: 5},
```

This is applied when the document is created, setting the initial value to be 0. Something else about this code might be shouting out at you. There's no validation!

VALIDATING THE DATA USING MONGOOSE

This controller has no validation code inside it, so what's to stop somebody from entering loads of empty or partial documents? Again, we started this off in the Mongoose schemas. In the schemas we set a `required` flag to `true` in a few of the paths. When this flag is set, Mongoose will not send the data to MongoDB.

Given the following base schema for locations, for example, we can see that `name` and `coords` are both required fields:

```
var locationSchema = new mongoose.Schema({
    name: {type: String, required: true},
    address: String,
    rating: {type: Number, "default": 0, min: 0, max: 5},
    facilities: [String],
    coords: {type: [Number], index: '2dsphere', required: true},
    openingTimes: [openingTimeSchema],
    reviews: [reviewSchema]
});
```

If either of these fields is missing, the `create` method will raise an error and not attempt to save the document to the database.

Testing this API route in Postman looks like figure 6.11. Note that the method is set to `post`, and that the data type selected (above the list of names and values) is `x-www-form-urlencoded`.

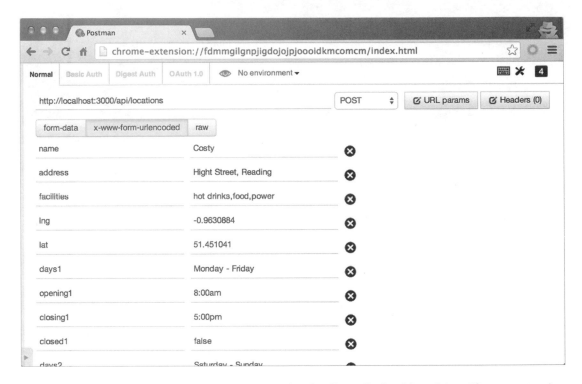

Figure 6.11   Testing a POST method in Postman, ensuring that the method and form data settings are correct

6.4.2   *Creating new subdocuments in MongoDB*

In the context of Loc8r locations, reviews are subdocuments. Subdocuments are created and saved through their parent document. Put another way, to create and save a new subdocument you have to

1   Find the correct parent document.
2   Add a new subdocument.
3   Save the parent document.

Finding the correct parent isn't a problem as we've already done that, and can use it as the skeleton for the next controller, `reviewsCreate`. When we've found the parent we can call an external function to do the next step, as shown in the following listing.

Listing 6.6   Controller for creating a review

```
module.exports.reviewsCreate = function(req, res) {
  var locationid = req.params.locationid;
  if (locationid) {
    Loc
      .findById(locationid)
      .select('reviews')
```

```
    .exec(
      function(err, location) {
        if (err) {
          sendJsonResponse(res, 400, err);
        } else {
          doAddReview(req, res, location);      ◁─┐
        }
      }
    );
  } else {
    sendJsonResponse(res, 404, {
      "message": "Not found, locationid required"
    });
  }
};
```

Successful find operation will call new function to add review, passing request, response, and location objects

This isn't doing anything particularly new; we've seen it all before. By putting in a call to a new function we can keep the code neater by reducing the amount of nesting and indentation, and also make it easier to test.

ADDING AND SAVING A SUBDOCUMENT

Having found the parent document, and retrieved the existing list of subdocuments, we then need to add a new one. Subdocuments are essentially arrays of objects, and the easiest way to add a new object to an array is to create the data object and use the JavaScript push method. The following code snippet demonstrates this:

```
location.reviews.push({
  author: req.body.author,
  rating: req.body.rating,
  reviewText: req.body.reviewText
});
```

This is getting posted form data, hence using req.body.

Once the subdocument has been added, the parent document must be saved because subdocuments cannot be saved on their own. To save a document Mongoose has a model method save, which expects a callback with an error parameter and a returned object parameter. The following code snippet shows this in action:

```
location.save(function(err, location) {
  var thisReview;
  if (err) {
    sendJsonResponse(res, 400, err);
  } else {
    thisReview = location.reviews[location.reviews.length - 1];    ◁─┐
    sendJsonResponse(res, 201, thisReview);
  }
});
```

❶ Find last review in returned array, as MongoDB will return entire parent document, not just new subdocument

The document returned by the save method is the full parent document, not just the new subdocument. To return the correct data in the API response—that is, the subdocument—we need to retrieve the last subdocument from the array ❶.

When adding documents and subdocuments you need to keep in mind any impact this may have on other data. In Loc8r adding a review will add a new rating. This new rating will impact the overall rating for the document. So on the successful save of a review we'll call another function to update the average rating.

Putting everything we have together in the doAddReview function, plus a little extra error trapping, gives us the following listing.

Listing 6.7 Adding and saving a subdocument

```
var doAddReview = function(req, res, location) {          ◁──  When provided with a
  if (!location) {                                               parent document ...
    sendJsonResponse(res, 404, {
      "message": "locationid not found"
    });
  } else {
    location.reviews.push({
      author: req.body.author,                            push new data
      rating: req.body.rating,                            into subdocument
      reviewText: req.body.reviewText                     array...
    });
    location.save(function(err, location) {               ◁──  before
      var thisReview;                                           saving it
      if (err) {
        sendJsonResponse(res, 400, err);
      } else {
        updateAverageRating(location._id);
        thisReview = location.reviews[location.reviews.length - 1];
        sendJsonResponse(res, 201, thisReview);
      }
    });
  }
};
```

On successful save operation call function to update average rating

Retrieve last review added to array and return it as JSON confirmation response

UPDATING THE AVERAGE RATING

Calculating the average rating isn't particularly complicated, so we won't dwell on it too long. The steps are

1 Find the correct document given a provided ID.
2 Loop through the review subdocuments adding up the ratings.
3 Calculate the average rating value.
4 Update the rating value of the parent document.
5 Save the document.

Turning this list of steps into code gives us something along the lines of the following listing, which should be placed in the reviews.js controller file along with the review-based controllers.

Listing 6.8 Calculating and updating the average rating

```
var updateAverageRating = function(locationid) {
  Loc
    .findById(locationid)
    .select('rating reviews')
    .exec(
      function(err, location) {
        if (!err) {
          doSetAverageRating(location);
        }
      });
};

var doSetAverageRating = function(location) {
  var i, reviewCount, ratingAverage, ratingTotal;
  if (location.reviews && location.reviews.length > 0) {
    reviewCount = location.reviews.length;
    ratingTotal = 0;
    for (i = 0; i < reviewCount; i++) {
      ratingTotal = ratingTotal + location.reviews[i].rating;
    }
    ratingAverage = parseInt(ratingTotal / reviewCount, 10);
    location.rating = ratingAverage;
    location.save(function(err) {
      if (err) {
        console.log(err);
      } else {
        console.log("Average rating updated to", ratingAverage);
      }
    });
  }
};
```

Find correct document given supplied ID

Loop through review subdocuments adding up ratings

Calculate average rating value

Update rating value of parent document

Save parent document

You might have noticed that we're not sending any JSON response here, and that's because we've already sent it. This entire operation is asynchronous and doesn't need to impact sending the API response confirming the saved review.

Adding a review isn't the only time we'll need to update the average rating. This is why it makes extra sense to make these functions accessible from the other controllers, and not tightly coupled to the actions of creating a review.

What we've just done here offers a sneak peak at using Mongoose to update data in MongoDB, so let's now move on to the PUT methods of the API.

6.5 *PUT methods: Updating data in MongoDB*

PUT methods are all about updating existing documents or subdocuments in the database, and then returning the saved data as confirmation. In the routes for Loc8r we have two PUT requests doing different things, listed in table 6.8.

Table 6.8   Two PUT requests of the Loc8r API for updating locations and reviews

Action	Method	URL path	Parameters	Example
Update a specific location	PUT	`/locations`	`locationid`	http://loc8r.com/api/locations/123
Update a specific review	PUT	`/locations/ locationid/ reviews`	`locationid reviewid`	http://loc8r.com/api/locations/123/reviews/abc

PUT methods are similar to POST methods because they work by taking form data posted to them. But instead of using the data to create new documents in the database, PUT methods use the data to update existing documents.

6.5.1   *Using Mongoose to update a document in MongoDB*

In Loc8r we might want to update a location to add new facilities, change the open times, or amend any of the other data. The approach to updating data in a document is probably starting to look familiar, following these steps:

1 Find the relevant document.
2 Make some changes to the instance.
3 Save the document.
4 Send a JSON response.

This approach is made possible by the way that an instance of a Mongoose model maps directly to a document in MongoDB. When your query finds the document you get a model instance. If you make changes to this instance and then save it, Mongoose will update the original document in the database with your changes.

USING THE MONGOOSE SAVE METHOD

We've actually already seen this in action, when updating the average rating value. The `save` method is applied to the model instance that the `find` function returns. It expects a callback with the standard parameters of an error object and a returned data object.

A cut-down skeleton of this approach is shown in the following code snippet:

```
Loc                                              Find document
  .findById(req.params.locationid)   <──┘        to update
  .exec(
    function(err, location) {                     Make change to model
      location.name = req.body.name;   <──┘        instance, changing a
      location.save(function(err, location) {      value of one path
        if (err) {
          sendJsonResponse(res, 404, err);   <──┘
        } else {
          sendJsonResponse(res, 200, location);   <──┘   Return success or
        }                                                failure response
```

Save document with Mongoose's save method

```
      });
    }
  );
};
```

Here we can clearly see the separate steps of finding, updating, saving, and responding. Fleshing out this skeleton into the locationsUpdateOne controller with some error trapping and the data we want to save gives us the following listing.

Listing 6.9   Making changes to an existing document in MongoDB

```
module.exports.locationsUpdateOne = function(req, res) {
  if (!req.params.locationid) {
    sendJsonResponse(res, 404, {
      "message": "Not found, locationid is required"
    });
    return;
  }
  Loc
    .findById(req.params.locationid)          Find location
    .select('-reviews -rating')               document by
    .exec(                                     supplied ID
      function(err, location) {
        if (!location) {
          sendJsonResponse(res, 404, {
            "message": "locationid not found"
          });
          return;
        } else if (err) {
          sendJsonResponse(res, 400, err);
          return;
        }
        location.name = req.body.name;
        location.address = req.body.address;
        location.facilities = req.body.facilities.split(",");
        location.coords = [parseFloat(req.body.lng),
  parseFloat(req.body.lat)];
        location.openingTimes = [{              Update
          days: req.body.days1,                 paths with
          opening: req.body.opening1,           values from
          closing: req.body.closing1,           submitted
          closed: req.body.closed1,             form
        }, {
          days: req.body.days2,
          opening: req.body.opening2,
          closing: req.body.closing2,
          closed: req.body.closed2,
        }];
        location.save(function(err, location) {
          if (err) {
            sendJsonResponse(res, 404, err);       Send appropriate
          } else {                                 response, depending
            sendJsonResponse(res, 200, location);  on outcome of save
          }                                        operation
```

Save instance

```
      });
    }
  );
};
```

There's clearly a lot more code here, now that it's fully fleshed out, but we can still quite easily identify the key steps of the update process.

The eagle-eyed among us may have noticed something strange in the select statement:

```
.select('-reviews -rating')
```

Previously we've used the `select` method to say which columns we *do want* to select. By adding a dash in front of a path name we're stating that we *don't want* to retrieve it from the database. So this `select` statement says to retrieve everything except the reviews and the rating.

6.5.2   *Updating an existing subdocument in MongoDB*

Updating a subdocument is exactly the same as updating a document, with one exception. After finding the document you then have to find the correct subdocument to make your changes. After this, the save method is applied to the document, not the subdocument. So the steps to updating an existing subdocument are

1 Find the relevant document.
2 Find the relevant subdocument.
3 Make some changes to the subdocument.
4 Save the document.
5 Send a JSON response.

For Loc8r the subdocuments we're updating are reviews, so when a review is changed we'll have to remember to recalculate the average rating. That's the only additional thing we'll need to add in, above and beyond the five steps. The following listing shows this all put into place in the `reviewsUpdateOne` controller.

> **Listing 6.10   Updating a subdocument in MongoDB**

```
module.exports.reviewsUpdateOne = function(req, res) {
  if (!req.params.locationid || !req.params.reviewid) {
    sendJsonResponse(res, 404, {
      "message": "Not found, locationid and reviewid are both required"
    });
    return;
  }
  Loc                                          ⟵┐ Find parent
    .findById(req.params.locationid)              document
    .select('reviews')
    .exec(
      function(err, location) {
        var thisReview;
```

```
              if (!location) {
                sendJsonResponse(res, 404, {
                  "message": "locationid not found"
                });
                return;
              } else if (err) {
                sendJsonResponse(res, 400, err);
                return;
              }
              if (location.reviews && location.reviews.length > 0) {
                thisReview = location.reviews.id(req.params.reviewid);    ⟵──┐ Find
                if (!thisReview) {                                            subdocument
                  sendJsonResponse(res, 404, {
                    "message": "reviewid not found"
                  });
                } else {
                  thisReview.author = req.body.author;              ┌ Make changes to
                  thisReview.rating = req.body.rating;              │ subdocument from
                  thisReview.reviewText = req.body.reviewText;      │ supplied form data
                  location.save(function(err, location) {
     Save parent ┌─▷ if (err) {
     document  ──┘      sendJsonResponse(res, 404, err);
                    } else {                                    ⟵──┐ Return a JSON
                      updateAverageRating(location._id);            response, sending
                      sendJsonResponse(res, 200, thisReview);   ⟵──┘ subdocument object on
                    }                                                basis of successful save
                  });
                }
              } else {
                sendJsonResponse(res, 404, {
                  "message": "No review to update"
                });
              }
            }
          }
        );
      };
```

The five steps for updating are clear to see in this listing: find the document, find the subdocument, make changes, save, and respond. Once again a lot of the code here's error trapping, but it's vital for creating a stable and responsive API. You really don't want to save incorrect data, send the wrong responses, or delete data you don't want to. Speaking of deleting data, let's move on to the final of the four API methods we're using: DELETE.

6.6   *DELETE method: Deleting data from MongoDB*

The DELETE method is, unsurprisingly, all about deleting existing documents or subdocuments in the database. In the routes for Loc8r we have a DELETE request for deleting a location, and another for deleting a review. The details are listed in Table 6.9.

We'll start by taking a look at deleting documents.

Table 6.9   Two DELETE requests of the Loc8r API for deleting locations and reviews

Action	Method	URL path	Parameters	Example
Delete a specific location	DELETE	`/locations`	`locationid`	http://loc8r.com/api/locations/123
Delete a specific review	DELETE	`/locations/locationid/reviews`	`locationid reviewid`	http://loc8r.com/api/locations/123/reviews/abc

6.6.1   *Deleting documents in MongoDB*

Mongoose makes deleting a document in MongoDB extremely simple by giving us the method `findByIdAndRemove`. This method expects just a single parameter—the ID of the document to be deleted.

The API should respond with a 404 in case of an error and a 204 in case of success. The following listing shows this all in place in the `locationsDeleteOne` controller.

Listing 6.11   Deleting a document from MongoDB given an ID

```
module.exports.locationsDeleteOne = function(req, res) {
  var locationid = req.params.locationid;
  if (locationid) {                          ┐ Call findByIdAndRemove
    Loc                                      │ method, passing in
      .findByIdAndRemove(locationid)    ◄────┘ locationid
      .exec(                            ◄──────── Execute method
        function(err, location) {
          if (err) {
            sendJsonResponse(res, 404, err);   ◄─┐
            return;                              │ Respond with
          }                                      │ success or
          sendJsonResponse(res, 204, null);  ◄───┘ failure
        }
    );
  } else {
    sendJsonResponse(res, 404, {
      "message": "No locationid"
    });
  }
};
```

That's the quick and easy way to delete a document, but you can break it into a two-step process and find it then delete it if you prefer. This does give you the chance to do something with the document before deleting if you need to. This would look like the following code snippet:

```
Loc
  .findById(locationid)
  .exec(
    function (err, location) {
      // Do something with the document
      Loc.remove(function(err, location){
```

```
        // Confirm success or failure
    });
  }
);
```

So there's an extra level of nesting there, but with it comes an extra level of flexibility should you need it.

6.6.2 Deleting a subdocument from MongoDB

The process for deleting a subdocument is no different from the other work we've done with subdocuments—everything is managed through the parent document. The steps for deleting a subdocument are

1 Find the parent document.
2 Find the relevant subdocument.
3 Remove the subdocument.
4 Save the parent document.
5 Confirm success or failure of operation.

Actually deleting the subdocument itself is really easy, as Mongoose gives us another helper method. You've already seen that we can find a subdocument by its ID with the id method like this:

```
location.reviews.id(reviewid)
```

Mongoose allows you to chain a remove method to the end of this statement like so:

```
location.reviews.id(reviewid).remove()
```

This will delete the subdocument from the array. Remember, of course, that the parent document will need saving after this to persist the change back to the database. Putting all the steps together—with a load of error trapping—into the reviewsDelete-One controller looks like the following listing.

Listing 6.12 Finding and deleting a subdocument from MongoDB

```
module.exports.reviewsDeleteOne = function(req, res) {
  if (!req.params.locationid || !req.params.reviewid) {
    sendJsonResponse(res, 404, {
      "message": "Not found, locationid and reviewid are both required"
    });
    return;
  }
  Loc                                          Find relevant
    .findById(req.params.locationid)     ◁──┐  parent document
    .select('reviews')
    .exec(
      function(err, location) {
        if (!location) {
```

```
          sendJsonResponse(res, 404, {
            "message": "locationid not found"
          });
          return;
        } else if (err) {
          sendJsonResponse(res, 400, err);
          return;
        }
        if (location.reviews && location.reviews.length > 0) {
          if (!location.reviews.id(req.params.reviewid)) {
            sendJsonResponse(res, 404, {
              "message": "reviewid not found"
            });
          } else {
            location.reviews.id(req.params.reviewid).remove();
            location.save(function(err) {
              if (err) {
                sendJsonResponse(res, 404, err);
              } else {
                updateAverageRating(location._id);
                sendJsonResponse(res, 204, null);
              }
            });
          }
        } else {
          sendJsonResponse(res, 404, {
            "message": "No review to delete"
          });
        }
      }
    );
};
```

Find and delete relevant subdocument in one step

Save parent document

Return appropriate success or failure response

Again, most of the code here's error trapping; there are seven possible responses the API could give and only one of them is the successful one. Actually deleting the sub-document is really easy; you just have to make absolutely sure that you're deleting the right one.

As we're deleting a review here, which will have a rating associated to it, we also have to remember to call the updateAverageRating function to recalculate the average rating for the location. This should only be called if the delete operation is successful, of course.

And that is it. We've now built a REST API in Express and Node that can accept GET, POST, PUT, and DELETE HTTP requests to perform CRUD operations on a MongoDB database.

6.7   *Summary*

In this chapter we've covered

- The best practices for creating a REST API, including URLs, request methods, and response codes

- How the POST, GET, PUT, and DELETE HTTP request methods map onto common CRUD operations
- Mongoose helper methods for creating the helper methods
- Interacting with the data through Mongoose models, and how one instance of the model maps directly to one document in the database
- Managing subdocuments through their parent documents because you cannot access or save a subdocument in isolation
- Making the API robust by checking for any possible errors you can think of, so that a request is never left unanswered

Coming up next in chapter 7 we're going to see how to use this API from inside the Express application, finally making the Loc8r site database-driven!

7
Consuming a REST API: Using an API from inside Express

This chapter covers

- Calling an API from an Express application
- Handling and using data returned by the API
- Working with API response codes
- Submitting data from the browser back to the API
- Validation and error traps

This chapter is an exciting one! Here's where we tie the front end to the back end for the first time. We'll remove the hard-coded data from the controllers, and end up showing data from the database in the browser instead. On top of this we'll push data back from the browser into the database via the API, creating new subdocuments.

The technology focus for this chapter is on Node and Express. Figure 7.1 shows where this chapter fits into the overall architecture and our grand plan.

In this chapter we'll discuss how to call an API from within Express, and how to deal with the responses. We'll make calls to the API to read from the database and write to the database. Along the way we'll look at handling errors, processing data, and creating reusable code by separating concerns. Toward the end we'll cover the

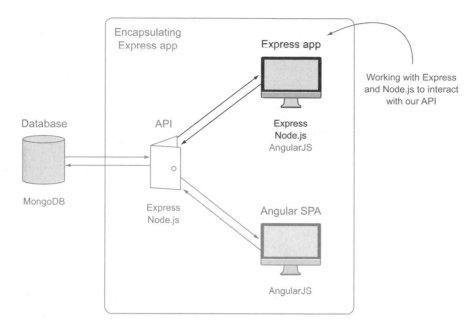

Figure 7.1 This chapter will focus on updating the Express application from chapter 4 to interact with the REST API developed in chapter 6.

various layers of the architecture to which we can add validation, and why these different layers are useful.

We'll start off by looking at how to call an API from the Express application.

7.1 How to call an API from Express

The first part we need to cover is how to call an API from Express. This isn't actually limited to our API; the approach can be used to call any API.

Our Express application needs to be able to call the API URLs that we set up in chapter 6—sending the correct request method, of course—and then be able to interpret the response. To help with doing this we'll use a module called request.

7.1.1 Adding the request module to our project

The request module is just like any of the other packages we've used so far, and can be added to our project using npm. To install the latest version and add it to the package.json file, head to terminal and type the following command:

```
$ npm install --save request
```

When npm has finished doing its thing, we can include request into the files that will use it. In Loc8r we only have one file that needs to make API calls, and that's the file with all of the controllers for the main server-side application. So right at the top of locations.js in app_server/controllers add the following line to `require request`:

```
var request = require('request');
```

Now we're good to go!

7.1.2   Setting up default options

Every API call with `request` must have a fully qualified URL, meaning that it must include the full address and not be a relative link. But this URL will be different for development and live environments.

To avoid having to make this check in every controller that makes an API call, we can set a default configuration option once at the top of the controllers file. To use the correct URL depending on the environment we can use our old friend the `NODE_ENV` environment variable.

Putting this into practice, the top of the controllers file should now look something like the following listing.

Listing 7.1   Adding request and default API options to the locations.js controllers file

```
var request = require('request');
var apiOptions = {
  server : "http://localhost:3000"          Set default server URL
};                                          for local development
if (process.env.NODE_ENV === 'production') {
  apiOptions.server = "https://getting-mean-loc8r.herokuapp.com";
}
```

If application running in production mode set different
base URL; change to be live address of application

With this in place every call we make to the API can reference `apiOptions.server` and will use the correct base URL.

7.1.3   Using the request module

The basic construct for making a request is really simple, being just a single command taking parameters for options and a callback like this:

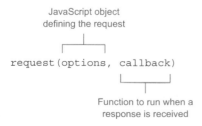

```
request(options, callback)
```

JavaScript object
defining the request

Function to run when a
response is received

The options specify everything for the request, including the URL, request method, request body, and query string parameters. These indeed are the options we'll be using in this chapter and they're detailed in table 7.1.

Table 7.1 Four common request options for defining a call to an API

Option	Description	Required
url	Full URL of the request to be made, including protocol, domain, path, and URL parameters	Yes
method	The method of the request, such as GET, POST, PUT, or DELETE	No—defaults to GET if not specified
json	The body of the request as a JavaScript object; an empty object should be sent if no body data is needed	Yes—ensures that the response body is also parsed as JSON
qs	A JavaScript object representing any query string parameters	No

The following code snippet shows an example of how you might put these together for a GET request. A GET request shouldn't have a body to send, but might have query string parameters.

```
var requestOptions = {
  url : "http://yourapi.com/api/path",          ◁── Define URL of API call to be made
  method : "GET",                               ◁── Set request method
  json : {},                                    ◁── Define body of request, even if it's an empty JSON object
  qs : {
    offset : 20                                 Optionally add any query string parameters that might be used by API
  }
};
```

There are many more options that you could specify, but these are the common four, and the ones we'll be using in this chapter. For more information on other possible options, take a look at the reference in the GitHub repository: https://github.com/mikeal/request.

The callback function runs when a response comes back from the API, and has three parameters: an error object, the full response, and the parsed body of the response. The error object will be null unless an error has been caught. Three pieces of data are going to be most useful in our code: the status code of the response, the body of the response, and any error thrown. The following code snippet shows an example of how you might structure a callback for the request function:

```
function(err, response, body) {
  if (err) {                                    If error has been passed
    console.log(err);                           through, do something with it
```

```
    } else if (response.statusCode === 200) {
      console.log(body);
    } else {
      console.log(response.statusCode);
    }
}
```

If response status code is 200 (request was successful), output JSON body of response

If response status wasn't 200, do something else

The full response object contains a huge amount of information, so we won't go into it here. You can always check it out yourself in a `console.log` statement when we start adding the API calls into our application.

Putting the parts together, the skeleton for making API calls looks like the following:

```
var requestOptions = {
  url : "http://yourapi.com/api/path",
  method : "GET",
  json : {},
  qs : {
    offset : 20
  }
};
request(requestOptions, function(err, response, body) {
  if (err) {
    console.log(err);
  } else if (response.statusCode === 200) {
    console.log(body);
  } else {
    console.log(response.statusCode);
  }
});
```

Define options for request

Make request, sending through options, and supplying a callback function to use responses as needed

Let's move on and put this theory into practice, and start building the Loc8r controllers to use the API we've already built.

7.2   Using lists of data from an API: The Loc8r homepage

By now the controllers file that will be doing the work should already have the `request` module required in, and some default values set. So now comes the fun part—let's update the controllers to call the API and pull the data for the pages from the database.

We've got two main pages that pull data: the homepage showing a list of locations, and a Details page giving more information about a specific location. Let's start at the beginning and get the data for the homepage from the database.

The current homepage controller contains just a `res.render` statement sending hard-coded data to the view. But the way we want it to work is to render the homepage after the API has returned some data. The homepage controller is going to have quite a lot to do anyway, so let's move this rendering into its own function.

7.2.1   *Separating concerns: Moving the rendering into a named function*

There are a couple of reasons for moving the rendering into its own named function. First, we decouple the rendering from the application logic. The process of rendering doesn't care where or how it got the data; if it's given data in the right format it will use it. Using a separate function helps us get closer to the testable ideal that each function should do just one thing. An additional bonus related to this is that it becomes reusable, so we can call it from multiple places.

The second reason for creating a new function for the homepage rendering is that the rendering process occurs inside the callback of the API request. As well as making the code hard to test, it also makes it hard to read. The level of nesting required makes for a rather large, heavily indented controller function. As a point of best practice you should try to avoid these, as they're hard to read and understand when you come back to them.

The first step is to make a new function called `renderHomepage` in the locations.js file in the app_server/controllers folder, and move the contents of the `homelist` controller into it. Remember to ensure it accepts the `req` and `res` parameters too. Listing 7.2 shows a very snipped down version of what we're doing here. You can now call this from the `homelist` controller, as also shown in the listing, and things will still work as before.

Listing 7.2   Moving the contents of the `homelist` controller into an external function

```
var renderHomepage = function(req, res){
  res.render('locations-list', {                          Include all code from
    title: 'Loc8r - find a place to work with wifi',      res.render call here
    ...                                                    (snipped down for brevity)
  });
};
module.exports.homelist = function(req, res){             Call new renderHomepage
  renderHomepage(req, res);                                function from homelist
};                                                         controller
```

This is a start, but we're not there yet—we want data!

7.2.2   *Building the API request*

We'll get the data we want by asking the API for it, and to do this we need to build the request. To build the request we need to know the URL, method, JSON body, and query string to send. Looking back at chapter 6, or indeed the API code itself, we can see that we need to supply the information shown in table 7.2.

Table 7.2   Information needed to make a request to the API for a list of locations

Parameter	Value
URL	`SERVER:PORT/api/locations`
Method	`GET`

Table 7.2   Information needed to make a request to the API for a list of locations (continued)

Parameter	Value
JSON body	`null`
Query string	`lng, lat, maxDistance`

Mapping this information into a request is quite straightforward. As we saw earlier in the chapter the options for a request are just a JavaScript object. For the time being we'll hard-code values for longitude and latitude into the options, as it's quicker and easier for testing. Later in the book we'll make the application location-aware. For now we'll choose coordinates close to where the test data is stored. The maximum distance is set to be 20 kilometers.

When we make the request we'll pass through a simple callback function to call the `renderHomepage` function so that we don't leave the browser hanging.

Putting this into code, into the `homelist` controller, looks like the following listing.

Listing 7.3   Update the `homelist` controller to call the API before rendering the page

```
module.exports.homelist = function(req, res){         Set path for API request
  var requestOptions, path;                            (server is already set
  path = '/api/locations';                             at top of file)
  requestOptions = {
    url : apiOptions.server + path,
    method : "GET",                              Set request options,
    json : {},                                   including URL, method,
    qs : {                                       empty JSON body, and
      lng : -0.7992599,                          hard-coded query
      lat : 51.378091,                           string parameters
      maxDistance : 20
    }
  };
  request(                                       Make request, sending
    requestOptions,                              through request options
    function(err, response, body) {
      renderHomepage(req, res);            Supplying callback to
    }                                      render homepage
  );
};
```

If you save this and run the application again, the homepage should display exactly as before. We might now be making a request to the API, but we're ignoring the response.

7.2.3   Using the API response data

Seeing as we're going to the effort of calling the API, the least we can do is use the data it's sending back. We can make this more robust later, but we'll start with making it work. In making it work we're going to assume that a response body is returned to the callback, and we can just pass this straight into the renderHomepage funtion, as highlighted in the following listing.

> **Listing 7.4   Update the contents of the `homelist` controller to use the API response**

```
request(
  requestOptions,
  function(err, response, body) {
    renderHomepage(req, res, body);
  }
);
```

> ◁── Pass body returned by request to renderHomepage function

Seeing as we coded the API, we know that the response body returned by the API should be an array of locations. The renderHomepage function needs an array of locations to send to the view, so let's try just passing it straight through, making the changes highlighted in bold in the following listing.

> **Listing 7.5   Update the `renderHomepage` function to use the data from the API**

```
var renderHomepage = function(req, res, responseBody) {
  res.render('locations-list', {
    title: 'Loc8r - find a place to work with wifi',
    pageHeader: {
      title: 'Loc8r',
      strapline: 'Find places to work with wifi near you!'
    },
    sidebar: "Looking for wifi and a seat? Loc8r helps you find places to
     work when out and about. Perhaps with coffee, cake or a pint? Let Loc8r
     help you find the place you're looking for.",
    locations: responseBody
  });
},
```

> ◁── Add additional responseBody parameter to function declaration

> ◁── Remove hard-coded array of locations and pass responseBody through instead

Can it really be that easy? Try it out in the browser and see what happens. Hopefully you'll get something like figure 7.2.

That looks pretty good, right? We need to do something about how the distance is displayed, but other than that all of the data is coming through as we wanted. Plugging in the data was quick and easy because of the work we did upfront designing the views, building controllers based on the views, and developing the model based on the controllers.

We've made it work. Now we need to make it better. There's no error trapping yet, and the distances need some work.

7.2.4   *Modifying data before displaying it: Fixing the distances*

At the moment the distances in the list are displaying 15 decimal places and no unit of measurement, so they're extremely accurate and totally useless! We want to say

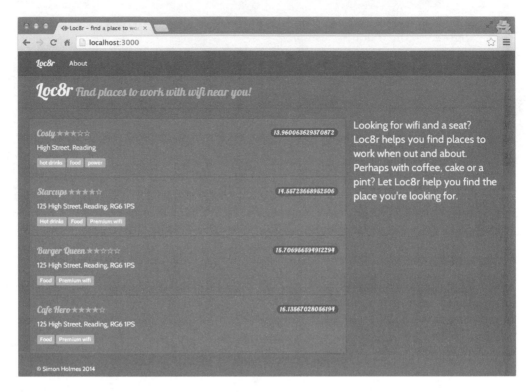

Figure 7.2   The first look at using data from the database in the browser—it's pretty close!

whether each distance is in meters or kilometers, and round the numbers off to the nearest meter or to one decimal place of a kilometer. This should be done before sending the data to the `renderHomepage` function, as that function should just be reserved for handling the actual rendering, not sorting out the data.

To do this we need to loop through the array of returned locations, formatting the distance value of each one. Rather than doing this inline we'll create an external function (in the same file) called `_formatDistance` that accepts a distance value and returns it nicely formatted.

Putting this all together looks like the following listing. Note that the framework of the `homelist` controller has been left out in this code snippet to keep things short, and the `request` statement still sits inside the controller.

Listing 7.6   Adding and using a function to format the distance returned by the API

```
request(
  requestOptions,
  function(err, response, body) {
    var i, data;
    data = body;
```

Assign returned
body data to a
new variable

```
    for (i=0; i<data.length; i++) {
      data[i].distance = _formatDistance(data[i].distance);
    }
    renderHomepage(req, res, data);
  }
);

var _formatDistance = function (distance) {
  var numDistance, unit;
  if (distance > 1) {
    numDistance = parseFloat(distance).toFixed(1);
    unit = 'km';
  } else {
    numDistance = parseInt(distance * 1000,10);
    unit = 'm';
  }
  return numDistance + unit;
};
```

Loop through array, formatting distance value of location

Send modified data to be rendered instead of original body

If supplied distance is over 1 km, round to one decimal place and add km unit

Otherwise convert to meters and round to nearest meter before adding m unit

If you make these changes and refresh the page you should see that the distances are now tidied up a bit and are actually useful, as shown in figure 7.3.

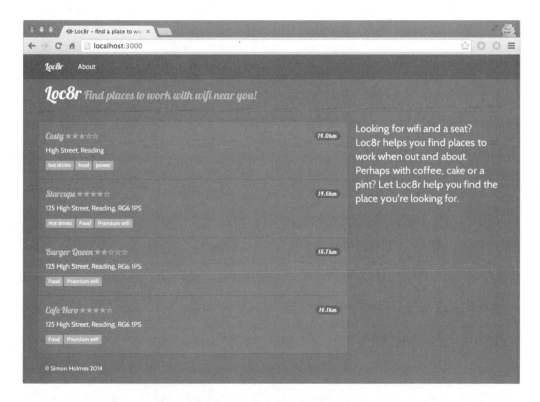

Figure 7.3   The homepage is looking better again after formatting the distances returned by the API.

That's better; the homepage is now looking more like we want it. For extra credit you can add some error trapping to the _formatDistance function to make sure that a distance parameter has been passed, and that it's a number.

7.2.5   *Catching errors returned by the API*

So far we've assumed that the API is always going to return an array of data along with a 200 success code. But this isn't necessarily the case. We coded the API to return a 200 status even if no locations are found nearby. As things stand, when this happens the homepage will display without any content in the central area. A far better user experience will be to output a message to the user that there are no places nearby.

We also know that our API can give 404 errors, so we'll need to make sure we handle these appropriately. We don't really want to show a 404 to the user in this case, because the error will not be due to the homepage itself being missing. The better option again here is to send a message to the browser in the context of the homepage.

Handling these scenarios shouldn't be too difficult; let's see how to do it, starting with the controller.

MAKING THE REQUEST CALLBACK MORE ROBUST

One of the main reasons for catching errors is to make sure that they don't cause code to fail. The first point of weakness is going to be in the request callback where we're manipulating the response before sending the data off to be rendered. This is fine if the data is always going to be consistent, but we don't have that luxury.

The request callback currently runs a for loop to format the distances no matter what data is returned by the API. We should really only run this when the API returns a 200 code and some results.

The following listing shows how we can easily achieve this by adding in a simple if statement, checking the status code and the length of the returned data.

Listing 7.7   Validate that the API has returned some data before trying to use it

```
request(
  requestOptions,
  function(err, response, body) {              Only run loop to
    var i, data;                               format distances if API
    data = body;                               returned a 200 status
    if (response.statusCode === 200 && data.length) {   and some data
      for (i=0; i<data.length; i++) {
        data[i].distance = _formatDistance(data[i].distance);
      }
    }
    renderHomepage(req, res, data);
  }
);
```

Updating this piece of code should prevent this callback from falling over and throwing an error if the API responds with a status code other than 200. The next link in the chain is the renderHomepage function.

DEFINING OUTPUT MESSAGES BASED ON THE RESONSE DATA

Just like the `request` callback, our original focus for the `renderHomepage` function is to make it work when passed an array of locations to display. Now that this might be sent different data types we need to make it handle the possibilities appropriately.

The response body could be one of three things:

- An array of locations
- An empty array, when no locations are found
- A string containing a message when the API returns an error

We already have the code in place to deal with an array of locations, so we need to address the other two possibilities. When catching these errors we also want to set a message that can be sent to the view.

To do this we need to update the `renderHomepage` function to also do the following:

- Set a variable container for a message.
- Check to see whether the response body is an array; if not, set an appropriate message.
- If the response is an array, set a different message if it's empty (that is, no locations are returned).
- Send the message to the view.

The following listing shows how this looks in code.

Listing 7.8   Outputting messages if the API doesn't return location data

```
var renderHomepage = function(req, res, responseBody){          Define a variable
  var message;                                                  to hold a message
  if (!(responseBody instanceof Array)) {              If response isn't array, set
    message = "API lookup error";                      message, and set responseBody
    responseBody = [];                                 to be empty array
  } else {
    if (!responseBody.length) {                        If response is array with
      message = "No places found nearby";              no length, set message
    }
  }
  res.render('locations-list', {
    title: 'Loc8r - find a place to work with wifi',
    pageHeader: {
      title: 'Loc8r',
      strapline: 'Find places to work with wifi near you!'
    },
    sidebar: "Looking for wifi and a seat? Loc8r helps you find places to
     work when out and about. Perhaps with coffee, cake or a pint? Let Loc8r
     help you find the place you're looking for.",
    locations: responseBody,
    message: message                        Add message to variables
  });                                       to send to view
};
```

The only surprise in there is when we set the `responseBody` to be an empty array if it was originally passed through as a string. We've done this to prevent the view from throwing an error. The view expects an array to be sent in the `locations` variable; it effectively ignores it if an empty array is sent, but will throw an error if a string is sent.

The last link in this chain is to update the view to display a message when one is sent.

UPDATING THE VIEW TO DISPLAY THE ERROR MESSAGES

So we're catching the errors from the API, and we're now also working with them to pass something back to the user. The final step is to let the user see the message by adding a placeholder into the view template.

We don't need to do anything fancy here—a simple `div` with a class of error to contain any messages will suffice. The following listing shows the `block content` section of the homepage view `locations-list.jade` in app_server/views.

> **Listing 7.9   Update the view to display an error message when needed**

```
block content
  #banner.page-header
    .row
      .col-lg-6
        h1= pageHeader.title
          small  #{pageHeader.strapline}
  .row
    .col-xs-12.col-sm-8
      .error= message          ← Add a div into main
      .row.list-group              content area and have
        each location in locations   it display a message if
          .col-xs-12.list-group-item  one is sent
            h4
              a(href="/location")= location.name
              small  
                +outputRating(location.rating)
              span.badge.pull-right.badge-default= location.distance
            p.address= location.address
            p
              each facility in location.facilities
                span.label.label-warning= facility
                 
    .col-xs-12.col-sm-4
      p.lead= sidebar
```

That's pretty easy—basic, but easy. It will certainly do for now. All that's left is to test it.

TESTING THE API ERROR TRAPPING

As with any new code, we now need to make sure that it works. A really easy way to test this is by changing the query string values that we're sending in the `requestOptions`.

To test the "no places found nearby" trap we can either set the `maxDistance` to a very small number (remembering that it's specified in kilometers), or set the `lng` and `lat` to a point where there are no locations. For example

```
requestOptions = {
  url : apiOptions.server + path,
  method : "GET",
  json : {},
  qs : {
    lng : 1,                      Change query string values
    lat : 1,                      sent in request to get no
    maxDistance : 0.002           results returned
  }
};
```

Fixing an interesting bug

Did you try testing the API error trapping by setting `lng` or `lat` to 0? You should have been expecting to see the "No places found nearby" message, but instead saw "API lookup error." This is due to a bug in the error trapping in our API code.

In the `locationsListByDistance` controller, check to see whether the `lng` and `lat` query string parameters have been omitted by using a generic "falsey" JavaScript test. Our code simply has this: `if (!lng || !lat)`.

In falsey tests like this, JavaScript looks for any of the values that it considers to be false, such as an empty string, undefined, `null`, and, importantly for us, 0. This introduces an unexpected bug into our code. If someone happened to be on the equator or on the Prime Meridian (that's the Greenwich Mean Time line) they'd receive an API error.

This can be fixed by verifying the falsey test to say, "If it's false but not zero." In code this looks like this: `if ((!lng && lng!==0) || (!lat && lat!==0))`.

Updating your controller in the API will remove this bug.

You can use a similar tactic to test the `404` error. The API expects all of the query string parameters to be sent, and will return a `404` if one of them is missing. So to quickly test the code you can just comment one of them out as shown in the following code snippet:

```
requestOptions = {
  url : apiOptions.server + path,
  method : "GET",
  json : {},
  qs : {                             Comment out one query
    // lng : -0.7992599,             string parameter in request
    lat : 51.378091,                 to help test what happens
    maxDistance : 20                 when API returns 404
  }
};
```

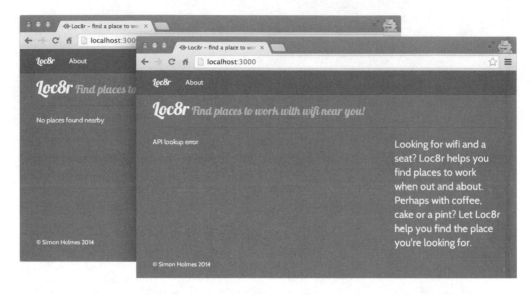

Figure 7.4   Showing the error message in the views after trapping the errors being returned by the API

Do these two things one at a time and refresh the homepage to see the different messages coming through. These are shown in figure 7.4.

That shows the homepage set up nicely. Our Express application is querying the API we built, which pulls data from the MongoDB database and passes it back to the application. When the application gets a response from the API, it works out what to do with it and either shows the data or an error message in the browser.

Now let's do the same thing for the Details page, this time working with single instances of data.

7.3   Getting single documents from an API: The Loc8r Details page

The Details page should display all of the information we have about a specific location, from the name and address, to ratings, reviews, facilities, and a location map. At the moment this is using data hard-coded into the controller, and looks like figure 7.5.

In this section we'll update the application to allow us to specify which location we want the details for, get the details from the API, and output them to the browser. We'll also add in some error trapping, of course.

7.3.1   Setting URLs and routes to access specific MongoDB documents

The current path we have to the Details page is just `/location`. This doesn't offer a way to specify which location we want to look at. To address this we can borrow the

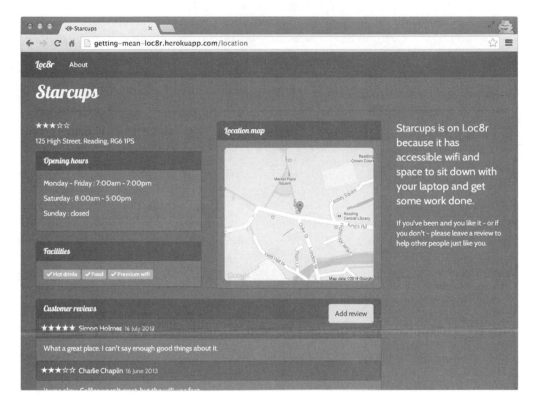

Figure 7.5   The Details page as it is now, using data hard-coded into the controller

approach from the API routes, where we specify the ID of the location document as a URL parameter.

The API route for a single location is /api/locations/:locationid. We can do the same thing for the main Express application and update the route to contain the `locationid` parameter. The main application routes for locations are in locations.js in the /routes folder. The following code snippet shows the simple change needed to update the location detail route to accept the `locationid` URL parameter:

```
router.get('/', ctrlLocations.homelist);
router.get('/location/:locationid', ctrlLocations.locationInfo);   ⟵─── Add locationid parameter to route for single location
router.get('/location/review/new', ctrlLocations.addReview);
```

Okay, great … but where do we get the IDs of the locations from? Thinking about the application as a whole, the homepage is the best place to start, as that's where the links for the Details page come from.

When the API for the homepage returns an array of locations, each location object contains its unique ID. This entire object is already passed to the view, so it shouldn't be too difficult to update the homepage view to add this ID as a URL parameter.

It's not difficult at all in fact! The following listing shows the little change that needs to be made in the locations-list.jade file to append the unique ID of each location to the link through to the Details page.

Listing 7.10   Update the list view to add the location ID to the relevant links

```
block content
  #banner.page-header
    .row
      .col-lg-6
        h1= pageHeader.title
          small  #{pageHeader.strapline}
  .row
    .col-xs-12.col-sm-8
      .error= message
      .row.list-group
        each location in locations
          .col-xs-12.list-group-item
            h4
              a(href="/location/#{location._id}")= location.name
              small  
                +outputRating(location.rating)
              span.badge.pull-right.badge-default= location.distance
            p.address= location.address
            p
              each facility in location.facilities
                span.label.label-warning= facility
                 
    .col-xs-12.col-sm-4
      p.lead= sidebar
```

As each location in array is looped through, pull unique ID from object and append it to href for link to Details page

If only everything in life was that easy. The homepage now contains unique links for each of the locations, and they all click through to the Details page. Now we just need to make them show the correct data.

7.3.2   *Separating concerns: Moving the rendering into a named function*

Just like we did for the homepage, we'll move the rendering of the Details page into its own named function. Again, this is to keep the rendering functionality separate from the API call and data processing.

The following listing shows a trimmed-down version of the new `renderDetailPage` function, and how it's called from the `locationInfo` controller.

Listing 7.11 Move the contents of the `locationInfo` controller into an external function

```
var renderDetailPage = function (req, res) {
  res.render('location-info', {
    title: 'Starcups',
    ...
  });
};
module.exports.locationInfo = function(req, res){
  renderDetailPage(req, res);
};
```

Create new function called renderDetailPage and move all contents of locationInfo controller into it

◁— Call new function from controller, remembering to pass it req and res parameters

Now we're set up with a nice, clear controller, ready to query the API.

7.3.3 Querying the API using a unique ID from a URL parameter

The URL for the API call needs to contain the ID of the location. Our Details page now has this ID as the URL parameter `locationid`, so we can get the value of this using `req.params` and add it to the `path` in the request options. The request is a GET request, and as such the `json` value will be an empty object.

Knowing all of this we can use the pattern we created in the homepage controller to build and make the request to the API. We'll call the `renderDetailPage` function when the API responds. All of this is shown together in the following listing.

Listing 7.12 Update the `locationInfo` controller to call the API

```
module.exports.locationInfo = function(req, res){
  var requestOptions, path;
  path = "/api/locations/" + req.params.locationid;
  requestOptions = {
    url : apiOptions.server + path,
    method : "GET",
    json : {}
  };
  request(
    requestOptions,
    function(err, response, body) {
      renderDetailPage(req, res);
    }
  );
};
```

Get locationid parameter from URL and append it to API path

Set all request options needed to call API

◁—| Call renderDetailPage function when API has responded

If you run this now you'll see the same static data as before, as we're not yet passing the data returned from the API into the view. You can add some console log statements into the `request` callback if you want to have a quick look at what's being returned.

If you're happy that all is working as it should, it's time for us to pass the data into the view.

7.3.4   *Passing the data from the API to the view*

We're currently assuming that the API is returning the correct data—we'll get around to error trapping soon. This data only needs a small amount of preprocessing: the coordinates are returned from the API as an array, but the view needs them to be named key-value pairs in an object.

The following listing shows how we can do this in the context of the request statement, transforming the data from the API before sending it to the renderDetailPage function.

Listing 7.13   Preprocessing data in the controller

```
request(
  requestOptions,
  function(err, response, body) {        Create copy of returned
    var data = body;              ◁       data in new variable
    data.coords = {
      lng : body.coords[0],              Reset coords property to be an
      lat : body.coords[1]               object, setting lng and lat using
    };                                    values pulled from API response
    renderDetailPage(req, res, data);   ◁
  }                                      Send transformed
);                                      data to be rendered
```

The next logical step is to update the renderDetailPage function to use this data rather than the hard-coded data. To make this work we need to make sure that the function accepts the data as a parameter, and then update the values passed through to the view as required. The following listing highlights the changes needed in bold.

Listing 7.14   Update renderDetailPage to accept and use data from the API

```
                                                       Add new parameter for
var renderDetailPage = function (req, res, locDetail) {  ◁  data in function definition
  res.render('location-info', {
    title: locDetail.name,                 Reference specific items of
    pageHeader: {title: locDetail.name},   data as needed in function
    sidebar: {
      context: 'is on Loc8r because it has accessible wifi and space to sit
      down with your laptop and get some work done.',
      callToAction: 'If you\'ve been and you like it - or if you don\'t -
      please leave a review to help other people just like you.'
    },
    location: locDetail            ◁    Pass full locDetail data object
  });                                    to view, containing all details
};
```

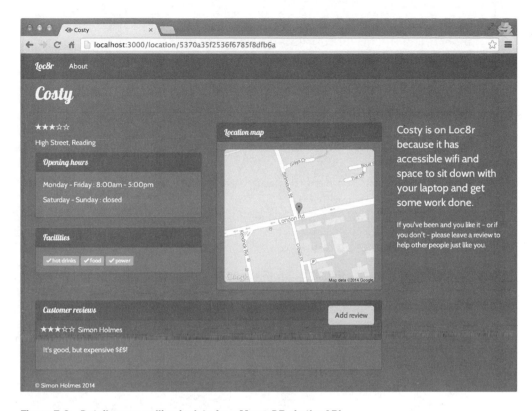

Figure 7.6   Details page pulling in data from MongoDB via the API

We're able to take the approach of sending the full object through like this, because we originally based the data model on what was needed by the view and the controller. If you run the application now you should see that the page loads with the data pulled from the database. A screenshot of this is shown in figure 7.6.

The eagle-eyed reader will have noticed a problem with the screenshot in figure 7.6. The review doesn't have a date associated with it.

7.3.5   Debugging and fixing the view errors

So, we have a problem with the view. It's not outputting the review date correctly. Perhaps we shouldn't have gotten overconfident about the fact that our data model was based on the view and controller? Let's take a look at what's going on.

Starting with a look at the Jade file location—info.jade in app_server/views—we can isolate the line that outputs this section:

```
small.reviewTimestamp #{review.timestamp}
```

Now we need to check the schema to see if we changed something when defining the model. The schema for reviews is in locations.js in app_api/models, and looks like the following code snippet:

```
var reviewSchema = new mongoose.Schema({
  author: String,
  rating: {type: Number, required: true, min: 0, max: 5},
  reviewText: String,
  createdOn: {type: Date, "default": Date.now}
});
```

Ah yes, here we can see that we changed the timestamp to be called `createdOn`, which is a more accurate name for the path.

Updating the Jade file using these values looks like the following:

```
small.reviewTimestamp #{review.createdOn}
```

Making these changes and refreshing the page gives us figure 7.7.

Figure 7.7   Pulling the name and date directly from the returned data; the format of the date isn't very user friendly

Success! Of sorts. The date is now showing, but not quite in the user-readable format that we'd like to see. We should be able to fix this using Jade.

FORMATTING DATES USING A JADE MIXIN

Back when we were setting up the views we used a Jade mixin to output the rating stars based on the rating number provided. In Jade, mixins are like functions—you can send parameters when you call them, run some JavaScript code if you wish, and have them generate some output.

Formatting dates is something that could be useful in a number of places, so let's create a mixin to do it. Our `outputRating` mixin is in the sharedHTMLfunctions.jade file in app_server/views/_includes. Let's add a new mixin called `formatDate` to that file.

In this mixin we'll largely use JavaScript to convert the date from the long ISO format into the more readable format of *Day Month Year*, for example *24 June 2014*. The ISO date object actually arrives here as a string, so the first thing to do is convert it into a JavaScript date object. When that's done we'll be able to use various JavaScript date methods to access the various parts of the date.

The following listing shows how this is done in a mixin—remember that lines of JavaScript in a Jade file must be prefixed with a dash.

Listing 7.15   Create a Jade mixin to format the dates

Set up array of values for names of months

Convert date provided from string to date object

Use JavaScript data methods to extract and convert required parts of date

Put parts back together in desired format and render output

```
mixin formatDate(dateString)
  -var date = new Date(dateString);
  -var monthNames = [ "January", "February", "March", "April", "May", "June",
    "July", "August", "September", "October", "November", "December" ];
  -var d = date.getDate();
  -var m = monthNames[date.getMonth()];
  -var y = date.getFullYear();
  -var output = d + ' ' + m + ' ' + y;
  =output
```

That mixin will now take a date and process it to output in the format that we want. As the mixin will render the output, we simply need to call it from the correct place in the code. The following code demonstrates this, again based on the same two isolated lines from the whole template:

Call mixin from its own line, passing creation date of review; make sure that new line is correctly indented

```
span.reviewAuthor #{review.author.displayName}
small.reviewTimestamp
  +formatDate(review.createdOn)
```

The call to the mixin should be placed on a new line, so you'll need to remember to take care with the indentation—the date should be nested inside the <small> tag.

Now the Details page is complete and looking like it should, as shown in figure 7.8.

Excellent; that's exactly what we wanted. If the URL contains an ID that's found in the database then the page displays nicely. But what happens if the ID is wrong, or isn't found in the database?

7.3.6   *Creating status-specific error pages*

If the ID from the URL isn't found in the database, the API will return a 404 error. This error originates from the URL in the browser, so the browser should also return a 404—the data for the ID wasn't found, so in essence the page cannot be found.

Using techniques we've already seen in this chapter we can quite easily catch when the API returns a 404 status, using response.statusCode in the request callback. We don't really want to deal with it inside the callback, so we'll just pass the flow into a new function that we can call, _showError.

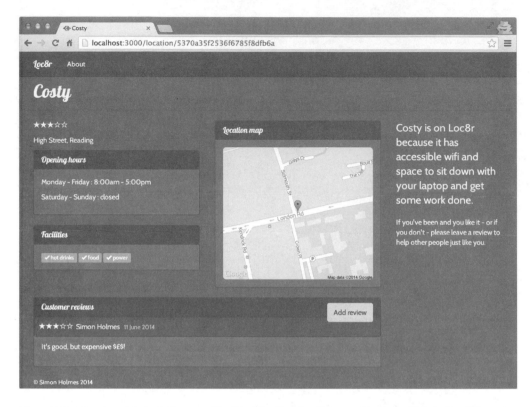

Figure 7.8   The complete Details page. The ID of the location is passed from the URL to the API, and the API retrieves the data and passes it back to the page to be formatted and rendered correctly.

CATCHING ALL ERROR CODES

Even better than just trapping for a 404 response, we can flip it over and look for any response from the API that isn't a 200 success response. We can pass the status code to the _showError function and let it figure out what to do. To enable the _showError function to keep control we'll also pass through the req and res objects.

The following listing shows how to update the request callback to render the Details page for successful API calls, and route all other errors to the catch-all function _showError.

Listing 7.16   Trap any errors caused by the API not returning a 200 status

```
request(
  requestOptions,
  function(err, response, body) {
    var data - body;
    if (response.statusCode === 200) {
```

Check for successful
response from API

```
      data.coords = {
        lng : body.coords[0],
        lat : body.coords[1]
      };
      renderDetailPage(req, res, data);
    } else {
      _showError(req, res, response.statusCode);
    }
  }
);
```

Continue with rendering page if check successful

If check wasn't successful, pass error through to _showError function

Great, so now we'll only try to render the Details page if we have something from the API to display. So what shall we do with the errors? Well, for now we just want to send a message to the users letting them know that there's a problem.

DISPLAYING ERROR MESSAGES

We don't want to do anything fancy here, just let the user know that something is going on and give them some indication of what it is. We have a generic Jade template already that's suitable for this; in fact, it's called generic-text.jade and expects just a title and some content. That will do us.

If you wanted to you could create a unique page and layout for each type of error, but for now we're good with just catching it and letting the user know. As well as letting the user know, we should also let the browser know by returning the appropriate status code when the page is displayed.

Listing 7.17 shows what the _showError function looks like, accepting a status parameter that, as well as being passed through as the response status code, is also used to define the title and content of the page. Here we have a specific message for a 404 page and a generic message for any other errors that are passed.

Listing 7.17   Create an error-handling function for API status codes that aren't 200

If status passed through is 404, set title and content for page

```
var _showError = function (req, res, status) {
  var title, content;
  if (status === 404) {
    title = "404, page not found";
    content = "Oh dear. Looks like we can't find this page. Sorry.";
  } else {
    title = status + ", something's gone wrong";
    content = "Something, somewhere, has gone just a little bit wrong.";
  }
  res.status(status);
  res.render('generic-text', {
    title : title,
    content : content
  });
};
```

Use status parameter to set response status

Send data to view to be compiled and sent to browser

Otherwise set a generic catch-all message

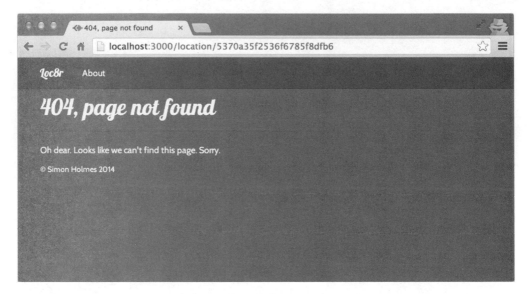

Figure 7.9   The 404 error page displayed when the location ID in the URL isn't found in the database by the API

This function can be reused from any of the controllers where we might find it useful. It's also built in such a way that we can easily add new, specific error messages for particular codes if we want to.

You can test the 404 error page by just slightly changing the location ID in the URL, and you should see something like figure 7.9.

That brings us to the end of the Details page. We can successfully display all of the information from the database for a given location, and also display a 404 message to the visitor if the location can't be found.

Following through the user journey, our next and final task is to add the ability to add reviews.

7.4   Adding data to the database via the API: Add Loc8r reviews

In this section we'll see how to take form data submitted by a user, process it, and post it to the API. Reviews are added to Loc8r by clicking the Add Review button on a location's Details page, filling in a form, and submitting it. At least that's the plan anyway. We currently have the screens to do this, but not the underlying functionality to make it happen. We're going to change that right now.

Here's a quick list of the things we're going to need to do:

1   Make the review form aware of which location the review will be for.
2   Create a route for the form to POST to.

3 Send the new review data to the API.

4 Show the new review in place on the Details page.

Note that at this stage in the development we don't have an authentication method in place, so we have no concept of user accounts.

7.4.1 *Setting up the routing and views*

The first item on our list is really about getting the ID of the location to the Add Review page in a way that we can use it when the form is submitted. After all, this is the unique identifier that the API will need to add a review.

The best approach for getting the ID to the page will be to contain it in the URL, like we did for the Details page itself.

DEFINING THE TWO REVIEW ROUTES

Getting the location ID into the URL will mean changing the route of the Add Review page to add a `locationid` parameter. While we're at it, we can deal with the second item on the list and create a route for the form to POST to. Ideally, this should have the same path as the review form, and be associated with a different request method and different controller.

The following code snippet shows how we can update the routes in index.js in the /routes folder:

> Insert locationid parameter into existing route for review form

```
router.get('/', ctrlLocations.homelist);
router.get('/location/:locationid', ctrlLocations.locationInfo);
router.get('/location/:locationid/reviews/new', ctrlLocations.addReview);
router.post('/location/:locationid/reviews/new', ctrlLocations.doAddReview);
```

> Create new route on same URL but using POST method and referencing different controller

Those are all of the routes we'll need for this section, but restarting the application will fail because the POST route references a controller that doesn't exist. We can fix this by adding a placeholder function into the controller file. Add the following code snippet into locations.js in app_server/controllers and the application will fire up successfully once again:

```
module.exports.doAddReview = function(req, res){
};
```

Now the application will start again, but if you click through to the Add Review page you'll get an error. Oh yes, we need to update the link to the Add Review page from the Details page.

FIXING THE LOCATION DETAIL VIEW

We need to add the location ID to the `href` specified in the Add Review button on the Details page. The controller for this page passes through the full data object as returned from the API, which, along with the rest of the data, will contain the `_id` field. This data object is called `location` when passed to the view.

The following code snippet shows a single line from the location-info.jade template in the app_server/views folder. This shows how to add the location ID to the link for the Add Review button.

```
a.btn.btn-default.pull-right(href="/location/#{location._id}/reviews/new")
| Add review
```

With that updated and saved, we can now click through to a review form for each individual location. There are just a couple of issues here: the form still doesn't post anywhere, and the name of the location is currently hard-coded into the controller.

UPDATING THE REVIEW FORM VIEW

Next we want to make sure that the form posts to the correct URL. When the form is submitted now, it just makes a GET request to the `/location` URL as shown in the following code snippet:

```
form.form-horizontal(action="/location", method="get", role="form")
```

This line is taken from the location-review-form.jade file in app_server/views. The `/location` path is no longer valid in our application, and we also want to use a POST request instead of a GET request. The URL we want to post the form to is actually the same as the URL for the Add Review: `/location/:locationid/reviews/new`.

A really easy way to achieve this is to set the action of the form to be an empty string, and set the method to be `post`, as shown in the following code snippet:

```
form.form-horizontal(action="", method="post", role="form")
```

Now when the form is submitted it will make a POST request to the URL of the current page.

CREATING A NAMED FUNCTION FOR RENDERING THE ADD REVIEW PAGE

As with the other pages, we'll move the rendering of the page into a separate named function. This allows us the separation of concerns we're looking for when coding, and prepares us for the next steps.

The following listing shows how this should look in the code.

> **Listing 7.18   Create an external function to hold the contents of the `addReview` controller**

```
var renderReviewForm = function (req, res) {
  res.render('location-review-form', {
    title: 'Review Starcups on Loc8r',
    pageHeader: { title: 'Review Starcups' }
  });
};
/* GET 'Add review' page */
module.exports.addReview = function(req, res){
  renderReviewForm(req, res);
};
```

Create new function render-
ReviewForm and move contents
of addReview controller into it

Call new function from within
addReview controller, passing
through same parameters

This might look a little odd, creating a named function and then having the call to that function be the only thing in the controller, but it will be very useful in just a moment.

GETTING THE LOCATION DETAIL

On the Add Review page we want to display the name of the location in order to retain a sense of context for the user. This means we want to hit the API again, give it the ID of the location, and get the information back to the controller and into the view. We've just done this for the Details page, albeit with a different controller. If we approach this right we shouldn't have to write much new code.

Rather than duplicating the code and having to maintain two pieces, we'll go for a DRY (don't repeat yourself) approach. The Details page and the Add Review page both want to call the API to get the location information and then do something with it. So why not create a new function that does just this? We've already got most of the code in the `locationInfo` controller, we just need to change how it calls the final function. Instead of calling the `renderDetailPage` explicitly, we'll make it a callback.

So we'll have a new function called `getLocationInfo` that will make the API request. Following a successful request, this should then invoke whatever callback function was passed. The `locationInfo` controller will now call this function, passing a callback function that simply calls the `renderDetailPage` function. Similarly, the `addReview` controller can also call this new function, passing it the `renderReviewForm` function in the callback.

This gives us one function making the API calls that will have different outcomes depending on the callback function sent through. The following listing shows this all in place.

> **Listing 7.19   Create a new reusable function to get location information**

```
var getLocationInfo = function (req, res, callback) {
  var requestOptions, path;
  path = "/api/locations/" + req.params.locationid;
  requestOptions = {
    url : apiOptions.server + path,
    method : "GET",
```

New function getLocationInfo
accepts callback as third
parameter and contains all
code that used to be in
locationInfo controller

```
      json : {}
    };
    request(
      requestOptions,
      function(err, response, body) {
        var data = body;
        if (response.statusCode === 200) {
          data.coords = {
            lng : body.coords[0],
            lat : body.coords[1]
          };
          callback(req, res, data);
        } else {
          _showError(req, res, response.statusCode);
        }
      }
    );
};

module.exports.locationInfo = function(req, res){
  getLocationInfo(req, res, function(req, res, responseData) {
    renderDetailPage(req, res, responseData);
  });
};

module.exports.addReview = function(req, res){
  getLocationInfo(req, res, function(req, res, responseData) {
    renderReviewForm(req, res, responseData);
  });
};
```

Following successful API response, invoke callback instead of named function

In locationInfo controller call getLocationInfo function, passing a callback function that will call renderDetailPage function upon completion

Also call getLocationInfo from addReview controller, but this time pass renderReviewForm in callback

> **TIP**   If this approach of creating your own callback handlers is new or confusing to you, take a look online at appendix D, particularly section D.4, "Understanding JavaScript callbacks."

And there we have a nice DRY approach to the problem. It would have been very easy to just copy and paste the API code from one controller to another, which, if we're being honest, is absolutely fine if you're figuring out your code and what you need to make it work. But when you see two pieces of code doing pretty much exactly the same thing, always ask yourself how you can make it DRY—it makes your code cleaner and easier to maintain.

DISPLAYING THE LOCATION DETAIL

We're forgetting one thing here. The function for rendering the form still contains hard-coded data instead of using the data from the API. A quick tweak to the function will change that, as is illustrated in the following listing.

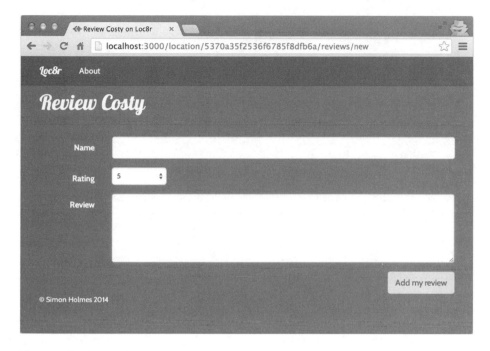

Figure 7.10 Add Review page pulling in the location name via the API, based on the ID contained in the URL

> **Listing 7.20 Removing hard-coded data from the `renderReviewForm` function**

```
var renderReviewForm = function (req, res, locDetail) {     ◁─┐
  res.render('location-review-form', {
    title: 'Review ' + locDetail.name + ' on Loc8r',
    pageHeader: { title: 'Review ' + locDetail.name }
  });
};
```

> **Update renderReview-Form function to accept new parameter containing data**

> **Swap out hard-coded data for data references**

And with that the Add Review page is looking good once again, displaying the correct name based on the ID found in the URL, as shown in figure 7.10.

7.4.2 POSTing the review data to the API

By now we have the Add Review page set up and ready to go, including the posting destination. We've even got the route and controller for the POST action in place. The controller, `doAddReview`, is just an empty placeholder, though.

The plan for this controller is as follows:

1 Get the location ID from the URL to construct the API request URL.
2 Get the data posted in the form and package it up for the API.

3 Make the API call.

4 Show the new review in place if successful.

5 Display an error page if not successful.

The only part of this that we haven't seen yet is passing the data to the API; so far we've just passed an empty JSON object to ensure that the response is formatted as JSON. Now we're going to take the form data and pass it to the API in the format it expects. We have three fields on the form, and three references that the API expects. All we need to do is map one to the other. The form fields and model paths are shown in table 7.3.

Table 7.3   Mapping the names of the form fields to the model paths expected by the API

Form field	API references
name	author
rating	rating
review	reviewText

Turning this mapping into a JavaScript object is pretty straightforward. We just need to create a new object containing the variable names that the API expects, and use `req.body` to get the values from the posted form. The following code snippet shows this in isolation, and we'll put it into the controller in just a moment:

```
var postdata = {
  author: req.body.name,
  rating: parseInt(req.body.rating, 10),
  reviewText: req.body.review
};
```

Now that we've seen how that works, we can add it into the standard pattern we've been using for these API controllers and build out the `doAddReview` controller. Remember that the status code the API returns for a successful POST operation is `201`, not the `200` we've been using so far with the GET requests. The following listing shows the `doAddReview` controller using everything we've learned so far.

Listing 7.21   `doAddReview` controller used to post review data to the API

```
module.exports.doAddReview = function(req, res){
  var requestOptions, path, locationid, postdata;
  locationid = req.params.locationid;                          Get location ID from URL
  path = "/api/locations/" + locationid + '/reviews';          to construct API URL
  postdata = {
    author: req.body.name,                                     Create data object
    rating: parseInt(req.body.rating, 10),                     to send to API using
    reviewText: req.body.review                                submitted form data
  };
```

```
requestOptions = {
  url : apiOptions.server + path,        Set request options, including path, setting
  method : "POST",                       POST method and passing submitted form
  json : postdata                        data into json parameter
};
request(                          ◁─────── Make the
  requestOptions,                          request
  function(err, response, body) {
    if (response.statusCode === 201) {     Redirect to Details page if
      res.redirect('/location/' + locationid);   review was added successfully
    } else {                               or show an error page if API
      _showError(req, res, response.statusCode);   returned an error
    }
  }
);
};
```

Now we can create a review and submit it, and then see it on the Details page, as shown in figure 7.11.

Now that it all works, let's take a quick look at adding form validation.

7.5   *Protecting data integrity with data validation*

Whenever an application accepts external input and adds it to a database you need to make sure that the data is complete and accurate—as much as you can, or as much as it makes sense to. For example, if someone is adding an email address you should check that it's a valid email format, but you can't programmatically validate that it's a *real* email address.

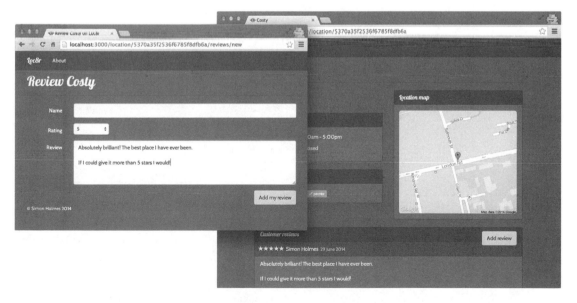

Figure 7.11   After filling in and submitting the review form, the review is shown in situ on the Details page.

In this section we're going to look at the ways we can add validation to our application, to prevent people from submitting empty reviews. There are three places that we can add validation:

- At the schema level, using Mongoose, before the data is saved
- At the application level, before the data is posted to the API
- At the client side, before the form is submitted

We'll look at each of these in turn, and add some validation at every step.

7.5.1 Validating at the schema level with Mongoose

Validating the data before saving it is arguably the most important stage. This is the final step, the one last chance to make sure that everything is as correct as it can be. This stage is particularly important when the data is exposed through an API; if we don't have control over all of the applications using the API we can't guarantee the quality of the data that we're going to get. So it's important to ensure that the data is valid before saving it.

UPDATING THE SCHEMA

When we first set up the schema in chapter 5, we looked at adding some validation in Mongoose. We set the `rating` path to be required, but we also want the `author` `displayName` and `reviewText` to be required. If any of these fields are missing, a review won't make sense. Adding this to the schema is simple enough, and looks like the following listing (the schema is in locations.js in the app_api/model folder).

> **Listing 7.22 Adding validation to reviews at the schema level**

```
var reviewSchema = new mongoose.Schema({
  author: {type: String, required: true}
  rating: {type: Number, required: true, min: 0, max: 5},
  reviewText: {type: String, required: true},
  createdOn: {type: Date, "default": Date.now}
});
```

Make each of these paths a required field because if any of them are missing, a review won't make sense

createdOn doesn't need to be required because Mongoose automatically populates it when a new review is created

Once this is saved we can no longer save a review without any review text. We can try, but we'll see the error page shown in figure 7.12.

On the one hand it's good that we're protecting the database, but it's not a great user experience. We should try to catch that error and let the visitor try again.

CATCHING MONGOOSE VALIDATION ERRORS

If you try to save a document with one or more required paths missing or empty, Mongoose will return an error. It does this without having to make a call to the database, as

Figure 7.12   Error message shown when trying to save a review without any review text, now that the schema says it's required

it's Mongoose itself that holds the schema and knows what is and isn't required. The following code snippet shows an example of such an error message:

```
{
  message: 'Validation failed',
  name: 'ValidationError',
  errors: {
    'reviews.1.reviewText': {
      message: 'Path `reviewText` is required.',
      name: 'ValidatorError',
      path: 'reviewText',
      type: 'required',
      value: ''
    }
  }
}
```

In the flow of the application this happens inside the callback from the save function. If we take a look at the save command inside the doAddReview function (in locations.js in app_api/controllers) we can see where the error bubbles up and where we set the 400 status. The following code snippet shows this, including a temporary console log statement to show the output of the error to terminal:

```
location.save(function(err, location) {
  var thisReview;
  if (err) {
    console.log(err);                      Mongoose validation errors are
    sendJSONresponse(res, 400, err);       returned through error object
                                           following attempted save action
```

```
  } else {
    updateAverageRating(location._id);
    thisReview = location.reviews[location.reviews.length - 1];
    sendJSONresponse(res, 201, thisReview);
  }
});
```

Our API uses the sendJSONresponse function to return this message as the response body, alongside the 400 status. So we can look for this information in our application by looking at the response body when the API returns a 400 status.

The place to do this is in the app_server, in the doAddReview function in controllers/locations.js, to be precise. When we've caught a validation error we want to let the user try again by redirecting to the Add Review page. So that the page knows that an attempt has been made, we can pass a flag in the query string.

The following listing shows this code in place, inside the request statement callback for the doAddReview function.

> **Listing 7.23   Trapping validation errors returned by the API**

```
request(
  requestOptions,                                    Add in check to see if status is
  function(err, response, body) {                    400, if body has a name, and if
    if (response.statusCode === 201) {               that name is ValidationError
      res.redirect('/location/' + locationid);
    } else if (response.statusCode === 400 && body.name && body.name ===
    "ValidationError" ) {                                                    ◁──
      res.redirect('/location/' + locationid + '/reviews/new?err=val');   ◁──
    } else {
      console.log(body);
      _showError(req, res, response.statusCode);      If true redirect to review
    }                                                 form, passing an error
  }                                                   flag in query string
);
```

So now when the API returns a validation error we can catch it and send the user back to the form to try again. Passing a value in the query string means that we can look for this in the controller that displays the review form, and send a message to the view to alert the user to the problem.

DISPLAY AN ERROR MESSAGE IN THE BROWSER

To display an error message in the view, we need to send a variable to the view if we see the err parameter passed in the query string. The renderReviewForm function is responsible for passing the variables into the view. When it's called it's also passed the req object, which contains the query object, making it quite easy to pass the err parameter when it exists. The following listing highlights the simple change required to make this happen.

Listing 7.24   Update the controller to pass a query string error string to the view

```
var renderReviewForm = function (req, res, locDetail) {
  res.render('location-review-form', {
    title: 'Review ' + locDetail.name + ' on Loc8r',
    pageHeader: { title: 'Review ' + locDetail.name },
    error: req.query.err
  });
};
```

Send new error variable to view, passing it query parameter when it exists

The query object is always part of the req object, regardless of whether it has any content. This is why we don't need to error trap this and check that it exists—if the err parameter isn't found it will just return undefined.

All that remains is to do something with this information in the view, letting the user know what the problem is. We'll show a message to the user at the top of the form, if a validation error was bubbled up. To give this some style and presence on the page we'll use a Bootstrap alert component; this is just a div with some relevant classes and attributes. The following code snippet shows the two lines needed added in place in the location-review-form view:

```
form.form-horizontal(action="", method="post", role="form")
  - if (error == "val")
    .alert.alert-danger(role="alert") All fields required, please try again
```

So now when the API returns a validation error we catch this and display a message to the user. Figure 7.13 shows how this looks.

This type of validation at the API level is important, and is generally a great place to start because it always protects a database against inconsistent or incomplete data, no matter the origin. But the experience for end users isn't always the best—they have to submit the form, and it makes a roundtrip to the API before the page reloads with an error. There's clearly room for improvement here, and the first step is to perform some validation at the application level before the data is passed to the API.

7.5.2   *Validating at the application level with Node and Express*

Validation at the schema level is the backstop, the final line of defense in front of a database. An application shouldn't rely solely on this, and you should try to prevent unnecessary calls to the API, reducing overhead and speeding things up for the user. One way to do this is to add validation at the application level, checking the submitted data before sending it to the API.

In our application, the validation required for a review is pretty simple; we can add some simple checks to ensure that each of the fields has a value. If this fails then we redirect the user back to the form, adding the same query string error flag as before. If the validation checks are successful then we allow the controller to continue into the request method. The listing on the next page shows the additions needed in the doAddReview controller in locations.js in the app_server/controllers folder.

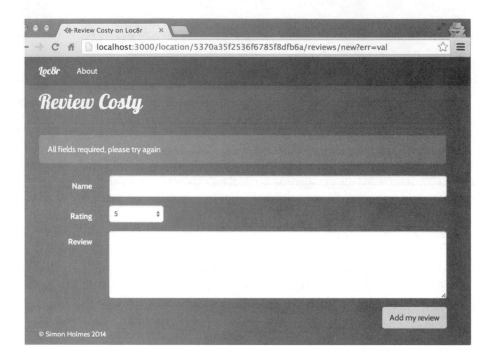

Figure 7.13   The validation error message showing in the browser, the end result of a process kicked off by Mongoose catching the error and returning it

Listing 7.25   Adding some simple validation to an Express controller

```
module.exports.doAddReview = function(req, res){
  var requestOptions, path, locationid, postdata;
  locationid = req.params.locationid;
  path = "/api/locations/" + locationid + '/reviews';
  postdata = {
    author: req.body.name,
    rating: parseInt(req.body.rating, 10),
    reviewText: req.body.review
  };
  requestOptions = {
    url : apiOptions.server + path,
    method : "POST",
    json : postdata
  };
  if (!postdata.author || !postdata.rating || !postdata.reviewText) {
    res.redirect('/location/' + locationid + '/reviews/new?err=val');
  } else {
    request(
      requestOptions,
      function(err, response, body) {
```

> If any of three required data fields are falsey, then redirect to Add Review page, appending query string used to display error message

> Otherwise continue as before

```
        if (response.statusCode === 201) {
          res.redirect('/location/' + locationid);
        } else if (response.statusCode === 400 && body.name && body.name ===
     "ValidationError" ) {
          res.redirect('/location/' + locationid + '/reviews/new?err=val');
        } else {
          console.log(body);
          _showError(req, res, response.statusCode);
        }
      }
    );
  }
};
```

The outcome for this will be the same as before—if the review text is missing then the user gets shown the error message on the Add Review page. The user doesn't know that we're no longer posting data to the API, but it's one less roundtrip and so it should be a faster experience. But we can make it even faster with the third tier of validation: browser-based validation.

7.5.3 *Validating in the browser with jQuery*

Just like application level validation speeds things up by not requiring a call to the API, client-side validation in the browser can speed things up by catching an error before the form is submitted to the application, by removing yet another call. Catching an error at this point will keep the user on the same page.

To get JavaScript running in the browser, we need to place it in the public folder in the application. Express treats the contents of this folder as static files to be downloaded to the browser instead of being run on the server. If you don't have a folder called javascripts in your public folder already, create one now. Inside this new folder create a new file called validation.js.

WRITING THE JQUERY VALIDATION

Inside this new validation.js file we'll put a jQuery function that will do the following:

- Listen for the submit event of the review form.
- Check to see that all of the required fields have a value.
- If one is empty, show an error message like we've used in the other types of validation, and prevent the form from submitting.

We won't dive into the semantics of jQuery here, assuming you have some familiarity with it or a similar library. The following listing shows the code to do this.

> **Listing 7.26   Creating a jQuery form validation function**

Check for any missing values →

```
$('#addReview').submit(function (e) {
  $('.alert.alert-danger').hide();
  if (!$('input#name').val() || !$('select#rating').val() ||
    !$('textarea#review').val()) {
```

← **Listen for submit event of review form**

Show or inject error message onto page if value is missing

```
   if ($('.alert.alert-danger').length) {
     $('.alert.alert-danger').show();
   } else {
     $(this).prepend('<div role="alert" class="alert alert-danger">All
   fields required, please try again</div>');
   }
   return false;          ◁——  Prevent form from submitting
 }                              if value is missing
});
```

For this to work we need to ensure that the form has an ID of `addReview` set so that the jQuery can listen for the correct event. We also need to add this script to the page so that the browser can run it.

ADDING THE JQUERY TO THE PAGE
We'll include this jQuery file at the end of the body, along with the other client-side JavaScript files. These are set in the `layout.jade` view in app_server/views, right at the very bottom. Add a new line below the others pointing to the new file, as shown in the following code snippet:

```
script(src='/bootstrap/js/bootstrap.min.js')
script(src='/javascripts/validation.js')
```

That's all there's to it. The form will now validate in the browser without the data being submitted anywhere, removing a page reload and any associated calls to the server.

> **TIP**   Client-side validation can seem like it's all that you need, but the other types are vital to the robustness of an application. JavaScript can be turned off in the browser, removing the ability to run this validation, or the validation could be bypassed and have data posted directly to either the form action URL or the API endpoint.

7.6   *Summary*

In this chapter we've covered

- Using the `request` module to make API calls from Express
- Making POST and GET requests to API endpoints
- Separating concerns by keeping rendering functions away from the API request logic
- Applying a simple pattern to the API logic in each controller
- Using the status code of the API response to check for success or failure
- Applying data validation in three places in the architecture, and when and why to use each

Coming up next in chapter 8 we're going to introduce Angular into the mix, and start playing with some interactive front-end components on top of the Express application.

Part 3

Adding a dynamic front end with Angular

AngularJS is one of the most exciting and fastest growing technologies of our time and is a key part of the MEAN stack. We've done a lot of work with Express so far, which is the server-side framework. Angular is the client-side framework, which enables us to build entire applications that run in the browser.

We'll get to know Angular in chapter 8, see what all the fuss is about, and get into the particular syntax semantics and jargon associated with it. Angular can have a steep learning curve, but it doesn't have to. As we get started with Angular in chapter 8, we'll see how to use it to build a component for an existing web page, including calling our REST API to get data.

Chapters 9 and 10 focus on how to use Angular to build a single page application. Building on what you've learned in chapter 8, we'll re-create Loc8r as an SPA. We'll focus on best practices throughout, learning how to build a modular application that is easily maintainable using components that can easily be reused. By the end of part 3 we will have a fully functioning single page application interacting with our REST API to create and read data.

Adding Angular
components to
an Express application

This chapter covers

- Getting to know Angular
- Adding Angular to an existing page
- Filtering lists of data
- Using an API for reading data
- Some Angular jargon: controllers, scope, filters, directives, services

Here it comes. It's now time to take a look at the final part in the MEAN stack: Angular! We're going to look at how to include Angular into the Express application, and develop a couple of components to improve our existing Loc8r application. As we go we'll discuss some of the semantics and key technical terms found in the Angular world. Unlike the other parts of the stack, Angular is opinionated, meaning that things have to be done in a certain way.

Figure 8.1 shows where we are in the overall plan, adding Angular into the front end of the existing Express application.

The approach taken in this chapter is what you'd do if you wanted to enhance a page, project, or application with a bit of Angular. Building a full application

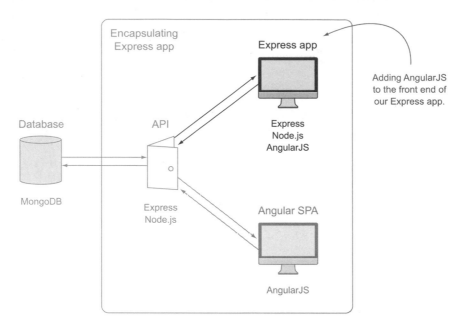

Figure 8.1   Chapter 8 focuses on adding Angular to the front end of the existing Express application.

entirely in Angular is coming up in chapters 9 and 10. We'll use this chapter to get to know Angular a bit too.

In this chapter we'll focus on improving the experience of the homepage. We'll use Angular to load the data into the list of locations, and add the ability for users to search and filter the list. To start off we'll use static data to get the hang of Angular before pulling data from the API, and using the HTML5 location APIs to get the geographical position of the user.

8.1   *Getting Angular up and running*

Angular is the second JavaScript framework in the MEAN stack, with Express being the other. Express, as we've seen, sits on the server, whereas Angular sits on the client side in the browser. Like Express, Angular helps you separate your concerns, dealing with views, data, and logic in distinct areas. The approach is very much in the MVC style, but Angular has been defined as an MVW framework, where the W stands for "whatever works for you." Sometimes it might be controllers, or the view-model, or services. It depends on what you're doing at any given point.

Now that you know a little bit about it, let's get on with the cool stuff. We'll start by playing a little with some basics of Angular, coming to terms with the concept of two-way data binding, including views, models, view-models, and controllers.

Angular is a client-side framework, so it doesn't take much installation. The process is covered in appendix A, but it's essentially as simple as downloading the latest stable version from http://angularjs.org.

8.1.1 Uncovering two-way data binding

So what does two-way data binding actually mean? Back in chapter 1 we talked briefly about how the data model and the view are bound together in Angular, and that both are live. This means that changes to the view update the model, and changes to the model update the view. Remember that we're not talking about any type of database here—all of this happens in the browser. Figure 8.2 illustrates this two-way binding.

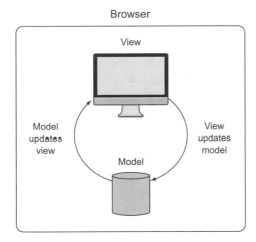

Figure 8.2   In Angular the view and model are bound together with two-way data binding, all in the browser.

Pictures may paint a thousand words, but examples are better yet. So let's look at our first bit of Angular coding.

STARTING WITH A PAGE OF HTML

Say we have a very simple HTML page, where we have an input box and somewhere to display the input. In the following code snippet we have an `input` field and an `<h1>` tag, and we want to take whatever text is entered into the input box and immediately display it after the `Hello` in the h1:

```
<!DOCTYPE html>
<html>
<head>
  <meta charset="utf-8">
  <title>Angular binding test</title>
</head>
<body>
  <input />
  <h1>Hello </h1>
</body>
</html>
```

If you're experienced in JavaScript or jQuery you're probably thinking about how you'd do this, possibly writing code to bind to keystroke events on the `input` field and then injecting that into the `<h1>` tag. It's doable, and it's not *that* hard. But with Angular you can actually do something like this without coding any JavaScript at all!

MAKING THE PAGE AN ANGULAR APPLICATION

To make the page an Angular application we have to include Angular in the page; Angular may be extremely clever but it cannot read your mind! Adding it's simple; it's just a single external JavaScript file that you can either download and reference directly or reference a CDN version.

Assuming we download and reference it locally we need to add it to the page as follows:

```
<script src="angular.min.js"></script>
```

Just referencing the file isn't enough; we need to tell Angular that this page is an Angular application. To do this we can add a simple attribute, `ng-app` to the opening `<html>` tag, like so:

```
<html ng-app>
```

This tells Angular that anything nested inside the `<html>` tag can be considered part of the application.

> **TIP**   `ng-app` can be assigned to any element on the page if you want to limit the area that Angular has access to. It's often put into the `<html>` tag so that Angular can work anywhere within the page.

BINDING INPUT AND OUTPUT

As mentioned, we're going to take the input from the form and show it in the HTML without writing any JavaScript. It sounds unlikely, but we're really going to do it. We just need to bind an Angular model to the input and the output, and Angular will do the rest. Both bindings will need to reference the same name, so that Angular knows that they share the same model.

First we bind the input to the model, giving it a name—for example, `myInput`—like this:

```
<input ng-model="myInput" />
```

Next we output the value of the model where we want it in the HTML. Angular uses double curly braces {{ }} to define these bindings. To bind the model variable into the view we simply put the name in between the double curly braces, like this:

```
<h1>Hello {{ myInput }}</h1>
```

Putting everything together, we should end up with the following listing.

> **Listing 8.1   Simple Angular binding, binding a model to input and output**

```
<!DOCTYPE html>
<html ng-app>
<head>
<script src="angular.min.js"></script>
  <meta charset="utf-8">
  <title>Angular binding test</title>
</head>
<body>
  <input ng-model="myInput" />
  <h1>Hello {{ myInput }}</h1>
</body>
</html>
```

Doesn't look like much, does it? But run it in a browser and try it out, as demonstrating it in screenshots doesn't really do it justice. If you run it in a browser and start typing in the input box you should see behavior like that shown in figure 8.3.

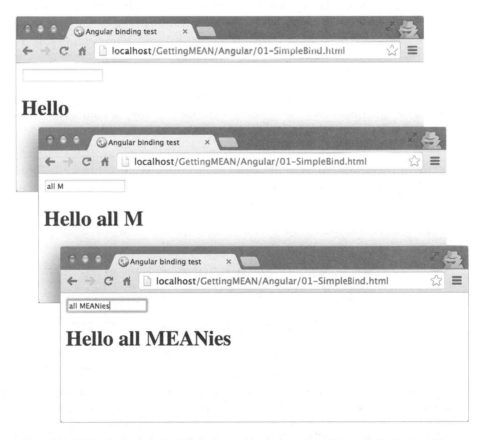

Figure 8.3   With simple data binding in Angular, as soon as text is typed into the input box it's output inside the <h1> tag. This is all achieved without having to write a single line of code.

This works because the Angular model is bound to both the input and the output. There may be two elements on the page, but there's only one model holding the data.

This example is all very well and good, but chances are that you want to do something more with Angular. And that's going to involve some coding.

8.1.2 Setting up for greatness (and JavaScript code)

To cover the necessary concepts and jargon for getting started with some Angular coding we'll go for the simple goal of assigning a default value to the `myInput` model. To do this we'll need to define our Angular application as a module, and create a controller to manage the scope. Don't worry if that didn't make sense—it will by the time we get to the end of this section.

CREATING AN ANGULAR APPLICATION AS A MODULE

To create and code an Angular application we need to define a module. A module is defined in JavaScript with a name that we choose, and this name is then referenced by the `ng-app` attribute in the HTML.

Let's start with this bit so that it's done. We simply add the name of the Angular application or module as a value of the `ng-app` attribute in the `<html>` tag. In the following code snippet we're saying that we'll be using an Angular application called `myApp`:

```
<html ng-app="myApp">
```

In an external JavaScript file we can create the definition for this application using a simple setter statement. We have to define the same name, of course, as follows:

```
angular.module('myApp', []);
```

This use of the setter syntax is the best practice for defining a module, but to make sense of a common approach that you'll likely see in online code samples take a look at the following sidebar.

A common but inferior approach

The best practice for defining a module is to use the setter syntax like this:

```
angular.module('myApp', []);          ◁—— This is good.
```

But it's quite common among online code examples to see this being assigned to a variable, like this:

```
var myApp = angular.module('myApp', []);          ◁—— This isn't so good.
```

The prevalence of this approach is largely due to the original Angular documentation showing this method, but it's slowly being changed as the documentation gets updated. It's better to use the setter syntax for a few reasons. It allows you to use the getter syntax for controllers and more that we'll see soon, and it makes the code easier to read and reduces the risk of reusing an existing variable name.

DEFINING A CONTROLLER

Once an application has been defined it can have controllers attached to it. A controller is defined in JavaScript and attached to a specific HTML element. The controller can then work inside the associated element.

For our example we'll attach the controller to the body. This is done using the Angular attribute ng-controller, giving it the name of the controller we want to use. The following code snippet provides the controller name myController:

```
<body ng-controller="myController">
```

Now it's the turn of the code. Having defined the application module using the setter syntax, we can use the getter syntax to define a controller. The following code snippet shows how to attach a controller called myController to an Angular module called myApp:

```
angular                                        Get myApp module.
  .module('myApp')
  .controller('myController', function() {     Assign controller myController,
    // controller code here                    including controller code in
  });                                          anonymous function.
```

This works well, but it would be better for readability, reusability, and testability to use a named function instead of an anonymous function. In the following code snippet we do just that, creating a new named function myController to hold the controller code:

```
var myController = function() {                Put controllers in
  // controller code here                      named functions for
};                                             better coding practice.
angular
  .module('myApp')
  .controller('myController', myController);
```

If you refresh the page at this point the mini-application should still work, taking the contents of the input and displaying it as you type. Next we'll look at scope to see how to give our model a default value.

INTRODUCING SCOPE

Angular applications have scopes just like JavaScript code does. Similar in concept to the JavaScript global scope, Angular has a *rootScope*. The rootScope is everything within an application, and is implicitly created with the ng-app directive in the HTML. The model for the first version of our "Hello world!" application was held within this scope.

Nested within the rootScope can be one or more child scopes. A child scope is also implicitly created whenever the ng-controller directive is added to the HTML. When we added the controller to the application we actually moved the model out of the rootScope and into the scope of the controller.

In Angular, scope ties together the view, model, and controller, as they all use the same scope. We've witnessed scope working with the model and view, even though we didn't know it. We can make it more obvious by playing with it in the controller.

The controller function can take a $scope parameter because the scope has already been created by Angular. This must be called $scope because behind the scenes it's dependent on the Angular provider $scopeProvider. This $scope parameter gives us direct access to the model. So setting a default value is as simple as using the standard JavaScript dot notation for accessing object properties. The following code snippet shows how we can update the controller function to accept the $scope parameter and use it to set a default value:

```
var myController = function($scope) {          ⟵  Accept $scope parameter
  $scope.myInput = "world!";                       to have access to scope.
};                                              ⟵  myInput is property of scope,
                                                   so it's easy to assign it a value.
```

Just because we've assigned it a default value, it doesn't set that value in stone. Updating the input field will still update the model and display it. Figure 8.4 shows this in action.

At the start of this section we said that we'd define our Angular application as a module and create a controller to manage the scope. That might not have made sense at the start, but hopefully it does now. These are the foundation building blocks of knowledge for Angular.

Figure 8.4   The controller assigns a default value via the scope, but we can still change that value using the input.

So now that we know what we're doing and where Angular is coming from, let's start adding some components to the Loc8r application.

8.2   *Displaying and filtering the homepage list*

In this section we're going to see how to add an Angular component to an application; in this case we're going to replace existing functionality. We're going to change the way the homepage is coded, using Angular to display the list of locations on the homepage rather than having Express deliver the HTML. Throughout the course of this section we'll cover quite a lot of Angular functionality that will be useful in most other projects, including filtering lists, data format filters, services, dependency injection, and using directives for adding in reusable HTML.

8.2.1   *Adding Angular to an Express application*

From what we've just learned in section 8.1 we know what we'll need to do to add Angular into the Loc8r application. We'll need to do the following:

- Download the Angular library file.
- Create a new JavaScript file for our code.
- Include these files in the HTML.
- Define the Angular application in the HTML.

This shouldn't take long, so let's get started.

ADDING THE JAVASCRIPT FILES TO THE PROJECT

As Angular is a client-side framework we need to ensure that Express sends the Java-Script files to the browser rather than trying to run them. The public folder is already set up to deliver static files, so that's the perfect place for adding a couple of new JavaScript files.

Inside the public folder create a new folder called Angular. Drop the downloaded minimized Angular library file in here. In the same folder create a new JavaScript file called loc8rApp.js—this will hold our Angular code for this chapter.

While we're here, let's create the Angular module setter for our application, which we'll call loc8rApp. In loc8rApp.js enter the following code snippet and save it:

```
angular.module('loc8rApp', []);
```

And that will do us for now. Next we need to update the views to include the JavaScript and define the Angular application.

SETTING UP THE HTML

Updating the views is pretty easy. We'll add everything we need at this stage to the layout.jade file so that any of the pages in the application can use Angular.

First let's add the two JavaScript file links in with the other external files at the bottom of the Jade file, as shown in the following listing.

Listing 8.2   Adding the Angular library and application code to the HTML

```
script(src='/angular/angular.min.js')
script(src='/angular/loc8rApp.js')
script(src='/javascripts/jquery-1.11.1.min.js')
script(src='/bootstrap/js/bootstrap.min.js')
script(src='/javascript/validation.js')
```

Then we just need to define the Angular application in the HTML, which we'll do in the <html> tag again. The following code snippet shows how to do this in Jade syntax, using the loc8rApp name:

```
html(ng-app='loc8rApp')
```

And with that, all pages of Loc8r are primed for some Angular action.

8.2.2 *Moving data delivery from Express to Angular*

If we're going to use Angular to display the list of locations, then Angular will need to have the data for that list. We'll start off validating the approach by using data hard-coded in Angular—much like we did when building the Express application—before eventually pulling it from the database.

To achieve this we need to do three things:

- Remove the API call from the Express controller for the homepage.
- Add some hard-coded data into the Angular application scope.
- Update the view template to bind to the Angular data.

We'll get going by updating Express.

REMOVING THE HOMEPAGE API CALL FROM EXPRESS

As it stands, pretty much everything in the Express controller for the homepage (homelist in app_server/controllers/locations.js) is concerned with hitting the API for the data. We can remove this and just call the renderHomepage function, as shown in the following code snippet:

```
module.exports.homelist = function(req, res){
  renderHomepage(req, res);
};
```

The renderHomepage function is also set to deal with incoming data, which is no longer needed. In the following listing we remove any references to responseBody and message.

Listing 8.3   Taking the dynamic content out of the renderHomepage Express function

```
var renderHomepage = function(req, res){
  res.render('locations-list', {
    title: 'Loc8r - find a place to work with wifi',
```

```
    pageHeader: {
      title: 'Loc8r',
      strapline: 'Find places to work with wifi near you!'
    },
    sidebar: "Looking for wifi and a seat? Loc8r helps you find places to
    work when out and about. Perhaps with coffee, cake or a pint? Let Loc8r
    help you find the place you're looking for."
  });
};
```

That's all we need to do for the controller function. Now we jump over to the Angular code for a moment to add some data into the scope.

ADDING HARD-CODED DATA INTO THE ANGULAR SCOPE

We're going to start off with hard-coding some data into the scope so that we can get the view sorted out. The first step is to create a function for our controller code in loc8rApp.js in /public/angular. We'll call this locationListCtrl, make sure we pass in the $scope parameter, and assign an array of location objects to a property called data.

The following listing shows how this looks with a couple of locations in it; you'll probably want to add a few more so that you can test the filtering.

Listing 8.4   Create an Angular controller and some test data in loc8rApp.js

```
var locationListCtrl = function ($scope) {          ◁      Create new function to
  $scope.data = {                                   ◁      hold Angular controller
    locations: [{                                           code, remembering to
      name: 'Burger Queen',                                 have function accept
      address: '125 High Street, Reading, RG6 1PS',         $scope parameter
      rating: 3,
      facilities: ['Hot drinks', 'Food', 'Premium wifi'],
      distance: '0.296456',
      _id: '5370a35f2536f6785f8dfb6a'                Create data property
    }, {                                             attached to $scope and
      name: 'Costy',                                 assign some location
      address: '125 High Street, Reading, RG6 1PS',  values to it
      rating: 5,
      facilities: ['Hot drinks', 'Food', 'Alcoholic drinks'],
      distance: '0.7865456',
      _id: '5370a35f2536f6785f8dfb6a'
    }]};
};
```

That's all we need to do in the controller to get the data into the scope so that the view can use it. We'll update the code soon to get the real data from the database. The last thing to remember is to attach the controller to the Angular application. To do this, we'll use the module getter syntax at the very bottom of the loc8rApp.js file, after the controller code, as shown in the following code snippet:

```
angular
  .module('loc8rApp')
  .controller('locationListCtrl', locationListCtrl);
```

Now the controller is attached to the application and pushing data into the scope. But the view doesn't define the Angular controller anywhere so it won't be used yet, and it's still using the Express data bindings. So let's jump back over to the Express application and update the homepage view.

UPDATE THE JADE VIEW TO BIND TO THE ANGULAR CONTROLLER

The Jade view is still currently trying to use the Express bindings, and will fail because we've deleted all of the code from Express. So we need to add the `ng-controller` directive to a relevant element, swap out the Jade loop for an Angular loop, and change the Jade data bindings to Angular data bindings.

The trick here is to use an Angular loop. Rather than using a `for` loop Angular has a directive called `ng-repeat` that allows us to repeat through the elements of an array. The `ng-repeat` directive will loop through an array, outputting the HTML and data bindings for each entry in the array. For more information, check out the following sidebar.

Using ng-repeat to loop through data objects

Angular's `ng-repeat` directive will loop through a given array, rendering the HTML for each of the pieces of data. For example, let's start with this simple controller adding an array of data to the scope:

```
var myController = function($scope) {
  $scope.items = ["one", "two", "three"];
};
```

You can output the items in the array using the `ng-repeat` directive like this:

```
<body ng-controller="myController">
  <ul>
    <li ng-repeat="item in items">{{ item }}</li>
  </ul>
</body>
```

The resulting output, omitting the attributes that Angular will add to the HTML elements, is this:

```
<ul>
  <li>one</li>
  <li>two</li>
  <li>three</li>
</ul>
```

Note that Angular will start the repetition on the element where you put the `ng-repeat` directive, so you must be careful to put it in the right place. In this example it would be very easy to accidentally put it into the `<ul>` tag instead of the `<li>` tag, but this would output the following markup:

```
<ul>
  <li>one</li>
</ul>
```

```
<ul>
  <li>two</li>
</ul>
<ul>
  <li>three</li>
</ul>
```

This is probably not what you were after. ng-repeat is extremely handy and very powerful, but just be careful you put it in the right place.

Everything we want to do is contained in the main content column of the page, so that's a good place to define the controller. Inside that controller all of the Jade data bindings and loops need to be swapped out for their Angular counterparts. The following listing runs through the changes made to make this happen.

Listing 8.5   Changing the Jade bindings to Angular bindings

```
.col-xs-12.col-sm-8(ng-controller="locationListCtrl")       ⟵─┐  Define Angular controller
  .error {{ message }}                                          │  on central column div
    .row.list-group
      .col-xs-12.list-group-item(ng-repeat="location in data.locations")
        h4
          a(href="/location/{{ location._id }}") {{ location.name }}
          small {{ location.rating }}                               Output
          span.badge.pull-right.badge-default {{ location.distance }}  details for
        p.address {{ location.address }}                          each location
        p
          span.label.label-warning.label-facility(ng-repeat="facility in
      location.facilities")
            | {{ facility }}                        Add nested ng-repeat loop to
                                                    output facilities for each location
```

Start ng-repeat for each item in locations array in $scope.data

That's the last piece of the puzzle for our first pass at getting Angular running in the homepage. We've added the scripts, defined the application in the HTML and JavaScript, created the controller, and bound the data into the HTML. So now when we reload the homepage, we get something like figure 8.5.

We can see from figure 8.5 that a few things need tweaking. We had been using Express to format the distance before sending it to the view, and had also used a Jade mixin to output rating stars instead of just a number. Angular gives us a couple of tools to achieve these things in a different way: filters and directives. We'll look at filters first.

8.2.3   Using Angular filters to format data

Filters allow you to specify your chosen format for a given piece of data. Angular has some built-in filters such as formatting a date, currency, and text. You can apply these filters directly within the data binding in the HTML. To apply one insert a pipe | after the value followed by the name of the filter.

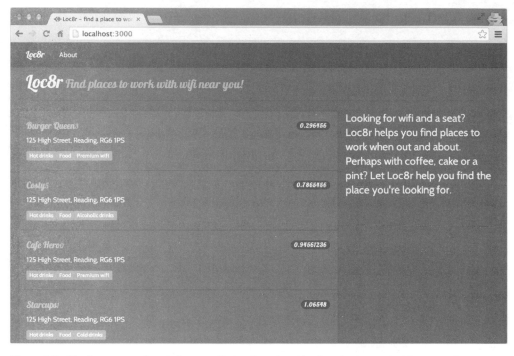

Figure 8.5   The homepage data being supplied and rendered by Angular instead of Express. There are some layout issues that need fixing.

The following code snippet shows an example of using the currency filter:

```
<div>{{ 123.2345 | currency }}</div>
<!-- Output: $123.23 -->
```

Some of the filters allow you to specify options. The currency filter can be told to output a different currency symbol, as shown in the following code snippet:

```
<div>{{ 123.2345 + 321.321 | currency:"£" }}</div>
<!-- Output: £444.56 -->
```

The filters aren't limited to working with numbers, of course; you can also work with strings and dates. A couple of quick examples are as follows:

```
<div>{{ "Let's shout" | uppercase }}</div>
<!-- Output: LET'S SHOUT -->
{{ timestamp | date:"d MMM yyyy" }}         ◁── Requires timestamp to be
<!-- Output: 21 Aug 2014 -->                     set in scope as date object
```

The built-in filters that come with Angular are pretty good. While it's very useful to have these at your disposal you may find you need to do something different, which is the case we have with Loc8r when we want to format the distances. The good news is, you can create your own custom filters for your application.

CREATING A CUSTOM FILTER

The Loc8r API returns distances as long numbers such as 0.296456. This distance is actually in kilometers, but doesn't explicitly state any unit of measurement. We want this to look better to the end user.

We've already solved this problem in Express, but now we need to solve it in Angular. As we're using JavaScript in the back end and the front end we can lift most of the code we need from Express and pop it into Angular.

In Express, in locations.js in app_server/controllers, we had two functions for formatting the data, _isNumeric and _formatDistance. We can keep the logic of these functions intact. The only change we need to make when we move it into the Angular application is to change the formatDistance function to return a function that does the processing, rather than doing the processing itself. The following listing shows the code we need to put into our Loc8rApp.js file.

Listing 8.6　Creating a custom filter to apply formatting to distances

_isNumeric helper function is copied directly from Express code

To be used as Angular filter formatDistance function must return a function that accepts distance parameter rather than accepting it itself

Contents of function remain same and can be copied directly from Express application

```
var _isNumeric = function (n) {
  return !isNaN(parseFloat(n)) && isFinite(n);
};
var formatDistance = function () {
  return function (distance) {
    var numDistance, unit;
    if (distance && _isNumeric(distance)) {
      if (distance > 1) {
        numDistance = parseFloat(distance).toFixed(1);
        unit = 'km';
      } else {
        numDistance = parseInt(distance * 1000,10);
        unit = 'm';
      }
      return numDistance + unit;
    } else {
      return "?";
    }
  };
};
```

This shows how to create a custom filter, but now we need to add it to the application and use it in the HTML.

ADDING AND USING CUSTOM FILTERS

When we have our custom filter built, we want to add it to our application so that we can use it. At the bottom of the loc8rApp.js file we can chain it to the Angular module getter syntax, where we registered the controller for the application. The principle is the same, but rather than defining a controller, this time we're defining a filter.

The following code snippet shows how this section of the file should now look:

```
angular
  .module('loc8rApp')
  .controller('locationListCtrl', locationListCtrl)
  .filter('formatDistance', formatDistance);
```

With this in place the filter is now available to the application, so we can reference it in the code, just like we would with any other filter. In the following code snippet we add the filter to the relevant place in the Jade template:

```
.col-xs-12.list-group-item(ng-repeat="location in data.locations")
  h4
    a(href="/location/{{ location._id }}") {{ location.name }}
    small {{ location.rating }}
    span.badge.pull-right.badge-default {{ location.distance | formatDistance
      }}
  p.address {{ location.address }}
```

This should now be formatting our distance nicely like before, and we should have something that looks like figure 8.6.

And that wraps up a quick tour of filters, taking a look at some of the native Angular filters and how to create your own. Next up on the to-do list is using directives for HTML snippets with the aim of adding back the rating stars.

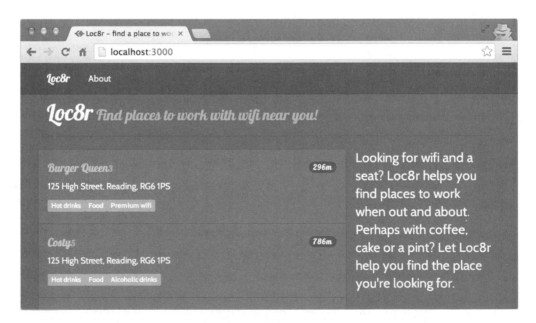

Figure 8.6   Custom Angular filter formats and displays the distances in the way we want

8.2.4   *Using Angular directives to create HTML snippets*

In Angular, directives essentially allow you to create HTML snippets. A single snippet can be used by as many different controllers and views as you like. This is a really handy feature for making your application more consistent and easier to maintain. And because these snippets run in the context of an Angular application, they also come with all of the data-binding goodness we've seen so far.

As an added bonus, browsers can cache directives that are saved as HTML files, helping to speed up your application when users switch between views. But let's back up a bit and start off by seeing how to add a directive to our application.

ADDING A DIRECTIVE TO AN ANGULAR APPLICATION

We'll start off in our Angular application to set up the code for a basic directive, and build up from there. A directive is added to an Angular application using the now-familiar module getter syntax and a named function. For the starting point of our directive we want to return a simple template that outputs the rating as a number, so in the browser it will look the same as it does now.

The following listing shows what needs to be added/updated in loc8rApp.js.

Listing 8.7   Creating a directive and adding it to the Angular module

```
var ratingStars = function () {
  return {
    template : "{{ location.rating }}"       Create new function ratingStars
  };                                          and return a basic template,
};                                            binding to rating of location

angular
  .module('loc8rApp')
  .controller('locationListCtrl', locationListCtrl)
  .filter('formatDistance', formatDistance)       Register directive
  .directive('ratingStars', ratingStars);         with application
```

This simple template is exactly the same as we currently have in the Jade template. *It's important that the name of the function is in camelCase*—you'll see why next when we update the Jade view to use this new directive.

ATTACHING A DIRECTIVE TO THE HTML TEMPLATE

Having a directive in the Angular application is all very well and good, but we need to tell the HTML where we want to use it. The default way to do this is to add an attribute into the tag that will contain the directive.

The attribute name is important, and must match that of the directive name, but in a different format. Unlike JavaScript, HTML isn't case sensitive, so it doesn't make sense to use camelCase here. Instead, the uppercase letters are converted to lowercase letters and prefixed with a dash. So the directive name `ratingStars` would be referenced in HTML as `rating-stars`.

In raw HTML, when applied to a div, it would look like the following:

```
<div rating-stars></div>
```

In our homepage we want to add this to a small tag. Jade templates allow us to add in attributes without a value, which is what we need here. In the following code snippet we do exactly this:

```
h4
  a(href="/location/{{ location._id }}") {{ location.name }}
  small(rating-stars)
```

Apply empty attribute name to small tag that will hold rating

This simple change allows Angular to bind the ratingStars directive to the small tag, inserting the contents within it. If you reload the page now you shouldn't actually see any changes, as all we've done is change the way that Angular outputs the number.

This number is a good start, but the idea of a directive is that it's reusable. What we have *is* reusable, but next we'll make it even more so by removing its reliance on having a value assigned to location.rating in the current scope. We'll do this by using what's known as an *isolate scope*.

PASSING VARIABLES TO DIRECTIVES WITH AN ISOLATE SCOPE

Our current template for showing the rating will only work when the directive is included in a scope that contains a value for location.rating. This might seem fine for now, but what if we want to show the rating stars for each review in a list of reviews? That's not likely to reference an object called location.rating, and even if it does it's not likely to be the piece of data we actually want to use.

To address this problem we can create an isolate scope for the directive by adding the scope option to the directive's definition. Listing 8.8 shows how to do this, creating a new scope variable thisRating for the directive. The value of '=rating' tells Angular to look for an attribute called rating on the same HTML element that defined the directive.

Listing 8.8   Updating the directive to use an isolate scope for the rating

```
var ratingStars = function () {
  return {
    scope: {
      thisRating : '=rating'
    },
    template : "{{ thisRating }}"
  };
};
```

Add scope option to directive definition to create isolate scope

Create new variable thisRating and tell Angular to get value from attribute called rating

Update template to use new variable

This directive now expects the HTML element to which it's bound to contain a `rating` attribute, which in turn holds the value of the rating. The following code snippet shows the update we need to make to the Jade template to make this happen:

```
h4
  a(href="/location/{{ location._id }}") {{ location.name }}
  small(rating-stars, rating="location.rating")
```

> Create new attribute called rating and give it rating value

This update means that wherever we want to use rating stars we can add two attributes to an HTML element, one to bind the directive and one to pass the rating value. So the directive is no longer dependent on a specific value existing in the parent scope.

After all that, it's still not showing stars. We'll address that now.

USING AN EXTERNAL HTML FILE FOR THE TEMPLATE

As a rule of thumb, unless a directive template is very simple it should exist in its own HTML file. Our directive to display rating stars will be a little more complex than just displaying the number sent to it, so we'll put it into an external HTML file. As well as separating concerns—keeping markup separate from application logic—this approach has the added bonus of browsers being able to cache HTML files.

To move a template into an external HTML file, the first thing to do is to take `template` out of the directive definition and replace it with `templateUrl`. `templateUrl` should hold the path to the HTML file. The following listing shows how we can update the `ratingStars` directive to use a file, /angular/rating-stars.html.

> **Listing 8.9 Update the directive to use an external file for the template**

```
var ratingStars = function () {
  return {
    scope: {
      thisRating : '=rating'
    },
    templateUrl: '/angular/rating-stars.html'
  };
};
```

> Change template to templateUrl and set path to HTML file we want to use

This HTML file doesn't exist yet, so we'll create that now. In the /public/angular folder create a file called rating-stars.html. In that file we'll start with the HTML needed to output a rating; the following code snippet shows the markup used to display a three-star rating:

```
<span class="glyphicon glyphicon-star"></span>
<span class="glyphicon glyphicon-star"></span>
<span class="glyphicon glyphicon-star"></span>
<span class="glyphicon glyphicon-star-empty"></span>
<span class="glyphicon glyphicon-star-empty"></span>
```

> **Classes output a solid star, giving three solid stars**
>
> **Classes output a hollow star, giving two hollow stars**

To make the template smart we can use an Angular binding to insert the `-empty` class suffix where appropriate. For example, if the rating is less than two, only the first star should be solid, and the remaining four hollow. We'll use the JavaScript ternary operator (a shorthand for a simple `if-else` conditional statement) to achieve this, as shown in the following listing.

Listing 8.10   Creating the Angular rating star template

```
<span class="glyphicon glyphicon-star{{ thisRating<1 ? '-empty' : ''}}"></span>
<span class="glyphicon glyphicon-star{{ thisRating<2 ? '-empty' : ''}}"></span>
<span class="glyphicon glyphicon-star{{ thisRating<3 ? '-empty' : ''}}"></span>
<span class="glyphicon glyphicon-star{{ thisRating<4 ? '-empty' : ''}}"></span>
<span class="glyphicon glyphicon-star{{ thisRating<5 ? '-empty' : ''}}"></span>
```

For each star, if `thisRating` is less than the number of stars, Angular will add the `-empty` suffix to the class. Reloading the page now gives us our stars back, as shown in figure 8.7.

That finalizes sorting out how to get the list to display correctly using Angular. But what we set out to do was add a text input so that we could filter the results. Let's do that now.

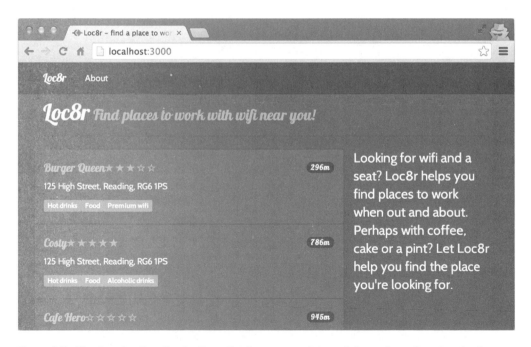

Figure 8.7   The Angular directive for the rating is now complete and shows the rating stars back in place.

FILTERING A LIST OF RESULTS WITH ANGULAR

Earlier in this chapter we saw how we could change the output of a particular piece of data by using a filter. Some quite astounding news is that we can do exactly the same thing with a list of results by adding a filter to the ng-repeat directive. We're actually going to filter the list of locations on the homepage without using any JavaScript.

The aim is for the list to be filtered according to whatever a user types in, so we're going to create an input box. We'll bind an input field to the model, and then apply this as a filter to the ng-repeat directive. It's really as simple as that.

The following listing shows how to set this up in the Jade template for the homepage.

> **Listing 8.11 Creating and applying the text filter for the list of results**

```
                                                           Create new input field
                                                           and bind it to model
                                                           with a name, textFilter
.col-xs-12.col-sm-8(ng-controller="locationListCtrl")
  label(for="filter") Filter results
  input#filter(type="text", name="filter", ng-model="textFilter")      ◁──┘
  .error {{ message }}
  .row.list-group
    .col-xs-12.list-group-item(ng-repeat="location in data.locations | filter
    : textFilter")
                                          ◁──┐  Apply filter to ng-repeat
                                              │  directive, referencing textFilter
```

That's all there is to it. Think of all the effort you'd have to go to if you wanted to manually program this functionality from scratch! Before we look at a screenshot we'll add a tweak to the CSS in public/stylesheets/style.css to prevent it from looking too cramped:

```
#filter {margin-left: 4px;}
```

Now we can see what it looks like and how it works in figure 8.8.

I think we can all agree that that's pretty neat. But we must not forget that the data for this is currently hard-coded into the controller. In the next section we'll see how to make use of our API and pull the data from the database.

8.3 *Getting data from an API*

In this section we're going to do a couple of things. First we're going to give ourselves a pat on the back for having the foresight to create a REST API for our database. When we've calmed down a bit we'll use our API from Angular to get the data for the homepage, and then also make the page location-aware. This step will mean that the application will start to show places that are near you, not just near the coordinates you hard-coded in.

Okay, let's get started. We'll begin by moving the data out of the controller and into a service.

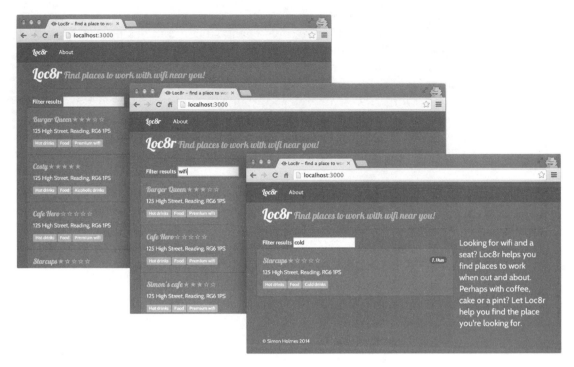

Figure 8.8   The text filter in action on the homepage, filtering the list of results as a user types

8.3.1   *Using services for data*

Services are self-contained units of functionality that can be combined to provide the complete functionality of a software application. You'll end up using services quite a lot in Angular, as most application logic should be deferred to services, making it reusable from multiple controllers. In our case here, we'll be creating a data service that we can use elsewhere.

When accessing data, a controller shouldn't care where the data comes from; it just needs to know who to ask for it. This is what we're going to do right now—move the data from the controller to a service, and have the controller call the service.

CREATING A SIMPLE DATA SERVICE

The method of defining a service in Angular shouldn't be much of a surprise by now. We'll create a named function and then register the service with the application.

So let's define a function called `loc8rData` and have it return the data that's currently being held in the controller. We'll then register it with our application. The following listing shows both of these steps.

Listing 8.12   Creating a simple data service and adding it to the module

```
var loc8rData = function () {
  return [{
      name: 'Burger Queen',
      address: '125 High Street, Reading, RG6 1PS',
      rating: 3,
      facilities: ['Hot drinks', 'Food', 'Premium wifi'],
      distance: '0.296456',
      _id: '5370a35f2536f6785f8dfb6a'
    }];
};
angular
  .module('loc8rApp')
  .controller('locationListCtrl', locationListCtrl)
  .filter('formatDistance', formatDistance)
  .directive('ratingStars', ratingStars)
  .service('loc8rData', loc8rData);
```

> Create new named function to return data
>
> Register service with application

That seems fairly intuitive, right? And in keeping with the patterns we've seen so far in this chapter.

USING A SERVICE FROM A CONTROLLER

To use a service from a controller we first have to pass the service to the controller. Passing the service in is easy—just add the name of the service as a parameter in the function definition for the controller.

When the service has been passed to the controller it can be used, just as you might expect. The following code snippet shows how to update the controller function to accept the service and use it:

```
var locationListCtrl = function ($scope, loc8rData) {
  $scope.data = { locations: loc8rData };
};
```

> Pass service name into controller function as parameter
>
> Call service, which will then return data

Reloading the application now shouldn't show any changes in the homepage. The change we've made here is behind the scenes getting ready for the next step: getting the data from our API.

8.3.2   *Making HTTP requests from Angular to an API*

Making HTTP requests from JavaScript is nothing particularly new. jQuery has had good Ajax support for a while, and in chapter 7 we used the request module to make HTTP requests from Node. Angular has a built-in service called $http to manage this type of request.

We'll now use the $http service to make the call to our API and retrieve the data for the homepage. This request will be asynchronous, of course, so we'll also see how to handle that.

ADDING AND USING THE $HTTP SERVICE

Adding the $http service to the application is very easy—in fact, we only need to use it in our data service. Remember that the controller shouldn't care how the data is obtained, it just knows who to ask.

There are two key things we need to know about the $http service to get started with it:

- The $http service is given to another service by passing it as a parameter to the function, much like we've done with $scope in the controller.
- The $http service has a get method that expects a single parameter—the URL—to be called.

If we put these two things together we can update our data service function loc8rData to look like the following code snippet (remember to put in coordinates near to you or the locations you've added):

Pass $http service into existing service function

```
var loc8rData = function ($http) {
  return $http.get('/api/locations?lng=-0.79&lat=51.3&maxDistance=20');
}
```

Remove hard-coded data and return $http.get call, ensuring that it's calling correct URL

So now, instead of returning some hard-coded data, the data service returns to the call the $http.get method. If you reload the page now expecting to see the data in the homepage you'll be disappointed. You'll even be able to see in the JavaScript console of your browser (depending on your browser) that an XHR request to the API has loaded and returned some data.

So why isn't the page showing the data? Well that's because the $http.get is asynchronous, and our controller is trying to use it in a synchronous way. Let's see how to use it properly.

HANDLING THE ASYNCHRONOUS NATURE OF $HTTP

Because $http goes off dealing with web services, there's no idea of how long it's going to take to execute. Nobody wants their entire JavaScript program to stop working while we're waiting for a response, so it makes sense that $http runs asynchronously.

Our controller code is currently just this:

```
var locationListCtrl = function ($scope, loc8rData) {
  $scope.data = { locations: loc8rData };
};
```

This is running synchronously, and as we've seen it will not work with $http. $http instead returns a promise with two methods: success and error. What this means is that rather than expecting the $http.get call to return data, it will invoke either its success method or its error method.

Let's clarify this with a bit of code. loc8rData now returns the $http.get method, so we'll start by invoking that. We then chain the success and error methods to it using the dot syntax. When loc8rData has received a response it will invoke either the success or error method, depending on the response.

The scaffolding for this looks like the following listing, which also shows how to take the data returned from a successful request and pass it into the scope.

Listing 8.13 Updating the controller to work asynchronously with the $http promises

```
var locationListCtrl = function ($scope, loc8rData) {
  loc8rData
    .success(function(data) {
      $scope.data = { locations: data };
    })
    .error(function (e) {
      console.log(e);
    });
};
```

Invoke loc8rData service, which returns $http.get call

On successful response, pass returned data into callback function

Apply this data to scope

If web service returned error, pass error to callback function

With that in place we'll once again be able to see the data from the database showing up on our homepage. This is the minimum functionality, but as the code is asynchronous it would be good to let the user know what's happening while the empty page displays and the $http request is being made.

TELLING THE USER WHAT'S GOING ON

A problem with asynchronous data calls in the client side is that a user will first see the page rendered without any content. This will last until the asynchronous call completes and returns some data. This isn't great! If your page remains free of data for even just a very short time users may well see the empty page and click the back button.

So when making asynchronous calls for data, always let the user know that you're doing something and that something is happening in the background. In Loc8r we'll do this by outputting a simple message, largely because we already have the HTML in place for it.

Inside the Jade template we already have a div set up to hold a message, as highlighted in bold in the following code snippet:

```
.col-xs-12.col-sm-8(ng-controller="locationListCtrl")
  label(for="filter") Filter results
  input#filter(type="text", name="filter", ng-model="textFilter")
  .error {{ message }}
```

This div and message were part of the original Jade template when we were using Express to generate the final HTML. We updated message to be an Angular binding when we set up the Angular controller instead. So we can use this message binding in the scope in our controller. The following listing shows how to update the scope to show a different message at different points in the process.

Listing 8.14 Setting an output message at various points in the process

```
var locationListCtrl = function ($scope, loc8rData) {
  $scope.message = "Searching for nearby places";
  loc8rData
    .success(function(data) {
      $scope.message = data.length > 0 ? "" : "No locations found";
      $scope.data = { locations: data };
    })
    .error(function (e) {
      $scope.message = "Sorry, something's gone wrong ";
    });
};
```

Set default message letting user know that we're doing something in background

If request returns successfully and there's some data, clear the message; otherwise let user know that nothing was found

If asynchronous call returns an error, let user know that something has gone wrong

Just something as simple as that can make a huge difference to the user experience. If you want to take it to the next level and include an Ajax Spinner—usually an animated GIF of a spinning wheel—go ahead! But we'll stick with what we've got for the time being because we've got something cool coming up.

Now we're going to make our application show places that are actually near you, not just near the coordinates that you hard-coded in.

8.3.3   Adding HTML geolocation to find places near you

The main premise of Loc8r is that it will be location-aware, and thus able to find places that are near you. So far we've been faking it by hard-coding geographic coordinates into the API requests. We're going to change that right now by adding in HTML5 geolocation.

To get this working we'll need to do the following:

- Add a call to the HTML5 location API into our Angular application.
- Only look for places when we have the location.
- Pass the coordinates to our Angular data service, removing the hard-coded location.
- Output messages along the way so the user knows what's going on.

Starting at the top, we'll add the geolocation JavaScript function by creating a new service.

CREATING AN ANGULAR GEOLOCATION SERVICE

Being able to find the location of the user feels like something that would be reusable, in this project and other projects. So to snap it off as a piece of standalone functionality we'll create another service to hold this. As a rule, any code that's interacting with APIs, running logic, or performing operations should be externalized into services. *Leave the controller to control the services, rather than perform the functions.*

We won't get distracted by diving into the details of how the HTML5/JavaScript geolocation API works right now. We'll just say that modern browsers have a method on the navigator object that you can call to find the coordinates of the user. The user has to give permission for this to happen. The method accepts two parameters, a success callback and an error callback, and looks like the following:

```
navigator.geolocation.getCurrentPosition(cbSuccess, cbError);
```

We'll need to wrap the standard geolocation script in a function so that we can use it as a service, and also error trap against the possibility that the current browser doesn't support this. The following listing shows the code needed to create the geolocation service and provide a getPosition method that the controller can call.

> **Listing 8.15 Create a geolocation service returning a method to get the current position**

Define function called getPosition that accepts three callback functions for success, error, and not supported

Create service called geolocation

```
var geolocation = function () {
  var getPosition = function (cbSuccess, cbError, cbNoGeo) {
    if (navigator.geolocation) {
      navigator.geolocation.getCurrentPosition(cbSuccess, cbError);
    }
    else {
      cbNoGeo();
    }
  };
  return {
    getPosition : getPosition
  };
};
```

If geolocation isn't supported, invoke not supported callback

If geolocation supported, call native method, passing through success and error callbacks

Return getPosition function so it can be invoked from controller

That code gives us a geolocation service, with a method getPosition that we can pass three callback functions to. This service will check to see whether the browser supports geolocation and then attempt to get the coordinates. The service will then call one of the three different callbacks depending on whether geolocation is supported and whether it was able to successfully obtain the coordinates.

The next step is to add it to the application.

ADDING THE GEOLOCATION SERVICE TO THE APPLICATION

To use our new geolocation service we need to register it with the application and inject it into the controller.

The following code snippet highlights in bold the addition we need to make to the module definition to register the service with the application.

```
angular
  .module('loc8rApp')
  .controller('locationListCtrl', locationListCtrl)
  .filter('formatDistance', formatDistance)
  .directive('ratingStars', ratingStars)
  .service('loc8rData', loc8rData)
  .service('geolocation', geolocation);
```

Once the `geolocation` service has been registered we then need to inject it into the `locationListCtrl` controller so that it can use it. To do this we just need to add the name of the service to the parameters being accepted by the controller function. The following code snippet demonstrates this (the contents of the controller aren't included in this snippet for the sake of brevity):

```
var locationListCtrl = function ($scope, loc8rData, geolocation) {    ◁─┐
  // controller code
};                                          Add name of geolocation service to
                                         parameters accepted by controller function
```

This approach is probably looking familiar by now. The next step is to get the controller to interact with the service.

USING THE GEOLOCATION SERVICE FROM THE CONTROLLER

The controller now has access to the geolocation service, so let's use it! Calling it will be pretty easy; we just need to call `geolocation.getPosition` and pass it the three callbacks we want to use.

Inside the controller we'll create three functions, one for each of the possible outcomes:

- Successful geolocation attempt
- Unsuccessful geolocation attempt
- Geolocation not supported

We'll also update the messages being displayed to the user, letting them know that the system is doing something. This is particularly important now because geolocation can take a second or two.

The following listing shows the controller after all of these updates are made, creating the new functions and calling the geolocation service to kick it off.

Listing 8.16   Updating the controller to use the new geolocation service

```
var locationListCtrl = function ($scope, loc8rData, geolocation) {
  $scope.message = "Checking your location";                       ◁─ ❶ Set default message

  $scope.getData = function (position) {
    $scope.message = "Searching for nearby places";
    loc8rData
      .success(function(data) {                                              ❷ Function
        $scope.message = data.length > 0 ? "" : "No locations found";        to run if
        $scope.data = { locations: data };                                   geolocation
      })                                                                      is successful
      .error(function (e) {
        $scope.message = "Sorry, something's gone wrong";
      });
  };
```

```
$scope.showError = function (error) {
  $scope.$apply(function() {
    $scope.message = error.message;
  });
};


$scope.noGeo = function () {
  $scope.$apply(function() {
    $scope.message = "Geolocation not supported by this browser.";
  });
};

geolocation.getPosition($scope.getData,$scope.showError,$scope.noGeo);
};
```

❸ Function to run if geolocation is supported but not successful

❹ Function to run if geolocation isn't supported by browser

Pass the function to our geolocation service ❺

The first thing we did here is tell users that we're finding their location by setting a default message ❶. We then created a function to run when geolocation is successful ❷. The native geolocation API passes a position object to this callback. This function will then call the loc8rData service to get the list of locations.

Next we have a function to run when geolocation is supported but not successful ❸. The native geolocation API passes an error object to the callback containing a message property that we can output to the user. Note the $scope.$apply() wrapper and take a look at the sidebar to see what it is and why it's there.

The noGeo function ❹ will run if geolocation isn't supported by the browser, and set a message to be output to the user. Note again the use of $scope.$apply().

Finally, we call our geolocation service ❺, passing the three callback functions as parameters.

About $scope.$apply()

In the code snippet that manages the geolocation functionality we use $scope.$apply() in two out of the three callbacks after updating a value in the scope. If we hadn't done this, the messages wouldn't have displayed in the browser. But why, and why only two of the callbacks?

$scope.$apply() is used when Angular may not know about some updates to the scope. This typically occurs after an asynchronous event, such as a callback or user action. The purpose of the function is to push changes in scope over to the view.

$scope.$apply() is actually used a lot in Angular, but most of the time you don't see it. We didn't use it with the success callback, because in that case the changes in scope were made within the returned promises of the $http service. Behind the scenes Angular wraps these promises inside a $scope.$apply() function so that you don't have to. Most of the native Angular events, in fact, are wrapped inside one, saving you time and effort most of the time.

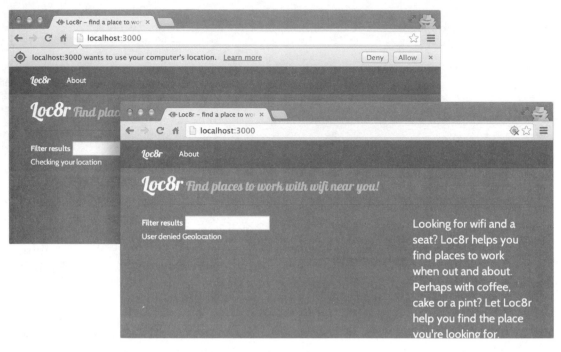

Figure 8.9   With geolocation added Loc8r will now ask your permission to know your location; if you say no then a simple message is displayed.

If you reload the application in your browser you'll now be prompted to share your location, which you can allow or deny. If you deny the browser access to your location the $scope.showError callback function will be invoked and an error message will be displayed on the screen. Figure 8.9 shows how this looks in Chrome.

If you say no to test this error message there is a good chance that your browser will remember this setting. If it does you can manage the settings in your browser's preferences or options to let you test what happens if you say yes.

If you do say yes then the application will call our data service to get the data from the API. This sounds good but we've missed one step: we haven't passed the coordinates to the data service yet, so it's still using the hard-coded lat and lng values. Let's change this now.

PASSING THE GEOLOCATION COORDINATES TO THE DATA SERVICE

We're almost there. The geolocation service is returning coordinates to the Angular application, so we now just need to get these coordinates over to our data service so that we can add them to the API call.

The first thing to do is modify the loc8rData service, wrapping the call to the API in a function so that we can pass data to it. We can't pass parameters into the loc8rData function itself because it's a service constructor. In the following listing we'll set up the new nested function to accept two parameters, lat and lng, and update the call to the API to use them.

Listing 8.17   Updating the `loc8rData` service to return a function instead of data

```
var loc8rData = function ($http) {
  var locationByCoords = function (lat, lng) {        ◄──
    return $http.get('/api/locations?lng=' + lng + '&lat=' + lat +
      '&maxDistance=20');                             ◄──
  };
  return {
    locationByCoords : locationByCoords              ◄──
  };
};
```

Create new function inside service function, accepting two parameters, lat and lng

Remove hard-coded values in API call and replace with lng and lat variables

Return locationByCoords function making it accessible as method of service

Our `loc8rData` service now has a method `locationByCoords` that the controller can access, passing it the coordinates. So let's make the update to the controller.

We've seen that the geolocation API returns a position parameter to the success callback, which in this case we've called `$scope.getData`. position is a JavaScript object containing various pieces of data, including a coords path that holds values for latitude and longitude.

The following listing shows how to update the `$scope.getData` function in the controller, modifying the call to the data service to use the new method and pass through the parameters.

Listing 8.18   Update the controller to pass the coordinates to the services

```
$scope.getData = function (position) {
  var lat = position.coords.latitude,
      lng = position.coords.longitude;
  $scope.message = "Searching for nearby places";
  loc8rData.locationByCoords(lat, lng)                  ◄──
    .success(function(data) {
      $scope.message = data.length > 0 ? "" : "No locations found";
      $scope.data = { locations: data };
    })
    .error(function (e) {
      $scope.message = "Sorry, something's gone wrong";
    });
};
```

Define variables to hold latitude and longitude values from position object

Instead of just calling loc8rData service name, update code to call new locationByCoords method, passing the lat and lng variables

And that's the last piece of the puzzle. Loc8r now finds your current location and lists the places near you, which was the whole idea from the very start. You can also filter the results on the homepage using the text input.

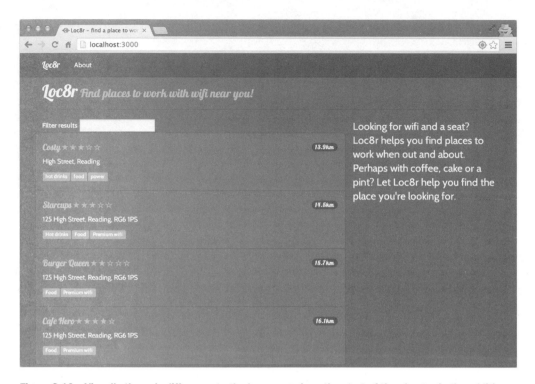

Figure 8.10   Visually the only difference to the homepage from the start of the chapter is the addition of the filter textbox; under the hood, however, the main content area is now being generated by Angular, which is also finding your actual location and displaying results close by.

Figure 8.10 shows the homepage now. It doesn't look much different from when we started this chapter, but the main content area of the homepage is now an Angular module.

And that's it. Nearly. As we've been merrily adding in Angular to the homepage we've actually introduced a bug on the Add Review page. Now we'll see what that bug is and how to fix it.

8.4   *Ensuring forms work as expected*

By adding Angular to the site template in layout.jade we've inadvertently created a bug in the form that adds a review. When we created the review form we kept the `action` blank, as this meant that the form would submit to the current URL. This is exactly what we wanted and has worked well for us so far. So, what's the problem?

When Angular encounters a form without an action it prevents the submit action from happening. In many ways this makes sense. If you're creating an Angular application and include a form, you'll probably want Angular to handle the form and manage the submission and destination. You don't want to manually prevent it from submitting each time, so Angular helps you out by doing it for you.

This is very helpful, except for the situation we find ourselves in now. The way to fix it is to add an action to the form; this will stop Angular from interfering with the form.

Step one is to pass the current URL to Jade from the controller. An easy way to get an accurate representation of the URL is via the `originalUrl` property of the `req` object. The following listing shows the update required to the `renderReviewForm` function in locations.js in the app_server/controllers folder.

Listing 8.19 Pass the URL from the review form controller

```
var renderReviewForm = function (req, res, locDetail) {
  res.render('location-review-form', {
    title: 'Review ' + locDetail.name + ' on Loc8r',
    pageHeader: { title: 'Review ' + locDetail.name },
    error: req.query.err,
    url: req.originalUrl
  });
};
```

Step two is to simply output this `url` parameter in the `action` attribute of the form definition in location-review-form.jade in the app_server/views folder. This is shown in the following code snippet:

```
form.form-horizontal(action="#{url}", method="post", role="form")
```

With those two small updates the form will continue to work as before and Angular will ignore it.

8.5   *Summary*

In this chapter we've covered

- Simple binding and two-way data binding
- The best practice of using the getter and setter syntax for defining a module and its components
- Defining controllers in code and HTML to manage the application
- How scope works in Angular, particularly the rootScope and controller-level scopes
- Creating HTML snippets with directives
- Using filters to modify the output of text and also entire repeated items of HTML
- Using services to add reusable pieces of functionality and work with data
- The $http service for making asynchronous calls to an API
- When and why to use $scope.$apply()
- Working with the HTML5 location API

Coming up next in chapter 9 we're going to start converting the whole of the Loc8r application into a single-page application using Angular. So take a deep breath and get ready—it's going to be a good one!

Building a single-page application with Angular: Foundations

This chapter covers

- Setting up Express to deliver a single-page application
- Best practices for organizing code in a large Angular application
- Using Angular to do the URL routing instead of Express
- Combining and minifying several Angular files into one

We saw in chapter 8 how to use Angular to add a component to an existing page. Over the next two chapters we're going to take Angular to the next level and use it to create a single-page application. This means that instead of running the entire application logic on the server using Express, we'll be running it all in the browser using Angular. By the end of this chapter we'll have the framework for an SPA in place, and have the first part up and running by using Angular to route to the homepage and display the content.

Figure 9.1 shows where we're at in the overall plan, recreating the main application as an Angular SPA.

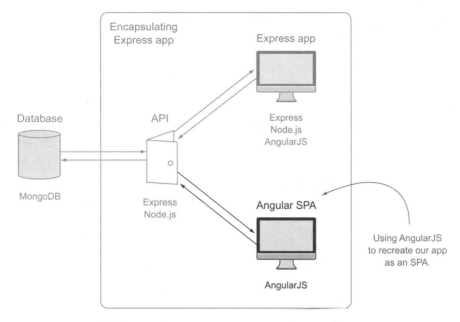

Figure 9.1 **This chapter will recreate the Loc8r application as an Angular SPA, moving the application logic from the back end to the front end.**

In a normal development process you probably wouldn't create an entire application on the server and then recreate it as an SPA. Ideally, your early planning phases will have defined whether or not you want an SPA, enabling you to start in the appropriate technology. For the learning process we're going through now it's a good approach; we're already familiar with the functionality of the site and the layouts have already been created. This will let us focus on the more exciting prospect of seeing how to build a full Angular application.

We'll start off by updating the encapsulating Express application to include a client-side application, before creating the homepage. As we go through the process of adding controllers, services, filters, and directives, we'll explore various best practices such as protecting the global scope, making reusable components, and minifying the code for better browser performance.

9.1 Setting the groundwork for an Angular SPA

In this section we'll be setting up a few things so that we can use the rest of the chapter to build the functionality of the SPA. In chapter 8 we put all of the Angular code for the homepage component into one file. This is okay to do for a relatively small one-off component, but you probably noticed that at around 140 lines or so it was already getting a bit hard to manage and find the piece of code you were looking for.

For reasons of manageability, code quality, and reusability, the best practice for building an Angular SPA is to have one file per piece of functionality. So each controller, service, directive, and filter should have its own file. That's the approach we're going to take here, which brings with it a need for good organization.

9.1.1   Getting base files in place

We need to get organized and get the base files for our application in the right place so that we can easily build it up. We'll start with creating a new folder at the root of the application to hold the SPA code.

CREATING AN APP_CLIENT FOLDER FOR THE CLIENT-SIDE APPLICATION

The very first thing we need to do is create a place inside our main Express application for the Angular SPA to live. We already have a naming convention for separating out the main parts of our application with folders called app_server and app_api. Adding to this family, create a new folder called app_client in the root of the application.

This is where we'll keep all of the application code for the Angular SPA. We want the JavaScript code that we'll put in the folder to be given to the browser to run, rather than running on the server. To make this happen we need to tell Express that this folder contains "static" content, to be delivered directly to the browser as it is, when requested.

You may remember from way back in the book that this is configured in the main Express app.js file. In there we already have the public folder set to be static. In the following code snippet we duplicate this line in app.js and set the folder name to be app_client:

```
app.use(express.static(path.join(__dirname, 'public')));
app.use(express.static(path.join(__dirname, 'app_client')));
```

Now whenever the browser requests a resource from our new folder it will be delivered directly as is.

CREATING THE MAIN SPA APPLICATION FILE

Inside the app_client folder we'll have a main application file. We saw in chapter 8 how to use the module setter and getter syntax, and this distributed file approach is where the syntax really starts to come into its own. The main file will contain the one and only module setter for our application.

In the app_client folder create a new file called app.js, and add the Angular module setter shown here:

```
angular.module('loc8rApp', []);
```

With the module setter in place we'll now be able to add controllers, filters, and more to the application by using the module getter syntax.

ADDING THE MAIN SPA APPLICATION FILE TO THE JADE LAYOUT

The Angular application will be needed in the browser, of course, and we no longer need the homepage component that we built in chapter 8. So we can update the reference in layout.jade (in app_server/views) as follows:

```
script(src='/angular/angular.min.js')
script(src='/app.js')
```

> Replace existing link to
> angular/loc8rApp.js with /app.js

That's it for the first round of basics. We've got somewhere to put our application code, and we created the module setter and added it to the Jade layout so that it will come down to the browser.

If you try it now though, you'll get a JavaScript error in your browser as it's still trying to use the Jade template for the homepage, but without the Angular component from chapter 8 attached to it.

We'll need to create some new application code to run the entire homepage, but first we need to let Angular take control of the routing.

9.2 Switching from Express routing to Angular routing

One of the principles of an SPA is that the page doesn't fully reload when a visitor navigates from one screen to another. The browser shouldn't make a request to the server every time a user clicks to look at a different page. But we also want visitors to be able to visit any of the URLs directly, and be shown the correct content the first time.

At the moment, when a user visits a URL for our site the browser sends a request to the server, which processes the request before sending the HTML for the page to the browser. See loop 1 in figure 9.2 for a visual of this process. This happens for every new page request while the user is on our site, with the server resending the entire page each time.

In an SPA, when a visitor first goes to a URL on the site the browser sends a request to the server. As loop 2 in figure 9.2 shows, the server then returns the full application to the browser, and it's this client-side application that processes the request before displaying the correct page to the visitor. When the user clicks to go to another page in the site, the application in the browser processes the request and changes what the user sees, rather than making another request to the server. This shorter process is shown in loop 3 in figure 9.2.

The interesting thing about this for us right now is how the browser knows what to display for different URLs. In Express we set up a bunch of routes that point to different controllers. In Angular we can actually do something similar, but first we need to stop Express from taking over.

9.2.1 Switching off the Express routing

As shown in figure 9.2, every page requested of the application is routed through Express. A URL request comes in and Express decides which controller should be

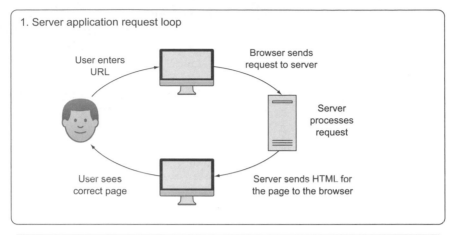

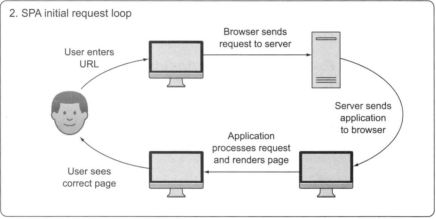

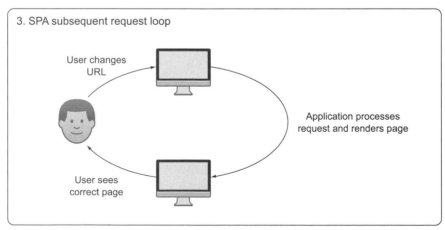

Figure 9.2   **Three different request loops associated with different approaches. Server applications hit the server for every new page request, but SPAs typically only hit the server for the initial page load. Subsequent requests are handled by the SPA itself.**

used to handle it. We want to move to a different approach, where Express will be used to deliver the containing page and Angular application, and Angular will do the rest of the routing.

To take control of the application routing away from Express we'll do two things:

- Create a new Express controller to deliver a basic template to the browser.
- Update the Express homepage route to use a new controller.

CREATING A NEW EXPRESS CONTROLLER TO DELIVER A PAGE TEMPLATE

Before updating the main Express route we'll give it a new controller to use. The question is: what do we want to send to the browser? In our SPA we want to keep the navigation and footer the same on all pages, and change the central content as the user clicks around. Our layout.jade template contains the header, footer, and a placeholder for the central content. Sounds like a perfect candidate to be reused.

The following code snippet shows the new controller to add to the end of the others.js file in app_server/controllers:

```
module.exports.angularApp = function(req, res){
  res.render('layout', { title: 'Loc8r' });
};
```

When we call this controller it will just send the layout to the browser. So next we need to call it.

CHANGING THE HOMEPAGE ROUTING

The route for the homepage is in the index file of app_server/routes, and we now need to update this to use our new controller. The following code snippet shows the update required to the routing:

> Set homepage route
> to use new controller

```
router.get('/', ctrlOthers.angularApp),
router.get('/location/:locationid', ctrlLocations.locationInfo);
router.get('/location/:locationid/review/new', ctrlLocations.addReview);
router.post('/location/:locationid/review/new', ctrlLocations.doAddReview);
```

What about the other Express routes?

The rest of the Express routes are effectively redundant now, and won't be used. You can delete them or comment them out if you wish. Leaving them in won't conflict with the Angular routing because all of the paths in Angular will be slightly different.

To avoid page reloads, the default behavior of Angular is to change the URL's paths after a #, which is traditionally a page anchor. The original intent of the # in a URL was to take a visitor to a specific point on a long page; Angular uses it to take a visitor to a specific point in an application.

In the Express version, the URL path for the About page looked like this:

```
/about
```

> **(continued)**
>
> With Angular routing set up, the URL path for the same page would look like this:
>
> ```
> /#/about
> ```
>
> We'll address this further in chapter 10 when we look at how to remove the # from Angular URLs for better deep linking.

Now visiting the homepage will give you a pretty bare page as shown in figure 9.3, with just the navigation and a footer (the footer at this stage is hidden behind the navigation due to the lack of content).

Let's move on to the next step and add some Angular routing.

9.2.2 Adding ngRoute (angular-route) to the application

Older versions of Angular had routing built in to the main library, but this has since been made an external dependency so that it can be maintained in its own right. So we'll need to download this and add it to our application.

As it's a core piece of functionality you can download the file from code.angularjs.org. This site maintains a folder for each release of Angular, so you can make sure you download the correct version. We're using Angular 1.2.19, so we can head to code.angularjs.org/1.2.19/ to see a list of possible downloads.

The module we want is called angular-route, so download the two following minified files:

- angular-route.min.js
- angular-route.min.js.map

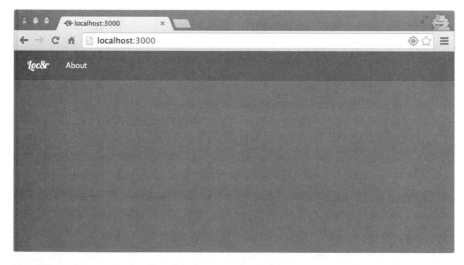

Figure 9.3 With Express only rendering the layout.jade template in the browser the homepage is quite bare, and ready for some Angular code.

Now it's time to add the files to the application.

ADDING THE ANGULAR-ROUTE FILES TO THE APPLICATION

We'll move these library files into the new app_client folder so that browsers can use them as static files. To keep things tidy create a new folder called lib inside app_client and place the two angular-route files in there. This will help keep library files separate from our application code.

The browser needs to know to get the JavaScript file, of course, so once again we need to add a link to the file inside layout.jade as shown in the following code snippet:

```
script(src='/angular/angular.min.js')
script(src='/lib/angular-route.min.js')
script(src='/app.js')
```

Now the browser knows about the JavaScript file and will download it, which will in turn reference the .map file to display more meaningful error messages if necessary. This is good, but our Angular application doesn't know that we want to use it, so let's address that now.

ADDING ANGULAR-ROUTE TO THE ANGULAR APPLICATION

To add angular-route to our Angular application we need to add it to the module definition as a dependency. The name of the file might be angular-route but the name of the module is ngRoute, so this is the dependency we need to add. This module generates a provider called $routeProvider that we can pass to an Angular config function. The config function is where we'll define the different routes for our application.

All of this is shown together in the following listing, which shows the updated contents of app_client/app.js in its entirety.

> **Listing 9.1 Adding `ngRoute` and `config` to the Angular application**

```
angular.module('loc8rApp', ['ngRoute']);          ◁⎯⎯   ❶ Add ngRoute as
                                                            module dependency
function config ($routeProvider) {
  $routeProvider
    .when('/', {
    })                                            ❷ Module config
    .otherwise({redirectTo: '/'});                   function to hold
}                                                    route definitions

angular
  .module('loc8rApp')                             ❸ Add config to module, passing
  .config(['$routeProvider', config]);   ◁⎯⎯        through $routeProvider as
                                                    dependency
```

The Angular syntax and use of dependency injection, modules, and providers can make this look more complicated than it is. Our module needs to use ngRoute to enable routing ❶, and the config function ❷ is where we define the routes. The module needs to be told about the config function ❸ using the module getter syntax.

The routing as it stands won't do much, but here the syntax is pretty clear. When the URL path '/' is called—that is, the homepage—it will do nothing; if a different URL is called, it will redirect to the homepage. As we go through this chapter we'll add more .when sections to this configuration so that we can show the different pages. But first, let's get the homepage doing something.

9.3   Adding the first views, controllers, and services

In this section we're going to reinstate the homepage functionality. To do this we'll need to create an Angular view and controller, and also use the services we created in chapter 8 for geolocation and hitting the data API.

In section 9.1 we talked about splitting the functionality into separate files, and that's what we're going to do here. Every view, controller, and service should be contained in its own separate file, and these files should be grouped together in logical folders. This means grouping them together based on what they do, rather than the file type. For example, the controller and view for the homepage are tightly bound to each other so we'll put them together in the same folder.

> **TIP: BEST PRACTICE**   Each view, controller, service, and filter should be contained in a separate file. The files should have a consistent naming convention, and be grouped together in functional folders.

With that in mind, let's start by creating a folder called home inside the app_client folder. This will house our homepage files, starting with the view.

9.3.1   Creating an Angular view

Here we're going to create the HTML template for the homepage content, attach it to the Angular routing, and display it on the page. So let's get straight into it and create the view.

CREATING THE VIEW TEMPLATE

We already know how the homepage should look and behave, and we've already got a template for it including some Angular bindings. That template is in Jade, but now we need to convert it to HTML making sure to replace any Jade binding with Angular equivalents. Inside the home folder in app_client create a new file for our view called home.view.html.

Listing 9.2 shows the contents of the home.view.html file after it has been converted from Jade. Note that for now we've removed the formatDistance filter from the location distance badge to prevent any errors; we'll add it back in later.

Listing 9.2   Angular view template for the homepage, home.view.html

```
<div id="banner" class="page-header">
  <div class="row">
    <div class="col-lg-6"></div>
      <h1>
```

```
        {{ pageHeader.title }}
        <small>{{ pageHeader.strapline }}</small>
      </h1>
    </div>
  </div>
```
Update pageHeader bindings to be Angular bindings

```
<div class="row">
  <div class="col-xs-12 col-sm-8">
    <label for="filter">Filter results</label>
    <input id="filter" type="text", name="filter", ng-model="textFilter">
    <div class="error">{{ message }}</div>
    <div class="row list-group">
      <div class="col-xs-12 list-group-item" ng-repeat="location in
      data.locations | filter : textFilter">
        <h4>
          <a href="/location/{{ location._id }}">{{ location.name }}</a>
          <small class="rating-stars" rating-stars
      rating="location.rating"></small>
          <span class="badge pull-right badge-default">{{ location.distance
      }}</span>
        </h4>
        <p class="address">{{ location.address }}</p>
        <p>
          <span class="label label-warning label-facility" ng-
      repeat="facility in location.facilities">
            {{ facility }}
          </span>
        </p>
      </div>
    </div>
  </div>
  <div class="col-xs-12 col-sm-4">
    <p class="lead">{{ sidebar.content }}</p>
  </div>
</div>
```
Remove formatDistance filter, for now

Update sidebar content to be Angular binding

This HTML isn't doing anything we haven't seen before, and when the data is plugged in we'll be back to our familiar homepage. The next step is to tell the Angular module to use this view for the homepage.

ASSIGNING A VIEW TO A ROUTE

Angular needs to know about our new view template, and when to apply it. For this we go back to our route config function in app_client/app.js. Inside the when statement for the homepage path, we specify a templateUrl option pointing to our new HTML file, as follows:

```
function config ($routeProvider) {
  $routeProvider
    .when('/', {
      templateUrl: 'home/home.view.html'
    })
    .otherwise({redirectTo: '/'});
}
```
Add templateUrl to route config to specify view template to use

With that in place Angular will now use the home.view.html template when the URL path is '/'. There's just one problem—we haven't told Angular where to show this template in the browser. Not to worry, that's just a very simple addition to the base HTML template.

DEFINING WHERE TO SHOW THE ANGULAR VIEW

In chapter 8 when we took some pieces of HTML and made them external, we included them back into the application as directives. What we're going to do here is the same, using a directive that comes with ngRoute. This directive is called ng-view and is used by Angular as a container in which the views can be switched.

Applying it is super simple. In layout.jade we already have a .container that currently holds the block content statement, designed to bring in the Jade content for individual pages. The following code snippet shows how we can add a new div with ng-view as an attribute inside the container for Angular to use:

```
.container
  div(ng-view)          Add empty div as
    block content       ng-view container, where
                        Angular inserts views
```

With that in place you can head to the browser and see what you've got. Not a lot, but more than before! There's no data attached to the view, but you should at least be able to see the Filter Results input box that's part of the view.

Next we'll give it some data by adding a controller.

9.3.2 Adding a controller to a route

The process of adding a controller to a route is also not particularly difficult. There are a few steps to take:

1 Create a controller in its own file.
2 Attach the controller to the Angular application.
3 Tell the route config function when to use the controller.
4 Tell the browser about the file.

Let's start at the beginning, creating the new file and the controller.

CREATING THE CONTROLLER

In the same folder as the home.view.html file create a new file home.controller.js— naming conventions don't come much more simple than this! In this file we'll use the module getter syntax to add a new controller to the application, and define a basic controller to add some data to the scope so that we can see the page header and sidebar content in the browser.

This step isn't really anything new to us, so let's look at the content of the new controller file in the following listing.

Listing 9.3   Creating the new homepage controller

```
angular                              Use module getter to
  .module('loc8rApp')                add new controller
  .controller('homeCtrl', homeCtrl); to application

function homeCtrl ($scope) {
  $scope.pageHeader = {                            Define new
    title: 'Loc8r',                                controller
    strapline: 'Find places to work with wifi near you!'  homeCtrl and
  };                                               bind some data
  $scope.sidebar = {                               for page header
    content: "Looking for wifi and a seat etc etc" and sidebar
  };
}
```

The new `homeCtrl` controller simply binds a few data elements that we used to send to
Jade from the Express controllers, but technically this is nothing alien to us after chapter 8. One thing that starts to become apparent when building up an application
using separate files is the great benefit of using the module getter/setter syntax. Each
controller, service, or filter can be added to the application from its own file. The
great benefit here is that you don't have to try to manage a full list of dependencies
from within the main app.js file.

ADDING A CONTROLLER TO THE ROUTE CONFIG FUNCTION

The route `config` function needs to know which controller to use for which path. This
is another simple step, adding a controller option to the `config` function for the
homepage path. The controller option takes the name of the controller to be used as
a string, as follows:

```
function config ($routeProvider) {
  $routeProvider
    .when('/', {                        Add controller option to
      templateUrl: 'home/home.view.html',  config for route, giving
      controller: 'homeCtrl'               name of controller as string
    })
    .otherwise({redirectTo: '/'});
}
```

We're nearly there—now we just need to tell the browser about the file so that it can
download it.

TELLING THE BROWSER ABOUT THE CONTROLLER FILE

No great surprises here; we need to add the script file to layout.jade so that the browser
will download it and Angular can use the contents. The following code snippet shows
the change needed to the bottom of layout.jade to add the new controller file:

```
script(src='/angular/angular.min.js')
script(src='/lib/angular-route.min.js')
script(src='/app.js')
script(src='/home/home.controller.js')
```

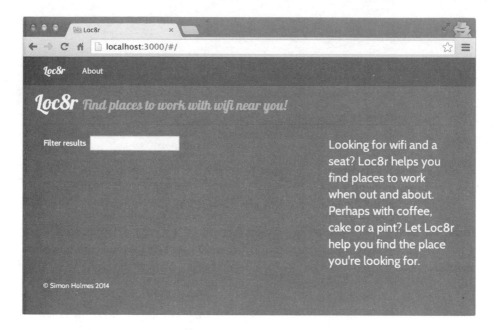

Figure 9.4   The first look at our SPA, setting the data for the homepage header and sidebar in the Angular `homeCtrl` controller

Now if you head over to the browser and view the homepage again you can see that the header and sidebar both have content showing. You should see something like the screenshot in figure 9.4.

Before we move on, we're going to update our controller to use a bit of best practice.

9.3.3   Controller best practice: Using the controllerAs syntax

Angular offers a way to create a *view model* that you can bind your data to, rather than attaching everything directly to the $scope object. There are a few advantages to following this approach. First, it forces you to contain your data correctly, avoiding the possibility of assigning a value directly to $scope. It also keeps your $scope object clean; you can still use it if you need to when publishing or subscribing to $scope events. So $scope should be reserved for special cases when it's actually needed, such as working with $scope.$apply.

So how does it work and what does it look like? Let's start with the route definition.

DECLARING CONTROLLERAS IN A ROUTE DEFINITION

The first step is to tell Angular that you want to use this controller with the controllerAs syntax. This is just a case of adding an option to the definition of the route. You specify an option of controllerAs and pass it the name of the ViewModel you want to use as a string.

Another piece of best practice is to choose a standard name; the typical choice is vm, which stands for ViewModel. The following code snippet shows this in place in the route definition:

```
function config ($routeProvider) {
  $routeProvider
    .when('/', {
      templateUrl: 'home/home.view.html',
      controller: 'homeCtrl',
      controllerAs: 'vm'
    })
    .otherwise({redirectTo: '/'});
}
```

> Add controllerAs option to route definition, passing variable name to be used as string

We'll use this vm variable in both the controller and the view, and put all of the data objects currently in $scope inside it.

DEFINING THE VIEWMODEL IN THE CONTROLLER

Behind the scenes, when you use a controller in an application it's generated using JavaScript's new method, creating a single instance. When the controllerAs syntax is used, Angular uses this inside the function, and binds it to $scope.

Using this in JavaScript can be problematic, as it's very context-sensitive. Each nested function will have its own this, rather than inheriting from the parent scope. To work around this issue, simply define a variable at the top of the controller, and assign this as the value.

We're going to declare a variable called vm as a matter of consistency and best practice, but it could be anything you want. The name of the variable defined here doesn't have to match that defined in the route definition.

When you've declared vm to be equal to this, you can update all of the data bindings, changing $scope to vm. With all of the references to $scope gone, you can now also remove $scope from the function definition. The updated home controller is shown in the following listing.

> **Listing 9.4   Updating the home controller to use vm and the controllerAs syntax**

```
function homeCtrl () {
  var vm = this;
  vm.pageHeader = {
    title: 'Loc8r',
    strapline: 'Find places to work with wifi near you!'
  };
  vm.sidebar = {
    content: "Looking for wifi and a seat? Etc etc…"
  };
}
```

> Remove $scope from function definition

> *Assign this to vm variable*

> Update data bindings to use vm instead of $scope

USING THE VIEWMODEL IN THE VIEW

The final step in using the controllerAs syntax is using the ViewModel variable in the view. The data in each data binding now lives inside the vm object, so all of the bindings must be updated. In the following listing you can see this in place for the home.view.html file.

Listing 9.5   Updating the home view to use vm data bindings

```
<div id="banner" class="page-header">
  <div class="row">
    <div class="col-lg-6"></div>
      <h1>
        {{ vm.pageHeader.title }}
        <small>{{ vm.pageHeader.strapline }}</small>
      </h1>
  </div>
</div>

<div class="row">
  <div class="col-xs-12 col-sm-8">
    <label for="filter">Filter results</label>
    <input id="filter" type="text", name="filter", ng-model="textFilter">
    <div class="error">{{ vm.message }}</div>#
    <div class="row list-group">
      <div class="col-xs-12 list-group-item" ng-repeat="location in
    vm.data.locations | filter : textFilter">
        <h4>
          <a href="/location/{{ location._id }}">{{ location.name }}</a>
          <small class="rating-stars" rating-stars
    rating="location.rating"></small>
          <span class="badge pull-right badge-default">{{ location.distance
    }}</span>
        </h4>
        <p class="address">{{ location.address }}</p>
        <p>
          <span class="label label-warning label-facility" ng-
    repeat="facility in location.facilities">
            {{ facility }}
          </span>
        </p>
      </div>
    </div>
  </div>
  <div class="col-xs-12 col-sm-4">
    <p class="lead">{{ vm.sidebar.content }}</p>
  </div>
</div>
```

Update data bindings, adding vm in front of each item

With that, the homepage is now back up and running using the `controllerAs` syntax. We'll use this approach for all controllers moving forward.

Now we're back to the task of getting the homepage working properly again, getting the visitor's location, and displaying a list of nearby results. In chapter 8 we created some services to work with the geolocation and data, and we're going to reintroduce those services to our SPA.

9.3.4 *Using services*

In chapter 8 we created two services, `geolocation` and `loc8rData`. We're going to lift these straight out of there and add them as services in our SPA. To add each service we'll need to:

1 Create a new file.
2 Paste in the service code.
3 Register the service with the application.
4 Add the file to layout.jade.
5 Invoke the service from the home controller.

CREATING THE SERVICE FILES

Sticking with our approach of keeping everything in separate files we'll create a new file for each of the services. These services could well be reused all over the site and aren't necessarily subcomponents of the homepage. So rather than put them in the home folder, create a new folder in app_client called common, and in that a new folder called services, giving us app_client/common/services.

Create a new file loc8rData.service.js in this folder and paste in the `loc8rData` service code from chapter 8 as shown in the following listing, remembering to also register it with the Angular application.

Listing 9.6 Create the `loc8rData` service

```
angular
  .module('loc8rApp')
  .service('loc8rData', loc8rData);

function loc8rData ($http) {
  var locationByCoords = function (lat, lng) {
    return $http.get('/api/locations?lng=' + lng + '&lat=' + lat +
      '&maxDistance=20');
  };
  return {
    locationByCoords : locationByCoords
  };
}
```

We'll tell the browser about this file in just a moment, but first we'll do the same thing for the `geolocation` service as shown in the next listing, this time in a new file called geolocation.service.js.

Listing 9.7 Create the `geolocation` service

```
angular
  .module('loc8rApp')
  .service('geolocation', geolocation);

function geolocation () {
  var getPosition = function (cbSuccess, cbError, cbNoGeo) {
```

```
    if (navigator.geolocation) {
      navigator.geolocation.getCurrentPosition(cbSuccess, cbError);
    }
    else {
      cbNoGeo();
    }
  };
  return {
    getPosition : getPosition
  };
}
```

There's nothing new in either of these files. We've just taken the code we've already created, put each service into its own file, and registered them with the Angular application. Now we need to tell the browser to download them.

GETTING THE FILES TO THE BROWSER

No major surprises here; we're going to add these two files to the list of scripts being included in layout.jade, as follows:

```
script(src='/angular/angular.min.js')
script(src='/lib/angular-route.min.js')
script(src='/app.js')
script(src='/home/home.controller.js')
script(src='/common/services/loc8rData.service.js')
script(src='/common/services/geolocation.service.js')
```

Pretty simple. Now we need to bring in the code to use the services.

USING THE SERVICES FROM THE CONTROLLER

Again, we've actually done the hard work already, as the code exists in the controller we created in chapter 8. So we're going to lift the code out of there and in to `homeCtrl` in our SPA.

The following listing shows the homepage controller after this has been done, including replacing all instances of `$scope` with `vm`. Remember, of course, to pass the names of the services into the controller so that it can use them.

Listing 9.8   Update the homepage controller to use the two services

```
function homeCtrl (loc8rData, geolocation) {          ⟵——  Pass names of services
  var vm = this;                                             into controller
  vm.pageHeader = {
    title: 'Loc8r',
    strapline: 'Find places to work with wifi near you!'
  };
  vm.sidebar = {
    content: "Looking for wifi and a seat? Etc etc"
  };
  vm.message = "Checking your location";
```

```
    vm.getData = function (position) {
      var lat = position.coords.latitude,
          lng = position.coords.longitude;
      vm.message = "Searching for nearby places";
      loc8rData.locationByCoords(lat, lng)
        .success(function(data) {
          vm.message = data.length > 0 ? "" : "No locations found nearby";
          vm.data = { locations: data };
        })
        .error(function (e) {
          vm.message = "Sorry, something's gone wrong";
        });
    };

    vm.showError = function (error) {
      vm.$apply(function() {
        vm.message = error.message;
      });
    };

    vm.noGeo = function () {
      vm.$apply(function() {
        vm.message = "Geolocation is not supported by this browser.";
      });
    };

    geolocation.getPosition(vm.getData,vm.showError,vm.noGeo);

}
```

Paste functionality from controller in chapter 8, replacing all instances of $scope with vm

That looks good, right? There's just one problem. $apply is a method of $scope, and vm doesn't inherit it and can't access it because vm is also a child of $scope. So we'll have to add $scope back in.

USE $SCOPE WHEN NEEDED

The controllerAs syntax that we're using is ideal for decluttering and avoiding abuse of $scope. Following this approach you only use $scope when you absolutely need it, which helps provide an additional layer of clarity and understanding to your code and the process going on behind it.

To use $scope.$apply in the home controller we just need to pass in $scope like any other dependency, and then change the current vm.$apply calls back to $scope.$apply. The following listing shows the changes needed (keep the rest of the code in place as it's omitted here for brevity).

Listing 9.9   Updates needed to use $scope.$apply in the home controller

```
function homeCtrl ($scope, loc8rData, geolocation) {

  vm.showError = function (error) {
    $scope.$apply(function() {
      vm.message = error.message;
    });
  };

  vm.noGeo = function () {
    $scope.$apply(function() {
```

Pass $scope into controller as dependency

Update instances of vm.$apply to be $scope.$apply

```
        vm.message = "Geolocation is not supported by this browser.";
      });
    };
}
```

Okay, *now* we're good to go. Now the scope will update again following the asynchronous actions of the geolocation service.

> **TIP: BEST PRACTICE**   Only use $scope when you actually need it; use the View-Model `controllerAs` approach where you can.

Trying out the site now will display a list of locations as shown in figure 9.5.

We're getting there—just a couple of tweaks to go, which we'll do by reintroducing the filters and directives.

9.3.5 *Using filters and directives*

The homepage now needs to output the rating stars and format the distances correctly. In chapter 8 we created a `formatDistance` filter and a `ratingStar` directive; we'll plug those in now. Going through things in this way should hopefully demonstrate the power and benefit of creating reusable modules and components that you can move around and plug into different projects as you need.

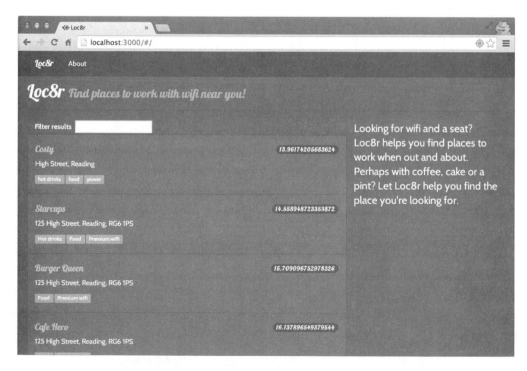

Figure 9.5   Homepage returning a list of locations using the `geolocation` and `loc8rData` services

Sticking with the "one component, one file" approach we'll create each filter and directive separately, as individual files, and make sure the browser knows about each of them, too.

CREATING THE formatDistance FILTER FILE

The `formatDistance` filter is designed to be reusable; we're currently only using it in the homepage but it could be used anywhere. So, like the services, we'll add it in the common folder. In the app_client/common folder create a new folder called filters. Inside the filters folder create a new file called formatDistance.filter.js.

In the new file we need to put the `formatDistance` function we created in chapter 8, along with the `_isNumeric` helper function it uses. We also need to register the function with the Angular application as a filter using the getter syntax. All of this together is shown in the following listing.

Listing 9.10 Create the formatDistance.filter.js file

```
angular
  .module('loc8rApp')
  .filter('formatDistance', formatDistance);

var _isNumeric = function (n) {
  return !isNaN(parseFloat(n)) && isFinite(n);
};

function formatDistance () {
  return function (distance) {
    var numDistance, unit;
    if (distance && _isNumeric(distance)) {
      if (distance > 1) {
        numDistance = parseFloat(distance).toFixed(1);
        unit = 'km';
      } else {
        numDistance = parseInt(distance * 1000,10);
        unit = 'm';
      }
      return numDistance + unit;
    } else {
      return "?";
    }
  };
}
```

CREATING THE ratingStars DIRECTIVE FILES

A directive requires two files, the JavaScript defining the directive and the HTML template to be used. The `ratingStars` directive is used in multiple places, so again we'll base it in the app_client/common folder.

Inside the common folder create a new folder called directive, and in the directive folder create a new subfolder called ratingStars, so we have app_client/common/directive/ratingStars. Copy the file /public/rating-stars.html that we created in chapter 8 into this folder, and to fit with our SPA module naming convention, rename it ratingStars.template.html.

NOTE   The folder and file naming convention we're using in Angular is informed by the "one function, one file" approach. Where we have one key function in a file, we'll name the file and containing folder after that function.

Now create a new file in the same folder called ratingStars.directive.js. This is where we'll hold the JavaScript code for the directive, and, of course, we also have to register it with the JavaScript application.

In the following listing we do exactly this, remembering to update the path of the template URL.

Listing 9.11   Create the `ratingStars` directive file

```
angular
  .module('loc8rApp')
  .directive('ratingStars', ratingStars);

function ratingStars () {
  return {
    restrict: 'EA',
    scope: {
      thisRating : '=rating'
    },
    templateUrl: '/common/directives/ratingStars/ratingStars.template.html'
  };
}
```

We've also added a little something new in there, the `restrict` attribute. This tells Angular to only use the `ratingStars` directive when the string `rating-stars` is found in particular places. In this instance the `E` and the `A` stand for element and attribute, respectively, so `rating-stars` can be its own element or an attribute of another element. Other options are `C` for class and `M` for comment, but the best practice is to stick with `EA`.

Before we move on we'll need to add the references to the `formatDistance` filter file and the `ratingStars` directive file in layout.jade so that the browser can download them.

SETTING UP THE HOMEPAGE VIEW

Next we need to make sure that the homepage view will make use of the directive and filter. We haven't made any changes to the HTML regarding the rating stars, but we did take the filter out of the `distance` element to prevent Angular from throwing errors.

So the following code snippet shows the only change we need to make in home.view.html, reintroducing the `formatDistance` filter:

```
<h4>
  <a href="/location/{{ location._id }}">{{ location.name }}</a>
  <small class="rating-stars" rating-stars rating="location.rating"></small>
  <span class="badge pull-right badge-default">{{ location.distance |
    formatDistance }}</span>
</h4>
```

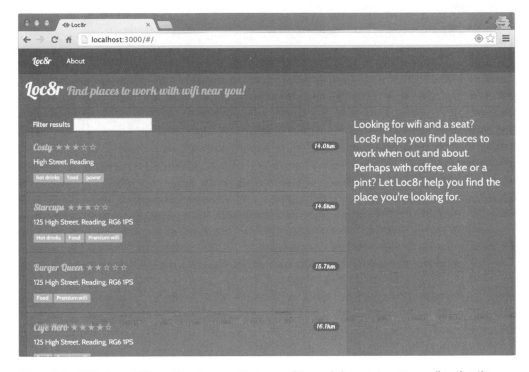

Figure 9.6 With the addition of the `formatDistance` filter and the `ratingStars` directive the homepage is looking good again.

And with that we're done with the homepage! So let's check it out in the browser. Figure 9.6 shows the homepage again with the rating stars back in and distance fixed.

Okay, good stuff. So we've got things set up to run an SPA with Angular, and we've got our first view up and running. But we've already added six JavaScript files to the template for the browser to download and we've only built the homepage. That's a lot of requests for a browser to have to make. And even worse, the files are all using global variables. So let's take a moment to look at some techniques and best practices we can use to address these issues, before continuing to build the application.

9.4 Improving browser performance

The modular approach that we're taking to coding is great for the maintainability of the codebase, but not so great for browsers if they have to go and download each of the little files separately. We've got quite a few already, and we've only done the homepage!

In this section we're going to

- Reduce the number of global variables.
- Reduce the number of files the browser downloads.
- Reduce the overall file size of the JavaScript.

Let's start with the global variables. We'll tackle this by wrapping each file in an *immediately invoked function expression* (IIFE).

9.4.1   Wrap each file in an IIFE

An IIFE is a way of encapsulating some JavaScript code in a unique scope, hiding the contents from the global scope. You can read more about this in appendix D (online).

In brief, an IIFE looks like the following code snippet, where we're wrapping a `console.log` statement:

```
(function() {
  console.log("Output immediately");
})();
```

This puts the `console.log` inside a function scope, and immediately invokes the function. And this is what we want to do with our application code. At the moment each file is running in the global scope. This is bad because it clutters the global scope, increases the risk of variable name collision, and exposes the application code to potential misuse.

> **NOTE** Our Angular application doesn't need the global scope to tie it together as everything is connected through the module getter/setter `angular.module-('loc8rApp')`.

In the following listing we can see how this looks in app_client/app.js.

> **Listing 9.12   Wrapping Angular application files in IIFEs, for example, app.js**

```
(function () {                          ←— Open IIFE

  angular.module('loc8rApp', ['ngRoute']);

  function config ($routeProvider) {
    $routeProvider
      .when('/', {
        templateUrl: 'home/home.view.html',
        controller: 'homeCtrl',
        controllerAs: 'vm'
      })
      .otherwise({redirectTo: '/'});
  }

  angular
    .module('loc8rApp')
    .config(['$routeProvider', config]);   ←— Close and invoke IIFE

})();
```

We haven't changed any of the actual code here, just wrapped the entire contents of the file in an IIFE. Now we just need to go through and wrap each of the JavaScript files we've created in this chapter in the same way:

- /app_client/common/directives/ratingStars/ratingStars.directive.js
- /app_client/common/filters/formatDistance.filter.js

- /app_client/common/services/geolocation.service.js
- /app_client/common/services/loc8rData.service.js
- /app_client/home/home.controller.js

That's it for the first goal of reducing global variables. *For the rest of this book we'll assume that each Angular JavaScript application file is wrapped in an IIFE.*

Now we want to look at reducing the number of files and the overall file size. This will involve minifying the scripts. If we try that right now our application will break, so let's see why that is, and what we can do about it.

9.4.2 *Manually injecting dependencies to protect against minification*

Minifying the code we have now will break the application. This is because we're injecting the names of the dependencies into controller and service functions as parameters. During minification these names get minified into single letters.

The definition for homeCtrl, for example, looks like this:

```
function homeCtrl ($scope, loc8rData, geolocation)
```

But if minified it would look something like this:

```
function homeCtrl(a,b,c){
```

Just to be clear, minification doesn't break JavaScript code. Each function we create would work independently. The problem arises with Angular because the parameters aren't mere parameters to be used solely in the context of the function. The parameters are also references to the names of other parts of the application, such as services. Looking at the example of the preceding code snippets, our application knows what the service loc0rData is, but doesn't know anything about a service called b.

We can protect against this by manually injecting the dependencies as strings, which won't get changed during a minify process. For this, Angular provides a $inject method against the constructors for controllers and services. The $inject method accepts an array of strings. These strings are the dependencies for a particular controller or service and match those being passed through as parameters.

This is one of those times when an example really sheds light on what we're talking about. In the following code snippet we add the dependency injection for the home-page controller, just before the definition of the function:

```
homeCtrl.$inject = ['$scope', 'loc8rData', 'geolocation'];
function homeCtrl ($scope, loc8rData, geolocation) {
```

The $inject method is applied to the name of the function, accepted as an array of the dependencies. The array should contain strings, because they don't get changed when code is minified. The contents of the array should be in the same order as the parameters in the function.

We only need to do one more thing for now, and that's to inject $http into our loc8rData service as follows:

```
loc8rData.$inject = ['$http'];
function loc8rData ($http) {
```

When organized and handled like this, dependency injection is quite simple. Just remember to do it for every controller or service that needs it. Now we're ready to minify the scripts.

9.4.3   *Using UglifyJS to minify and concatenate scripts*

To minify and concatenate the Angular application scripts we're going to use a third-party tool called UglifyJS. The aim is that when the Node application starts up in Express, UglifyJS will take the source files of our Angular application and put them all into one file and compress it. We'll update our application to use this single output file, instead of the multiple files we're using at the moment.

So let's get started, and install UglifyJS.

INSTALLING UGLIFYJS

Adding a new npm module and updating package.json is quite easy—we've done it a few times already.

Open a command line at the root folder of the application, where the package.json file is. In the command line run the following:

```
$ npm install uglify-js --save
```

This will install the UglifyJS module and add it to package.json.

ADDING UGLIFYJS TO THE APPLICATION

Now that the installation is done, it's time to bring it into the application. We're going to do this right down in the root of the application in /app.js, where everything starts. UglifyJS needs to be required in, and we also need to reference a default Node module called fs. This stands for filesystem—we'll need access to the filesystem to save the new uglified file.

The following listing shows the changes needed to /app.js to bring the two modules in.

> **Listing 9.13   Adding UglifyJS to the Node application**

```
var express = require('express');
var path = require('path');
var favicon = require('serve-favicon');
var logger = require('morgan');
var cookieParser = require('cookie-parser');
var bodyParser = require('body-parser');
require('./app_api/models/db');
var uglifyJs = require("uglify-js");
var fs = require('fs');
```

Great, we've got it in place. Let's use it!

UGLIFYING JAVASCRIPT FILES

We'll use UglifyJS to combine all of our Angular application files into one and then minify them. This process happens in memory, so once the combined file is generated we'll use the filesystem to save it.

We want this to happen quite early on when the application starts, so we'll insert the code quite high up in the main app.js file in the root of the project. Just below the view engine declaration will do. There are three distinct sections of the code we want to add in:

1 List all of the files we want to combine in an array.
2 Call UglifyJS to combine and minify the file in memory.
3 Save the uglified code into the public folder.

In the following listing we can see the code we need to add, starting off by defining an array of the files we want to uglify.

Listing 9.14 Uglifying and saving the new file

```
routeapp.set('views', path.join(__dirname, 'app_server', 'views'));
app.set('view engine', 'jade');
var appClientFiles = [
  'app_client/app.js',
  'app_client/home/home.controller.js',
  'app_client/common/services/geolocation.service.js',
  'app_client/common/services/loc8rData.service.js',
  'app_client/common/filters/formatDistance.filter.js',
  'app_client/common/directives/ratingStars/ratingStars.directive.js'
];
var uglified = uglifyJs.minify(appClientFiles, { compress : false });

fs.writeFile('public/angular/loc8r.min.js', uglified.code, function (err){
  if(err) {
    console.log(err);
  } else {
    console.log('Script generated and saved: loc8r.min.js');
  }
});
```

Step 1: define array of files to uglify

Run uglifyJs .minify process on array of files

Save generated file

Now when you restart the Node application you'll find that a new file, loc8r.min.js has been added to the folder public/angular. At this stage the minified file is 2,160 bytes, down from around 3,575 for the individual files. So as well as reducing the number of requests the browser has to make from six to one, we've reduced the file size by around 40%. Saving 1.5 kb might not seem like a lot at the moment, but remember that our application is currently very small, and only deals with the homepage.

Of course, the browser won't get the benefit if we don't tell it about the new file.

USING THE NEW MINIFIED FILE IN THE HTML

Swapping out the separate files for a single file in the HTML is a snap. We just need to update layout.jade, commenting out the individual files and adding in the new minified file, as shown in the following code snippet:

**Add in reference to new
concatenated minified file**

**Comment
out
individual
files**

```
script(src='/angular/loc8r.min.js')     ⟵
//- script(src='/app.js')
//- script(src='/common/services/loc8rData.service.js')
//- script(src='/common/services/geolocation.service.js')
//- script(src='/common/directives/ratingStars/ratingStars.directive.js')
//- script(src='/common/filters/formatDistance.filter.js')
//- script(src='/home/home.controller.js')
```

Why comment out, rather than delete? It's a lot harder to debug a single minified file than the original individual files. All errors will be on line 1, function and variable names will be changed, and so on. So if we're having problems we can flip back to using the individual files for debugging. Then we'll be shown filenames and line numbers in a useful way again.

It's possible to automate some of this by using a build system or task runner such as Gulp or Grunt. You could set these up to only build the minified file when you want to deploy to production. Or you could set them up to watch for changes to certain files and create the minified version on-the-fly. They can even generate a source map, which maps the minified file back to the originals for easier debugging.

We're not going to cover Gulp or Grunt in detail here, but they're definitely worth exploring.

PREVENTING A NODEMON RECURSIVE LOOP

Everything is working as it should, but if you start the application up using nodemon you'll notice that the application restarts several times right at the beginning. This is because nodemon restarts the application when the files change, and we're rebuilding the minified file every time the application starts. So perhaps this loop isn't such a big surprise.

We can fix this by telling nodemon to ignore changes to any files in the public folder. This folder contains static resources to be served to the browser, so we don't need an application rebuild to reflect any updates.

Passing configuration options to nodemon is a simple case of creating a nodemon.json file in the root folder of the application. Using the following code snippet will set it to verbose mode (so you get lots of information in the console) and crucially sets it to ignore everything in the public folder:

```
{
  "verbose": true,
  "ignore": ["public/*"]
}
```

Now if you restart the application using nodemon you'll see some different messages in terminal, and most importantly it won't restart several times!

Right, let's get on with building the application and adding some more pages.

9.5 *Summary*

In this chapter we've covered

- Setting Express to deliver the SPA
- Using Angular routing instead of Express to deliver the pages
- Attaching views and controllers to routes
- Using the `controllerAs` syntax
- The best practice of using separate files for everything
- Protecting the global scope using IIFEs
- Dependency injection
- Minifying and concatenating the separate files into one small application file

Coming up next in chapter 10 we'll build upon our SPA foundation, and look at new things like adding additional pages, removing the # from URLs, using route parameters, adding prebuilt AngularUI components, and pushing data back to the database. In short: lots of cool stuff.

Building an SPA with Angular: The next level

This chapter covers

- Making pretty URLs
- Adding multiple views to an SPA
- Going from one page to another without reloading the application
- Using AngularUI to get Twitter Bootstrap components as preconfigured Angular directives

In this chapter we're continuing on with the work we started in chapter 9 by building a single-page application. By the end of this chapter the Loc8r application will be a single Angular application that uses our API to get the data.

Figure 10.1 shows where we're at in the overall plan, still re-creating the main application as an Angular SPA.

We'll start off by decoupling the Angular application from the server-side application—it's still being incorporated into a Jade template. As part of this we'll see how to make pretty URLs, removing the #. When this is done we'll create the missing pages and functionality and see how to inject HTML into a binding, use URL

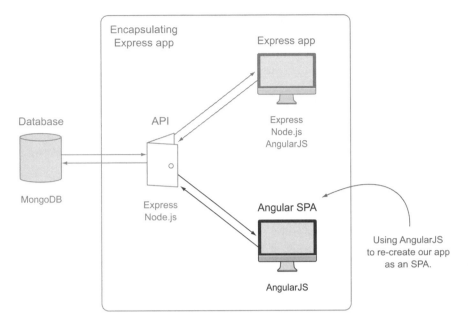

Figure 10.1   This chapter continues the work we started in chapter 9 of re-creating the Loc8r application as an Angular SPA, moving the application logic from the back end to the front end.

parameters in routes, and use prebuilt directives based on Twitter Bootstrap components. Along the way we'll keep an eye on best practices, of course.

10.1   A full SPA: Removing reliance on the server-side application

As our application stands right now, the navigation, page framework, header, and footer are all held in a Jade template. To use this template we have a controller in app_server. This works okay and might be just right for some scenarios. But to have a real SPA we want everything to do with the client-side application in app_client. The theory here is that the entire SPA could easily be moved and hosted anywhere, if you wanted to take it out of the encapsulating Express application, to a CDN for example.

To achieve this we'll start by creating the host HTML page in app_client and updating the Express routing to point to this. Following on from this we'll take the sections of the HTML page and make them into reusable components as directives. Finally we'll look at a way of making pretty URLs by removing the #.

10.1.1   Creating an isolated HTML host page

Okay, so the first step here is to create the host HTML page in a way that doesn't rely on the server application routes and controllers.

CREATE A NEW INDEX.HTML

The HTML we want to start with is the same as that already being generated by the layout.jade file. If we grab that and convert it to HTML it will look like the following listing. Save this file in app_client/index.html.

> **Listing 10.1   Host page converted into HTML**

```html
<!DOCTYPE html>
<html ng-app="loc8rApp">
  <head>
    <meta name="viewport" content="width=device-width, initial-scale=1.0">
    <title>Loc8r</title>
    <link rel="stylesheet" href="/bootstrap/css/amelia.bootstrap.css">
    <link rel="stylesheet" href="/stylesheets/style.css">
  </head>
  <body>
    <div class="navbar navbar-default navbar-fixed-top">
      <div class="container">
        <div class="navbar-header"><a href="/" class="navbar-brand">Loc8r</a>
          <button type="button" data-toggle="collapse" data-target="#navbar-
            main" class="navbar-toggle"><span class="icon-bar"></span><span
            class="icon-bar"></span><span class="icon-bar"></span></button>
        </div>
        <div id="navbar-main" class="navbar-collapse collapse">
          <ul class="nav navbar-nav">
            <li><a href="/#about">About</a></li>
          </ul>
        </div>
      </div>
    </div>
    <div class="container">
      <div ng-view>
      </div>
      <footer>
        <div class="row">
          <div class="col-xs-12"><small>&copy; Simon Holmes 2014</small></div>
        </div>
      </footer>
    </div>
    <script src="/angular/angular.min.js"></script>
    <script src="/lib/angular-route.min.js"></script>
    <script src="/lib/angular-sanitize.min.js"></script>
    <script src="/angular/loc8r.min.js"></script>
    <script src="//ajax.googleapis.com/ajax/libs/jquery/1.10.2/
      jquery.min.js"></script>
    <script src="/bootstrap/js/bootstrap.min.js"></script>
    <script src="/javascript/validation.js"></script>
  </body>
</html>
```

Nothing magical here, so let's move on and update the application to actually use this.

ROUTING TO THE STATIC HTML FILE FROM EXPRESS

Let's take a moment to think about when we want to send this index.html file to the browser. Definitely when someone visits the homepage, that's given. But if we can get rid of the # from the URLs, which we're going to look at in a couple of pages, we'll want to show it for all manner of URLs.

As we're using Angular to do the routing, we don't want to double up on that and also manage the routes in Express too. But we don't want to return this HTML file for all of the requests, because we're also serving the API requests from this application, and delivering static resources (such as CSS, Javascript, and images). So what shall we do?

You may remember that Express routing stops at the first match, after all middleware is applied. If no route match is found it continues through. We can use this feature to our advantage here. By disabling all of the routes for app_server, no requests to those URLs will match and so they'll fall through to the end.

At the end we can capture all unmatched URL requests and send our new HTML file. The following code snippet shows the changes we need to make to app.js to make this happen, including commenting out the original routes:

```
// require('./routes')(app);
require('./app_api/routes')(app);      ⟵  Comment out or delete the line
                                           requiring server application routes

app.use(function(req, res) {
  res.sendfile(path.join(__dirname, 'app_client', 'index.html'));
});

              Add catchall app.use function to respond to any
            requests that make it this far by sending HTML file
```

If you restart the application and head to the homepage you'll see that it works just as it did before, but now we've removed the reliance on the server application routes and controllers to deliver the base HTML page.

> **TIP**　When using this approach all unmatched URLs will respond by sending the HTML file that loads the Angular application. So your Angular routing should deal with unknown requests in a suitable manner.

Now let's make all of that HTML part of the Angular application.

10.1.2 *Making reusable page framework directives*

So we're now sending a basic HTML page to deliver our application, but this page has quite a lot of markup in it. This markup would be better off inside the application so that we can work with it more easily in Angular. Remember that with Angular you want to build the DOM, rather than manipulate it afterwards as you would with jQuery.

From the HTML page we'll take the footer and navigation and turn them into directives, so that we can include them on any page we want to. We'll do the same for the page header, which is currently in the homepage view.

You may remember from chapter 8 that a directive is comprised of two main parts. Each directive will have a JavaScript file to define it and a view template to display it. In turn, each JavaScript file will have to be added to app.js so that the application can use it, and each directive will be placed as an element (or an attribute of an element) into host views where required.

MAKING A FOOTER DIRECTIVE

The footer is the most basic component we have because it requires just a small amount of HTML. There's a slight catch. If you want to use a directive as an element, you can't give it the name of an existing tag. So we can't call the footer directive `footer` and try to include it in the site as `<footer>` because the HTML specification already contains a `footer` tag.

So we'll call our footer `footerGeneric` and create a folder in app_client/common/ directives called footerGeneric. In this folder we'll put both the HTML and JavaScript files required for the directive.

Starting off with the HTML we can create a file called footerGeneric.template.html and paste in the HTML for a footer, as shown in the following code snippet:

```
<footer>
  <div class="row">
    <div class="col-xs-12"><small>&copy; Simon Holmes 2014</small></div>
  </div>
</footer>
```

Next we need to create the associated JavaScript file as footerGeneric.directive.js. In the following listing we use this file to define the new directive, register it with the main application, and assign the HTML file we've just created as the view template.

> **Listing 10.2 Defining the generic footer as a directive: footerGeneric.directive.js**

```
(function () {

  angular
    .module('loc8rApp')
    .directive('footerGeneric', footerGeneric);

  function footerGeneric () {
    return {
      restrict: 'EA',
      templateUrl: '/common/directives/footerGeneric/
      ➥ footerGeneric.template.html'
    };
  }

})();
```

When that file is in place and saved, remember to add it to the `appClientFiles` array in app.js. Now when we want to include a footer in one of our Angular pages we can use the new element `<footer-generic></footer-generic>`.

MOVING THE NAVIGATION INTO A DIRECTIVE

The navigation directive is very similar in approach to the footer. It contains more HTML but doesn't need to do anything clever with the data. So we'll just create another folder called navigation in the same place as the footer directive folder, app_client/common/directives.

This folder will host the HTML and JavaScript files again. The following listing shows the HTML we need for the navigation template.

> **Listing 10.3 Navigation HTML: navigation.template.html**

```
<div class="navbar navbar-default navbar-fixed-top">
  <div class="container">
    <div class="navbar-header"><a href="/" class="navbar-brand">Loc8r</a>
      <button type="button" data-toggle="collapse" data-target="#navbar-main"
       class="navbar-toggle"><span class="icon-bar"></span><span class="icon-
       bar"></span><span class="icon-bar"></span></button>
    </div>
    <div id="navbar-main" class="navbar-collapse collapse">
      <ul class="nav navbar-nav">
        <li><a href="/about">About</a></li>
      </ul>
    </div>
  </div>
</div>
```

The next listing shows the JavaScript definition for the navigation directive.

> **Listing 10.4 Defining the navigation directive: navigation.directive.js**

```
(function () {

  angular
    .module('loc8rApp')
    .directive('navigation', navigation);

  function navigation () {
    return {
      restrict: 'EA',
      templateUrl: '/common/directives/navigation/navigation.template.html'
    };
  }

})();
```

Don't forget to add the JavaScript file to the array in app.js! The main reasons for creating these separate files and folders are maintainability and reusability. If each file and folder does one thing, it's easier to know where to go to fix or update something. It's also easier to take a component from one project to another.

CREATING A DIRECTIVE FOR THE PAGE HEADER

The page header is slightly different as a directive. It needs to display different data on different pages. Like we did with the rating-stars directive we'll create an isolate scope in Angular and pass the data through.

As before, create a new folder called pageHeader and create the empty HTML and JavaScript files we'll need. We'll start with the HTML that is in the following code snippet. We can lift this directly from the homepage view template, but we need to change the data binding. As we're using an isolate scope we won't have direct access to the data in vm. Instead, we'll say that we want the data for the title and strapline to be held in an object called content. For example

```html
<div id="banner" class="page-header">
  <div class="row">
    <div class="col-lg-6"></div>
      <h1>
        {{ content.title }}
        <small>{{ content.strapline }}</small>
      </h1>
  </div>
</div>
```

Directive will expect title and strapline to be passed through as properties of object called content

Next up we define the directive as we've done with the others, this time adding the scope option back in as shown in listing 10.5. We'll use the scope option to pass through the content object that the HTML expects. To pass the content object through, this directive expects to receive it from the binding when it's used.

Listing 10.5   Defining the page header directive: pageHeader.directive.js

```javascript
(function () {

  angular
    .module('loc8rApp')
    .directive('pageHeader', pageHeader);

  function pageHeader () {
    return {
      restrict: 'EA',
      scope: {
        content : '=content'
      },
      templateUrl: '/common/directives/pageHeader/pageHeader.template.html'
    };
  }

})();
```

Define isolate scope, passing through content object

When we use this directive in a controller view we'll need to pass through the content object as an attribute of the element. For example, we'll be using it like this:

```html
<page-header content="vm.pageHeader"></page-header>
```

Using an isolate scope like this protects the directive from any changes in scope names. So long as you pass it the content it expects it doesn't care what you called it before. Once again this makes code really reusable.

Again, don't forget to add this file to the appClientFiles array in the Express app.js file.

FINAL HOMEPAGE TEMPLATE

Now that we've created all of the directives we can add them to our homepage view template as shown in the following listing. The new directives are shown in bold, but to keep the DOM structure intact we've also had to add a little bit of the container markup from the index.html file.

> **Listing 10.6   Complete homepage view template**

```
<navigation></navigation>

<div class="container">
  <page-header content="vm.pageHeader"></page-header>

  <div class="row">
    <div class="col-xs-12 col-sm-8">
      <label for="filter">Filter results</label>
      <input id="filter" type="text", name="filter", ng-model="textFilter">
      <div class="error">{{ vm.message }}</div>
      <div class="row list-group">
        <div class="col-xs-12 list-group-item" ng-repeat="location in
    vm.data.locations | filter : textFilter">
          <h4>
            <a href="#/location/{{ location._id }}">{{ location.name }}</a>
            <small class="rating-stars" rating-stars
    rating="location.rating"></small>
            <span class="badge pull-right badge-default">{{ location.distance
    | formatDistance }}</span>
          </h4>
          <p class="address">{{ location.address }}</p>
          <p>
            <span class="label label-warning label-facility" ng-
    repeat="facility in location.facilities">
              {{ facility }}
            </span>
          </p>
        </div>
      </div>
    </div>
    <div class="col-xs-12 col-sm-4">
      <p class="lead">{{ vm.sidebar.content }}</p>
    </div>
  </div>

  <footer-generic></footer-generic>
</div>
```

Using directives like this—so long as they're named well—makes it really easy to understand the structure of your view at a glance, without getting bogged down in loads of markup.

We've taken all the markup from the index.html file, so what does that look like now?

FINAL INDEX.HTML FILE

Having taken all of the HTML markup and moved it into directives and views, there's not much left in the index.html file. But that's exactly what we wanted. As the controllers and views are now managing the entire content of a page we need to move the ng-view directive into the body tag.

We can see this in action in the following listing, with the new minimal index.html file.

Listing 10.7   Final index.html file

```
<!DOCTYPE html>
<html ng-app="loc8rApp">
  <head>
    <meta name="viewport" content="width=device-width, initial-scale=1.0">
    <title>Loc8r</title>
    <link rel="stylesheet" href="/bootstrap/css/amelia.bootstrap.css">
    <link rel="stylesheet" href="/stylesheets/style.css">
  </head>
  <body ng-view>
    <script src="/angular/angular.min.js"></script>
    <script src="/lib/angular-route.min.js"></script>
    <script src="/angular/loc8r.min.js"></script>
    <script src="//ajax.googleapis.com/ajax/libs/jquery/1.10.2/
      jquery.min.js"></script>
    <script src="/bootstrap/js/bootstrap.min.js"></script>
    <script src="/javascript/validation.js"></script>
  </body>
</html>
```

> ng-view directive now sits in body tag so that we can control full page in Angular

Now we really do have an SPA. We have a single minimal HTML file, with everything else being managed by Angular. Figure 10.2 shows the browser view and the HTML source.

Next we're going to look at an option for removing the # from URLs.

10.1.3   Removing the # from URLs

A common request for SPAs is to have pretty URLs. Our URLs aren't bad, but they do all have that # in them. Angular provides a method of removing them from the address bar, but please note that this doesn't work well with Internet Explorer 9 or below. If you need to support early versions of Internet Explorer, don't use this part.

The HTML5 spec allows browsers to push states into the navigation history. The main reason for this is to give browsers a way to use the back button in an SPA, preventing the back button from taking them straight away from the site they're looking at.

Angular routing can make use of this. We just have to switch it on!

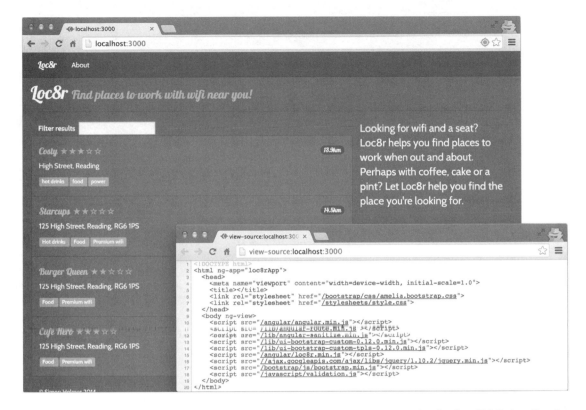

Figure 10.2 Now a real SPA, the source of the HTML page is minimal but the application is still fully functional.

USING $LOCATIONPROVIDER AND THE HTML5 MODE

To make use of this HTML5 mode we need to add a new provider to the Angular application configuration. We're already using $routeProvider, and now we need to pass in $locationProvider. This is native to Angular so we don't have to download any additional libraries.

Enabling the HTML5 mode will be a simple one-liner, like this:

```
$locationProvider.html5Mode(true);
```

In the following listing we make some changes to app_client/app.js to update the template URLs, pass $locationProvider into config, and set the html5Mode to be true.

> **Listing 10.8 Enabling the HTML5 history API**

```
(function () {

  angular.module('loc8rApp', ['ngRoute']);

  function config ($routeProvider, $locationProvider) {
    $routeProvider
```

Accept
$locationProvider as
a parameter in config

```
        .when('/', {
          templateUrl: 'home/home.view.html',
          controller: 'homeCtrl',
          controllerAs: 'vm'
        })
        .otherwise({redirectTo: '/'});                    Set html5Mode
                                                          to be true
      $locationProvider.html5Mode(true);
    }
                                                          Add $location-
    angular                                               Provider as
      .module('loc8rApp')                                 dependency
      .config(['$routeProvider', '$locationProvider', config]);    for config

})();
```

Now when you reload the application, in a modern browser, the URL for the homepage will no longer end in #/. Instead, it will be nice and clean on your domain. If you load it in IE9, the page will still work, but it will have the #.

WORKING WITH INTERNET EXPLORER

This type of routing won't work in IE8 or 9 as they don't have access to the HTML5 API. The application will still be usable in these browsers and Angular will fall back to using the #. So navigating through the application works just fine, albeit with the /#/ element in the URL.

The problem arises if someone copies and pastes a deep link without a hash and tries to use it in IE9. Internet Explorer will just render the homepage, as that's the way our default routing is set up.

Now, you didn't hear this from me, but here's a nasty little fix that you can put right at the top of the homepage controller if you want to. When the homepage controller runs it will check to see what the path name of the URL is. If it's not for the homepage—that is, just a /—it will take the path name, prefix it with a #, and redirect the page, as follows:

```
if (window.location.pathname !== '/') {
  window.location.href = '/#' + window.location.pathname;
}
```

I did say it was nasty. If someone pastes a URL without a # into IE9 they'll get a flicker as the homepage starts to load before Angular redirects to the correct route. It's not ideal, so think hard before going down this route if you need to support older versions of Internet Explorer.

Right, that's enough of nasty hacking! Let's get back to it and add another page to our application.

10.2 *Adding additional pages and dynamically injecting HTML*

The concept of an SPA is that the server delivers one page to the browser, and the client-side application does everything else. In this section we're going to see how to include additional pages by adding the About page. We'll also deal with an issue that arises when you try to inject HTML into an Angular binding.

10.2.1 Adding a new route and page to the SPA

You've probably got an idea of how this is going to work, using the config in app.js to add the route, pointing to a new template and controller. If that is what you were thinking then you were spot on!

UPDATING THE NAVIGATION LINK

The first step we need to take is to update the About entry in the main navigation. It currently points to /about, but that's not good for the Angular routing. Even though we're using the HTML5 mode and you don't see the # in the URL, the paths all need to come after a #. So all we need to do is update navigation.template.html, inserting a # into the About link as shown in the following code snippet:

```
<ul class="nav navbar-nav">
  <li><a href="/#about">About</a></li>          ⟵─┤  Add # to About
</ul>                                                 page link
```

Well, that was an easy first step. Next we'll jump into Angular and add the routing definition.

ADDING THE ROUTE DEFINITION

Now we need to add a route to the Angular $routeProvider configuration in app_client/app.js. To do this we can duplicate the entry for the homepage and change the path, template URL, and controller name.

Just like we did when creating the About page on the server side we'll define a reusable generic view for a simple page of text. In the following listing we can see the new route added to config making all of the required changes.

Listing 10.9 Add a new Angular route definition for the About page

```
function config ($routeProvider, locationProvider) {
  $routeProvider
    .when('/', {
      templateUrl: 'home/home.view.html',
      controller: 'homeCtrl',
      controllerAs: 'vm'                                    Set new path to
    })                                                      be /about          Define path for
    .when('/about', {                        ⟵─                               generic view
      templateUrl: '/common/views/genericText.view.html',  ⟵─                 template
      controller: 'aboutCtrl',                                    ⟵─
      controllerAs: 'vm'              ⟵─              Keep            Tell route to use
    })                                                controllerAs    controller called
    .otherwise({redirectTo: '/'});                    set to 'vm'     'aboutCtrl'
  $locationProvider.html5Mode(true);
}
```

Seeing this in place gives us a good idea of what we need to do next. This route contains a controller and a view template that don't exist yet. Let's deal with the controller first.

CREATING THE CONTROLLER

This is going to be a new controller, so it needs a new file. So in app_client create a folder called about, and in there create a new file called about.controller.js. This will hold the controller for the About page.

In this file we'll create an IIFE to protect the scopes, attach the controller to the loc8rApp application, and, of course, define the controller. The controller in this case is fairly simple—we just need to set the page title and the page content. For the content we'll take what we're using in Express. This is in the about export in app_server/controllers/main.js. Your text should have some line breaks in as \n; you'll need them in to follow through the rest of this section.

In the following listing we can see the complete code for the about.controller.js file. I've trimmed down the text in the main content area to save ink and trees.

> **Listing 10.10   Creating the Angular controller for the About page**

```
(function () {

  angular
    .module('loc8rApp')
    .controller('aboutCtrl', aboutCtrl);

  function aboutCtrl() {
    var vm = this;

    vm.pageHeader = {
      title: 'About Loc8r',
    };
    vm.main = {
      content: 'Loc8r was created to help people find places to sit down and
      get a bit of work done.\n\nLorem ipsum dolor sit amet, consectetur
      adipiscing elit.'
    };
  }

})();
```

As controllers go this is pretty simple. No magic going on here; we're just using the vm variable to hold the view model data like we did with the homepage controller. We, of course, need to make sure the application knows about this file. The following code snippet shows us adding it to the appClientFiles array in the main app.js file in Express:

```
var appClientFiles = [
  'app_client/app.js',
  'app_client/home/home.controller.js',
  'app_client/about/about.controller.js',
```

```
    'app_client/common/services/geolocation.service.js',
    'app_client/common/services/loc8rData.service.js',
    'app_client/common/filters/formatDistance.filter.js',
    'app_client/common/directives/ratingStars/ratingStars.directive.js'
];
```

When the Node application restarts our new file will be added to the single minified file we're now using. But if we try to view the page now it will just be empty, as we haven't created the view template yet.

CREATING THE NEW COMMON TEMPLATE

For this new generic text template we've already defined in the route `config` where the file will be: /app_client/common/views/genericText.view.html. So go ahead and create this file. From our original Jade templates we also know what the markup needs to be. Converting the Jade to an Angular template and adding in our layout directives gives us the following:

```
<navigation></navigation>

<div class="container">
  <page-header content="vm.pageHeader"></page-header>

  <div class="row">
    <div class="col-md-6 col-sm-12">
      <p>{{ vm.main.content }}/p>
    </div>
  </div>

  <footer-generic></footer-generic>
</div>
```

Again, nothing unusual here. Just some HTML and standard Angular bindings. If we take a look at this page in the browser we'll see that the content is coming through, but the line breaks aren't displaying, as illustrated in figure 10.3.

This isn't ideal. We want our text to be readable, and shown as originally intended. If we can change the way the distances appear on the homepage using a filter, why not do the same thing to fix the line breaks? Let's give it a shot and create a new filter.

10.2.2 Creating a filter to transform the line breaks

So, we want to create a filter that will take the provided text and replace each instance of \n with a <br/> tag. We've actually already solved this problem in Jade, using a JavaScript `replace` command as shown in the following code snippet:

```
p !{(content).replace(/\n/g, '<br/>')}
```

With Angular we can't do this inline; instead we need to create a filter and apply it to the binding.

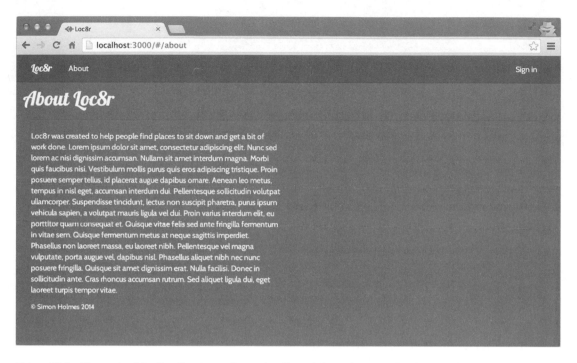

Figure 10.3   The content for the About page is coming through from the controller, but the line breaks are being ignored.

CREATING ADDHTMLLINEBREAKS FILTER

This is likely to be a common filter, so we'll put it in the common filters folder alongside formatDistance.filter.js. Again, the contents of the file need to be wrapped in an IIFE, and the filter needs to be registered with the application.

The filter itself is fairly straightforward, returning a function that accepts incoming text and replaces each \n with a `<br/>`. Create a new file called addHtmlLineBreaks .filter.js and enter the contents shown in the following code snippet:

```
(function () {

  angular
    .module('loc8rApp')
    .filter('addHtmlLineBreaks', addHtmlLineBreaks);

  function addHtmlLineBreaks () {
    return function (text) {
      var output = text.replace(/\n/g, '<br/>');
      return output;
    };
  }

})();
```

Before you can do anything with this new filter remember to add it to the `appClient-Files` array in the Express app.js. When you've done that, let's try using it.

APPLYING THE FILTER TO THE BINDING

Applying a filter to a binding is pretty simple—we've already done it a few times. In the HTML we just add the pipe character (|) after the data object being bound, and follow it with the name of the filter like this:

```
<p>{{ vm.main.content | addHtmlLineBreaks }}</p>
```

Simple, right? But if we try it in the browser all isn't quite as we'd hoped. As we can see in figure 10.4, the line breaks are being replaced with `<br/>` but they're being displayed as text instead of being rendered as HTML.

Figure 10.4 The `<br/>` tags being inserted with our filter are being rendered as text rather than HTML tags.

Hmmmm. Not quite what we wanted, but at least the filter seems to be working! There's a very good reason for this output: security. Angular protects you and your application from malicious attacks by preventing HTML from being injected into a data binding. Think about when we let visitors write reviews for locations, for example. If they could put any HTML in that they wanted, someone could easily insert a `<script>` tag and run some JavaScript hijacking the page.

But there's a way to let a subset of HTML tags through into a binding, which we'll look at now.

10.2.3 *Sending HTML through an Angular binding*

We're not the first to have a legitimate reason to want to pass some HTML into a binding, so Angular has an answer to this. We can use a service called angular-sanitize, which allows a certain subset of HTML tags to be included in a data binding.

DOWNLOADING NG-SANITIZE

In chapter 9 we downloaded angular-route from code.angularjs.org, and now we need to do the same for angular-sanitize. Find the correct branch again for the release of

Angular you're using (1.2.19 in my case) and download the two minimized angular-sanitize files *angular-sanitize.min.js* and *angular-sanitize.min.js.map*. Put these files alongside the angular-route files in /app_client/lib.

When they're in place, bring them to the browser by adding a reference to the JavaScript file in index.html as shown in the following code snippet:

```
<script src="/angular/angular.min.js"></script>
<script src="/lib/angular-route.min.js"></script>
<script src="/lib/angular-sanitize.min.js"></script>
<script src="/angular/loc8r.min.js"></script>
```

Okay, next up we need to tell the application we want to use the service.

ADDING NGSANITIZE AS AN APPLICATION DEPENDENCY

To tell our application that we want to use angular-sanitize we use the same approach that we used for ngRoute and add it as a dependency in the module setter. In this case the name of the service exposed to the application is ngSanitize, so as shown in the following code snippet, add this to the array of dependencies in app_clients/app.js:

```
angular.module('loc8rApp', ['ngRoute', 'ngSanitize']);
```

Now that this is available to the application we don't have to update the controller or the filter. But we don't necessarily want every single data binding to go through the sanitizer; rather, we want to hand pick which should be allowed to parse some HTML. Angular is looking out for us again here, because to use ngSanitize you have to bind your data to a directive, rather than an inline data binding.

BINDING TO THE HTML ELEMENT AS A DIRECTIVE

So ngSanitize doesn't just interfere with all data bindings in all templates, it exposes a directive that you bind to. This directive is called ng-bind-html. As with other directives this is added as an attribute of an HTML element, with the binding and filter passed through as the value.

In the following code snippet we can see how to use this, passing in our content data binding and the addHtmlLineBreaks filter. This is in the genericText.view.html file:

```
<div class="row">
  <div class="col-md-6 col-sm-12">
    <p ng-bind-html="vm.main.content | addHtmlLineBreaks"></p>
  </div>
</div>
```

This time if you reload the page in the browser you should see the line breaks in place, looking like figure 10.5.

Great news; it's always nice to see a win and have a few pieces of a puzzle fall into place. In this little section we've seen how to add a new page to an SPA, and also how to inject HTML into an Angular binding. Next we're going to look at a more interesting page and get the Details page running in our SPA.

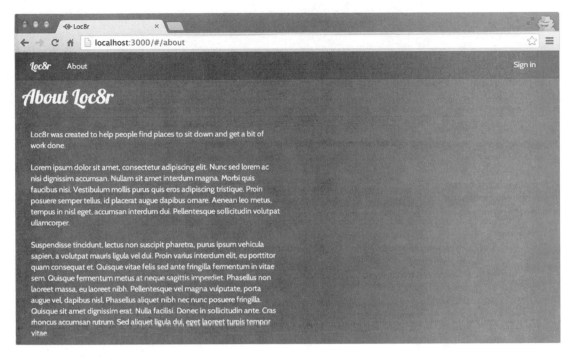

Figure 10.5 Using the `addHtmlLineBreaks` filter in conjunction with `ngSanitize` we now see the line breaks rendering as intended.

10.3 More complex views and routing parameters

In this section we're going to add the Details page to the Angular SPA. One of the crucial aspects here will be retrieving the location ID from the URL parameter to ensure we get the correct data. Using URL parameters in this way is common practice, and is a very useful technique to know in any framework. We'll also have to update the data service to hit the API asking for specific location details. As we translate the Jade view into an Angular template we'll also discover some additional things that Angular does to help us lay out things.

Before we get into the fun stuff we need to get the basic route, controller, and view in place.

10.3.1 Getting the page framework in place

We've done this a couple of times now, so we'll speed through it here. We need to add the route `config` and create the controller and view files it defines. The controller will also need to add it to application files so that we can use it.

DEFINING THE PAGE ROUTE

In app_client/app.js we need to add in the new route. As we want to accept a URL parameter we'll define the route in the same way we did in Express, by putting a locationid variable at the end of the path, preceded by a semi-colon. The new route in situ is shown in the following listing.

Listing 10.11   Add the Details page route to the Angular application configuration

```
function config ($routeProvider, locationProvider) {
  $routeProvider
    .when('/', {
      templateUrl: 'home/home.view.html',
      controller: 'homeCtrl',
      controllerAs: 'vm'
    })
    .when('/about', {
      templateUrl: '/common/views/genericText.view.html',
      controller: 'aboutCtrl',
      controllerAs: 'vm'
    })
    .when('/location/:locationid', {
      templateUrl: '/locationDetail/locationDetail.view.html',
      controller: 'locationDetailCtrl',
      controllerAs: 'vm'
    })
    .otherwise({redirectTo: '/'});
  $locationProvider.html5Mode(true);
}
```

CREATING THE CONTROLLER FILE

The Details page template and controller are going to be tightly coupled; they're not likely to work with any other templates or controllers. Bearing this in mind we'll put them together in the same folder. Create a new folder called locationDetail in app_client and set up the controller framework shown in the following listing in a new file called locationDetail.controller.js.

Listing 10.12   Controller framework for the Details page

```
(function () {

  angular
    .module('loc8rApp')
    .controller('locationDetailCtrl', locationDetailCtrl);

  function locationDetailCtrl () {
    var vm = this;

    vm.pageHeader = {
      title: 'Location detail page'
    };
  }

})();
```

The crucial step that's easy to forget: *add this file to the* appClientFiles *array in the Express app.js file.*

CREATING THE VIEW TEMPLATE

Inside the same folder as the controller file create the view template file called locationDetail.view.html. For now we'll just put the standard page framework in here, as you can see in the following code snippet:

```
<navigation></navigation>

<div class="container">
  <page-header content="vm.pageHeader"></page-header>

  <footer-generic></footer-generic>
</div>
```

UPDATING THE LINKS IN THE HOMEPAGE LIST

The files are now in place, but we also need to be able to navigate to the Details pages from the homepage listing. Like we did with the About link, we need to add a # to the front of the links in the list so that Angular can access them.

In home.view.html find the line that renders the location name—it's nested in the <h4> tag. As demonstrated in the following code snippet add a /# to the front of the href:

```
<h4>
  <a href="/#/location/{{ location._id }}">{{ location.name }}</a>
```

And there we go, that's the basics in place. Let's see about getting that URL parameter and using it to get the correct data.

10.3.2 *Using URL parameters in controllers and services*

Getting and using a URL parameter is a pretty common requirement, so it's no major surprise that Angular has a built-in service to help here. That service is called $routeParams and it's super easy to use.

USING $ROUTEPARAMS TO GET URL PARAMETERS

To use $routeParams in a controller we need to inject it as a dependency and pass it into the function. Once it's in the controller, $routeParams surfaces as an object holding any URL parameters it has matched. It's so easy to use; let's just look at it in code, updating the locationDetailCtrl function as shown in the following code snippet:

```
locationDetailCtrl.$inject = ['$routeParams'];
function locationDetailCtrl ($routeParams) {
  var vm = this;
  vm.locationid = $routeParams.locationid;
  vm.pageHeader = {
    title: vm.locationid
  };
}
```

Inject $routeParams service into controller, protecting against minification

Pass $routeParams into controller so we can use it

Get locationid from $routeParams and save it in view model

Use locationid in page title

Figure 10.6 Using `$routeParams` **we can get the location ID from the URL and use it in a controller, shown here by outputting it in the page header.**

See? How easy was that? We can see in the screenshot in figure 10.6 that the location ID is being taken from the URL and output in the page header. This is not where we want to end up, but it's good to see it working.

Let's use that location ID to get some data from the API so that we can make the page useful again. To do so we'll need to create the data service to hit the right API.

CREATING THE DATA SERVICE TO CALL THE API

In the API we built in chapter 6 we created an end point that would accept a location ID and return the associated data. The URL path for this is /api/location/:locationid. To interrogate this URL we'll add a new method to our `loc8rData` service.

The following listing shows how simple this is, adding and exposing a new `locationById` method that accepts a `locationid` parameter. The method then uses the `locationid` in the `$http` call to the API end point.

Listing 10.13   Add a method to the data service to call the API

```
function loc8rData ($http) {
  var locationByCoords = function (lat, lng) {
    return $http.get('/api/locations?lng=' + lng + '&lat=' + lat +
    '&maxDistance=20');
  };

  var locationById = function (locationid) {            Create new locationById
    return $http.get('/api/locations/' + locationid);   method, accepting
  };                                                     locationid parameter
                                                         ... that uses
  return {                                               locationid in
    locationByCoords : locationByCoords,                 a call to API
    locationById : locationById        Expose locationById
  };                                   method so that we
}                                      can call it from
                                       controller
```

USING THE SERVICE TO GET DATA

To use the service we need to inject the `loc8rData` service into the controller. Once it's there we can follow the pattern we used on the homepage when we hit the API to get the list of locations. As a reminder, the data service using the `$http` method is asynchronous; upon completion it will invoke either the `success` or `error` promise.

In the following listing we inject `loc8rData` into the `locationDetailCtrl` function, and call the `locationById` method passing the location ID as the parameter. On a successful completion of the request we save the returned data to the view model in `vm.data.location` and display the location name in the page header.

Listing 10.14   Using the service from the controller to get the location data

```
locationDetailCtrl.$inject = ['$routeParams', 'loc8rData'];    ⟩  Inject loc8rData
function locationDetailCtrl ($routeParams, loc8rData) {            service as
  var vm = this;                                                   dependency
  vm.locationid = $routeParams.locationid;                         and pass to
                                                                   controller

     loc8rData.locationById(vm.locationid)
       .success(function(data) {                  If request is successful save
         vm.data = { location: data };            returned data in view model
         vm.pageHeader = {
           title: vm.data.location.name           Output location name
         };                                       to page header
       })
       .error(function (e) {          If request isn't successful output
         console.log(c);              error message to browser console
       });
}
```

Call locationById method, passing location ID as parameter

So that's pretty powerful and pretty easy. We can see it working in the browser in figure 10.7, outputting a location name in the page header.

Figure 10.7   Proving that we're getting data from the API by outputting the location name in the page header

That's another good step complete. Now we need to put the view together.

10.3.3 *Building the Details page view*

The next step is to rebuild the view. We've got a Jade template with Jade data-bindings, and we need to transform this into HTML with Angular bindings. There are quite a few bindings to put in place and some loops using `ng-repeat`. We'll also use the `rating-stars` directive again to show the overall rating and the rating for each review. And we'll need to allow line breaks in the review text by using the `addHtml-LineBreaks` filter.

GETTING THE MAIN TEMPLATE IN PLACE

The following listing shows everything in place with the bindings in bold. This code should be added to the locationDetail.view.html file, between the page header and footer. There are some pieces we've left out, such as the opening times, which we'll fill in when we've got this in place and tested.

> **Listing 10.15   Angular view for the Details page**

```html
<div class="row">
  <div class="col-xs-12 col-md-9">
    <div class="row">
      <div class="col-xs-12 col-sm-6">
        <p class="rating" rating-stars rating="vm.data.location.rating"></p>        ⟵  Use rating-stars
        <p>{{ vm.data.location.address }}</p>                                            directive to show
        <div class="panel panel-primary">                                               average rating for
          <div class="panel-heading">                                                   location
            <h2 class="panel-title">Opening hours</h2>
          </div>
          <div class="panel-body">
            <!-- Opening times to go here -->
          </div>
        </div>
        <div class="panel panel-primary">
          <div class="panel-heading">
            <h2 class="panel-title">Facilities</h2>
          </div>
          <div class="panel-body">
            <span class="label label-warning label-facility" ng-
repeat="facility in vm.data.location.facilities">
              <span class="glyphicon glyphicon-ok"></span>        Loop through
              {{ facility }}                                      facilities
            </span>
          </div>
        </div>
      </div>
      <div class="col-xs-12 col-sm-6 location-map">
        <div class="panel panel-primary">
          <div class="panel-heading">
            <h2 class="panel-title">Location map</h2>
          </div>
          <div class="panel-body">
```

```
        <img src="http://maps.googleapis.com/maps/api/staticmap?center={{
    vm.data.location.coords[1] }},{{ vm.data.location.coords[0]
    }}&amp;zoom=17&amp;size=400x350&amp;sensor=false&amp;markers={{
    vm.data.location.coords[1] }},{{ vm.data.location.coords[0]
    }}&amp;scale=2" class="img-responsive img-rounded">
        </div>
      </div>
    </div>
  </div>
  <div class="row">
    <div class="col-xs-12">
      <div class="panel panel-primary review-panel">
        <div class="panel-heading"><a href="" class="btn btn-default pull-
  right">Add review</a>
          <h2 class="panel-title">Customer reviews</h2>
        </div>
        <div class="panel-body review-container">
          <div class="review" ng-repeat="review in
    vm.data.location.reviews">
            <div class="row">
              <div class="well well-sm review-header">
                <span class="rating" rating-stars rating="review.rating"></
    span>
                <span class="reviewAuthor">{{ review.author }}</span>
                <small class="reviewTimestamp">{{ review.createdOn }}</
    small>
              </div>
              <div class="col-xs-12">
                <p ng-bind-html="review.reviewText | addHtmlLineBreaks"></p>
              </div>
            </div>
          </div>
        </div>
      </div>
    </div>
  </div>
  <div class="col-xs-12 col-md-3">
    <p class="lead">{{ vm.data.location.name }} is on Loc8r because it has
    accessible wifi and space to sit down with your laptop and get some work
    done.</p>
    <p>If you've been and you like it - or if you don't - please leave a
    review to help other people just like you.</p>
  </div>
</div>
```

Annotations in code:
- **Loop through reviews** → `<div class="review" ng-repeat="review in vm.data.location.reviews">`
- **Using rating-stars directive to show rating for each review** → `<span class="rating" rating-stars rating="review.rating"></span>`
- **Apply addHtmlLineBreaks filter to review text and bind as HTML** → `<p ng-bind-html="review.reviewText | addHtmlLineBreaks"></p>`

Now that's quite a long code listing! But that's to be expected, as there's quite a lot going on in the Details page. If you look at the page in the browser you'll see there are a few things that could be fixed. We're not showing the opening times yet, the reviews are coming through oldest first, and data of the reviews needs formatting.

ADDING IF-ELSE STYLE LOGIC WITH NG-SWITCH TO SHOW THE OPENING TIMES

It's not unusual to want some type of if-else logic in a template, to let you show different chunks of HTML depending on a certain parameter. For each opening time we want to display the days in the range, and either a closed message or the opening and closing times. In our Jade template we had a bit of logic, a simple `if` statement checking whether `closed` was `true`, as shown in the following code snippet:

```
if time.closed
| closed
else
| #{time.opening} - #{time.closing}
```

We want to do something similar in our Angular view. Instead of using `if`, Angular works along the line of JavaScript's `switch` method, where you define which condition you want to check at the top, and then provide different options depending on the value of the condition.

The key directives here are `ng-switch-on` for defining the condition to switch on, `ng-switch-when` for providing a specific value, and `ng-switch-default` for providing a backup option if none of the specific values matched. We can see all of these in action in the following listing, where we add the opening times to the HTML view.

Listing 10.16   Using `ng-switch` to display the opening times

```
<div class="panel-heading">
  <h2 class="panel-title">Opening hours</h2>
</div>
<div class="panel-body">
  <p ng-repeat="time in vm.data.location.openingTimes" ng-switch
    on="time.closed">
    {{ time.days }} :
    <span class="opening-time" ng-switch-when="true">closed</span>
    <span class="opening-time" ng-switch-default>{{ time.opening + " - " +
    time.closing }}</span>
  </p>
</div>
```

Run switch based on value of time.closed

When time.closed is true just output closed

Otherwise default action is to output opening and closing times

And with that we now have a bit of logic in the view. Note that as all of the `ng-switch` commands are directives they need to be added to HTML tags. Okay, let's get the reviews showing most recent first.

CHANGING THE DISPLAY ORDER OF A LIST USING THE ORDERBY FILTER

To help us order things in an `ng-repeat` list, Angular comes with a native filter called `orderBy`. Note that `orderBy` can only be used on arrays, so if you want to sort an object it needs to be converted to an array first.

The `orderBy` filter can take a couple of arguments. First, you need to state what the list is to be ordered on. This can be a function, but the more common use is to provide a property name of the list being sorted. This is what we're going to do, using the `createdOn` property of each review.

The second argument is optional, and defines whether you want to reverse the order or not. This is a Boolean value and defaults to `false` if left out. We'll set it to `true` as we want to show the latest date first.

The following listing shows how we update the view template to add the filter to the ng-repeat directive.

Listing 10.17 Showing the reviews by date using the orderBy filter

```
<div class="review" ng-repeat="review in vm.data.location.reviews |
    orderBy:'createdOn':true">
  <div class="well well-sm review-header">
    <span class="rating" rating-stars rating="review.rating"></span>
    <span class="reviewAuthor">{{ review.author }}</span>
    <small class="reviewTimestamp">{{ review.createdOn }}</small>
  </div>
  <div class="col-xs-12">
    <p ng-bind-html="review.reviewText | addHtmlLineBreaks"></p>
  </div>
</div>
```

> Add orderBy filter to ng-repeat, specifying sort property and reverse setting

And now if you reload the page you should see your reviews showing in the correct order with most recent first. It's a little hard to tell though, as the date format is not exactly user friendly. Let's fix it.

FIXING THE DATE FORMAT USING THE DATE FILTER

Another filter that comes with Angular is the date filter, which will format a given date in the style that you want. This takes just one argument: the format for your date.

To apply your formatting you send a string describing the output you want. There are too many different options to go into here, but the format is quite easy to get the hang of. To get the format "1 December 2014" we'll send the string 'd MMMM yyyy' as shown in the following listing.

Listing 10.18 Applying a date filter to format the review dates

```
<div class="review" ng-repeat="review in vm.data.location.reviews |
    orderBy:'createdOn':true">
  <div class="well well-sm review-header">
    <span class="rating" rating-stars rating="review.rating"></span>
    <span class="reviewAuthor">{{ review.author }}</span>
    <small class="reviewTimestamp">{{ review.createdOn | date : 'd MMMM yyyy'
    }}</small>
  </div>
  <div class="col-xs-12">
    <p ng-bind-html="review.reviewText | addHtmlLineBreaks"></p>
  </div>
</div>
```

And with that we're done with the layout and formatting of the Details page. The next and final step is to allow reviews to be added, but we're going to drop the concept of an extra page to do this. Instead we're going to do it in a modal overlay on the Details page, to provide a slicker experience.

10.4   *Using AngularUI components to create a modal popup*

In this final section we're going to see how to add third-party components to an Angular application, and how to post form data. In Loc8r we'll now enable users to add reviews directly from the Details page, by creating a modal popup that displays when users click the Add Review button. The modal will display the review form, allowing users to input their name, rating, and review. When users submit their reviews we'll post them to the API so that they're saved in the database, and add them to the reviews on the page. All of this will happen without leaving the Details page.

The first step then is to create a modal popup to display when somebody clicks the Add Review button.

10.4.1   *Getting AngularUI in place*

Rather than creating a modal from scratch and figuring out all of the controlling code behind it, we can leverage the hard work of the AngularUI team. They've created a number of Bootstrap components written in pure Angular. These components rely only on Angular, no longer jQuery or Bootstrap's own JavaScript.

DOWNLOADING ANGULARUI

You can get your hands on AngularUI at http://angular-ui.github.io/bootstrap/. You can download the entire library, which defines around 20 components. This is a bit overkill if you just want to use a single component in your application. So you can instead choose to create your own custom build by clicking the Build button. You can then select the components you want—just Modal in our case as shown in figure 10.8— and download the modules.

Using a custom build like this will dramatically reduce the file size; in this case we've gone from 65 kb to 13 kb. Open the zip file you've downloaded and copy the two minified JavaScript files to the lib folder in app_client.

Now you can reference them in index.html along with the other library files, before our main application file, as shown in the following code snippet:

```
<script src="/angular/angular.min.js"></script>
<script src="/lib/angular-route.min.js"></script>
<script src="/lib/angular-sanitize.min.js"></script>
<script src="/lib/ui-bootstrap-custom-0.12.0.min.js"></script>
<script src="/lib/ui-bootstrap-custom-tpls-0.12.0.min.js"></script>
<script src="/angular/loc8r.min.js"></script>
```

With the files added we can now use them in the application.

USING ANGULARUI IN THE APPLICATION

To use AngularUI components in our application we need to define it as a dependency at the application level. When this is done we need to define the modal component as a dependency of the controller for the page we'll use it in.

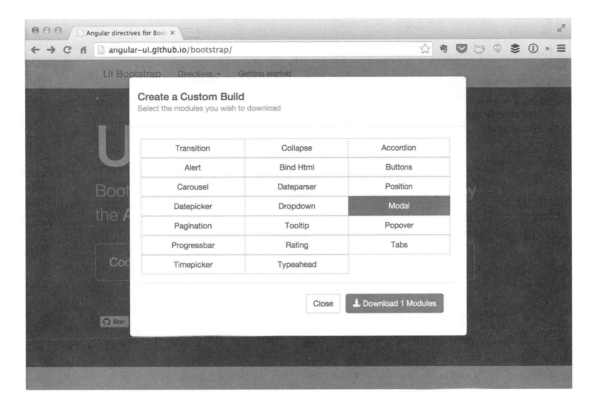

Figure 10.8   Create a custom build of AngularUI using just the component you need.

First, to add AngularUI as an application dependency we simply need to add `'ui.bootstrap'` to the array of dependencies in app_client/app.js, as shown in the following code snippet:

```
angular.module('loc8rApp', ['ngRoute', 'ngSanitize', 'ui.bootstrap']);
```

And now that they're in the application, we tell the controller that we want to use the modal component by injecting a $modal dependency, as shown in the following code snippet. Remember that we need to pass it as a parameter into the controller function and add it to the $inject array.

```
locationDetailCtrl.$inject = ['$routeParams', '$modal', 'loc8rData'];
  function locationDetailCtrl ($routeParams, $modal, loc8rData) {
```

With those two pieces in place we can now carry on and create the modal.

10.4.2 *Adding and using a click handler*

Reminding ourselves of what we want to achieve, the aim is to pop up a modal dialogue box when a user clicks the Add Review button. So we need to add a click handler to the button, create the corresponding function in the controller, and then look at how to create the modal.

ADDING THE NG-CLICK HANDLER

To listen for a click that calls a method in our Angular application, rather than use href or onclick we should use Angular's click handler ng-click. This behaves in a similar way to onclick, but gives access to your view model methods.

In the following code snippet we add an ng-click handler to the Add Review button in locationDetail.view.html that will call a function in our view model called popupReviewForm:

```
<a ng-click="vm.popupReviewForm()" class="btn btn-default pull-right">Add
    review</a>
```

Okay, the next step is to create the popupReviewForm method in the controller.

ADDING THE METHOD CALLED BY THE CLICK HANDLER

Creating the method in the controller is a simple case of declaring vm.popupReview-Form as a function. In the following listing we add the new function and set it to fire a simple alert so that we can test that the ng-click and the method are working together as expected.

> **Listing 10.19   Adding the method to the controller**

```
function locationDetailCtrl ($routeParams, $modal, loc8rData) {
  var vm = this;
  vm.locationid = $routeParams.locationid;

  loc8rData.locationById(vm.locationid)
    .success(function(data) {
      vm.data = { location: data };
      vm.pageHeader = {
        title: vm.data.location.name
      };
    })
    .error(function (e) {
      console.log(e);
    });

  vm.popupReviewForm = function () {
    alert("Let's add a review!");
  };
}
```

So if we make these changes and navigate to a location Details page on our site we should see an alert when we click the Add Review button. Figure 10.9 shows this in action, proving that we've linked the button and the method correctly.

Figure 10.9   Testing that the Add Review click handler works by using a simple Alert box

10.4.3   *Creating a Bootstrap modal with AngularUI*

Now it's time to create the modal dialogue box. Even though we're not doing it here, it's quite conceivable that you'd have several actions on a page that could fire a modal window. To prevent any cross-contamination of code each modal is created as a new instance, with its own template and controller.

So we're going to look at how to define an instance, and then add the view and controller.

DEFINING AN ANGULARUI MODAL INSTANCE

We're going to use the popupReviewForm handler from the previous section to define a new modal instance. We'll assign a template URL and a controller against this just like we do for a directive or route definition.

The syntax for this is the following:

```
vm.popupReviewForm = function () {
  var modalInstance = $modal.open({
    templateUrl: '/reviewModal/reviewModal.view.html',
    controller: 'reviewModalCtrl as vm',
  });
};
```

Note that we're using a different approach to the controllerAs syntax here. The modal component can use the approach but doesn't currently support using the controllerAs option to specify it. Instead, we define the view model name inline, just like we would if defining it inside an HTML element.

ADDING THE MODAL VIEW

To create the HTML for the review modal we'll blend a combination of the review form we've already got and the template markup for a Bootstrap modal. For good measure we'll add in some data bindings to the form fields, and define a function we can use to cancel the modal.

If we put all this together we end up with the following listing. Save this as a new file in the location we specified as the template URL in listing 10.19: reviewModal .view.html in app_client/reviewModal/.

Listing 10.20   HTML view for the modal popup

```
<div class="modal-content">
  <form id="addReview" name="addReview" role="form" class="form-horizontal">
    <div class="modal-header">
      <button type="button" ng-click="vm.modal.cancel()" class="close"><span
      aria-hidden="true">x</span><span class="sr-only">Close</span></button>      ⟵
      <h4 id="myModalLabel" class="modal-title">Add your review for {{
      vm.locationName }}</h4>
    </div>
    <div class="modal-body">
      <div class="form-group">
        <label for="name" class="col-xs-2 col-sm-2 control-label">Name</label>
        <div class="col-xs-10 col-sm-10">
          <input id="name" name="name" required="required" ng-
  model="vm.formData.name" class="form-control"/>
        </div>
      </div>
      <div class="form-group">
        <label for="rating" class="col-xs-10 col-sm-2 control-label">Rating</
  label>
        <div class="col-xs-12 col-sm-2">
          <select id="rating" name="rating" ng-model="vm.formData.rating"
  class="form-control input-sm">
            <option>5</option>
            <option>4</option>
            <option>3</option>
            <option>2</option>
            <option>1</option>
          </select>
        </div>
      </div>
      <div class="form-group">
        <label for="review" class="col-sm-2 control-label">Review</label>
        <div class="col-sm-10">
          <textarea id="review" name="review" rows="5" required="required"
  ng-model="vm.formData.reviewText" class="form-control"></textarea>
        </div>
      </div>
    </div>
    <div class="modal-footer">
      <button ng-click="vm.modal.cancel()" type="button" class="btn btn-
  default">Cancel</button>
      <button type="submit" class="btn btn-primary">Submit review</button>
    </div>
  </form>
</div>
```

Add Close button and specify method in view model to trigger

Add model data bindings for form fields

In Cancel button trigger same method as Close button

Nothing too complex here, just a lot of markup. To use the view, of course, we'll need to create the controller.

CREATING THE MODAL CONTROLLER

When we defined the modal in the location view controller we specified a controller name that we'd use: `reviewModalCtrl`. Now it's time to create that in a file called reviewModal.controller.js, alongside the view we've just created.

We'll start off with the basic controller construct. A modal controller has a dependency on `$modalInstance`—created by the AngularUI component—that we'll inject. `$modalInstance` has a `dismiss` method that we can invoke when either the Cancel or Close button is clicked. To do this we'll create the `vm.modal.cancel` method we reference in the view, and use it to dismiss the modal. All of this is tied together in the following listing.

Listing 10.21 Starting point for the review modal controller

```
(function () {

  angular
    .module('loc8rApp')
    .controller('reviewModalCtrl', reviewModalCtrl);

  reviewModalCtrl.$inject = ['$modalInstance'];        Inject $modalInstance
  function reviewModalCtrl ($modalInstance) {          into controller
    var vm = this;

    vm.modal = {                                       Create vm.modal.cancel()
      cancel : function () {                            method and use it to call
        $modalInstance.dismiss('cancel');              $modalInstance.dismiss method
      }
    };

  }

})();
```

When that's in place, remember to add it to the array of scripts to concatenate in the Express app.js file. If you now reload the page and click the Add Review button you should see the modal popup display, as shown in Figure 10.10. Clicking on the Cancel button, or anywhere outside the modal, should dismiss it.

That's a great start, but the name of the location doesn't display in the modal header. Let's fix that by passing data into the modal.

10.4.4 Passing data into the modal

Passing data from the page controller into the view model of the modal controller is a three-step process:

1 In the modal definition resolve the variables we want to use.
2 Inject these as dependencies into the modal controller.
3 Map them to objects in the modal view model.

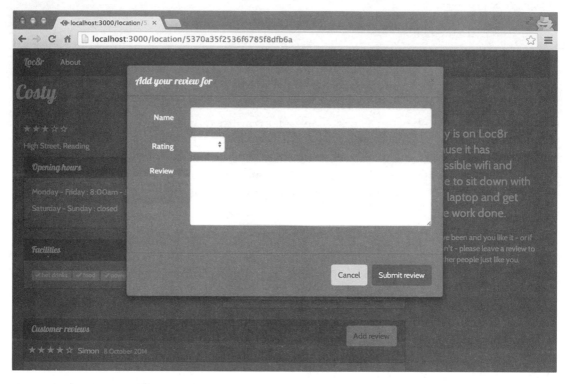

Figure 10.10   The modal popup in action, showing the review form

RESOLVING VARIABLES IN THE MODAL INSTANCE DEFINITION

The first step in passing data to the modal controller is to get the variables into the modal instance definition. This is done using a `resolve` option. The `resolve` option is mapped to an object containing one or more parameters that you want to use in the modal. Each parameter should be mapped to a function that returns a value or an object.

We want to have access to the location ID and the location name in our modal, so we'll resolve a parameter called `locationData`, and have it return an object containing both the location ID and the name. The following listing shows the additions we need to make to the modal instance definition.

Listing 10.22   Using `resolve` to pass variable values into the modal

```
var modalInstance = $modal.open({
  templateUrl: '/reviewModal/reviewModal.view.html',        Add resolve option,
  controller: 'reviewModalCtrl as vm',                       mapping to object
  resolve : {
    locationData : function () {                              Add parameter that
                                                              maps to function
```

```
      return {
        locationid : vm.locationid,
        locationName : vm.data.location.name
      };
    }
  }
});
```

> **Function should
> return an object
> or single value**

This will enable the modal controller to use a `locationData` parameter, if we inject it as a dependency.

DEPENDENCY INJECTING THE RESOLVED PARAMETERS AND ADDING TO THE VIEW MODEL

For the modal controller to use the parameter we've just created, we need to inject it as a dependency. We'll do this exactly like we would any other dependency injection, as shown in the following code snippet. We'll also take this opportunity to save the parameter as a property of the view model.

```
reviewModalCtrl.$inject = ['$modalInstance', 'locationData'];
function reviewModalCtrl ($modalInstance, locationData) {
  var vm = this;
  vm.locationData = locationData;
}
```

> **Inject new
> parameter
> from modal
> definition**

> **Save parameter
> into view model**

With that in place, we can now use the values of the `locationData` parameter in the modal.

USING THE DATA PASSED THROUGH

Now that we have the data available in the modal view model we can use it in a binding in the modal view. The following code snippet shows how we update the modal title to display the location name:

```
<h4 id="myModalLabel" class="modal-title">Add your review for {{
    vm.locationData.locationName }}</h4>
```

By reloading the page in the browser and clicking the Add Review button again you can see the data in action, as shown in figure 10.11.

Okay, we're looking good. The final thing we need to do is hook up the form, so that when it's submitted a review is added.

10.4.5   *Using the form to submit a review*

Now is the time to make our review form work and actually add a review to the database when it's submitted. To get to this end point we have a few steps involved:

1   Have Angular handle the form when it's submitted.
2   Validate the form so that only complete data is accepted.
3   Add a POST handler to our `loc8rData` service.
4   POST the review data to the service.
5   Push the review into the list in the Details page.

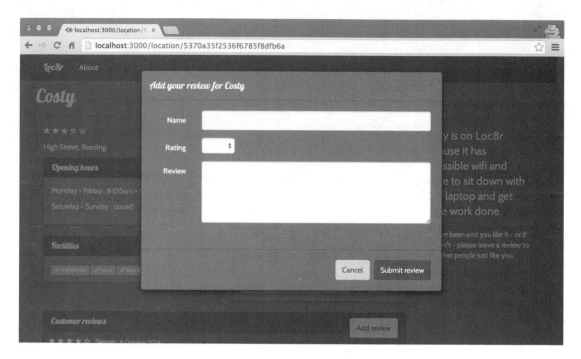

Figure 10.11   Displaying the name of the location inside the modal popup

ADDING ONSUBMIT FORM HANDLERS

When working with a form in HTML you'd typically have an action and a method to tell the browser where to send the data and the HTTP request method to use. You might also have an onSubmit event handler if you wanted to do anything with the form data using JavaScript before it was sent.

In an Angular SPA we don't want the form to submit to a different URL taking us to a new page. We want Angular to handle everything. For this we can use Angular's ng-submit listener to call a function in the view model. The following code snippet shows how this is used, adding it into the form definition, calling a function in the controller that we'll write in just a moment:

```
<form id="addReview" name="addReview" role="form" ng-submit="vm.onSubmit()"
    class="form-horizontal">
```

Next we need to create the corresponding onSubmit function inside the review modal controller. To test that it's working we'll simply log the form data to the console and then return false to prevent the form from submitting. When we built the view for the form we used a property on the view model for each input. Well we actually went one better and put each item as a child property of vm.formData, which makes it nice and easy to get all of the data together. The following code snippet shows the starting point for the onSubmit function to be added to the review modal controller:

```
vm.onSubmit = function () {          Output all form data to console
  console.log(vm.formData);    ◁——  to test that function is working
  return false;            ◁——
};                               Return false to prevent form from
                                 submitting and reloading page
```

Now that we can capture the form data we'll add in some validation.

VALIDATING THE SUBMITTED FORM DATA

Before we blindly send every form submission to the API to save to the database, we want to do some quick validation to ensure that all of the fields are filled in. If any of them aren't filled in we'll display an error message. Your browser may prevent forms from being submitted with empty required fields; if this is the case for you, temporarily remove the required attribute from the form fields to test the Angular validation.

When a form is submitted we'll start off by removing any existing error messages before checking whether each data item in the form is truthy. If any return false— that is, have no data—we'll set a form error message in the view model and return false. If all of the data exists we'll continue to log it to the console as before.

The following listing shows how we need to change the onSubmit function in the review modal controller to handle this validation piece.

Listing 10.23 Adding some basic data validation to the onSubmit handler

```
vm.onSubmit = function () {              Reset any existing
  vm.formError = "";               ◁——  error messages.
  if(!vm.formData.name || !vm.formData.rating || !vm.formData.reviewText) {
    vm.formError = "All fields required, please try again";
    return false;
  } else {                   Otherwise log submitted        If any form fields
    console.log(vm.formData);  data to console.              are false set an
    return false;                                           error message.
  }
};
```

Now that we're creating an error message we want to show it to users when it's generated. For this we'll add a new Bootstrap alert div into the modal view template, and bind the message as the content. We only want to show the div when there's an error message to display, so we'll add an Angular directive called ng-show. ng-show accepts an expression as the value, and if it evaluates as truthy it will display the element, otherwise it will hide it.

So for us, we can use it to check whether vm.formError has a value, and only show the alert div if it has. The following code snippet shows the addition we need

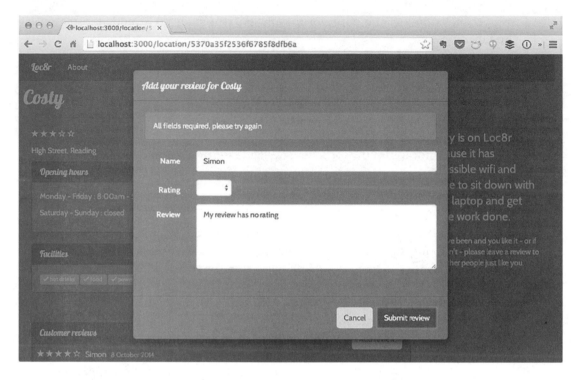

Figure 10.12 When an incomplete form is submitted, an error message is displayed.

to make to the review modal view template, adding the alert right near the top of the modal body:

```
<div class="modal-body">
  <div role="alert" ng-show="vm.formError" class="alert alert-danger">{{
    vm.formError }}</div>
  <div class="form-group">
```

We can see this in action in figure 10.12.

UPDATING THE DATA SERVICE TO ACCEPT NEW REVIEWS

Before we can use this form to post review data we need to add a method to our data service that talks to the correct API endpoint and can post the data. We'll call this new method `addReviewById` and have it accept two parameters: a location ID and the review data.

The contents of the method will be just the same as the others, except we'll be using `post` instead of `get` to call the API. The following listing highlights in bold the changes required to the `loc8rData` function in loc8rData.service.js.

Listing 10.24   Adding a new `addReviewById` method to the data service

```
function loc8rData ($http) {
  var locationByCoords = function (lat, lng) {
    return $http.get('/api/locations?lng=' + lng + '&lat=' + lat +
      '&maxDistance=20');
  };

  var locationById = function (locationid) {
    return $http.get('/api/locations/' + locationid);
  };

  var addReviewById = function (locationid, data) {
    return $http.post('/api/locations/' + locationid + '/reviews', data);
  };

  return {
    locationByCoords : locationByCoords,
    locationById : locationById,
    addReviewById : addReviewById
  };
}
```

Brilliant; now we can use this data service from our modal.

SENDING THE FORM DATA TO THE DATA SERVICE

So we've got our form data being posted and we've got a data service ready to post it to the API. Let's hook these two up. We'll use the data service just like we've done before; using this new method is no different. We start off by calling the method, which will resolve to either a success or error promise as the data service is using the asynchronous $http method.

To keep the code tidy we'll move this functionality into its own function called doAddReview. This is all shown in the following listing, including the important part of injecting the loc8rData service into the controller.

Listing 10.25   Sending complete form data to the data service

```
reviewModalCtrl.$inject = ['$modalInstance', 'loc8rData', 'locationData'];
function reviewModalCtrl ($modalInstance, loc8rData, locationData) {      ◁──┐
  var vm = this;
  vm.locationData = locationData;                        Inject loc8rData service
                                                                   as dependency
  vm.onSubmit = function () {
    vm.formError = "";
    if (!vm.formData.name || !vm.formData.rating || !vm.formData.reviewText)
      {
      vm.formError = "All fields required, please try again";
      return false;                                            On successful
    } else {                                                   form submission
      vm.doAddReview(vm.locationData.locationid, vm.formData);  ◁──  send details to
    }                                                          new function
  };
```

```
vm.doAddReview = function (locationid, formData) {
  loc8rData.addReviewById(locationid, {
    author : formData.name,
    rating : formData.rating,
    reviewText : formData.reviewText
  })
    .success(function (data) {
      console.log("Success!");
    })
    .error(function (data) {
      vm.formError = "Your review has not been saved, try again";
    });
  return false;
};

vm.modal = {
  cancel : function () {
    $modalInstance.dismiss('cancel');
  }
};

}
```

New function formats data and sends it to new service method

If service returns as successful, outputs a message to console

Otherwise use formError to display an alert message in modal

And now we can send reviews to the database. Just one last thing to make it slick: when the review is sent we want to close the modal popup and add the review to the list.

CLOSING THE MODAL AND DISPLAYING THE REVIEW

Closing the modal and adding the new review to the list are closely tied together. We could just use the dismiss method as we've done for the Close and Cancel buttons, but there's a better way.

The modal instance has a close method as well as a dismiss method. The close method can actually pass some data back to the parent controller. We can use this to pass the review data from the modal controller up into the location view controller. When a new review is posted to the API, we set it up so that the response to a successful posting would return the review object from the database.

We know that this data will be in the correct format to be displayed in the page so it's the best source of data to send back to the parent controller. So we need to call the modal close method in the success callback of the addReviewById call. Instead of calling it directly we'll create a helper method like we did for the Cancel button. It all comes together in the following listing.

Listing 10.26   Passing review data into the modal's close method

```
vm.doAddReview = function (locationid, formData) {
  loc8rData.addReviewById(locationid, {
    author : formData.name,
    rating : formData.rating,
    reviewText : formData.reviewText
  })
```

```
      .success(function (data) {
        vm.modal.close(data);
      })
      .error(function (data) {
        vm.formError = "Your review has not been saved, please try again";
      });
    return false;
};

vm.modal = {
  close : function (result) {
    $modalInstance.close(result);
  },
  cancel : function () {
    $modalInstance.dismiss('cancel');
  }
};
```

When new review has been successfully added to database, send returned data to modal close helper method

Create helper method to call modal instance close method, passing through supplied data

The question now arises: How do we use this data? Good question! The `close` method returns a promise to the parent controller where we defined the modal instance in the first place. We can hook into this promise, and when it's resolved simply push the new review into the array of reviews as shown in the following listing.

Listing 10.27 Resolving the modal instance promise to update the review list

```
vm.popupReviewForm = function () {
  var modalInstance = $modal.open({
    templateUrl: '/reviewModal/reviewModal.view.html',
    controller: 'reviewModalCtrl as vm',
    resolve : {
      locationData : function () {
        return {
          locationid : vm.locationid,
          locationName : vm.data.location.name
        };
      }
    }
  });

  modalInstance.result.then(function (data) {
    vm.data.location.reviews.push(data);
  });
};
```

When modal promise is resolved...

Push returned data into array of reviews; Angular binding will do the rest

As the array of reviews is bound to the view template, Angular will automatically update the list of reviews showing. And because we set it up to order by the newest review first, this review will appear at the top of the list as shown in figure 10.13. How easy is that?

And that's it. Our Angular SPA is complete. So let's take a look at what we've learned.

Figure 10.13   Add a review in the modal, and when submitted, the modal closes and the review appears at the top of the list without the page reloading.

10.5 *Summary*

In this chapter we've covered

- Taking the whole application code into the client
- Making pretty URLs using the HTML5 history API
- Adding multiple views to the application
- Safely binding text containing HTML elements
- Using URL parameters
- Adding `if` style logic using `ng-switch` and `ng-show`
- Using prebuilt AngularUI components
- Posting data to the API using the `$http` service

Coming up next in the final chapter we are going to see how to manage authenticated sessions, by adding the ability for users to register and log in before leaving reviews.

Part 4

Managing authentication and user sessions

The ability to identify individual users is a key piece of functionality for most web applications. Visitors should be able to register their details so that they can log back in as returning users at a later date. When users are registered and logged in, the application should be able to make use of the data.

In chapter 11 we'll look at how authentication works in the MEAN stack. The focus will be on managing this when you have all of the application code in the browser as an Angular SPA. Authentication touches every technology layer of the application; we'll cover saving user data to the database, securing API endpoints, and managing a session in the browser.

By the end of part 4 we'll have a fully functioning user registration and login system added to our Loc8r application, which uses the active user's data during the session.

Authenticating users, managing sessions, and securing APIs

This chapter covers

- Adding authentication in the MEAN stack
- Using Passport to manage authentication in Express
- Generating JSON Web Tokens in Express
- Registering and logging in a user
- Securing API endpoints in Express
- Using local storage and Angular to manage a user session

In this chapter we're going to improve upon the existing application by making users log in before they can leave reviews. This is an important topic, as many web applications need to let users log in and manage a session.

Figure 11.1 shows where we're at in the overall plan, now working with the MongoDB database, Express API, and Angular single-page application.

Our first stop will be an overview of how to approach authentication in a MEAN stack application, before updating Loc8r one piece at a time, working through the architecture from back to front. So we'll update the database and data schemas

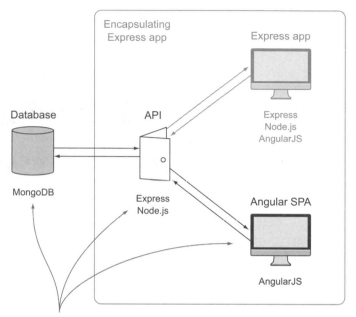

Working with the MongoDB database,
the Express and Node.js API, and the
Angular SPA to bring authentication
to the application

Figure 11.1   This chapter adds an authentication system to the application that touches most parts of the architecture, such as the database, API, and front-end SPA.

first, before upgrading the API, and finally modifying the front end. By the end of the chapter we'll be able to register new users, log them in, maintain a session, and do actions that only logged-in users can complete.

11.1 *How to approach authentication in the MEAN stack*

How to manage authentication in a MEAN application is seen as one of the great mysteries of the stack, particularly when using an SPA. This is largely because the entire application code is delivered to the browser, so how do you hide some of it? How do you define who can see or do what?

11.1.1 *Traditional server-based application approach*

Much of the confusion arises because people are very familiar with the traditional approach of application authentication and user session management.

In a traditional setup, the application code sits and runs on the server. For users to log in they enter their username and password into a form that gets posted to the server. The server then checks against a database to validate the login details. Assuming

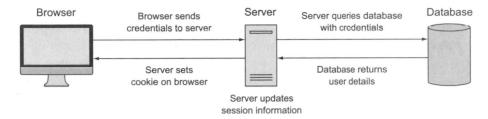

Figure 11.2 In a traditional server application the server and database validate user credentials and add them to users' sessions on the server.

the login is okay, the server will set a flag or session parameter in users' sessions on the server to declare that they're logged in.

The server may or may not set a cookie on users' browsers with the session information. This is quite common, but isn't technically required to manage the authenticated session—it's the server that maintains the vital session information. This flow is illustrated in figure 11.2.

When users then request a secure resource or try to submit some data to the database, it's the server that validates their session and whether or not it can continue. The two flows are illustrated in figures 11.3 and 11.4.

That's what the traditional approach looks like, but does it work for the MEAN stack?

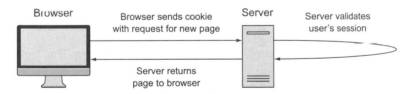

Figure 11.3 In a traditional server application the server validates users' sessions before continuing with a secure request.

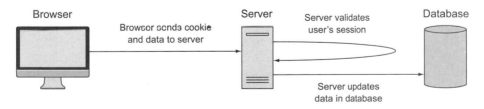

Figure 11.4 In a traditional server application the server validates users' sessions before pushing data to a database.

USING THE TRADITIONAL APPROACH IN THE MEAN STACK

This traditional approach isn't a very neat fit for the MEAN stack. The approach relies on the server reserving some resources for each user so that it can maintain the session information. You may remember from all the way back in chapter 1 that Node and Express don't maintain sessions for each user—the entire application for all users runs on a single thread.

That said, a version of the approach can be used in the MEAN stack if you're using a server-side application based on Express, like we built up in the book through chapter 7. Rather than using server resources to maintain session information, Express can use a database to store the data. MongoDB can be used; another popular option for this is Redis, which is a lightning-fast key-value store.

We're not going to cover that approach in this book; we're going to look at the more complicated scenario of adding authentication to an SPA hitting an API for data.

11.1.2 *Full MEAN stack approach*

Authentication in the MEAN stack poses two problems:

- The API is stateless as Express and Node have no concept of user sessions.
- The application logic is already delivered to the browser, so you can't limit the code that gets delivered.

The logical solution to these problems is to maintain some kind of session state in the browser, and let the application decide what it can and cannot display to the current user. This is the only fundamental change in approach. There are a few technical differences, but this is the only major shift.

A great way to securely keep user data in the browser in order to maintain a session is to use a JSON Web Token (JWT). We'll look at these in more detail later in this chapter when we start using them, but in essence a JWT is a JSON object encrypted into a string that's meaningless to the human eye, but can be decoded and understood by both the application and the server.

Let's see how this looks at a high level, starting with the login process.

MANAGING THE LOGIN PROCESS

Figure 11.5 illustrates the flow of a login process. Users post their credentials to the server (via an API); the server validates these using the database, and returns a token to the browser. The browser will save this token to reuse it later.

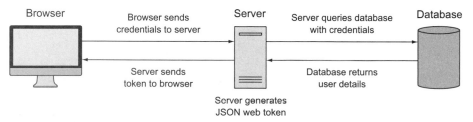

Figure 11.5   The login flow in a MEAN application, returning a JSON Web Token to the browser after the server validates user credentials

This is very similar to the traditional approach, but instead of storing each user's session data on the server, it's stored in the browser.

CHANGING VIEWS DURING AN AUTHENTICATED SESSION

While users are in a session, they'll need to be able to change a page or view, and the application will need to know what they should be allowed to see. So here, as illustrated in figure 11.6, the application will decode the JWT and use the information to show the appropriate data to users.

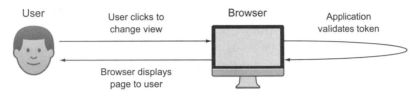

Figure 11.6   Using data inside the JWT, the SPA can determine which resources users can use or see.

This is where the change from the traditional approach is really obvious. The server is completely unaware that users are doing anything, until they need to access the API and database.

SECURELY CALLING AN API

If parts of the application are restricted to authenticated users, then it's quite likely that there will be some database actions that can only be used by authenticated users. As the API is stateless, it has no idea of who is making each call, unless you tell it. The JWT comes back into play here. As figure 11.7 shows, the token will be sent to the API endpoint, which will decode the token before validating whether the user is permitted to make that call.

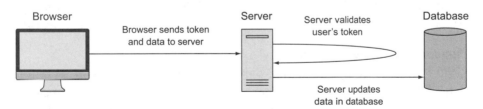

Figure 11.7   When calling an authenticated API endpoint, the browser sends the JWT along with the data; the server decodes the token to validate a user's request.

Okay, so that covers the approach at a high level, and now we've got a good idea what we're aiming for. We'll make the first step toward building this into our Loc8r application by setting up MongoDB to store user details.

11.2   Creating a user schema for MongoDB

Usernames and passwords naturally have to be stored in the database. To do that in the MEAN stack we need to create a Mongoose schema. Passwords should never—absolutely never—be stored in a database as plain text, as doing so presents a massive security breach if the database is ever compromised. So we'll have to do something else as we generate the schema.

11.2.1   One-way password encryption: Hashes and salts

The thing to do here is run a one-way encryption on the password. One-way encryption prevents anyone from decrypting the password, while still making it quite easy to validate a correct password. When users try to log in, the application can encrypt a given password and see if it matches the stored value.

Just encrypting isn't quite enough, though. If several people used the word "password" as their password (it happens!) then the encryption for each will be the same. Any hackers looking through the database could see this pattern and identify potentially weak passwords.

This is where the concept of a *salt* comes in. A salt is a random string generated by the application for each user that's combined with the password before encryption. The resulting encrypted value is called the *hash*, as illustrated in figure 11.8.

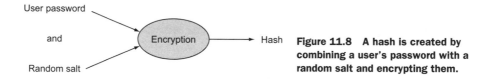

Figure 11.8   A hash is created by combining a user's password with a random salt and encrypting them.

The salt and the hash are both stored in the database rather than just a single "password" field. Using this approach, all hashes should be unique, and passwords are well protected.

11.2.2   Building the Mongoose schema

We'll start by creating the file that will hold the schema and `require` it into the application. In the folder app_api/models/ let's create a new file called users.js.

Next we'll pull that into the application by referencing it in the db.js file in the same folder. It should be required alongside the existing line that brings in the locations model, as shown in the following code snippet:

```
// BRING IN YOUR SCHEMAS & MODELS
require('./locations');
require('./users');
```

Okay, now we're ready to build the basic schema.

BASIC USER SCHEMA

What do we want in the user schema? We know we need a display name to show on reviews, plus a hash and a salt for the password. Let's also add an email address, and have this be the unique identifier that users log in with.

In the new user.js file we'll require Mongoose and define a new userSchema as shown in the following listing.

Listing 11.1   Basic Mongoose schema for users

```
var mongoose = require( 'mongoose' );

var userSchema = new mongoose.Schema({
  email: {
    type: String,              Email should be
    unique: true,              required and unique
    required: true
  },
  name: {                      Name is also required, but
    type: String,              not necessarily unique
    required: true
  },
  hash: String,               Hash and salt are
  salt: String                both just strings
});
```

The email and name will both be set from the registration form, but the hash and salt will both be created by the system. The hash, of course, will be derived from the salt and the password supplied via the form.

Now we'll see how to set the salt and the hash, using a piece of Mongoose functionality we haven't touched on yet: methods.

11.2.3   Setting encrypted paths using Mongoose methods

Mongoose allows us to add methods to a schema, which get exposed as model methods. Such methods give the code direct access to the model attributes.

The ideal outcome is to be able to do something along the lines of the following pseudocode:

```
                                          Instantiate
                                          user model
var User = mongoose.model('User');    ←┐
var user = new User();                 ◁──┘    Create
user.name = "User's name";                     new user
user.email = "test@example.com";               Set name and
user.setPassword("myPassword");       ◁        email values
user.save();          ◁               
                      Save new         Call a setPassword
                      user             method to set password
```

Let's see how we can add a method to Mongoose to achieve this.

ADDING A METHOD TO A MONGOOSE SCHEMA

Methods can be added to a schema *after* the schema has been defined, *before* the model is compiled. In the application code, methods are designed to be used once the model has been instantiated.

Adding a method to a schema is fairly straightforward, simply by chaining onto .methods of the schema. It's also easy to pass in an argument. See the following snippet, for example, which will be the outline for the actual setPassword method:

```
userSchema.methods.setPassword = function(password){
  this.salt = SALT_VALUE;
  this.hash = HASH_VALUE;
};
```

Unusually for a snippet of JavaScript, this in a Mongoose method actually refers to the model itself. So in the preceding example setting this.salt and this.hash in the method would actually set them in the model.

Before we can save anything, though, we need to generate a random salt value and encrypt the hash. Fortunately, there's a native Node module for that: crypto.

USING THE CRYPTO MODULE FOR ENCRYPTION

Encryption is such a common requirement there's a module built into Node called crypto. It comes with several methods for managing the encryption of data; we'll look at the following two:

- randomBytes—To generate a cryptographically strong string of data to use as the salt
- pbkdf2Sync—To create the hash from the password and the salt; pbkdf2 stands for *password-based key derivation function 2*, an industry standard

We're going to use these methods to create a random string for the salt, and for encrypting the password and salt into the hash. The first step is to require crypto in the top of the users.js file:

```
var mongoose = require( 'mongoose' );
var crypto = require('crypto');
```

Second, we'll update the setPassword method to set the salt and the hash for users. To set the salt we'll use the randomBytes method to generate a random 16-byte string. Then we'll use the pbkdf2Sync method to create the encrypted hash from the password and the salt. Here it is all shown together:

```
userSchema.methods.setPassword = function(password){          Create a random
  this.salt = crypto.randomBytes(16).toString('hex');         string for salt
  this.hash = crypto.pbkdf2Sync(password, this.salt, 1000,
    ➥ 64).toString('hex');                                    Create
};                                                            encrypted hash
```

Now when the setPassword method is called and supplied with a password, the salt and the hash will be generated for users, and added to the model instance. The password is never saved anywhere, and not even stored in memory.

11.2.4 *Validating a submitted password*

The other aspect of storing a password is being able to retrieve it when users try to log in—we need to be able to validate their credentials. Having encrypted the password we can't decrypt it, so what we need to do is use the same encryption on the password the user is trying to log in with, and see if it matches the stored value.

We can do the hashing and validation in a simple Mongoose method. Add the following method to users.js. It will be called from a controller once a user has been found with a given email address, and will return `true` or `false` depending on whether the hashes match:

```
userSchema.methods.validPassword = function(password) {
  var hash = crypto.pbkdf2Sync(password, this.salt, 1000, 64).toString('hex');
  return this.hash === hash;
};
```

That's it—it's pretty simple, right? We'll see these methods in action when we generate the API controllers.

The final thing the controller will need help to do is generate a JSON Web Token to include some of the model data.

11.2.5 *Generating a JSON Web Token*

A JWT (pronounced "jot") is used to pass data around, in our case between the API on the server and the SPA in the browser. A JWT can also be used by the server that generated the token to authenticate a user, when it's returned in a subsequent request.

Let's take a quick look at the parts of a JWT.

THREE PARTS OF A JWT

A JWT is comprised of three random-looking, dot-separated strings. These can be quite long; here's a real-world example:

```
eyJ0eXAiOiJKV1QiLCJhbGciOiJIUzI1NiJ9.eyJfaWQiOiI1NTZiZWRmNDhmOTUzOTViMT1hNjc1
ODgiLCJlbWFpbCI6InNpbW9uQGZ1bGxzdGFja3RyYWluaW5nLmNvbSIsIm5hbWUiOiJTaW1vbiBIb
2xtZXMiLCJleHAiOjE0MzUwNDA0MTgsImlhdCI6MTQzNDQzNTYxOH0.GD7UrfnLk295rwvIrCikbk
AKctFFoRCHotLYZwZpdlE
```

This is pretty meaningless to the human eye, but you should be able to spot the two dots and therefore the three separate parts. These three parts are

- *Header*—An encoded JSON object containing the type and the hashing algorithm used
- *Payload*—An encoded JSON object containing the data, the real body of the token
- *Signature*—An encrypted hash of the header and payload, using a "secret" that only the originating server knows

Note that the first two parts aren't encrypted—they're *encoded*. This means that it's easy for the browser—or indeed other applications—to decode them. Most modern browsers have a native function called `atob()` that will decode a Base64 string. A sister function called `btoa()` will encode *to* a Base64 string.

The third part, the signature, is encrypted. To decrypt it you need to use the secret that was set on the server; this secret should remain on the server and never be revealed in public.

The good news is that there are libraries to deal with all of the complicated parts of the process. So let's install one of these libraries into our application and create a schema method to generate a JWT.

GENERATING A JWT FROM EXPRESS

The first step toward generating a JWT is to include an npm module called `jsonwebtoken` from the command line:

```
$ npm install jsonwebtoken --save
```

Then we need to `require` it at the top of the users.js file:

```
var mongoose = require( 'mongoose' );
var crypto = require('crypto');
var jwt = require('jsonwebtoken');
```

Finally, we need to create a schema method, which we'll call `generateJwt`. To generate a JWT we'll need to provide the payload—that is, the data—and a secret value. In the payload we'll send the user's `_id`, `email`, and `name`. We should also set an expiry date for the token, after which the user will have to log in again to generate a new one. We'll use a reserved field in a JWT payload for this, `exp`, which expects the expiry data as a Unix number value.

To generate a JWT, we simply need to call a `sign` method on the `jsonwebtoken` library, sending the payload as a JSON object and the secret as a string. This will return a token, which we can then return out of the method. The following listing shows this all in place.

Listing 11.2   Create a schema method to generate a JWT

```
userSchema.methods.generateJwt = function() {          Create expiry date object
  var expiry = new Date();                             and set for seven days
  expiry.setDate(expiry.getDate() + 7);       ◁

  return jwt.sign({                    ◁            Call jwt.sign method and
    _id: this._id,                                  return what it returns
    email: this.email,           Pass payload
    name: this.name,             to method
    exp: parseInt(expiry.getTime() / 1000),    ◁
  }, 'thisIsSecret' );     ◁                          Including exp as Unix
};                        Send secret for hashing     time in seconds
                          algorithm to use
```

When this `generateJwt` method is called, it will use the data from the current user model to create a unique JWT and return it.

There's just one problem with this code: the secret shouldn't really be visible in the code, so let's quickly deal with that now.

If you're going to be pushing your code around in version control, like GitHub for example, you don't want to have the secret published. Exposing your secret dramatically weakens your security model—with your secret anybody could issue fake tokens that your application believes to be genuine. To keep secrets a secret, it's often a good idea to set them as environment variables.

Here's an easy way to do it, that lets you keep track of environment variables in the code on your machine. First create a file in the root of the project called .env, and set the secret as follows:

```
JWT_SECRET=thisIsSecret
```

In this case the secret is `thisIsSecret`, but it can be whatever you want it to be, so long as it's a string. Now we need to make sure this file isn't included in any Git commits by adding a line to the `.gitignore` file in the project. As a minimum the `.gitignore` file should have the following content:

```
# Dependency directory
node_modules

# Environment variables
.env
```

To read and use this new file to actually set environment variables, we'll need to install and use a new npm module called `dotenv`. We'll do this with the following command in terminal:

```
$ npm install dotenv --save
```

The `dotenv` module should be required into the app.js file as the very first line in the file as shown here:

```
require('dotenv').load();
var express = require('express');
```

Now all that remains is to update the user schema to replace the hard-coded secret with the environment variable, highlighted in bold in the following snippet:

```
userSchema.methods.generateJwt = function() {
  var expiry = new Date();
  expiry.setDate(expiry.getDate() + 7);

  return jwt.sign({
    _id: this._id,
    email: this.email,
    name: this.name,
    exp: parseInt(expiry.getTime() / 1000),    Don't keep secrets in
  }, process.env.JWT_SECRET);    ◁───    code; use environment
};                                          variables instead
```

Of course your production environment will need to know about this environment variable too. You may remember the command from when we set the database URI on Heroku. It's the same thing here, so run the following command in terminal:

```
$ heroku config:set JWT_SECRET=thisIsSecret
```

And that's the last step. So with the MongoDB and Mongoose side of things covered, next we'll look at using Passport to manage authentication.

11.3 Creating an authentication API with Passport

Passport is a Node module by Jared Hanson that's designed to make authentication in Node easy. One of its key strengths is that it can accommodate several different methods of authentication, called *strategies*. Examples of these strategies include

- Facebook
- Twitter
- OAuth
- Local username and password

You can find many more different strategies by searching for "passport" on the npm website. Using Passport you can easily use one or more of these approaches to let users log in to your application. For Loc8r, we're going to use the *local* strategy as we're storing usernames and password hashes in the database.

We'll start by installing the modules.

11.3.1 Installing and configuring Passport

Passport is separated out into a core module and separate modules for each of the strategies. So we'll install the core module and the local strategy module via npm, using the following commands in terminal:

```
$ npm install passport --save
$ npm install passport-local --save
```

When both of those are installed we can create the configuration for our local strategy.

CREATING A PASSPORT CONFIG FILE

It's the API in our application that will be using Passport, so we'll create the config inside the app_api folder. Inside app_api create a new folder called config, and inside that create a new file named passport.js.

At the top of this file we'll need to require Passport and the local strategy module, as well as Mongoose and the user model. This is shown in the following snippet:

```
var passport = require('passport');
var LocalStrategy = require('passport-local').Strategy;
var mongoose = require('mongoose');
var User = mongoose.model('User');
```

Now we can configure the local strategy.

CONFIGURING A LOCAL STRATEGY

To set a Passport strategy you use a `passport.use` method and pass it a new strategy constructor. This constructor takes an options parameter and a function that does most of the work. The skeleton of this looks like the following:

```
passport.use(new LocalStrategy({},
  function(username, password, done) {
  }
));
```

By default a Passport local strategy expects and uses the fields `username` and `password`. We have `password` so that one's okay, but instead of `username` we're using `email`. Passport allows you to override the username field in the options object as shown in the following snippet:

```
passport.use(new LocalStrategy(
    usernameField: 'email'
  },
  function(username, password, done) {
  }
));
```

Next is the main function, which is really just a Mongoose call to find users given the username and password supplied into the function. Our Mongoose function will need to do the following:

- Find a user with the email address supplied.
- Check whether the password is valid.
- Return the user object if the user is found and the password is valid.
- Otherwise return a message stating what's wrong.

As the email address is set to be unique in the schema we can use the Mongoose `findOne` method. The other interesting point to note is that we'll make use of the `validPassword` schema method we created earlier to check whether the supplied password is correct.

The following listing shows the local strategy in its entirety.

Listing 11.3 Full Passport local strategy definition

```
passport.use(new LocalStrategy({
    usernameField: 'email'                                    Search MongoDB
  },                                                          for user with
  function(username, password, done) {                        supplied email
    User.findOne({ email: username }, function(err, user) {   address
      if (err) { return done(err); }
      if (!user) {                          If no user is found,
        return done(null, false, {          return false and a
          message: 'Incorrect username.'    message
        });
      }
```

```
        if (!user.validPassword(password)) {
          return done(null, false, {
            message: 'Incorrect password.'
          });
        }
        return done(null, user);
      });
    }
));
```

If password is incorrect, return false and a message
Call validPassword method, passing supplied password
If we've got to the end we can return user object

Now that we have Passport installed and a strategy configured, we need to register it with the application.

ADDING PASSPORT AND THE CONFIG TO THE APPLICATION

To add our Passport settings to the application we need to do three things in app.js:

1   Require Passport.
2   Require the strategy config.
3   Initialize Passport.

There's nothing complicated about any of these three things; the important thing is *where* they go in app.js.

Passport should be required before the database models, and the configuration after the database models. Both should be in place before the routes are defined. If we reorganize the top of app.js slightly, we can bring in Passport and the config as follows:

```
require('dotenv').load();
var express = require('express');
var path = require('path');
var favicon = require('serve-favicon');
var logger = require('morgan');
var cookieParser = require('cookie-parser');
var bodyParser = require('body-parser');
var uglifyJs = require("uglify-js");
var fs = require('fs');
var passport = require('passport');          // Require Passport before model definition

require('./app_api/models/db');
require('./app_api/config/passport');         // Require strategy after model definition

var routes = require('./app_server/routes/index');
var routesApi = require('./app_api/routes/index');
```

The strategy needs to be defined after the model definitions, because it needs the user model to exist.

Passport should be initialized in app.js after the static routes have been defined, and before the routes that are going to use authentication—in our case the API routes. The following snippet shows this in place:

```
app.use(express.static(path.join(__dirname, 'public')));
app.use(express.static(path.join(__dirname, 'app_client')));

app.use(passport.initialize());

app.use('/api', routesApi);
```

With that in place, Passport is now installed, configured, and initialized in our application. What we'll do now is create the API endpoints we need to let users register and log in.

11.3.2 Creating API endpoints to return JSON Web Tokens

To enable users to log in and register via our API, we'll need to have two new endpoints. To do this we'll need to add two new route definitions and two new corresponding controllers. When we've got endpoints in place we can test them using Postman and also validate that the registration endpoint has worked by using the Mongo shell to look inside the database. First up, adding the routes.

ADDING THE AUTHENTICATION ROUTE DEFINITIONS

The route definitions for the API are held in the index.js file in app_api/routes, so that's where we'll start. Our controllers are separated out into logical collections, currently locations and reviews. It makes sense to add a third collection for the authentication. The following snippet shows this added at the top of the file:

```
var ctrlLocations = require('../controllers/locations');
var ctrlReviews = require('../controllers/reviews');
var ctrlAuth = require('../controllers/authentication');
```

We haven't created this controllers/authentication file yet; we'll do that in the next step when we code up the related controllers. Next we'll add the route definitions themselves toward the end of the file (but before the `module.exports` line). We want two, one each for registration and login, which we'll create at /api/register and /api/login, respectively as shown in the following snippet:

```
router.post('/register', ctrlAuth.register);
router.post('/login', ctrlAuth.login);
```

These both need to be post actions, of course, as they're accepting data, and remember that we don't need to specify the /api part of the routes as that's added when the routes are required inside app.js. Now we need to add the controllers before we can test.

CREATING THE REGISTER CONTROLLER

We'll look at the register controller first, but to start with we need to create the file specified in the route definitions. So in the app_api/controllers folder create a new file, authentication.js, and enter the code in the following snippet to require the things we're going to need and bring in the sendJSONresponse function again:

```
var passport = require('passport');
var mongoose = require('mongoose');
var User = mongoose.model('User');

var sendJSONresponse = function(res, status, content) {
  res.status(status);
  res.json(content);
};
```

The registration process won't actually use Passport at all. We can do what we need with Mongoose, as we've already set up the various helper methods on the schema.

The register controller will need to do the following:

1 Validate that the required fields have been sent.
2 Create a new model instance of `User`.
3 Set the name and email address of the user.
4 Use the `setPassword` method to create and add the salt and the hash.
5 Save the user.
6 Return a JWT when saved.

This seems like quite a lot of things to do, but fortunately it's all pretty easy—we've done the hard work already by creating the Mongoose methods. Now we just need to tie it all together. The following listing shows the complete code for the register controller.

Listing 11.4   Register controller for the API

```
module.exports.register = function(req, res) {
  if(!req.body.name || !req.body.email || !req.body.password) {        Respond with
    sendJSONresponse(res, 400, {                                       an error status
      "message": "All fields required"                                 if not all
    });                                                                required fields
    return;                                                            are found
  }

  var user = new User();                    Create a new user
                                            instance and set
  user.name = req.body.name;                name and email
  user.email = req.body.email;

  user.setPassword(req.body.password);      ◁⎤  Use setPassword method
                                                to set salt and hash
  user.save(function(err) {                 ◁⎤  Save new user
    var token;                                  to MongoDB
    if (err) {
      sendJSONresponse(res, 404, err);
    } else {
      token = user.generateJwt();           Generate a JWT using
      sendJSONresponse(res, 200, {          schema method and
        "token" : token                     send it to browser
      });
    }
  });
};
```

In terms of this piece of code there's nothing particularly new or complex here, but it really highlights the power of the Mongoose methods. This registration controller could have been really complex had everything been written in line, which would have been tempting if we'd started here instead of with Mongoose. But as it is, the controller is easy to read and understand—just what you want from your code. Next up, the login controller.

CREATING THE LOGIN CONTROLLER

The login controller will rely on Passport to do the difficult stuff. We'll start by simply validating that the required fields have been filled, and then hand over everything to Passport. Passport will do its thing—attempting to authenticate the user using the strategy we specify—and then tell us whether it was successful or not. If it was successful we can use the `generateJwt` schema method again to create a JWT before sending it to the browser.

All of this, including the syntax required to initiate the `passport.authenticate` method, is shown in the following listing. This should be added to the new authentication.js file.

Listing 11.5 Login controller for the API

```
module.exports.login = function(req, res) {
  if (!req.body.email || !req.body.password) {
    sendJSONresponse(res, 400, {           Validate that
      "message": "All fields required"      required fields
    });                                      have been
    return;                                  supplied
  }

  passport.authenticate('local', function(err, user, info){   ◁──  Pass name of
    var token;                                                       strategy and
                                                                     a callback to
    if (err) {                                                       authenticate
      sendJSONresponse(res, 404, err);      Return an error if       method
      return;                               Passport returns
    }                                       an error

    if(user){
      token = user.generateJwt();           If Passport
      sendJSONresponse(res, 200, {          returned a user
        "token" : token                     instance, generate
      });                                    and send a JWT
    } else {                                          Otherwise return
      sendJSONresponse(res, 401, info);               info message (why
    }                                                 authentication failed)
  })(req, res);      ◁──
};                        Make sure that req and res
                          are available to Passport
```

With the login controller we can see that once again all of the complicated work is abstracted out, this time primarily by Passport. This leaves the code really easy to read, follow, and understand, which should always be a goal to have in mind when coding.

Now that we've built these two endpoints in our API, let's test them.

TESTING THE ENDPOINTS AND CHECKING THE DATABASE

When we built the bulk of the API back in chapter 6 we tested the endpoints with Postman. We can do the same here. Figure 11.9 shows testing the register endpoint, and how it returns a JWT. The URL to test is localhost:3000/api/register, creating form

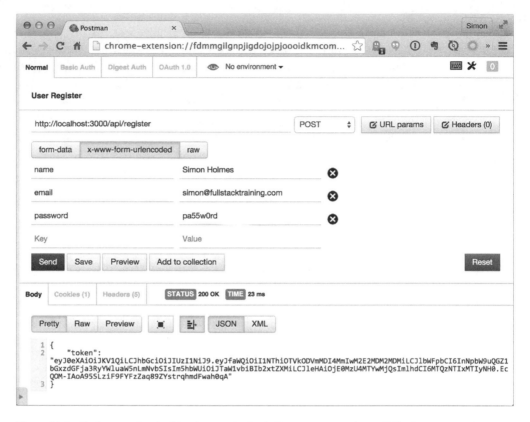

Figure 11.9 Trying out the /api/register endpoint in Postman, returning a JWT when successful

fields for name, email, and password. Remember to select the x-www-form-urlencoded form type.

Figure 11.10 shows testing of the login endpoint, including the return of a Passport error message as well as a JWT when successful. The URL for this test is localhost:3000/api/register and requires email and password form fields.

As well as seeing in the browser that JWTs are returned when expected, we can also take a look in the database and check to see whether the user has been created. We'll go back to the Mongo shell for this, which we haven't used for a while:

```
$ mongo
> use Loc8r
> db.users.find()
```

Or you can find a particular user by specifying the email address of course:

```
> db.users.find({email : "simon@fullstacktraining.com"})
```

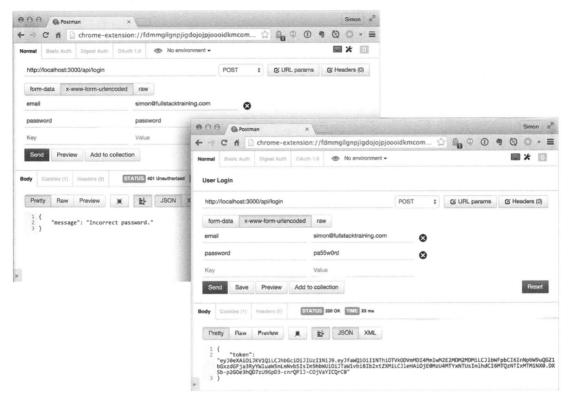

Figure 11.10   Using the api/login endpoint in Postman, testing correct and incorrect credentials

Whichever you use you should see one or more user documents returned from the database, looking something like this:

{ **"hash"** : "1255e9df3daa899bee8d53a42d4acf3ab8739fa758d533a84da5eb1278412f7a7bdb36e888ae b80a9eec4fb7bbe9bcef038f01fbbf4e6048e2f4494be44bc3d5", **"salt"** : "40368d9155ea690cf9fc08b49f328e38", **"email"** : "simon@fullstacktraining.com", **"name"** : "Simon Holmes", **"_id"** : ObjectId("558b95d85f0282b03a603603"), "__v" : 0 }

I've made the path names bold to make them easier to pick out in print, but you should be able to see all of the expected data there.

Now that we've created the endpoints to enable users to register and log in, the next thing we're going to look at is how to restrict certain endpoints to authenticated users only.

11.4   Securing relevant API endpoints

It's a pretty common requirement in web applications to limit access to API endpoints to authenticated users only. In Loc8r, for example, we want to make sure that only registered users can leave reviews. To do this there are really two parts:

- Only allow users sending a valid JWT with their request to call the new review API.
- Inside the controller validate that the user exists and can create a review.

We'll start by adding authentication to the routes in Express, before getting into the controller.

11.4.1   Adding authentication middleware to Express routes

In Express, middleware can be added to routes, as you'll see in just a moment. This middleware gets in the middle of the route and the controller. So once a route is called, the middleware is activated before the controller, and can prevent the controller from running or change the data being sent.

We want to use middleware that will validate the supplied JWT, and then extract the payload data and add it to the `req` object for the controller to use. It's no surprise that there's an npm module for this and it's called `express-jwt`, so let's install it now with the following command in terminal:

```
$ npm install express-jwt --save
```

Now we can use it in the routes file.

SETTING UP THE MIDDLEWARE

To use `express-jwt` we need to `require` it and configure it. When included, `express-jwt` exposes a function that can be passed an options object, which we'll use to send the secret and also specify the name of the property we want to add to the `req` object to hold the payload.

The default property added to `req` is `user`, but in our code `user` is an instance of the Mongoose `User` model. So we'll set it to `payload` to avoid confusion and maintain consistency—it's what it's called in Passport and inside the JWT after all.

Open up the API routes file, app_api/routes/index.js, and add the setup to the top of the file, highlighted in bold in the following snippet:

```
var express = require('express');
var router = express.Router();
var jwt = require('express-jwt');          ◁─── Require express-jwt
var auth = jwt({                                 module
  secret: process.env.JWT_SECRET,          ◁─── Set secret using same
  userProperty: 'payload'                        environment variable as before
});                                        ◁─── Define property on
                                                 req to be payload
```

Now that the middleware is configured, we can add the authentication to the routes.

ADDING AUTHENTICATION MIDDLEWARE TO SPECIFIC ROUTES

Adding middleware to the route definitions is really simple. We simply need to reference it in the router commands, in between the route and the controller. It really does go in the middle!

The following snippet shows how to add it to the post, put, and delete review methods, while leaving get open—the reviews are supposed to be readable by the public:

```
router.post('/locations/:locationid/reviews', auth,
    ➥ ctrlReviews.reviewsCreate);
router.get('/locations/:locationid/reviews/:reviewid',
    ➥ ctrlReviews.reviewsReadOne);
router.put('/locations/:locationid/reviews/:reviewid', auth,
    ➥ ctrlReviews.reviewsUpdateOne);
router.delete('/locations/:locationid/reviews/:reviewid', auth,
    ➥ ctrlReviews.reviewsDeleteOne);
```

So that's the middleware configured and applied. In just a moment we'll take a look at how to use it in the controller, but first let's see how to deal with an invalid token that the middleware rejects.

DEALING WITH AUTHENTICATION REJECTION

When the supplied token is invalid—or perhaps doesn't exist at all—the middleware will actually throw an error to prevent the code from continuing. So what we need to do is catch this error, and return an unauthorized message and status (401).

The best place to add this is with the other error handlers in app.js. We'll add it as the first error handler so that generic handlers don't intercept it. The following snippet shows the new error handler to be added to app.js:

```
// error handlers
// Catch unauthorised errors
app.use(function (err, req, res, next) {
  if (err.name === 'UnauthorizedError') {
    res.status(401);
    res.json({"message" : err.name + ": " + err.message});
  }
});
```

With that in place and the app restarted we can test that the rejection occurs by using Postman again, this time submitting a review. We can use the same POST request that we had when first testing the API, the result of which is shown in figure 11.11.

As expected, trying to call the newly protected API endpoint without including a valid JWT in the request returns an unauthorized status and message. Just what we wanted. Let's move on to what happens when a request is authorized by the middleware and continues on to the controller.

11.4.2 *Using the JWT information inside a controller*

In this section we're going to see how to use the data from the JWT that has just been extracted by the middleware in Express and added to the req object. We're going to

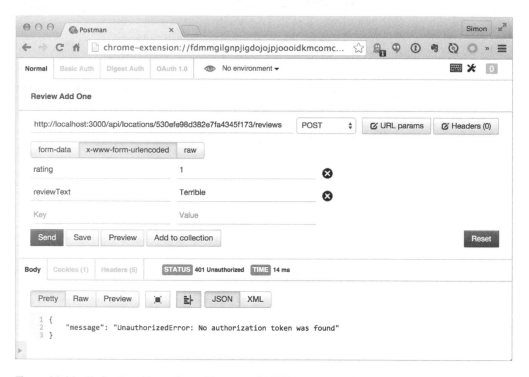

Figure 11.11   Trying to add a review without a valid JWT now results in a 401 response.

use the email address to get the user's name from the database, and add it to the review document.

ONLY RUN THE MAIN CONTROLLER CODE IF THE USER EXISTS

The first thing to do, as shown in listing 11.6, is to take the `reviewsCreate` controller and wrap the contents in a new function that we'll call `getAuthor`. This new function should accept the `req` and `res` objects, with the existing controller code in a callback.

The whole point of the `getAuthor` function will be to validate that the user exists in the database, and return the user's name for use in the controller. So we can pass this through as `userName` to the callback, and in turn pass it through to the `doAddReview` function.

Listing 11.6   Update the create review controller to get the user's name first

```
module.exports.reviewsCreate = function(req, res) {
  getAuthor(req, res, function (req, res, userName) {
    if (req.params.locationid) {
      Loc
        .findById(req.params.locationid)
        .select('reviews')
        .exec(
          function(err, location) {
```

Call getAuthor function, and pass original controller code in as a callback; pass user's name into callback

```
                if (err) {
                  sendJSONresponse(res, 400, err);
                } else {
                  doAddReview(req, res, location, userName);     ◁─┐  Pass user's
                }                                                   │  name into
              }                                                    │  doAddReview
            );                                                     │  function
        } else {
          sendJSONresponse(res, 404, {
            "message": "Not found, locationid required"
          });
        }
    });        ◁─┤  Close getAuthor
};                   function
```

Looking at this highlights the two things we still need to do: write the `getAuthor` function and update the `doAddReview` function. Let's write the `getAuthor` function, so that we can see how to get the JWT data.

VALIDATING THE USER AND RETURNING THE NAME

The idea of the `getAuthor` function is to validate that the email address is associated with a user on the system, and return the name to use. It will need to do the following:

- Check that there's an email address in the `req` object.
- Use the email address to find a user.
- Send the user's name to the callback function.
- Trap errors and send appropriate messages.

The full code for the `getAuthor` function is in listing 11.7. The very first thing to do is check for the `payload` property on `req`, and in turn check that it has an `email` property. Remember that `payload` is the property we specified when we added authentication to the Express routes. After that it's simply a case of using `req.payload.email` in a Mongoose query, passing the user's name through to the callback if successful.

Listing 11.7 Use data from the JWT to query the database

```
var User = mongoose.model('User');                    ◁─┐  Ensure the User
var getAuthor = function(req, res, callback) {            │  model is available
  if (req.payload && req.payload.email) {          ◁────
    User
      .findOne({ email : req.payload.email })     ◁───    Validate that JWT
      .exec(function(err, user) {                          information is on
        if (!user) {                                       request object
          sendJSONresponse(res, 404, {
            "message": "User not found"
          });                                      Use email address
          return;                                  to find user
        } else if (err) {
          console.log(err);
          sendJSONresponse(res, 404, err);
          return;
        }
```

```
        callback(req, res, user.name);          ◁──┐  Run callback, passing
      });                                           │  user's name

  } else {
    sendJSONresponse(res, 404, {
      "message": "User not found"
    });
    return;
  }
};
```

Now when the callback is invoked it will run what was the original code in the controller, finding a location and passing the information to the doAddReview function. It's also now passing the username to the function, so let's quickly update doAddReview to use the user's name and add it to the review documents.

SETTING THE USER'S NAME ON REVIEWS

The change to the doAddReview function is really simple, and is shown in listing 11.8. We were already saving the author of the review, getting the data from req.body .author. Now we have another parameter being passed to the function, and can use this instead. The updates are highlighted in bold.

Listing 11.8   Saving the username in the review

```
var doAddReview = function(req, res, location, author) {    ◁──┐  Add an author
  if (!location) {                                              │  parameter to
    sendJSONresponse(res, 404, "locationid not found");         │  function definition
  } else {
    location.reviews.push({
      author: author,            ◁──┐  Use author parameter
      rating: req.body.rating,       │  when creating review
      reviewText: req.body.reviewText │  subdocument
    });
    location.save(function(err, location) {
      var thisReview;
      if (err) {
        sendJSONresponse(res, 400, err);
      } else {
        updateAverageRating(location._id);
        thisReview = location.reviews[location.reviews.length - 1];
        sendJSONresponse(res, 201, thisReview);
      }
    });
  }
};
```

That simple change brings us to the end of the back-end work. We've created a new user schema, generated and consumed JWTs, created an authentication API, and secured some other API routes. That's quite a lot already! And now we're going to move to the front end and focus on integrating this into the Angular app.

11.5 Creating Angular authentication service

In an Angular app, just like any other application, authentication is likely to be needed across the board, in several different places. So really the obvious thing to do is create an authentication service that can be used anywhere it's needed.

This service should be responsible for everything related to authentication, including saving and reading a JWT, returning information about the current user, and calling the login and register API endpoints.

We'll start by looking at how to manage the user session.

11.5.1 Managing a user session in Angular

Let's assume for a moment that a user has just logged in, and the API has returned a JWT. What should we do with the token? Since we're running an SPA, we could just keep it in the application memory. This will be okay unless the user decides to refresh the page, which reloads the application, losing anything in memory. Not ideal.

So next we look to save the token somewhere a bit more robust, allowing the application to read it whenever it needs to. The question is, should we use cookies or local storage?

COOKIES VERSUS LOCAL STORAGE

The traditional approach to saving user data in a web application is to save a cookie, and that's certainly an option. But cookies are really there to be used by server applications, with each request to the server sending the cookies along in the HTTP header to be read. In an SPA we don't really need this; the API endpoints are stateless and don't get or set cookies.

So let's look somewhere else, toward local storage, which is really designed for client-side applications. With local storage the data stays in the browser and doesn't get transmitted with requests.

Local storage is also really easy to use with JavaScript. Look at the following snippet that would set and get some data:

```
window.localStorage['my-data'] = 'Some information';
window.localStorage['my-data']; // Returns 'Some information'
```

Right, so that's settled; we'll use local storage in Loc8r to save the JWT.

CREATING A SERVICE TO SAVE AND READ A JWT IN LOCAL STORAGE

We'll start building the authentication service by creating the methods to save a JWT in local storage and read it back out again. We've just seen how easy it is to work with `localStorage` in JavaScript, so now we just need to wrap this in an Angular service that exposes two methods, `saveToken` and `getToken`.

No real surprises here, but the `saveToken` method should accept a value to be saved, and `getToken` should return a value. First we'll create a new file called authentication.service.js inside app_client/common/services. Listing 11.9 shows the contents of the new service, including the first two methods. In Angular it's best practice to use

`$window` instead of the native `window` object—primarily for testing reasons—so we'll inject it into the service. The service also needs to be registered with the application, and must return the methods.

> **Listing 11.9   Create the authentication service with the first two methods**

```
(function () {
  angular
    .module('loc8rApp')
    .service('authentication', authentication);     Register new service
                                                    with application

  authentication.$inject = ['$window'];       Inject $window
  function authentication ($window) {         service

    var saveToken = function (token) {              Create a saveToken
      $window.localStorage['loc8r-token'] = token;  method to save a value
    };                                              to localStorage

    var getToken = function () {                    Create a getToken
      return $window.localStorage['loc8r-token'];   method to read a value
    };                                              from localStorage

    return {
      saveToken : saveToken,        Expose methods
      getToken : getToken           to application
    };
  }
})();
```

And there we go, a pretty simple service to handle saving `loc8r-token` to `local-Storage` and reading it back out again. Don't forget to add a reference to this file in the `appClientFiles` array in app.js!

Next we'll look at logging in and registering.

11.5.2 *Allowing users to sign up, sign in, and sign out*

To use the service to enable users to register, log in, and log out, we'll need to add three more methods. Let's start with registering and logging in.

CALLING THE API TO REGISTER AND LOG IN

We'll need two methods to register and log in, which will post the form data to the `register` and `login` API endpoints we created earlier in this chapter. When successful these endpoints both return a JWT, so we can use the `saveToken` method to save them.

The following snippet shows the two new methods to add to the service. Don't forget that `register` and `login` will also need to be added to the `return` statement to expose the methods. Here's the code:

```
register = function(user) {
  return $http.post('/api/register', user).success(function(data){
    saveToken(data.token);
  });
};
```

```
login = function(user) {
  return $http.post('/api/login', user).success(function(data) {
    saveToken(data.token);
  });
};
```

Remember that $http returns promises, which is why we chain the success method to the request. Now to look at signing out.

DELETING LOCALSTORAGE TO SIGN OUT

The user session in the Angular application is managed by saving the JWT in local-Storage. If the token is there, is valid, and hasn't expired, then we can say that the user is logged in. We can't change the expiry date of the token from within the Angular app—only the server can do that. What we can do is delete it.

So to enable users to log out we can create a new logout method in the authentication service to remove the Loc8r JWT, as shown in the following snippet:

```
logout = function() {
  $window.localStorage.removeItem('loc8r-token');
};
```

This will simply remove the loc8r-token item from the browser's localStorage. Again, don't forget that logout will have to be added to the return statement so that it can be exposed to the application.

Now we have methods to get a JWT from the server, save it in localStorage, read it from localStorage, and also delete it. So the next question is: How do we use it in the application to see that a user is logged in to get data out of it?

11.5.3 *Using the JWT data in the Angular service*

The JWT saved in the browser's localStorage is what we use to manage a user's session. It will be used to validate whether a user is logged in. If a user is logged in, the application can also read the user information stored inside.

First we'll add a method to check whether somebody is logged in.

CHECKING THE LOGGED-IN STATUS

To check whether a user is currently logged in to the application, we need to check to see if the loc8r-token exists in localStorage. We can use the getToken method for that. But the existence of a token isn't enough. Remember that the JWT has expiry data embedded in it, so if a token exists we'll need to check that too.

The expiration date and time of the JWT is part of the payload, which is the second chunk of data. Remember that this part is just an encoded JSON object; it's encoded rather than encrypted, so we can decode it. In fact, we've already talked about the function to do this: atob.

So, stitching this all together, we want to create a method that

1 Gets the stored token
2 Extracts the payload from the token

3   Decodes the payload

4   Validates that the expiry date hasn't passed

This method should simply return `true` if a user is logged in, and `false` if not. The following snippet shows this put together in a method called `isLoggedIn`:

```
var isLoggedIn = function() {
  var token = getToken();

  if(token){
    var payload = JSON.parse($window.atob(token.split('.')[1]));

    return payload.exp > Date.now() / 1000;
  } else {
    return false;
  }
};
```

Annotations:
- **Get token from storage**
- **If token exists get payload, decode it, and parse it to JSON**
- **Validate whether expiry date has passed**

There's not much code there, but it's doing a lot. And once we've referenced it in the `return` statement in the service, the application will be able to quickly check whether a user is logged in at any given point.

The next and final method to add to the authentication service will get some user information from the JWT.

GETTING USER INFORMATION FROM THE JWT

We want the application to be able to get a user's email address and name from the JWT. We've just seen in the `isLoggedIn` method how to extract data from the token, and our new method will do exactly the same thing.

So we'll create a new method called `currentUser`. The first thing this will do is validate that there's a user logged in by calling the `isLoggedIn` method. If there's a user logged in it will get the token by calling the `getToken` method, before extracting and decoding the payload and returning the data we're after. The following snippet shows how this looks:

```
var currentUser = function() {
  if(isLoggedIn()){
    var token = getToken();
    var payload = JSON.parse($window.atob(token.split('.')[1]));
    return {
      email : payload.email,
      name : payload.name
    };
  }
};
```

With that done and referenced in the `return` statement the Angular authentication service is complete. Looking back over the code you can see how this is pretty generic and easy to copy from one application to another. All you'd probably have to change is the name of the token and the API URLs, so we've got a nice reusable Angular service.

Now that the service is in the application, we can use it. So let's keep moving forward and create the login and register pages.

11.6 Creating register and login pages

Everything we've done so far is great, but without a way for visitors to the website to actually register and log in it would be pretty useless! So that's what we'll do now.

In terms of functionality we want a register page for new users to set their details and sign up, and a login page for returning users to input their username and password. When users have gone through either of these processes and are successfully authenticated, the application should send them back to the page they were on when they started the process.

Let's begin with register page.

11.6.1 Building the register page

To develop a working registration page there are a few things to do:

1 Define the route in the Angular application config.
2 Create the view for the page.
3 Create the controller for the page.
4 Get it to redirect to the previous page when successful.

And, of course, we'll want to test it when it's done. Step one is to define the route.

DEFINING THE ROUTE IN THE ANGULAR APP

First we'll define the route for the registration page in the Angular application config, which is in app_client/app.js. The route will be /register, and we'll put the view file in a new folder hierarchy of app_client/auth/register/.

So the new route to add to the config looks like the following snippet:

```
.when('/register', {
  templateUrl: '/auth/register/register.view.html',
  controller: 'registerCtrl',
  controllerAs: 'vm'
})
```

There's nothing new or exciting here, so save that and we'll move on to creating the view.

BUILDING THE REGISTRATION VIEW

Okay, so now we're going to build the view for the registration page. Aside from the normal header and footer there are a few things we're going to need. Primarily we'll need a form to allow visitors to input their name, email address, and provide a password. In this form we should also have an area to display any errors, and on the page we'll also pop in a link to the login form, in case users realize that they're already logged in.

The following listing shows the view all pieced together. Notice how the input fields have the credentials in the view model bound to them using `ng-model`.

Listing 11.10   Full view for the registration page

```
<navigation></navigation>

<div class="container">
  <page-header content="vm.pageHeader"></page-header>                      Link to switch
                                                                          to login page
  <div class="row">
    <div class="col-md-6 col-sm-12">
      <p class="lead">Already a member? Please <a href="/#login">log in</a>
      ➥ instead.</p>
      <form ng-submit="vm.onSubmit()">
        <div role="alert" ng-show="vm.formError" class="alert alert-
        ➥ danger">{{ vm.formError }}</div>
        <div class="form-group">
          <label for="name">Full name</label>                              Input for
          <input type="text" class="form-control" id="name"                user's
        ➥ placeholder="Enter your name" ng-model="vm.credentials.name">     name
          </div>
        <div class="form-group">
          <label for="email">Email address</label>                         Input for
          <input type="email" class="form-control" id="email"              email
        ➥ placeholder="Enter email" ng-model="vm.credentials.email">       address
          </div>
        <div class="form-group">
          <label for="password">Password</label>                           Input for
          <input type="password" class="form-control" id="password"        password
        ➥ placeholder="Password" ng-model="vm.credentials.password">
          </div>
          <button type="submit" class="btn btn-default">Register!</button>
        </form>
      </div>
    </div>

  <footer-generic></footer-generic>
</div>
```

A div to display errors →

Again, the important thing to note here is that a user's name, email, and password are bound to the view model in the object `vm.credentials`. Now to look at the flip-side of this and code up the corresponding controller.

CREATING THE REGISTRATION CONTROLLER SKELETON

Based on the view, we'll need to set up a few things in the register controller. We'll need the title text for the page header of course, and a `vm.onSubmit` function to handle the form submission. We'll also give all of the credentials properties a default empty string value.

Listing 11.11 shows all this. But there's one more thing. When users have registered we want a way to send them back to the page they were on before. To do this we'll use a query string parameter called `page`. So on any page that we create a link to the register URL, we'll include a query string stating the current URL; for example, something like this: /#register?page=/about.

In the controller, also included as part of listing 11.11, we'll capture this as vm.returnPage, providing a default of the homepage if the query string can't be found. To get the query string we'll need to inject Angular's $location service into the controller.

Listing 11.11   Skeleton of the register controller

```
(function () {

  angular
    .module('loc8rApp')
    .controller('registerCtrl', registerCtrl);          Inject $location and
                                                         authentication
  registerCtrl.$inject = ['$location','authentication'];  services into
  function registerCtrl($location, authentication) {    controller
    var vm = this;

    vm.pageHeader = {
      title: 'Create a new Loc8r account'
    };

    vm.credentials = {
      name : "",            Instantiate
      email : "",           credentials
      password : ""
    };
                                                        Get page to
                                                        return to from
    vm.returnPage = $location.search().page || '/';  ◁─┘ query string

    vm.onSubmit = function () {     Create a placeholder
    };                             for onSubmit function

  }
})();
```

One thing to notice is how we get the page parameter from the query string by running a search on the $location. Now that we're getting that returnPage value we should make sure that we pass it through if the user chooses to click on the login link in the page. To do that we simply need to update the link in the view highlighted in bold in the following snippet:

```
<p class="lead">Already a member? Please <a href="/#login?page={{
vm.returnPage }}">log in</a> instead.</p>
```

Now that we've got that set up we can look at coding up the onSubmit function.

HANDLING THE REGISTER FORM SUBMISSION

When the register form is submitted the first thing the code should do is validate that all of the fields have been filled in. If any are missing we can show the error in the form, just like we did when adding reviews. When this basic validation is passed, we can move on with registering a user.

To register a user we'll call the register method in the authentication service, passing it the credentials. Remember that the register method uses the $http service, so it will return promises that we can chain to. So if the method returns an error we can display this on the form. But if registration was successful we'll clear the query string object and then set the application path to be the `returnPage` we captured earlier. This will redirect the user to that path.

All of this is shown in the following snippet, which is to be added to the register controller:

```
vm.onSubmit = function () {
  vm.formError = "";
  if (!vm.credentials.name || !vm.credentials.email ||
      !vm.credentials.password) {              If any credentials
    vm.formError = "All fields required, please try again";   are missing, show
    return false;                                              an error
  } else {                       Otherwise continue
    vm.doRegister();             to register
  }
};

vm.doRegister = function() {            Call authentication
  vm.formError = "";                    register method,
  authentication                        passing credentials
    .register(vm.credentials)
    .error(function(err){
      vm.formError = err;               Show a form error
    })                                  if registration fails
    .then(function(){
      $location.search('page', null);        If registration was
      $location.path(vm.returnPage);         successful clear query
    });                                      string and redirect user
};
```

Don't forget to add this controller file to the `appClientFiles` array in app.js. With this in place you can try out the register page and functionality by starting the application running and heading to http://localhost:3000/register.

When you've done this and successfully registered as a user, open up the browser development tools and look for the resources. As illustrated in figure 11.12 you should be able to see a `loc8r-token` under the Local Storage folder.

Okay, so we've added the ability for a new user to register. Now let's enable a returning user to log in.

11.6.2 *Building the login page*

The approach to the login page is very similar to the register page. It's mainly copying and pasting so we'll go through the steps quite quickly.

First we need to add the new route to app.js:

```
.when('/login', {
  templateUrl: '/auth/login/login.view.html',
  controller: 'loginCtrl',
  controllerAs: 'vm'
})
```

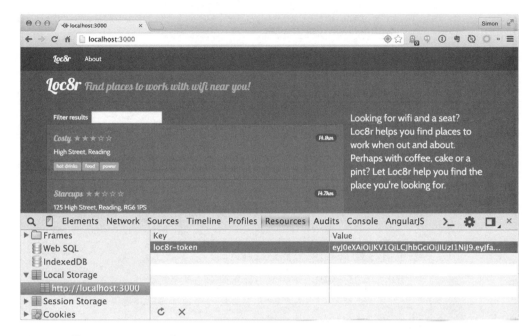

Figure 11.12 Finding the `loc8r-token` in the browser

Then we need to create the view file, login.view.html. We can see from the route where we want this to be. It's very similar to the register view, so it's probably easiest to duplicate that and edit it. All we need to do is remove the name input and change a couple of pieces of text. The following snippet highlights the changes in bold we need to make in the login view:

```
<div class="col-md-6 col-sm-8">
  <p class="lead">Not a member? Please <a href="/#register?page={{
    ➥ vm.returnPage }}">register</a> first.</p>
  <form ng-submit="vm.onSubmit()">
    <div role="alert" ng-show="vm.formError" class="alert alert-danger">{{
      ➥ vm.formError }}</div>
    <div class="form-group">
      <label for="email">Email address</label>
      <input type="email" class="form-control" id="email" placeholder="Enter
      ➥ email" ng-model="vm.credentials.email">
    </div>
    <div class="form-group">
      <label for="password">Password</label>
      <input type="password" class="form-control" id="password"
      ➥ placeholder="Password" ng-model="vm.credentials.password">
    </div>
    <button type="submit" class="btn btn-default">Sign in!</button>
  </form>
</div>
```

Change login link to be a register link

Note that name input is removed

Change text on button

And finally the login controller, which again is very similar to the register controller. The changes we need to make are

- Change the name of the controller.
- Change the page title.
- Remove references to the name field.
- Rename doRegister to doLogin.
- Call the login method of the authentication service instead of the register method.

So let's create login.controller.js as a copy of register.controller.js and make the changes. The following snippet shows the content of the file (without the IIFE wrapper for brevity), and highlights in bold the changes made:

```
angular
  .module('loc8rApp')
  .controller('loginCtrl', loginCtrl);              ← Change name
                                                      to loginCtrl
loginCtrl.$inject = ['$location','authentication'];
function loginCtrl($location, authentication) {
  var vm = this;

  vm.pageHeader = {
    title: 'Sign in to Loc8r'                        ← Change
  };                                                   page title

  vm.credentials = {                                 ←
    email : "",
    password : ""
  };                                                   Remove
                                                       references
  vm.returnPage = $location.search().page || '/';      to name
                                                       credential
  vm.onSubmit = function () {
    vm.formError = "";
    if (!vm.credentials.email || !vm.credentials.password) {  ←
      vm.formError = "All fields required, please try again";
      return false;
    } else {
      vm.doLogin();                                  ←
    }                                                  Rename
  };                                                   doRegister
                                                       to doLogin
  vm.doLogin = function() {                           ←
    vm.formError = "";
    authentication
      .login(vm.credentials)                         ← Call login method
      .error(function(err){                            instead of register
        vm.formError = err;
      })
      .then(function(){
        $location.search('page', null);
        $location.path(vm.returnPage);
      });
  };
}
```

That was easy! There's no need to dwell on this, as functionally it works just like the register controller. Just remember to add it to the `appClientFiles` array in app.js so that it's included in the application code.

Now we'll move onto the final stage and actually make use of the authenticated session in the Angular application.

11.7 *Working with authentication in the Angular app*

Once you have a way to authenticate users, the next step is to make use of that information. In Loc8r we're going to do two things:

- Change the navigation based on whether the visitor is logged in or not.
- Use the user information when creating reviews.

Let's tackle the navigation first.

11.7.1 *Updating navigation*

One thing currently missing from the navigation is a sign-in link. So we'll add one in the conventional place—the top right of the screen. But when a user is logged in, we don't want to display a sign-in message; it would be better to display the user's name and give an option to sign out.

That's what we'll do in this section, starting by adding a right-hand section to the navigation bar.

ADDING A RIGHT-HAND SECTION TO THE NAVIGATION

The navigation for Loc8r is set up as a directive that we include in every page; the files are in common/directives/navigation. The following snippet highlights in bold the markup we need to add to the template to put a sign-in link on the right-hand side:

```
<div id="navbar-main" class="navbar-collapse collapse">
  <ul class="nav navbar-nav">
    <li><a href="/#about">About</a></li>
  </ul>
  <ul class="nav navbar-nav navbar-right">
    <li><a href="/#login/">Sign in</a></li>
  </ul>
</div>
```

This will be our starting point. But to apply some logic behind this—for example, to display a user's name when logged in—we're going to need to add a controller to the directive.

USING A CONTROLLER WITH A DIRECTIVE

So far the directives we've used have consisted of a directive definition and HTML template. But it's possible to link a controller to a directive to give even more functionality, so that's what we'll do here.

This is done by adding a `controller` property to the directive definition, which can be set with the inline version of the `controllerAs` syntax. Because a directive is nested inside other pages with a view model already defined, a view model name other than vm is required to avoid conflicts. The following snippet shows how to add a controller to a directive definition, supplying a view model name of navvm:

```
function navigation () {
  return {
    restrict: 'EA',
    templateUrl: '/common/directives/navigation/navigation.template.html',
    controller: 'navigationCtrl as navvm'
  };
}
```

Okay then, let's create the related controller.

CREATING THE NAVIGATION CONTROLLER

First we'll create a new file in the same folder as the directive definition and template called navigation.controller.js; let's add this to the appClientFiles array in app.js. This controller will need to do a few things, and talk to the authentication service quite a lot. But the first thing it needs to do is get the current URL path so that we can add it to the "Sign in" link—remember that we want the user to be sent back to their original page after logging in.

So we'll create the new controller definition and pass in the native $location service and our authentication service, as we know we'll need both. For coding consistency we'll name the view model in the function vm—this is an internal reference for the controller function and doesn't have to match what's in the template.

The following snippet shows the starting point of the navigation controller, and exposes the current path as vm.currentPath:

```
(function () {
  angular
    .module('loc8rApp')
    .controller('navigationCtrl', navigationCtrl);

  navigationCtrl.$inject = ['$location', 'authentication'];
  function navigationCtrl($location, authentication) {
    var vm = this;

    vm.currentPath = $location.path();

  }
})();
```

With the current path exposed we can now use this in the template to add to the sign-in link as a query string value like this:

```
<li><a href="/#login/?page={{ navvm.currentPath }}">Sign in</a></li>
```

Now when users log in or register successfully they'll be returned to their starting point to continue whatever it was they were doing. Our next step is for signed-in users to show their name and a logout option instead of the link to sign in.

SHOWING A USER'S NAME AND A LOGOUT LINK: THE CONTROLLER

A secondary purpose of this part of navigation is to validate to users that they're logged in by displaying their name instead of the sign-in link. While we're at it we'll also add a dropdown option to enable users to sign out.

So this is where we actually get to use the methods of our authentication service, and some of the data from the JWT saved in local storage. In this navigation controller we want to know whether a user is logged in or not—to display the correct navigation item and also the user's name. Listing 11.12 shows the controller updated with calls to the isLoggedIn and currentUser methods on the authentication service.

We also want a logged-in user to be able to sign out. Again we created a method for this in the authentication service, so we just need a way to call this before redirecting users to the page they were on when they started the process. We could redirect to a specific confirmation page, but the homepage will do for now. This is also part of the controller code in the following listing.

> **Listing 11.12 Using the authentication services methods in the navigation controller**

```
function navigationCtrl($location, authentication) {
  var vm = this;

  vm.currentPath = $location.path();                       Find out whether
                                                           visitor is logged in
  vm.isLoggedIn = authentication.isLoggedIn();       ◄─
                                                           Get current
  vm.currentUser = authentication.currentUser();   ◄─    user's name

  vm.logout = function() {
    authentication.logout();          Create a logout function;
    $location.path('/');              redirect to homepage
  };                                  when complete
}
```

With the functions in place we can update the view accordingly.

SHOWING THE USER'S NAME AND A LOGOUT LINK: THE HTML TEMPLATE

To display the correct navigation item depending on the user's logged-in status we'll use Angular's native ng-show and ng-hide directives, and look up the value of isLoggedIn from the controller. If isLoggedIn returns true then we'll hide the sign-in link and display the other markup.

Creating a dropdown menu with Bootstrap takes a fair amount of markup, so the following snippet highlights the important parts in bold:

```
                                                        Hide sign-in link for
                                                          logged-in users
<ul class="nav navbar-nav navbar-right">
  <li ng-hide="navvm.isLoggedIn"><a href="/#login/?page={{ navvm.currentPath
    ➥ }}">Sign in</a></li>                                              ◄─
  <li ng-show="navvm.isLoggedIn" class="dropdown">   ◄─  Show dropdown nav
                                                         for logged-in users
```

```
    <a href="" class="dropdown-toggle" data-toggle="dropdown">{{
➥     navvm.currentUser.name }} <span class="caret"></span></a>
    <ul class="dropdown-menu" role="menu">
      <li><a href="" ng-click="navvm.logout()">Logout</a></li>
    </ul>
  </li>
</ul>
```

Display user's name

Add logout link to dropdown menu

When that's all in place we'll have a fully functioning authentication system in Loc8r, which validates the current visitor's status and displays some of the saved information in the browser. And now we move onto the final piece of functionality: adding a user's name to a review.

11.7.2 Adding user data to a review

The main use case for authentication in Loc8r is to only accept reviews from registered and logged-in users. There's some housekeeping to do, like only showing the Add Review button to logged-in users, and removing the name field from the form. The new and important part in this section is how to pass the JWT from the loc8rData service to the API endpoint. Let's start with the fun stuff and then we'll tidy up afterwards.

PASSING A JWT TO A SECURE API ENDPOINT

A JWT is sent with the request to an API endpoint as an HTTP header called Authorization. In Loc8r the call to add a review is in the loc8rData service, which is in app_client/common/services. The call itself uses the $http.post method.

Adding an HTTP header to the method is a simple case of adding a headers object to the call, as part of an options parameter as shown in listing 11.13. The options parameter comes after the URL and data parameters, and the content of the Authorization header should be the word Bearer followed by a space and the JWT. We'll need to inject our authentication service into this service to get the token. All of this is highlighted in bold in the following listing.

> **Listing 11.13   Update the data service to pass the JWT**

```
loc8rData.$inject = ['$http', 'authentication'];          Inject authentication
function loc8rData ($http, authentication) {               service
  var locationByCoords = function (lat, lng) {
    return $http.get('/api/locations?lng=' + lng + '&lat=' + lat +
➥     '&maxDistance=20');
  };

  var locationById = function (locationid) {
    return $http.get('/api/locations/' + locationid);
  };

  var addReviewById = function (locationid, data) {
    return $http.post('/api/locations/' + locationid + '/reviews', data, {
```

```
      headers: {
        Authorization: 'Bearer '+ authentication.getToken()
      }
    });
  };
  return {
    locationByCoords : locationByCoords,
    locationById : locationById,
    addReviewById : addReviewById
  };
}
```

Add an options parameter to pass a new HTTP header containing JWT

With this header in place the API endpoint for adding a review will now be able to read the JWT it's expecting, and validate the user accordingly. Now we'll quickly tidy up, first only showing the Add Review button when a user is logged in.

SHOWING DIFFERENT BUTTONS BASED ON THE CURRENT USER'S STATUS

Here we're going to show different content in a page depending on whether the current visitor is logged in or not. When a user is on a location detail page we only want to show the Add Review button if they're logged in. If the user isn't logged in, we can change this button to be a prompt to log in.

Based on some of the things we've done earlier in this chapter, such as using currentPath and isLoggedIn along with ng-show and ng-hide, the following snippet highlights in bold the changes to make in the locationDetail.view.html file:

```
<div class="panel-heading">
  <a ng-show="vm.isLoggedIn" ng-click="vm.popupReviewForm()" class="btn
      btn-default pull-right">Add review</a>
  <a ng-hide="vm.isLoggedIn" href="/#/login?page={{ vm.currentPath }}"
      class="btn btn-default pull-right">Login to add review</a>
  <h2 class="panel-title">Customer reviews</h2>
</div>
```

That's pretty straightforward from a view perspective; we just need to make sure that the corresponding controller has the view model methods isLoggedIn and current-Path. As the following snippet shows we just need to pass in the $location and authentication services and define the methods. Note that this snippet only shows a part of the controller; the rest of the code should be left as is:

Inject $location and authentication services

```
locationDetailCtrl.$inject = ['$routeParams', '$location', '$modal',
    'loc8rData', 'authentication'];
function locationDetailCtrl ($routeParams, $location, $modal, loc8rData,
    authentication) {
  var vm = this;
  vm.locationid = $routeParams.locationid;

  vm.isLoggedIn = authentication.isLoggedIn();

  vm.currentPath = $location.path();
```

Create isLoggedIn method to get current visitor state

Get current URL path of visitor

Figure 11.13   The two different states of the Add Review button, depending on whether the user is logged in or not

With those changes saved the button will behave differently for logged-in users. Both states are shown in figure 11.13.

This is good and works nicely. But when the user clicks the button to add a review, the form in the modal popup still contains an input for the user's name.

REMOVING THE NAME FIELD FROM THE REVIEW FORM

We no longer need users to enter their name into the form, as the API will take it from the JWT. So we can *delete* the following snippet from the reviewModal.view.html file:

```
<div class="form-group">
  <label for="name" class="col-xs-2 col-sm-2 control-label">Name</label>
  <div class="col-xs-10 col-sm-10">
    <input id="name" name="name" required="required" ng-
    model="vm.formData.name" class="form-control"/>
  </div>
</div>
```

Without the form field, we no longer need to validate for it, or send the value to the API, so we can also delete references to it from the controller. The following snippet highlights in bold the pieces to be deleted from reviewModal.controller.js:

```
vm.onSubmit = function () {
  vm.formError = "";
  if (!vm.formData.name || !vm.formData.rating || !vm.formData.reviewText) {
    vm.formError = "All fields required, please try again";
    return false;
  } else {
    vm.doAddReview(vm.locationData.locationid, vm.formData);
  }
};

vm.doAddReview = function (locationid, formData) {
  loc8rData.addReviewById(locationid, {
    author : formData.name,
    rating : formData.rating,
    reviewText : formData.reviewText
  })
```

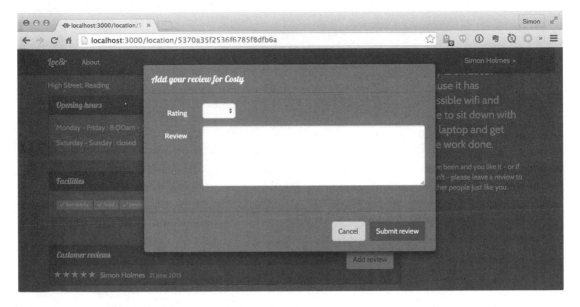

Figure 11.14 The final review form without a name field. Note the user's name in the top right and the logged-in version of the Add Review button.

```
    .success(function (data) {
      vm.modal.close(data);
    })
    .error(function (data) {
      vm.formError = "Your review has not been saved, please try again";
    });
  return false;
};
```

Figure 11.14 shows how the review form now looks without the name field.

And with that update we've completed the authentication section. Users must be logged in to add a review, and through the authentication system the review will be given the correct username.

11.8 Summary

In this chapter we've covered

- How to approach authentication in the MEAN stack
- Encrypting passwords with hashes and salts
- Using Mongoose model methods to add functions to schemas
- How to create a JSON Web Token with Express
- Managing authentication on the server with Passport
- Making routes in Express available to authenticated users only

- Using local storage to manage a user session in the browser
- How to use JWT data inside Angular
- Adding controllers to Angular directives
- Passing a JWT from Angular to an API via HTTP headers

And that brings us to the end of the book. By now you should have a good idea of the power and capabilities of the MEAN stack and be empowered to get building some cool stuff!

You now have a platform to build REST APIs, server-side web applications, and browser-based single-page applications. You can create database-driven sites, APIs, and applications, and publish them to a live URL.

When starting your next project remember to take a little time to think about the best architecture and user experience. Spend a little time planning to make your development time more productive and enjoyable. And never be afraid to refactor and improve your code and application as you go.

If you're looking for the next thing to learn, take a look a Gulp at www.gulpjs.com, a great build system for automating activities such as code linting, minification, and concatenation. Depending on your projects you may want to delve deeper into Angular, Express, Node, Mongo, or Mongoose.

Really, we've just scratched the surface of what these amazing technologies can offer. So please, dive in, build things, try stuff, keep learning, and, most importantly, have fun!

appendix A
Installing the stack

This appendix covers

- Installing Node and npm
- Installing Express globally
- Installing MongoDB
- Installing Angular

Before you can build anything on the MEAN stack you'll need to install the software to run it. This is really easy to do on Windows, Mac OS X, and the more popular Linux distributions like Ubuntu.

As Node underpins the stack, that's the best place to start. Node now also ships with npm included, which will be very useful for installing some of the other software.

A.1 Installing Node and npm

The best way to install Node and npm depends on your operating system. When possible it's recommended to download an installer from the Node website at http://nodejs.org/download/. This location always has the latest version as maintained by the Node core team.

A.1.1 Installing Node on Windows

Windows users should simply download an installer from the Node website.

A.1.2   Installing Node on Mac OS X

The best option for Mac OS X users is to simply download an installer from the Node website. Alternatively, you can install Node and npm using the Homebrew package manager, as detailed on Joyent's Node wiki on GitHub at https://github.com/joyent/node/wiki/Installing-Node.js-via-package-manager.

A.1.3   Installing Node on Linux

There aren't any installers for Linux users, but you can download binaries from the Node website if you're comfortable working with them.

Alternatively, Linux users can also install Node from package managers. Package managers don't always have the latest version, so be aware of that. A particularly out-of-date one is the popular apt system on Ubuntu. There are instructions for using a variety of package managers, including a fix for apt on Ubuntu, on Joyent's Node wiki on GitHub at https://github.com/joyent/node/wiki/Installing-Node.js-via-package-manager.

A.1.4   Verifying installation by checking version

Once you have Node and npm installed you can check the versions you have with a couple of terminal commands:

```
$ node --version
$ npm --version
```

These will output the versions of Node and npm that you have on your machine. The code in this book is built using Node 4.2.1 and npm 2.2.0.

A.2   Installing Express globally

To be able to create new Express applications on-the-fly from the command line, you need to install Express generator. You can do this from the command line, using npm. In terminal you simply run the following command:

```
$ npm install -g express-generator
```

If this fails due to a permissions error you'll need to run this as an administrator. On Windows right-click the command prompt icon and select Run As Administrator. Now try the preceding command again in this new window. On Mac and Linux you can prefix the command with sudo as shown in the following code snippet; this will prompt you for a password:

```
$ sudo npm install -g express-generator
```

When the generator has finished installing Express you can verify it by checking the version number from terminal:

```
$ express --version
```

The version of Express used in the code samples in this book is 4.9.0.

If you run into any problems with this installation process, the documentation for Express is available on its website at http://expressjs.com/.

A.3 Installing MongoDB

MongoDB is also available for Windows, Mac OS X, and Linux. Detailed instructions about all of the following options are available in the MongoDB online documentation at http://docs.mongodb.org/manual/installation/.

A.3.1 Installing MongoDB on Windows

There are some direct downloads available from http://docs.mongodb.org/manual/installation/ for Windows, depending on which version of Windows you're running.

A.3.2 Installing MongoDB on Mac OS X

The easiest way to install MongoDB for Mac OS X is to use the Homebrew package manager, but if you prefer, you can also choose to install MongoDB manually.

A.3.3 Installing MongoDB on Linux

There are also packages available for a few Linux distributions as detailed at http://docs.mongodb.org/manual/installation/. If you're running a version of Linux that doesn't have MongoDB available in a package, you can choose to install it manually.

A.3.4 Running MongoDB as a service

Once you have MongoDB installed, you'll probably want to run it as a service so that it automatically restarts whenever you reboot. Again, there are instructions for doing this in the MongoDB installation documentation.

A.3.5 Checking the MongoDB version number

MongoDB installs not only itself, but also a Mongo shell, so that you can interact with your MongoDB databases through the command line. You can check the version number of MongoDB and the Mongo shell independently. To check the shell version, run the following in terminal:

```
$ mongo --version
```

To check the version of MongoDB run this:

```
$ mongod --version
```

This book uses version 2.4.6 of both MongoDB and the Mongo shell.

A.4 Installing Angular

Angular doesn't take much installation because it's really just a library file that you need to download and place in the correct spot in your folder structure. You can download Angular from its homepage at http://angularjs.org/.

It will give you some options when starting the download. You want to download the *minified* build of the *stable* branch. The version used throughout this book is 1.2.19.

When downloaded, create a new folder called angular inside your application's public folder and place the JavaScript file in there.

appendix B
Installing and preparing
the supporting cast

This appendix covers

- Adding Twitter Bootstrap and a custom theme
- Installing Git
- Installing a suitable command-line interface
- Signing up for Heroku
- Installing Heroku toolbelt

There are several technologies that can help with developing on the MEAN stack, from front-end layouts to source control and deployment tools. This appendix covers the installation and setup of the supporting technologies used throughout this book. As the actual install instructions tend to change over time, this appendix will point you toward the best place to get the instructions and anything you need to look out for.

B.1   Twitter Bootstrap

Bootstrap is not really installed as such, but rather added to your application. This is as simple as downloading the library files, unzipping them, and placing them into the application.

The first step is to download Bootstrap. You can get this from www.getbootstrap.com. Make sure that you download the distribution zip and not the source. At the time of writing Bootstrap is on version 3.0.2 and the distribution zip contains three folders: css, fonts, and js.

Once you have it downloaded and unzipped, the files need to be moved into the public folder in your Express application. To keep the files together and the top level clean, create a new folder called Bootstrap in the public folder and copy the unzipped files into there. The public folder in your application should now look like figure B.1.

Figure B.1   The structure and contents of the public folder after Bootstrap has been added

That will give you access to the default look and feel of Bootstrap, but you probably want your application to stand out from the crowd a bit. You can do this by adding in a theme.

B.1.1   Getting the Amelia theme

The Loc8r application in this book uses a Bootstrap theme called Amelia from Bootswatch. Since writing this Bootswatch has removed the Amelia theme from their website, but you can download both the original CSS file and the minified version from my GitHub repository at https://github.com/simonholmes/amelia. Once you've downloaded the amelia.bootstrap.css and amelia.bootstrap.min.css files, you can copy them into the /public/bootstrap/css folder in your application.

B.1.2   Tidying up the folders

If you wish you can tidy up your Bootstrap folder by removing some of the duplicates. You'll notice that there are readable and minified versions of the CSS and JavaScript files, and also a pair of default Bootstrap-theme CSS files. Unless you're going to hack around in the files you only really need the minified versions.

B.2 Installing Git

The source code for this book is managed using Git, so the easiest way to access it is with Git. Also, Heroku relies on Git for managing the deployment process and pushing code from your development machine into a live environment. So you need to install Git if you don't already have it.

You can verify if you have it with a simple terminal command:

```
$ git --version
```

If this responds with a version number then you already have it installed and can move onto the next section. If not, then you'll need to install Git.

A good starting point for Mac OS X and Windows users who are new to Git is to download and install the GitHub user interface from https://help.github.com/articles/set-up-git.

You don't need a GUI though, and you can install just Git by itself using the instructions found on the main Git website at http://git-scm.com/downloads.

B.3 Installing a suitable command-line interface

You can get the most out of Git by using a CLI, even if you've downloaded and installed a GUI. Some are better than others, and you can't actually use the native Windows command prompt, so if you're on Windows then you'll definitely need to run something else. Here's what I use in a few different environments:

- Mac OS X Mavericks and later: native terminal
- Mac OS X pre-Mavericks (10.8.5 and earlier): iTerm
- Windows: GitHub shell (this comes installed with the GitHub GUI)
- Ubuntu: native terminal

If you have other preferences and the Git commands work, then by all means use what you already have and you're used to.

B.4 Setting up Heroku

This book uses Heroku for hosting the Loc8r application in a live production environment. You can do this too—for free—so long as you sign up, install the toolbelt, and log in through terminal.

B.4.1 Signing up for Heroku

To use Heroku you'll need to sign up for an account, of course. For the purposes of the application you'll be building through this book a free account will be fine. Simply head over to www.heroku.com and follow the instructions to sign up.

B.4.2 *Installing Heroku toolbelt*

Heroku toolbelt contains the Heroku command-line shell and a utility called Fore-man. The shell is what you'll use from terminal to manage your Heroku deployment, and Foreman is very useful for making sure what you've built on your machine is set up to run properly on Heroku. You can download the toolbelt for Mac OS X, Windows, and Linux from toolbelt.heroku.com.

B.4.3 *Logging in to Heroku using terminal*

Once you've signed up for an account and installed the toolbelt on your machine, the last step is to log in to your account from terminal. Enter the following command:

```
$ heroku login
```

This will prompt you for your Heroku login credentials, and will most likely generate a new SSH public key and upload it for you. Now you're all set up and ready to go with Heroku.

appendix C
Dealing with all
of the views

This appendix covers
- Removing the data from all views, except the homepage
- Moving the data into the controllers

Chapter 4 covers setting up the controllers and the views for the static, clickable prototype. The "how" and "why" are covered in that chapter in more detail, so this appendix will really focus on what the end results should be.

C.1 Moving the data from the views to the controllers

Part of this includes moving the data back down the MVC flow from the views into the controllers. The example in chapter 4 deals with this in the Loc8r homepage, but it needs to be done for the other pages too. We'll start with the Details page.

C.1.1 Details page

The Details page is the largest and most complex of the pages, with the most data requirements, but following the homepage is the most logical place for it to go. The first step is setting up the controller.

The controller for this page is called `locationInfo` in the locations.js file in app_server/controllers. When you've analyzed the data in the view, and collated it into a JavaScript object, your controller will look something like the following listing.

Listing C.1 `locationInfo` **controller**

```javascript
module.exports.locationInfo = function(req, res){
  res.render('location-info', {
    title: 'Starcups',
    pageHeader: {title: 'Starcups'},
    sidebar: {
      context: 'is on Loc8r because it has accessible wifi and space to sit
    down with your laptop and get some work done.',
      callToAction: 'If you\'ve been and you like it - or if you don\'t -
    please leave a review to help other people just like you.'
    },
    location: {
      name: 'Starcups',
      address: '125 High Street, Reading, RG6 1PS',
      rating: 3,
      facilities: ['Hot drinks', 'Food', 'Premium wifi'],
      coords: {lat: 51.455041, lng: -0.9690884},
      openingTimes: [{
        days: 'Monday - Friday',
        opening: '7:00am',
        closing: '7:00pm',
        closed: false
      },{
        days: 'Saturday',
        opening: '8:00am',
        closing: '5:00pm',
        closed: false
      },{
        days: 'Sunday',
        closed: true
      }],
      reviews: [{
        author: 'Simon Holmes',
        rating: 5,
        timestamp: '16 July 2013',
        reviewText: 'What a great place. I can\'t say enough good things
    about it.'
      },{
        author: 'Charlie Chaplin',
        rating: 3,
        timestamp: '16 June 2013',
        reviewText: 'It was okay. Coffee wasn\'t great, but the wifi was
    fast.'
      }]
    }
  });
};
```

Include latitude and longitude coordinates to use in Google Map image

Add array of open times, allowing for different data on different days

Array for reviews left by other users

A part to note here is the latitude and longitude being sent through. You can get your current latitude and longitude from this website: http://www.where-am-i.net/.

You can geocode an address—that is, get the latitude and longitude of it—from this website: http://www.latlong.net/convert-address-to-lat-long.html. Your views will actually be using the `lat` and `lng` to display a Google Map image of the correct location, so it's worthwhile doing this for the prototype stage.

UPDATING THE VIEW

As this is the most complex, data-rich page, it stands to reason that it will have the largest view template. You've already seen most of the technicalities in the homepage layout, such as looping through arrays, bringing in includes, and defining and calling mixins. There are a couple of extra things to look out for in this template though, both of which are annotated and highlighted in bold.

First, this template uses an `if-else` conditional statement. This looks like JavaScript without the brackets. Second, the template uses a JavaScript `replace` function to replace all line breaks in the text of reviews with `<br/>` tags. This is done using a simple regular expression, looking for all occurrences of the characters `\n` in the text. The following listing shows the `location-info.jade` view template in full.

Listing C.2 `location-info.jade` view template in app_server/views

```
extends layout

include _includes/sharedHTMLfunctions        ←  Bring in sharedHTMLfunctions
                                                 include, which contains
block content                                    outputRating mixin
  .row.page-header: .col-lg-12
      h1= pageHeader.title
  .row
    .col-xs-12.col-md-9
      .row
        .col-xs-12.col-sm-6
          p.rating
            +outputRating(location.rating)   ←  Call outputRating mixin,
          p= location.address                   sending it rating of
          .panel.panel-primary                  current location
            .panel-heading
              h2.panel-title Opening hours
            .panel-body
              each time in location.openingTimes
                p                                        Loop through
                  | #{time.days} :                       array of open
                  if time.closed                         times, checking
                    | closed                             whether location
                  else                                   is closed using an
                    | #{time.opening} - #{time.closing}  inline if-else
          .panel.panel-primary                           statement
            .panel-heading
              h2.panel-title Facilities
            .panel-body
              each facility in location.facilities
```

```
                    span.label.label-warning
                      span.glyphicon.glyphicon-ok
                      |  #{facility}
                      |  
                .col-xs-12.col-sm-6.location-map
                  .panel.panel-primary
                    .panel-heading
                      h2.panel-title Location map
                    .panel-body
                      img.img-responsive.img-rounded(src="http://maps.googleapis.com/
➡ maps/api/
➡ staticmap?center=#{location.coords.lat},#{location.coords.lng}&
➡ zoom=17&size=400x350&sensor=false&markers=#{location.coords.lat},
➡ #{location.coords.lng}&scale=2")                        ◁─┐
                  .row                                          │
                    .col-xs-12                                  │
                      .panel.panel-primary.review-panel         │
                        .panel-heading
                          a.btn.btn-default.pull-right(href="/location/review/new") Add
➡ review
                          h2.panel-title Customer reviews
                        .panel-body.review-container
                          each review in location.reviews    ◁───┐
                            .row                                   │
                              .review                              │
                                .well.well-sm.review-header
                                  span.rating
                                    +outputRating(review.rating)  ◁─┘
                                  span.reviewAuthor #{review.author}
                                  small.reviewTimestamp #{review.timestamp}
                              .col-xs-12
                                p !{(review.reviewText).replace(/\n/g, '<br/>')}
      .col-xs-12.col-md-3
        p.lead #{location.name} #{sidebar.context}
        p= sidebar.callToAction
```

Build URL for Google Maps static image, inserting lat and lng using Jade variables

Loop through each review, calling outputRating mixin again to generate markup for stars

Code replaces any line breaks in review text with <br/> tag so that renders as intended by author

A question that may arise from this is, why replace line breaks with <br/> tags every time? Why don't you just save the data with <br/> tags in? That way you only have to run the replace function once, when the data is saved. The answer is that HTML is just one method of rendering text; it just happens to be the one we're using here. Further down the line you may want to pull this information into a native mobile application. You don't want the source data tainted with HTML markup that you don't use in that environment. So the answer, really, is to keep the data clean.

C.1.2   Add Review page

The Add Review page is really simple at the moment; there's only one piece of data in it: the title in the page header. So updating the controller shouldn't pose much of a problem. See the following listing for the full code of the addReview controller, in locations.js in the app_server/controllers folder.

Listing C.3 `addReview` **controller**

```
module.exports.addReview = function(req, res){
  res.render('location-review-form', {
    title: 'Review Starcups on Loc8r',
    pageHeader: { title: 'Review Starcups' }
  });
};
```

Not much to talk about here; we've just updated the text inside the titles. The following listing shows the corresponding view, `location-review-form.jade`, in app_server/views.

Listing C.4 `location-review-form.jade` **template**

```
extends layout

block content
  .row.page-header
    .col-lg-12
      h1= pageHeader.title
  .row
    .col-xs-12.col-md-6
      form.form-horizontal(action="/location", method="get", role="form")
        .form-group
          label.col-xs-2.col-sm-2.control-label(for="name") Name
          .col-xs-10.col-sm-10
            input#name.form-control(name="name")
          label.col-xs-10.col-sm-2.control-label(for="rating") Rating
          .col-xs-12.col-sm-2
            select.form-control.input-sm(name="rating")
              option 5
              option 4
              option 3
              option 2
              option 1
        .form-group
          label.col-sm-2.control-label(for="review") Review
          .col-sm-10
            textarea#review.form-control(name="review", rows="5")
        button.btn.btn-default.pull-right Add my review
    .col-xs-12.col-md-4
```

Again, nothing complicated or new here, so let's move on to the About page.

C.1.3 *About page*

The About page doesn't contain a huge amount of data either, just a title and some content. So let's pull that out of the view and into the controller. Note that the content in the view currently has some <br/> tags in it, so replace each <br/> tag with \n when you put it into the controller. These are highlighted in bold in the following listing; the about controller is in app_server/controllers/others.js.

Listing C.5 about controller

```
module.exports.about = function(req, res){
  res.render('generic-text', {
    title: 'About Loc8r',
    content: 'Loc8r was created to help people find places to sit down and
➥ get a bit of work done.\n\nLorem ipsum dolor sit amet, consectetur
➥ adipiscing elit. Nunc sed lorem ac nisi dignissim accumsan. Nullam
➥ sit amet interdum magna. Morbi quis faucibus nisi. Vestibulum mollis
➥ purus quis eros adipiscing tristique. Proin posuere semper tellus, id
➥ placerat augue dapibus ornare. Aenean leo metus, tempus in nisl eget,
➥ accumsan interdum dui. Pellentesque sollicitudin volutpat ullamcorper.'
  });
};
```

Aside from removing the HTML from the content there's not much going on here. So let's take a quick look at the view, and we'll be done. The following listing shows the final generic-text view that is used for the About page in app_server/views—the view will have to use the same piece of code as we saw in the reviews section to replace the \n line breaks with HTML <br/> tags.

Listing C.6 `generic-text.jade` template

```
extends layout

block content
  #banner.page-header
    .row
      .col-md-6.col-sm-12
        h1= title
  .row
    .col-md-6.col-sm-12
      p !{(content).replace(/\n/g, '<br/>')}    ◁—— Replace all line
                                                     breaks with <br/>
                                                     tags when rendering
                                                     HTML
```

This is a really simple, small, reusable template for whenever you just want to output some text on a page.

index

Node.js in Action

Mike Cantelon, Marc Harter,
 T.J. Holowaychuk, Nathan Rajlich

ISBN: 9781617290572
416 pages
$44.99
October 2013

Node.js in Practice

by Alex Young, Marc Harter

ISBN: 9781617290930
424 pages
$49.99
December 2014

Express in Action
Node applications with Express and its companion tools

by Evan M. Hahn

ISBN: 9781617292422
245 pages
$39.99
November 2015

For ordering information go to www.manning.com

MORE TITLES FROM MANNING

AngularJS in Action

by Lukas Ruebbelke

ISBN: 9781617291333
192 pages
$44.99
July 2015

Secrets of the JavaScript Ninja

by John Resig, Bear Bibeault

ISBN: 9781933988696
392 pages
$39.99
December 2012

Amazon Web Services in Action

by Michael Wittig, Andreas Wittig

ISBN: 9781617292880
424 pages
$49.99
September 2015

For ordering information go to www.manning.com